"Revelation is notoriously difficult to interpret, hence many preachers are afraid to preach it. Enter this accessible treatment of the book by Danny Akin written with the pastor and his preaching in mind. Akin is himself a consummate expositor, and preachers will find in this volume practical help in sermon preparation. If you want to know how to preach Revelation and how to preach Christ from Revelation, this book is for you. I highly recommend it."

David L. Allen, dean, School of Preaching, Southwestern Baptist Theological Seminary, Fort Worth, Texas

"Revelation is not easy to understand, but Dr. Akin has succeeded in writing a commentary that is a great gift to pastors and leaders in the church. With precise exposition, clear points of application, and thoughtful questions, this book is both theologically driven and accessible. I cannot recommend this book enough!"

Matt Carter, pastor of preaching at the Austin Stone Community Church in Austin, Texas, and co-author of *The Real Win*, *Creation Unraveled*, and *Creation Restored*

"This commentary is an insightful, responsible, theologically rich commentary that inspires worship as well as study. Danny Akin, a wise and respected scholar, avoids the silly speculation and the pastoral irrelevance of many commentaries on this book. Instead, Akin helps us to see from Patmos the unveiling of our Lord. Such a revelation is just what we need for this hour."

Russell Moore, director of the Public Theology Project at *Christianity Today*

CHRIST-CENTERED

Exposition

NT / COMMENTARY

AUTHOR Daniel L. Akin

SERIES EDITORS David Platt, Daniel L. Akin, and Tony Merida

CHRIST-CENTERED
Exposition

EXALTING JESUS IN

REVELATION

HOLMAN
REFERENCE
NASHVILLE, TENNESSEE

SERIES DEDICATION

Dedicated to Adrian Rogers and John Piper. They have taught us to love the gospel of Jesus Christ, to preach the Bible as the inerrant Word of God, to pastor the church for which our Savior died, and to have a passion to see all nations gladly worship the Lamb.

—David Platt, Tony Merida, and Danny Akin
March 2013

AUTHOR'S DEDICATION

Dedicated to W. A. Criswell, who fueled my passion for the Apocalypse and the return of King Jesus.

CONTENTS

ACKNOWLEDGMENTS

I would like to thank Shane Shaddix, Mary Jo Haselton, and Kim Humphrey, each of whom made significant contributions to this volume. You have blessed and enriched my life.

SERIES INTRODUCTION

Augustine said, "Where Scripture speaks, God speaks." The editors of the Christ-Centered Exposition Commentary series believe that where God speaks, the pastor must speak. God speaks through His written Word. We must speak from that Word. We believe the Bible is God breathed, authoritative, inerrant, sufficient, understandable, necessary, and timeless. We also affirm that the Bible is a Christ-centered book; that is, it contains a unified story of redemptive history of which Jesus is the hero. Because of this Christ-centered trajectory that runs from Genesis 1 through Revelation 22, we believe the Bible has a corresponding global-missions thrust. From beginning to end, we see God's mission as one of making worshipers of Christ from every tribe and tongue worked out through this redemptive drama in Scripture. To that end we must preach the Word.

In addition to these distinct convictions, the Christ-Centered Exposition Commentary series has some distinguishing characteristics. First, this series seeks to display exegetical accuracy. What the Bible says is what we want to say. While not every volume in the series will be a verse-by-verse commentary, we nevertheless desire to handle the text carefully and explain it rightly. Those who teach and preach bear the heavy responsibility of saying what God has said in His Word and declaring what God has done in Christ. We desire to handle God's Word faithfully, knowing that we must give an account for how we have fulfilled this holy calling (Jas 3:1).

Second, the Christ-Centered Exposition Commentary series has pastors in view. While we hope others will read this series, such as parents, teachers, small-group leaders, and student ministers, we desire to provide a commentary busy pastors will use for weekly preparation of biblically faithful and gospel-saturated sermons. This series is not academic in nature. Our aim is to present a readable and pastoral style of commentaries. We believe this aim will serve the church of the Lord Jesus Christ.

Third, we want the Christ-Centered Exposition Commentary series to be known for the inclusion of helpful illustrations and theologically driven applications. Many commentaries offer no help in illustrations, and few offer any kind of help in application. Often those that do offer illustrative material and application unfortunately give little serious attention to the text. While giving ourselves primarily to explanation, we also hope to serve readers by providing inspiring and illuminating illustrations coupled with timely and timeless application.

Finally, as the name suggests, the editors seek to exalt Jesus from every book of the Bible. In saying this, we are not commending wild allegory or fanciful typology. We certainly believe we must be constrained to the meaning intended by the divine Author Himself, the Holy Spirit of God. However, we also believe the Bible has a messianic focus, and our hope is that the individual authors will exalt Christ from particular texts. Luke 24:25-27,44-47 and John 5:39,46 inform both our hermeneutics and our homiletics. Not every author will do this the same way or have the same degree of Christ-centered emphasis. That is fine with us. We believe faithful exposition that is Christ centered is not monolithic. We do believe, however, that we must read the whole Bible as Christian Scripture. Therefore, our aim is both to honor the historical particularity of each biblical passage and to highlight its intrinsic connection to the Redeemer.

The editors are indebted to the contributors of each volume. The reader will detect a unique style from each writer, and we celebrate these unique gifts and traits. While distinctive in their approaches, the authors share a common characteristic in that they are pastoral theologians. They love the church, and they regularly preach and teach God's Word to God's people. Further, many of these contributors are younger voices. We think these new, fresh voices can serve the church well, especially among a rising generation that has the task of proclaiming the Word of Christ and the Christ of the Word to the lost world.

We hope and pray this series will serve the body of Christ well in these ways until our Savior returns in glory. If it does, we will have succeeded in our assignment.

David Platt
Daniel L. Akin
Tony Merida
Series Editors
February 2013

Revelation

When God Speaks from Heaven

REVELATION 1:1-8

Main Idea: Those who hear and obey God's Word concerning who Jesus is and what He does will be blessed by the Lord.

I. **Receive the Blessing for the True Disciple (1:1-3).**
   A. The blessing comes from God's prophetic revelation from Jesus (1:1-2).
   B. The blessing comes in the church's public reading of God's Word (1:3).
   C. The blessing comes with our personal response of obedience (1:3).

II. **Welcome the Greeting from the Triune God (1:4-6).**
   A. The Father is perfect in His person (1:4).
   B. The Spirit is perfect in His presence (1:4).
   C. The Son is perfect in His provision (1:5-6).
      1. In His revelation (1:5)
      2. In His resurrection (1:5)
      3. In His rule (1:5)
      4. In His redemption (1:5)
      5. In His reign (1:6)

III. **Look for the Coming of the Triumphant Lord (1:7-8).**
   A. His coming will be seen (1:7).
   B. His coming will bring sorrow (1:7).
   C. His coming will be in strength (1:8).

If ever there was a book that could be described as "a riddle, wrapped in a mystery, inside an enigma," it is the last book in the Bible, the book of Revelation.[1] And yet it is the only book in the Bible with a direct blessing for those who read it, listen to it, and obey it (1:3). Why? Because this is a book in which God speaks directly from heaven. And it is a book that talks about heaven's favorite subject: the Lord Jesus Christ. Indeed

---

[1] This is a phrase used by Winston Churchill to describe Russia in the 1930s, but it applies just as well to John's apocalyptic vision.

I believe the *theme* of the book could be described as **the majesty and glory of the warrior Lamb, King Jesus, who is coming again to rule and reign forever!** I believe the book addresses the future, but I believe the book is even more interested in exalting Jesus. Regardless of how you understand the book, if you miss this, you have missed its main message.

Revelation is a book that has puzzled, confused, and frustrated the minds of the best biblical scholars. Neither John Calvin nor Martin Luther wrote a commentary on it, and Luther was quite harsh in his evaluation of Revelation's value, saying,

> My spirit cannot accommodate itself to this book. There is one sufficient reason for the small esteem in which I hold it—that Christ is neither taught nor recognized. (Preface to Luther's Bible, 1522)

Wow! One wonders if Luther was reading the same book we have in our Bible. Revelation is certainly a *mystery*, but it is also a *masterpiece*. It does not constitute an unsolvable puzzle but contains a definite promise and a magnificent portrait of the coming again of the Lord Jesus.

In 404 verses, with 285 Old Testament citations and as many as 550 Old Testament allusions, we discover not a closed book but an open book—one to be read and not rejected. Daniel 12:4 says, "Keep these words secret and seal the book until the time of the end," but Revelation 22:10 says, "Don't seal the prophetic words of this book, because the time is near." Revelation is to be explored, examined, and embraced, for in it we discover a marvelous message whose theme is the theme of the Bible: the greatness and the glory of Jesus. From 1:1 to 22:21 the Apocalypse is from Jesus and about Jesus. As He is the focus of the Bible, so He is the focus of this book.

Revelation 1:1-8 constitutes the prologue or introduction of the book. Here our God speaks from heaven with power and promise to His saints on the earth. How does He want us to respond?

Receive the Blessing for the True Disciple
REVELATION 1:1-3

Revelation is a unique book because it comprises three different literary genres. It is an apocalypse (v. 1), a prophecy (v. 3), and a letter (v. 4). That God intended for us to read and understand it is made clear when He tells us twice in verse 3 that there is a blessing for those who read, hear, and keep the words of this prophecy. God intended to bless, comfort, and encourage His people in every generation to be faithful and persevere, especially during times of persecution and suffering. Revelation had a word of blessing for the first-century church just as it has a word of blessing for the twenty-first-century church. To miss this is to immediately get off on the wrong hermeneutical foot in interpreting this book.

The Blessing Comes from God's Prophetic Revelation from Jesus (1:1-2)

The book begins with "The revelation of Jesus Christ." The word *revelation* is the title of the book and translates the Greek word *apokalupsis*, which means "to reveal, unveil, uncover, or disclose." This is the only time the word appears in the entire book. It tells us God is pulling back the curtain in order to show us something previously hidden and unknown. He is letting us catch a glimpse of what goes on behind the scenes in the realm of spiritual conflict. That the book is an apocalypse tells us it is highly metaphorical and symbolic. The images and symbols represent real truths and real things, but we err if we interpret them in an overly literal sense. Symbols are meant to be symbolic.

This is a revelation of, from, and about Jesus Christ. Three times John uses the phrase "Jesus Christ" in 1:1-5 but never again in the rest of the book. Notice the divine or heavenly chain of communication of this great unveiling: God → Jesus Christ → angel → John → His slaves or servants (Gk *doulos*). Revelation is a blessed gift from God the Father, which He gave to His Son, which the Lord Jesus graciously shares with us.

The things in this revelation "must quickly" or will soon "take place." This phrase occurs seven times in Revelation and emphasizes imminence and expectancy. We must put this phrase in biblical and theological context. Hebrews 1:2 teaches we are now in "these last days." James 5:9 tells us, "The judge stands at the door." First John 2:18 affirms, "It is the last hour." Alan Johnson says,

> In eschatology and apocalyptic literature, the future is always viewed as imminent. . . . The church in every age has always lived with the expectancy of the consummation of all things in its own day. "Imminent" describes an event that is "possible any day, impossible no day." (*Revelation*, 22)

To make this apocalyptic vision known, Jesus "sent it and signified it through His angel." *Angel* (Gk *angelos*) means "messenger." Angels are mentioned 67 times in Revelation, which accounts for one quarter of the references to them in the Bible (Johnson, *Revelation*, 22). Through these beings the Lord made His message known. He signified it by signs and symbols, visions and revelations.

To whom was the angel sent? Most immediately, he was sent to the apostle John, who was an old man residing on "the island called Patmos" (v. 9). Here John is referred to, not as an apostle, but as a slave. John will be faithful to testify, to bear witness "to God's word and to the testimony about Jesus Christ, in all he saw" (v. 2). What an insightful way to talk about the Bible! It is from Genesis to Revelation "God's Word." Further, the heart of its message is the "testimony about" or witness to Jesus Christ. But it comes to us from faithful human servants like John who tell us all they see, exactly what God wants us to have. That is why I often say the simplest way to describe the Bible is "the Word of God written in the words of men."

The Blessing Comes in the Church's Public Reading of God's Word (1:3)

The book of Revelation both begins and ends with a blessing, and there are seven proclamations of blessing in all (1:3; 14:13; 16:15; 19:9; 20:6; 22:7,14). "Blessed" (Gk *makarios*) calls to remembrance the Beatitudes from the Sermon on the Mount (Matt 5–7). John tells us here that there is a blessing that should and will accompany the right public reading of God's Word. Because of this, and because the Bible is the infallible and inerrant Word of God, I believe it is a sin to read it poorly.

The one who reads Scripture publicly has a special and sacred assignment. In the first century many were illiterate, and few could afford even a portion of Holy Scripture. And the public reading and use of a book in corporate worship was a sign and test of *canonicity*. A perfect book should be read well in private but especially in public.

John says those who hear what is read will hear "the words of this prophecy." The idea of "prophecy" also appears seven times in Revelation (1:3; 11:6; 19:10; 22:7,10,18,19). Grant Osborne is helpful:

> Revelation must be characterized not as apocalyptic but as prophetic-apocalyptic. Its purpose is not merely to outline the future intervention of God or to portray the people of God

symbolically in light of that divine reality but to call the saints to accountability on that basis. This is a prophetic book of warning as well as comfort to the church. (*Revelation*, 59)

Therefore, the words of Revelation demand a response from those who hear.

The Blessing Comes with Our Personal Response of Obedience (1:3)

The purpose of Revelation is not to titillate our imagination to wild speculative interpretations. It is to inspire and motivate us to faithfulness and obedience: "To Him who loves us and has set us free from our sins by His blood and made us a kingdom of priests to His God and Father" (vv. 5-6). John wants us to read, hear, and keep what is written in Revelation because in doing so we will be blessed, and the time is near. What we hear, we need to obey. What we believe, we need to live out. The nearness of the Lord's return is meant to challenge us to live faithful lives. "In other words," Osborne explains, "in light of the fact that 'the time is near,' we are called to live decisively and completely for God" (*Revelation*, 59). The *Life Application Bible Commentary* says it like this:

> The phrase "the time is near" is like the phrase "what must soon take place" in 1:1 and refers to imminence. Believers must be ready for Christ's second coming. The Last Judgment and the establishment of God's kingdom are certainly near. No one knows when these events will occur, so all believers must be prepared. They will happen quickly, with no second chance to change minds or sides. (Barton, "Revelation," 4)

This is why the blessing is reserved for those who personally respond and obey, and this is why we must heed the words given to us in this wonderful book.

Welcome the Greeting from the Triune God
REVELATION 1:4-6

The Bible teaches us that God loves us because "God is love" (1 John 4:8,16). The Bible also teaches that God loved us in Jesus when our Savior died on the cross and "set us free from our sins" (Rev 1:5; see Gal 2:20; Eph 5:25).

Revelation 1:4-6 constitutes a greeting or salutation from the Trinity. Craig Keener says we could title this section "From God with Love" (Keener, *Revelation*, 68). Each member of the Godhead addresses us in this "elaborate triadic formula for the Trinity" (Johnson, "Revelation," 420). Each is characterized in rich theological and practical instruction.

John now takes up his pen to write "to the seven ["seven" appears 54 times in Revelation] churches in Asia," that is, Asia Minor or modern Turkey (Wilson, *Charts*, 47–49). It is here that John, almost certainly John the apostle, is named as the author. Exiled to the island of Patmos during the reign of emperor Domitian (AD 81–96), he is an old man and the last living apostle. He has been sent here to labor and die because of his witness for Jesus. Perhaps he, like the seven historical churches he addresses, needed assurance, comfort, encouragement, and instruction.

As we will see again and again, numbers are highly important and symbolic in Revelation, with none more significant than the number seven. It stands for that which is perfect, complete, or full. John writes to seven literal churches in and around Ephesus, but this book and these letters (2:1–3:22) are for various local churches and the church universal throughout the church's history. John greets them in the name of the triune God and offers praise to Him who has poured out His grace on all the believers in these places. "Praise God from whom all blessings flow" (see v. 3) comes to mind as we delve into verses 4-6.

The Father Is Perfect in His Person (1:4)

Grace—God's unmerited favor; all that He does in redemption for underserved sinners—and peace—blessing and wholeness; Shalom—combine a Greek and Hebrew greeting, with the order being important. Peace "with God" (Rom 5:1) and the peace "of God" (Phil 4:7) flow out of the amazing grace of God, what Paul calls "the surpassing grace of God" (2 Cor 9:14). This grace, Paul also says, "has appeared, bringing salvation for all people" (Titus 2:11). All members of the Godhead are avenues, conduits, for the flow of grace and peace in our direction. John begins with the fountainhead, God the Father.

God is described as "the One who is, who was, and who is coming." The focus is on His perfection as He relates to time and eternity. This title appears only in Revelation (see 4:8; 11:17; 16:15) but reflects the language of Exodus 3:14 and the great I AM declaration. Additional allusions may be found in Isaiah (41:4; 43:10; 44:6; 48:12). He is the God of the present, the past, and the future, the God who is the incomparable, sovereign Lord over history, who is thus able to bring prophecy to fulfillment and to deliver his people despite overwhelming odds, whether from Egypt, Babylon or the nations. (Beale, *Revelation*, 188)

Some have suggested John may also be countering a popular pagan slogan of his day: "Zeus was, Zeus is, Zeus will be" (Mounce, *Revelation*, 46). With a word of helpful application, Charles Swindoll says, "God is just as much in control of our unknown future and unnerving present as He is of our unpleasant past" (*Insights*, 28). Robert Mounce adds, "An uncertain future calls for one who by virtue of His eternal existence exercises sovereign control over the course of history" (*Revelation*, 46). Little things or big things, all things are under His rule and control.

The Spirit Is Perfect in His Presence (1:4)

Grace and peace also run in our direction "from the seven spirits [also 3:1; 4:5; 5:6] before His throne." There is debate over exactly who the seven spirits are. Some believe this is a reference to the seven archangels of Jewish tradition (Uriel, Raphael, Raguel, Michael, Saragâêl, Gabriel, and Remiel) (Mounce, *Revelation*, 47). Others see them "as part of a heavenly entourage that has a special ministry" to the Lamb, the Lord Jesus (ibid., 48). I believe, however, the reference is to the Holy Spirit. When this phrase is used in Revelation 5:6, His divine omnipresence is in view. Further, the phrase should be understood in light of Isaiah 11:2 and Zechariah 4:1-6,10, where similar phrases speak more clearly to the Spirit of God (Osborne, *Revelation*, 61).

The Holy Spirit of God, John tells us, is in front of God's throne. The Spirit who energizes and equips the churches for service is the Spirit who proceeds from the very throne of God. We are indeed made sufficient for every assignment, every challenge, for the God who lives in us (1 Cor 6:19) is the God who is before the throne! The One who is in heaven is the One who also is in us!

The Son Is Perfect in His Provision (1:5-6)

Revelation may be about eschatology and the future, but even more than that it is a book about the glory and greatness of the warrior Lamb (see Rev 5) and the King of kings and Lord of lords (19:16), the Lord Jesus Christ. Even those with differing theological perspectives can agree on this.

Though it is unusual, John places the Son last in this greeting from the Trinity for emphasis. Indeed he will say more about the Son here than he does the Father and the Holy Spirit put together because the focus of Revelation is on Him! Five tremendous truths concerning who He *is* and what He *does* are highlighted and explained in verses 5-6.

In His Revelation. Jesus is "the faithful witness," the trustworthy revealer of the Father (John 14:9). By His perfect, sinless life and by His words and works, He showed us the character of God. By His present ministry among the churches (Rev 2–3) He reveals the continuing interest and concern of the Father. Gordon Fee makes the interesting observation that in Psalm 89:37 "'the moon' is called 'a faithful witness in the sky,'" and "that language is now transferred to Christ." Further,

> The word translated "witness" (*martyrus*), which eventually
> came to mean "martyr," is here a forensic term, and thus a
> live metaphor for John, reflecting Christ's having stood trial
> and then being sentenced to death. Indeed, this language
> will occur again only in 2:10 and 13, where it clearly refers to
> those who have borne witness "unto death." Thus "Antipas,
> my faithful witness, . . . was put to death in your city" (2:13). In
> turn these linguistic realities are what caused the Greek word
> to make its way into English not as a word for "witness" but as
> a reference to someone who is put to death by others. (Fee,
> *Revelation*, 7)

In His Resurrection. Jesus is "the firstborn from the dead" (Col 1:15,18). Jesus did what no person has ever done: He died, rose from the dead, and stayed alive. However, He is not the only one who will do this; He is the *firstborn*, the first of a new order, the pledge and promise of our resurrection (see 1 Cor 6:14). The language of the *firstborn* is messianic and Davidic (see Ps 89:27: "And I will make Him [Messiah] my Firstborn, the highest of the kings of the earth"). Jesus is first in *time* but also in *importance* as God's firstborn over death. Jesus Himself puts it in perspective in 1:18 when He says, "[I am] the Living One. I was dead, but look—I am alive forever and ever, and I hold the keys of death and Hades."

In His Rule. "The ruler of the kings of the earth" is a recurring theme in Revelation (11:15; 17:15; 19:16). It is not "He will be" but rather "He is!" All authorities, spiritual and earthly, are under His dominion and rule (see Matt 28:16-20). That is true now, and it will be made crystal clear when He comes again (19:11-21). Larry Helyer and Richard Wagner are helpful in providing context and application at this point:

> Talk about being countercultural! This title flies directly in the face of the Roman imperial cult with its claims about the divine Caesar and *Roma* (the Latin name for Rome). John's work portrays the truth as presented in the Bible: All glory and dominion belong to the rightful king (Jesus)—all the more reason for the faithful to remain steadfast. (*Revelation*, 109)

In His Redemption. John identifies Jesus as "Him who loves us and has set us free from our sins by His blood." Jesus loved us (Gal 2:20) and He continually loves us. How do we know? We know it because of the cross! By His bloody and brutal death, He set us free, loosed us once and for all from our sins. He died as our penal substitute. He *lived* the life we should have lived but did not. He *died* the death we should have died but now do not have to. He *paid* the penalty we should pay but cannot. And He gives us a salvation we do not deserve but can freely receive. The KJV and NKJV say He "washed us," viewing sin as a *stain*, and that is certainly true. However, the best manuscripts do render the text as He "loosed" or "set us free" where sin is viewed as a *chain*. I delight in saying it this way:

> He freed us from sin's *penalty*—our *justification*.
> He is freeing us from sin's *power*—our *sanctification*.
> He will free us from sin's *presence*—our *glorification*.

Philip Bliss the hymn writer got it right: "Guilty, vile, and helpless we; / Spotless Lamb of God was He; / Full atonement! Can it be? / Hallelujah, what a Savior!"

In His Reign. Lastly, Jesus "made us a kingdom, priests to His God and Father—the glory and dominion are His forever and ever. Amen." Blood-freed sinners now fill His kingdom to the glory of the Father. To be fully forgiven would be more than enough, but He does even more. Drawing on Exodus 19:5-6, John informs us we have entered the dominion of King Jesus as kings (we reign) and priests (we serve). First Peter 2:5 calls us a "holy priesthood." We serve, worship, and bear witness to the kingdom of our Christ that is both now and not yet. It is real and it is happening right now. However, its full manifestation awaits His second coming. John can only conclude these verses of glorious doxology to our redeeming King with one word: "Amen." It means "it is so" or "so let it be!" (Mounce, *Revelation*, 50). It is a fitting end to this wonderful description of our King. We behold Him for who He is and simply must agree.

Look for the Coming of the Triumphant Lord
REVELATION 1:7-8

John concludes his prologue with a brief word on what Paul calls "the blessed hope and appearing of the glory of our great God and Savior, Jesus Christ" (Titus 2:13). Having discussed His work of redemption, he now draws attention to His day of consummation, "when he will return in triumph and bring history to a close" (Mounce, *Revelation*, 50). Allusions to the Old Testament dominate these two short verses.

His Coming Will Be Seen (1:7)

The call to "Look!" (traditionally "Behold") is a call to pay attention, appearing 25 times in Revelation. We as readers are beckoned to pay attention because what follows is important. "He is coming with the clouds" (see Matt 11:2-3; John 3:31) draws from Daniel 7:13 (see Matt 24:30; Acts 1:9) where the prophet "saw One like a son of man coming with the clouds of heaven." He who is coming is literally, historically, and visibly "coming with the clouds," which is also an atheological symbol for the presence of God (Exod 13:21; 16:10). He who is coming is Jesus Christ (Rev 1:5-6), "and every eye will see Him." This is not the coming of God incognito, which was the case, to some degree, when He came the first time. No, His authority, deity, and sovereignty will be put on full display for all to see. The whole earth will see this!

His Coming Will Bring Sorrow (1:7)

John now combines Daniel 7:13 with Zechariah 12:10 and notes that the audience to this epiphany will include those "who pierced Him." In that day Israel will see and understand that they (and we) crucified their Messiah. And "all the families of the earth will mourn over Him. This is certain. Amen." Yes, Israel will mourn and the nations will mourn. But by God's grace some, including Jews and Gentiles, will mourn in repentance and salvation (5:9-10; 7:1-17; see Zech 13:1; Rom 11:25-26). Others, however, will mourn in remorse as the just and righteous judgment of God is poured out in the great day of wrath (Rev 6:16-17), what is called "the great tribulation" (7:14). Amazingly, they will seek death, not deliverance (6:16). Repentance will not be found in their hearts (9:21).

His Coming Will Be Strength (1:8)

Three of the many titles of God appear in verse 8, where we see one of the only two times God speaks directly in the entire book of Revelation (see 21:5-6). These titles serve as a revelation of His person and power. They also serve as a confirmation and guarantee that these things will surely come to pass. The "Amen" of verse 7 affirmed this. This divine confession settles it!

First, "'I am the Alpha and Omega,' says the Lord God." These are the first and last letters of the Greek alphabet. We would say "the A to Z." The phrase is expanded in 22:13 and applied directly to Jesus. What is said of God can be said of Him because He is God. There we read, "I am the Alpha and the Omega, the First and the Last, the Beginning and the End." The emphasis in 1:7 falls particularly on God's omniscience. "He knows . . . the certainty of this promise" (MacArthur, *Revelation 1–11*, 34).

The second title, "The One who is, who was, and who is coming" (see v. 4), indicates that our God is the eternal and everlasting One. There never was a time when He was not, and there will never be a time when He is not. Stephen Smalley notes the phrase "is repeated from verse 4, and forms an inclusion at the end of the address with its opening." Further,

> The advent theme of verse 7 centered in the returning Christ, is picked up here once again, and set within the total context of the judgment and salvation brought by the living Godhead. . . . John is saying that God is in control of his world, and of all the human activity within it; he is the eternal origin and goal of history in its entirety. (*Revelation*, 58)

Third, our God is "the Almighty" (Gk *pantokrator*), a claim that appears 10 times in the New Testament. Nine of those are in Revelation (1:8; 4:8; 11:17; 15:3; 16:7,14; 19:6,15; 21:22; see 2 Cor 6:18 where it is in a quotation). The title again emphasizes God's sovereignty and omnipotence. This God has absolute authority, control, and power. He is "in control of this world and the next" (Osborne, *Revelation*, 72). This is no finite deity. This is no God in process on the way to completion and perfection. These titles leave no room for "open theism" and a God who is not absolutely omniscient in the fullest sense that word can bear. It is hard to imagine how God Himself could make this clearer!

Conclusion

Several years ago a colleague told me about an interesting experience he had on the mission field when ministering to an underground and persecuted church in a totalitarian country. Out of curiosity he asked, "What are your favorite books in the Bible?" To his surprise the answer was Daniel and Revelation. When he asked why, they said, "Because they teach us in the end our God wins!" Those faithful brothers and sisters in Christ are right. Revelation, in particular, teaches us that Jesus is "the ruler of the kings of the earth" and that "the glory and dominion" are our God's forever. He is "the One who is, who was, and who is coming, the Almighty." This is a God who is victorious. This is a God you can trust. This is a God who will do what He promises. This is what we learn when God speaks from heaven.

—◦—

Excursus: A Run Through Revelation: An Overview/Outline

Introduction: The Christ of Communication (1:1-8)
(He is the God who reveals His will to His people.)
Vision 1: The Christ of the Churches (1:9–3:22)
(He is the God who rebukes and refreshes His churches.)

To Ephesus He says, "Remember your first love." (2:1-7)

To Smyrna He says, "Remain faithful to your God." (2:8-11)

To Pergamum He says, "Repent of false teaching." (2:12-17)

To Thyatira He says, "Remain fast among false teachings." (2:18-29)

To Sardis He says, "Repent from incomplete service." (3:1-6)

To Philadelphia He says, "Rest in the promise of God." (3:7-13)

To Laodicea He says, "Repent from your indifference." (3:14-22)

Vision 2: The Christ of the Cosmos (4:1–16:21)
(He is the God who reclaims the earth for His kingdom.)
    The vision in heaven (4:1–5:14)
    The destruction on the earth (6:1–16:21)
        The seal judgments (6:1-17)
        Detailed explanation (7:1-17)
            The 144,000 Jewish evangelists
        The trumpet judgments (8:1–9:21)
        Detailed explanation (10:1–15:8)
            The two witnesses (10:1–11:18)
            The war in heaven (11:19–12:17)
            The beast and false prophet (13:1-18)
            A description of the end (14:1–15:8)
        The bowl judgments (16:1-21)
Vision 3: The Christ of Conquest (17:1–21:8)
(He is the God who repays the ungodly for their sin.)
    Judgment on false religion (17:1-18)
    Judgment on evil commercialism (18:1-24)
    Justice in Christ's return to the earth (19:1-21)
    Justice in Christ's reign on the earth (20:1-6)
    Justice in Christ's consignment of Satan and sinners to
        the lake of fire (20:7-15)
    Joy in Christ's call of His saints to the new heaven and
        new earth (21:1-8)
Vision 4: The Christ of Consummation (21:9–22:5)
(He is the God who reigns for all eternity.)
    The description of eternity (21:9-27)
    The delights of eternity (22:1-5)
Conclusion: The Christ of Challenge (22:6-21)
(He is the God who requests all to come to Him.)
    He invites the church. (22:5-9)
    He invites the world. (22:10-19)
    He invites the individual believer. (22:20-21)
              (Adapted from Tenney, *Revelation,* 32–41)

Reflect and Discuss

1. Read through the book of Revelation. What would you say is the main theme of the book?
2. Why is it important to remember the symbolic nature of Revelation? Where should we look for help interpreting the symbols?
3. What does it mean to have the expectation of the imminent return of Christ? How does this affect the way we live?
4. Why does it matter how Scripture is read publicly? What blessings come when God's Word is rightly handled? What are the dangers of poor readings of Scripture? What characterizes good public reading?
5. John's Revelation is prophetic and apocalyptic. What does it mean to "keep what is written" in such a book?
6. How would you explain God's relationship to time, as described in Revelation 1:4? How does God's relationship to time bring comfort to the believer?
7. What role does the Holy Spirit play in bringing "grace and peace" to those who are believers in Christ?
8. Discuss the importance of who Jesus is and what He has done in each of the following: revelation, resurrection, rule, redemption, and reign.
9. Why is it significant that Jesus' return will be seen by all? What false teachings does this truth rule out?
10. Verse 8 contains several names for God. What do these names mean for you in your Christian walk? What are some other names for God revealed in Scripture?

A Vision of the Exalted and Glorified Christ

REVELATION 1:9-20

Main Idea: Even in the midst of suffering and hardship, the church of Christ can look to the risen Savior and receive encouragement to both persevere and worship.

I. **The Plan of Christ Involves Suffering and Service (1:9-11).**
   A. We suffer for His kingdom (1:9).
   B. We serve His church (1:10-11).
II. **The Person of Christ Should Awe and Inspire (1:12-16).**
   A. Sense His presence (1:12).
   B. Marvel at His portrait (1:13-16).
III. **The Power of Christ Should Overwhelm and Encourage (1:17-20).**
   A. He lives forever (1:17-18).
   B. He has authority over death (1:18).
   C. He has a plan (1:19).
   D. He helps His people understand His Word (1:20).

The book of Revelation is unique in so many ways. It is the only book in the New Testament where the writer is told to write at the direct command of the Lord who appears to him (1:10-11,19). It was written at the end of the first century, when the church faced persecution from without and compromise from within. It was written by the last living apostle, John, who also gave us a Gospel and three canonical letters that bear his name. It was written from an island called Patmos in the Aegean Sea, which is about 70 miles southwest of Ephesus. John was a prisoner there, having been exiled under the reign of Emperor Domitian (AD 81–96) because of his faithful witness to Jesus (v. 9).

Three times in the 22 chapters of Revelation, at strategic moments, great visions of the exalted Christ take the stage. Some scholars even believe Revelation was written as a three-act or seven-act play patterned after the Greek theater (Osborne, *Revelation*, 29).

1:12-16	The exalted Christ who walks among His churches
5:5-14	The warrior Lamb on the throne in heaven
19:11-21	The King of kings who is coming again

For people who need to be encouraged to persevere when persecuted and need to be challenged to remain faithful and not compromise, these visions are timely and much-needed medicine.

Before examining the first vision in 1:9-20, we must ask an important question: What interpretive method should we employ for Revelation? Basically, four views have been set forth:

- *Preterism*—The book addresses details and events in the first century.
- *Idealism*—The book addresses timeless truths and does not deal with historical events.
- *Historicism*—The book is a chronicle of Western church history.
- *Futurism*—The book (chs. 4–22 or 6–22) speaks primarily to future events at the end of history and leading into the eternal state (chs. 21–22).

There are elements of truth in each of these views. Personally, I try to draw what I see are the best elements from all four. The result is that I take a modified futurist approach (I am not a classic dispensationalist), or what some call an eclectic approach. In this regard, I fall in line with New Testament scholars like Greg Beale, D. A. Carson, Robert Mounce, and Grant Osborne. That does not mean I will be in agreement with these men on every interpretive point, but I do agree with them overall. Osborne summarizes this perspective well:

> The solution is to allow the preterist, idealist, and futurist methods to interact in such a way that the strengths are maximized and the weaknesses minimized. . . . For instance, the beast of 13:1-8 refers both to the "many antichrists" throughout church history and to the final Antichrist at the end of history . . . the futurist rather than the idealist position is primary. My study of ancient apocalyptic and of the Book of Revelation has led me to believe that John's visions (esp. chps. 4–22) were primarily intended to describe the events that will end world history. The saints in these chapters are believers alive in that final period, and the beast is the Antichrist who will lead the "earth-dwellers"/unbelievers in a final pogrom against all the people of God. The seals, trumpets, and bowls symbolize a final series of judgments by which God will turn the evil deeds of the nations back upon their heads (the Roman legal principle of *lex talionis*, the law

of retribution) to prove his sovereignty once and for all and to give them a final chance to repent (9:20-21; 11:13; 14:6-7; 16:9,11). But the preterist school is also correct, because the visions use the events of the future to address John and his readers in the present. Most of the imagery used to describe the beast and Babylon the Great comes from actual first-century parallels. The beast is a final Nerolike figure, and Babylon is the final unholy Roman Empire. One of my definitions for apocalyptic is "the present addressed through parallels with the future." John's readers were being asked to identify with the people at the end of history and gain perspective for their present suffering through the future trials of God's people. This leads us to the idealist position, also intended in the text, for these final events are also timeless symbols meant to challenge the church in every era. (*Revelation*, 21–22)

I believe this hermeneutical approach is both balanced and wise. It allows apocalyptic literature to do what it is intended to do, and at the same time it helps us avoid wild speculation that often, if not always, proves embarrassing and foolish. We will move through the 22 chapters with what I hope is a sane and tame premillennialism. My cards are on that table!

The Plan of Christ Involves Suffering and Service
REVELATION 1:9-11

A study on the book of Revelation may possibly be titled, "The Normal Christian Life: Prosperity Gospelers Need Not Apply." The apostle John had been faithful both to preach the Word of God and to proclaim the testimony of Jesus Christ (see 1:2). David Platt points out this idea appears three other times in Revelation (6:9; 12:17; 20:4), and every time it refers to Christians who are suffering because they are speaking and witnessing about Jesus ("Danger"). Christians will be attacked, exiled, slaughtered, beheaded. Serving Christ will not be easy. It is costly! John's reward for being such a faithful witness was imprisonment and being sent away to die alone. There was no health and wealth for this follower of Jesus.

Patmos was a ten-by-six-mile mountainous island in the Aegean Sea off the coast of Asia Minor (modern Turkey). It may have been a penal colony for exiled criminals banished and sentenced to hard labor in the rock quarries. Though the island was inhabitable and had a sizable population, it is all but certain John was sent there (ca. AD 95, according to Eusebius) as a criminal against the state. John MacArthur summarizes what might well have been John's situation:

> According to the Roman historian Tacitus, exile to such islands was a common form of punishment in the first century. At about the same time that John was banished to Patmos, Emperor Domitian exiled his own niece, Flavia Domitilla, to another island. Unlike Flavia Domitilla, whose banishment was politically motivated, John was probably sent to Patmos as a criminal (as a Christian, he was a member of an illegal religious sect). If so, the conditions under which he lived would have been harsh. Exhausting labor under the watchful eye (and ready whip) of a Roman overseer, insufficient food and clothing, and having to sleep on the bare ground would have taken their toll on a ninety-year-old man. It was on the bleak, barren island, under those brutal conditions, that John received the most extensive revelation of the future ever given. (*Revelation 1–11*, 41)

For the apostle John, service to the Lord Jesus meant suffering and even death. We will find throughout the book that the gospel demands such devotion from all of Christ's people.

We Suffer for His Kingdom (1:9)

John begins by calling himself not an apostle but a "brother and partner." He knew that there is *partnership* in suffering for Jesus. He is not alone. He is no Lone Ranger. His Lord had suffered, and his brother James was martyred. Paul and Peter were likewise dead. John knew that many share as partners in the Lord's work. He could therefore take heart; we suffer as family.

There is also *pain* in suffering for Jesus. "Tribulation" means pressure, trouble, affliction. It is a part of the normal Christian life. Tribulation need not sidetrack our walk with Christ. John, like Peter, Paul, and the Lord, received his greatest revelation and climbed his highest spiritual mountain during a time of extreme suffering and persecution for Christ. Second Timothy 3:12 reminds us, "All those who want to live a godly life in Christ Jesus will be persecuted."

There is *privilege* in suffering for Jesus. John speaks of a "kingdom." Jesus inaugurated His kingdom as a suffering Savior. We enter the kingdom and serve as suffering saints. Reigning and suffering are not mutually exclusive. It is the way of Jesus. It is also to be our way.

There is *purpose* in suffering for Jesus. "Endurance" or perseverance means to abide under a heavy load, to stay with it, to hang in there, not to throw in the towel or drop out of the race. All of this is in Him, in Jesus, according to His will, His plan. John's exile to Patmos was no accident. It did not catch God by surprise anymore than any crisis or tribulation we face catches Him off guard or unprepared. It is in Christ, of Christ, and for Christ. Jesus provided the needed strength for John, and He will do the same for us. James 1:4 reminds us to let "endurance do its complete work, so that you may be mature and complete, lacking nothing."

Being witness to God's Word, all of it, and staying faithful in our testimony to Jesus may cost us. We may suffer unjustly. When that happens, remember what Jesus said: "A slave is not greater than his master. If they persecuted Me, they will also persecute you" (John 15:20).

We Serve His Church (1:10-11)

John tells us he "was in the Spirit on the Lord's day." The phrase "in the Spirit" occurs four times in Revelation (1:10; 4:2; 17:3; 21:10). Like Old Testament prophets he was in a supernatural state of inspiration as he wrote. He was "caught up in an ecstatic experience" (Ladd, *Commentary*, 31). Nothing in the text indicates John sought it. It was a divine seizing by God.

"The Lord's day" is almost certainly Sunday, or perhaps Easter Sunday. It was the day of worship. It was resurrection day, and John was worshiping the Lord. Suddenly John heard a loud voice behind him like a trumpet (see 4:1). It was sharp, clear, and loud—a clarion call. Some say the voice is that of an angel, but what follows clearly identifies the speaker as the Lord Jesus Christ. He is commanded to write on a scroll what he saw and send it to the seven churches. These seven churches were especially dear to the heart of God and the heart of John. These were actual historical churches in Asia. The number seven also stands for completeness. It would also indicate their representative nature of the various types of churches that exist throughout the history of the church. Christ had a word for His churches that is detailed in chapters 2–3. He tells John to write, and John does—one of the most magnificent books of all time. John received a command from his Lord and obeyed. And by obeying, he served well Christ's church.

The Person of Christ Should Awe and Inspire
REVELATION 1:12-16

In Song of Songs 5:10-16 there is a poetic description of Solomon as the shepherd-king and husband. Some have said it is almost apocalyptic. Now in Revelation we find another portrait of a shepherd-king and husband (7:17; 19:7-10) that is most definitely apocalyptic, and it may be the most magnificent picture in all of Scripture of the Lord Jesus Christ.

Sense His Presence (1:12)

John turned to see the One whose voice was like a trumpet, who spoke directly to him with a commission to address the seven churches. What John saw would encourage his heart. It would also knock him off his feet and nearly take his life (v. 17).

John sees "seven golden lampstands." Moses constructed a seven-branched lampstand for the tabernacle (Exod 37:17-24). Zechariah had a vision of a seven-branched golden lampstand that represented the "eyes of the Lord, which range throughout the earth" (Zech 4:10). Verse 20 tells us that in Revelation they are the seven churches. As lampstands they held small oil lamps. From them light, God's light, was to go out to a dark and evil world. For us the assignment is the same. We are to be "the light of the world" (Matt 5:14).

John also saw a person in the midst of the lampstands. His identity is no secret: it is the Son of Man, the Lord Jesus. Both His title and His location are significant. The title goes back to Daniel 7:13-14. This is Jesus' favorite self-designation. It occurs 81 times in the Gospels. It identifies Him as the heavenly Messiah who is also human and who will receive an eternal kingdom. His location is among the lampstands. He is there with them. He knows what they are going through. He is watching and He is working in His churches. Though they may fail Him, He will not fail them. To sense His presence would encourage and sustain them. He is right there in the middle of all they experience. And what a One it is who is with them, as verses 13-16 make clear!

Marvel at His Portrait (1:13-16)

Jesus is unveiled in all His glory and splendor. What John saw, human words can only approximate. Our attention is again drawn to Daniel 7 due to His appearance as well as His threefold office as Prophet, Priest, and King. What unfolds in the vision of Christ bears this out. John saw the unveiled, glorified, and exalted Jesus.

In His clothing He is our *priest* (v. 13). He is dressed "in a long robe and with a gold sash wrapped around His chest." This is the clothing of the priest in the Old Testament (Exod 28:4). It signifies Jesus as our great high priest and points to His work of atonement and intercession on our behalf (see Heb 7:25).

In His wisdom He is *profound* (v. 14). "His head and hair were white like wool—white as snow." The significance of these words and their Old Testament connections are powerful and must not be missed. John Piper, with great insight, puts it in proper perspective:

> This is remarkable, because in that same chapter in Daniel (7) where John gets this picture of "one like a son of man" (vv. 13-14), God the Father is described like this in verse 9: "The Ancient of Days took his seat; his vesture was like white snow, and the hair of his head like pure wool." In other words John is describing the Son of Man in terms used for God himself. John wants us to see something here about the age of Christ and the wisdom and dignity that come with age—everlasting age!
>
> In American culture today, we respect the process of aging less and less. A person is admired if he can keep looking young, not if he has the dignity of age. The Bible saw it another way. Proverbs 16:31 says, "A white head is a crown of glory," so much so that in the law God commanded, "You will rise up before the white head, and honor the face of an old man, and you shall fear your God; I am the Lord" (Leviticus 19:32).
>
> One of the reasons we don't want to grow old is that we associate age with the fading of powers that make life worth living—the capacity to see and hear and think clearly and move about and not have pain. But all of those things do not belong to aging *as aging*. They belong to aging in a futile and fallen world of sin. Once God does away with sin and the

curse, and establishes the new heavens and the new earth, aging will not have any of these negative connotations. It will only be associated with growing wisdom and insight and maturity. All the strength will still be there. All the mental powers. All the sight and hearing and agility. Nothing that is great about youth will be left behind. There will only be added all the powers and beauties and depth of age.

This is what John saw in Jesus. He was like the Ancient of Days with all the wisdom of eternity and all the maturity and steadiness of age, but he was not weak or weary or faltering in his step. ("Look at Jesus")

That His eyes are "like a fiery flame" speaks of penetrating insight and omniscient intelligence. In fiery holiness, the true condition of each church, each Christian is transparent to the gaze of His eyes (see 19:12).

In His strength He is *permanent* (v. 15): "His feet were like fine bronze as it is fired in a furnace." He is strong, solid, and stable (see Ps 110:1; Heb 10:13).

In His announcement He is *powerful* (v. 15): "His voice like the sound of cascading waters." It is a voice of awesome power and pervasive authority. It echoes forth His majesty and sovereignty like the waves that continually crash against the rocks of Patmos.

For His servants He is *protective* (v. 16). The "right hand" is the hand of authority and honor. What is in His hand is His possession and has His protection (see John 10:28). The "seven stars" (see v. 20) are His servants who are protected. They most likely are angels who have a specific relationship to the church (see 1 Cor 11:10), though many believe they represent the pastor of each church. Regardless, they belong only to Him. They are His and under His protection.

In His judgments He is *perfect* (v. 16). "A sharp double-edged sword came from His mouth" (see Heb 4:12), the Tracian sword—long, broad, and heavy; sharp on both sides (mentioned six times in Revelation: 1:16; 2:12,16; 6:8; 19:15,21). The sword is the Word of God, divine in judgment, power, and authority. It both cuts and cures, hurts and heals.

In His appearance He is *praiseworthy* (v. 16): "His face was shining like the sun at midday." This speaks of His brilliance, holiness, majesty, and awesomeness. John saw Jesus as He, the Son of God, truly is. He is an awesome God, a powerful God, a majestic God. He is a God worthy of our worship, worthy of our service, worthy of all we can give Him. He is a God whose presence gives us assurance. The Lord knows what is happening in His churches, for He is continually among them. Our Lord is an awesome God, sufficient for every need we may have.

The Power of Christ Should Overwhelm and Encourage
REVELATION 1:17-20

To see Jesus today as He is (glorified) and us as we are (sinners) is more than we can take. In our sinful condition the magnificence of His glory would overwhelm us as it did John. It would be too much. We would not survive. John nearly died. Verses 17-20, following 13-16, help show us why. This is the Lord, the Savior, King Jesus.

He Lives Forever (1:17-18)

John "fell at His feet like a dead man," but Jesus laid His right hand on him with gentle authority. He said, "Don't be afraid," literally the command to "stop being afraid." "I am the First (*protos*) and the Last (*eschatos*)." This is said of God in Isaiah 44:6 and 48:12 and also of Jesus in Revelation 1:17; 2:8; and 22:13. He is God, absolute Lord both of creation and history. He starts and He finishes. He is before all and He is after all. All is under His sovereign control.

He is the "Living One," declaring, "I was dead, but look—I am alive forever and ever." He was dead (once in the past), but He beckons us to look and see that He is alive forever and ever. He died once and for all on the cross, but He will never die again. Atonement, perfect atonement, has been made. Amen!

He Has Authority Over Death (1:17-18)

"Hades" is similar to the Old Testament *Sheol*, meaning the grave, the place of all the dead, or (as it is used in Revelation) the place of the wicked dead. "Death" claims the body. "Hades" claims the soul but not unless Jesus says so! He has the keys. He has the authority. Jesus holds "the keys of death and Hades." He alone opens and closes this door.

He Has a Plan (1:19)

I believe this verse unlocks the key to the book of Revelation. It tells us how the book unfolds, and it tells us how God's eschatological plan will take place. James Hamilton says it "serves as a preview of the overarching structure of the book of Revelation" (*Revelation*, 51).

"What you have seen" looks to Revelation 1:9-20.
"What is" looks to chapters 2–3.
"What will take place after this" looks to chapters 4–22.

As we work through the book, we will see a general chronological progression, not a direct line. At times we step back in history or take some interludes, but all the while the book moves toward the consummation of history and the eternal state.

He Helps His People Understand His Word (1:20)

Jesus now becomes our teacher and interpreter. He informs us that the seven stars are the seven angels of the seven churches, and the seven lampstands are the seven churches we see in chapters 2–3. Many times, but not every time, symbols will be explained for us. This is a blessing and an act of divine grace. Christ gives us spiritual insight at this point as we prepare to move ahead. Then, as now, He looks for those who have ears to hear what the Spirit says (2:7,11,17,29; 3:6,13,22). This Word was made clear in chapter 1; of that there is no doubt. Were we listening?

Conclusion

Revelation, rightly understood, had a word for the first-century church. Rightly understood, it has had a word for the church throughout history. And rightly understood, it has a word for the church today and tomorrow. At the heart of that word, that message, is this: Gaze on the exalted and glorified Christ. He walks among His churches and His people as the glorious Son of Man (1:13). He is, as John Piper well says,

> the one with power over the nations and with everlasting dominion and glory. He is the great high priest that has put away the sins of his people once and for all. He is as aged and wise and mature as the great white-crowned Ancient of Days, yet with eyes that are aflame with the fire of youth and energy and hope and exhilaration for his unstoppable plans for you and for this church and for the world.
>
> Gaze upon Jesus and let his royal power and his priestly forgiveness and his ancient wisdom and his fiery hope fill you with confidence afresh that [in the past] has not been in vain, and that [in the future] will be the appointed brush-stroke on the canvas of your life and on the canvas of history till the great mosaic of God's work is done. ("Look at Jesus")

So, do not fear *time*. He is the First and the Last.
Do not fear *life*. It is He who is alive forevermore.
Do not fear *dying*. He holds the keys to the grave and death.

Reflect and Discuss

1. Briefly explain the different interpretive methods used to understand the book of Revelation. What are the strengths and weaknesses of each?
2. How does the book of Revelation contradict the false teachings of the prosperity gospel?
3. In what way is suffering and persecution a corporate event? What does it mean to be partners with those who are being persecuted?
4. Why is it a privilege to suffer for Christ? How does this logic go against worldly interests?
5. Why is Jesus' presence in the midst of the lampstands/churches comforting to us?
6. What parallels are there between Revelation 1 and Daniel 7? What do these suggest about who Christ is?
7. What is most striking to you about the portrait of Jesus as seen in verses 13-16? Why?
8. Why does Jesus emphasize His eternality when revealing Himself to John? What significance does this carry for the rest of Revelation?
9. Verses 17-18 show Jesus' authority over death. How does this reinforce Paul's point in 1 Corinthians 15?ß
10. Do you agree that the message of Revelation is to "gaze on the exalted and glorified Christ"? How else might you summarize the book's message?

When a Church Loses Its Love for Jesus

REVELATION 2:1-7

Main Idea: Though Jesus is pleased with our obedience, He is jealous for hearts that maintain a devoted love for Him that fuels good works.

I. **Christ Is Characterized by His Protection (2:1).**
 A. Christ cares.
 B. Christ is there.
II. **The Church Is Commended for Its Purity (2:2-3,6).**
 A. Jesus is pleased with our good deeds (2:2).
 B. Jesus is pleased with our faithful dedication (2:3).
 C. Jesus is pleased with our sound doctrine (2:2,6).
III. **The Church Is Criticized for Its Passion (2:4).**
 A. Jesus is honest with His people.
 B. Jesus is jealous for His people.
IV. **The Church Is Corrected with a Plan (2:5).**
 A. Remember from where you have fallen.
 B. Repent of your sin.
 C. Return to where you first fell in love.
V. **The Church Is Challenged with a Promise (2:7).**
 A. We can conquer by perseverance.
 B. We will celebrate in paradise.

A Word About the Seven Churches of Revelation 2–3

Chapters 2–3 of Revelation address the seven churches John greeted in chapter 1. They are each unique in their circumstances, makeup, and situation. John, however, addresses them in a common manner, and we can highlight certain characteristics they share:

1. All seven churches follow a distinct and similar pattern:
 a. A characteristic of *Christ* drawn from Revelation 1 (and other texts)
 b. A word of *commendation* and praise if appropriate
 c. *Criticism* for their sins

      d. A word of *correction* and *warning*

      e. A *challenge* and promise drawn from Revelation 19–22 (and other texts)

  6. These were seven *historical churches* located in Asia Minor (modern Turkey) at the end of the first century AD.

  7. These churches were in and around Ephesus, the major city of the province of Asia at that time.

  8. These churches were located on a major postal/travel route and are addressed in a counterclockwise order in terms of their location.

  9. Each of their messages has a word of wisdom and application for all churches throughout history until Jesus comes again. These seven churches do not represent seven ages or dispensations of the church (usually seen as the church in the West).

  10. The chart on the next page helps us see the parallels and patterns in the seven letters.

The first of these churches to be addressed is the church at Ephesus, for whom the Lord Jesus has some difficult words.

Introduction

Few things are more hurtful and painful than when a spouse says to their mate, "I don't love you anymore." Sometimes there is shock. Often there are tears. To hear the one you have covenanted with for life say, "I have lost my passion for you; I no longer desire you; my feelings for you have grown cold," rips at the heart and wounds the soul. We may sing a song that says, "You've lost that lovin' feeling," but we all know this is nothing to sing about.

Now, looking in from the outside, we may not actually know what is going on in a marriage. I often say, "No one knows what goes on behind closed doors." And sometimes, in fact most times, love for another is lost not in a moment but over time. It takes place slowly, not quickly. We may not even realize it is happening.

This was true of the first-century church in Ephesus. By all outward appearances things were good. However, in this instance looks were deceiving, and the Lord who walked among them knew it. Like many churches, this church was doing many good things. But they had somehow neglected and lost the most important thing: Christ and the gospel. Their condition was critical but not hopeless. The Christ who loved

The Seven Churches of Revelation: A Comparison

The Church	Christ	Commendation	Criticism	Correction	Challenge
Ephesus (2:1-7)	Holds the seven stars in His right hand, walks among the seven golden lampstands (1:20)	Works, toil, endurance, intolerance of evil, judgment of false teachers in word and actions	You left your first love.	Remember, repent, and return to your first works or be extinguished.	You will eat from the tree of life in paradise (22:2).
Smyrna (2:8-11)	The First and the Last, who died and came to life (1:17-18)	Tribulation, poverty, and slander			Do not fear, be faithful; you will receive the crown of life and not experience the second death (20:6,14; 21:8).
Pergamos (2:12-17)	Has the sharp double-edged sword (1:16)	Faithfulness, honor for the name of Jesus, refusal to deny faith in Christ	You hold the teachings of Balaam (spiritual compromise) leading to idolatry and sexual immorality, and the teachings of the Nicolaitans.	Repent or face My sword.	Receive My hidden manna, a white stone, and a new name (19:12).

The Church	Christ	Commendation	Criticism	Correction	Challenge
Thyatira (2:18-29)	Has eyes like a flame of fire and feet like burnished bronze (1:14-15)	Works, love, faith, service, and patient endurance	You tolerate Jezebel, a false prophetess who led you into idolatry and sexual immorality.	Repent and hold fast what you have until I come.	You will receive authority over the nations, and the morning star (20:1-6; 22:16).
Sardis (3:1-6)	Has the seven spirits of God and the seven stars (1:4,20)	Works, undefiled clothes	You are spiritually dead.	Wake up, strengthen what remains, remember: repent.	You will be clothed in white garments, not blotted out of the book of life. I will confess your name (19:8,14; 20:12,15).
Philadelphia (3:7-13)	Holy and true One who has the key of David and who opens and shuts (1:8)	Works, keeping of Jesus' word, refusal to deny His name		Just keep holding onto what you have.	You will be kept from the hour of temptation, made a pillar in God's temple, and receive the name of God, new Jerusalem, and Jesus' new name (19:12;21:2;22:4).
Laodicea (3:14-22)	The Amen, the faithful and true witness, the beginning of God's creation (1:5)		You are lukewarm, wretched, pitiable, poor, blind, and naked.	Buy refined gold from Jesus and white clothing, eye salve. Be zealous and repent.	You will have communion with Christ and sit on His throne (20:4-6).

them and had freed them from their sins (1:5) was there to cure them
if they would listen.

Christ Is Characterized by His Protection
REVELATION 2:1

The exalted Christ has been revealed to us in all of His glory in 1:13-
16. Both His work of atonement (1:5) and His vindicating resurrection
(1:5,18) have been highlighted. This Christ is sufficient for every need
His churches might have. John, on behalf of Christ, writes to the angel
who watches over the church at Ephesus.

Ephesus was a city of significance in the first century politically, commercially, and religiously, though its significance was waning. Politically,
it was the capital of Asia and known as the "Supreme Metropolis of Asia."
Commercially, the great highways converged there, and a major seaport
was still in place, but silt deposited by the Cayster River was building
in the mouth of the harbor and would eventually be the death of the
city's importance. Some have referred to Ephesus as "the Vanity Fair
of the Ancient World" (Barclay, *Revelation*, 59). Religiously, the city was
the center for the worship of the fertility goddess Diana (Roman) or
Artemis (Greek). The temple dedicated to Diana came to be known
as one of the "Seven Wonders of the Ancient World" and a source
of intense civic pride. Thousands of priests and priestesses served in
the temple, many as religious prostitutes. One of Ephesus's own philosophers, Heraclitus, was known as the weeping philosopher, and he
lamented over the immorality and wickedness of the city, saying that its
citizens were "fit only to be drowned, and that the reason he could never
laugh or smile was because he lived amidst such terrible uncleanness"
(Johnson, *Revelation*, 1983, 41).

Paul, Aquila, and Priscilla evangelized and founded the church at
Ephesus (Acts 18:18-19; 19:1-10). Paul believed the city to be so significant as a gospel outpost that he labored there for at least two years (Acts
19:10). His ministry was not uneventful and included a riot related to
the temple of Diana. Later Paul would meet with their elders at Miletus
(Acts 20:17-38), and he wrote one of his prison letters to them in the
early 60s. Paul, Timothy, and now John had ministered to this church.
What a heritage! What a danger! Here is a second-generation church
that apparently was living off the prestige and momentum of the past.
The past was great, but their present condition was spiritually perilous.

Christ Cares

Jesus is described in two ways in verse 1. First, He "holds [present tense] the seven stars in His right hand." He is in possession of His "church angels" with divine authority. He is responsible for them, and they, like us, are accountable to Him. Ladd says,

> The Greek verb used here . . . [indicates] that Christ holds his churches firmly in his hand, that they should not be snatched away (see John 10:28). (Ladd, *Commentary*, 38)

Every church Jesus purchased with His own blood is dear to Him.

Christ Is There

John says, secondly, Christ "walks [present tense] among the seven gold lampstands." Our Lord walks about among His people, His church. He is no absentee landlord or disinterested deity. He is there, up close and personal, intimately present.

For contemporary believers, this promise remains. Christ is our sustainer and protector. He is our vigilant watchman. He sees what we do, hears what we say, and knows how we think and what is in our heart. This brings great assurance. It also brings great accountability.

The Church Is Commended for Its Purity
REVELATION 2:2-3,6

The church at Ephesus was active and busy in doing many good things. Our Lord accurately and fairly assesses and takes note of these. In fact, every church should seek to emulate the church at Ephesus at this point. Three things, in particular, are recognized and commended by our Lord: its works, labor, and endurance.

Jesus Is Pleased with Our Good Deeds (2:2)

This community was busy for the Lord. Mounce says, "The Ephesians had toiled to the point of exhaustion and borne patiently the hostility of a society at odds with their goals and efforts" (Mounce, *Revelation*, 68). Further, "they could not tolerate evil." Holiness and purity mattered to them. Scripture, not the culture, guided their moral behavior. Purity of life was a hallmark of this community of faith. I like the way *The Message* phrases it: "I see what you've done, your hard, hard work, your refusal to quit. I know you can't stomach evil."

Jesus Is Pleased with Our Dedication (2:3)

Jesus says of the Ephesians, "You also possess endurance and have toler-ated many things [NIV, "endured hardship"] because of My name and have not grown weary." Life was not easy for these followers of the cruci-fied Galilean. Swindoll notes:

> The Ephesian Christians faced special challenges. Because they refused to bow the knee to the goddess Diana or the images of the emperor, they found themselves maligned, slandered, boycotted, and abused. Not unlike Jewish merchants in Berlin in the 1930's Christians in Ephesus would have been the objects of physical violence, social ostracism, and economic repression. Yet they endured. They bore up under the load. Clearly, Ephesus had been taught well by its predecessors, Paul, Timothy, and John. (*Insights*, 38)

These were not fair-weather fans of Christ and His cross, and the Lord took note of their dedication.

Jesus Is Pleased with Our Sound Doctrine (2:2,6)

This church was theologically orthodox and evangelical to the core. They took confessional identity and doctrinal fidelity seriously. One of the evidences that they would not "tolerate evil" is that "they tested those who call themselves apostles and are not, and have found them to be liars." I suspect the tests or theological exams they gave related to things like these:

- What do you believe about Jesus—His person and work?
- What is the gospel, and how are people born again?
- Do you believe a holy life should complement our confession of Christ?
- Do you teach anything contrary to or in addition to the Word of God and the witness of the 12 apostles?

I think this to be the case because these are the types of issues that arise in virtually every generation. Further, in verse 6 they are commended because they "hate the practices of the Nicolaitans, which I also hate." Many people imagine Jesus is always meek and mild, only ever saying positive things about everyone. But from His own lips, Jesus tells us there is something He hates!

Exactly who the Nicolaitans were we cannot be sure. It would seem idolatry and immorality were at the roots of their practices.

―――

Excursus: The Nicolaitans

In the New Testament only two passages refer to the Nicolaitans—Revelation 2:6 and 2:15. Likewise, the church fathers Irenaeus, Clement, and Tertullian mention the Nicolaitans only briefly. The New Testament shows that the Nicolaitans were a sect whose teachings were repudiated in Ephesus (2:6), yet they had several adherents in Pergamum (2:15).

Irenaeus (*Against Heresies* 1.26.3) identified the Nicolaitans as the heretical followers of Nicolaus, the proselyte of Antioch (Acts 6:5): "The Nicolaitans are the followers of that Nicolaus who was one of the seven first ordained to the diaconate by the apostles. They lead lives of unrestrained indulgence. The character of these men is very plainly pointed out in the Apocalypse of John when they are represented as teaching that it is a matter of indifference to practice adultery, and to eat things sacrificed to idols."

Hippolytus added that one of the seven appointed apostles lapsed from the true doctrine (*The Refutation of All Heresies* 7.24). Clement of Alexandria identified the followers of Nicolaus as a Gnostic sect who, "abandoning themselves to pleasure like goats, as if insulting the body, led a life of self-indulgence" (*The Stromata* 2.20). Tertullian asserted that the Nicolaitans aimed at destroying the happiness of sanctity by their lust and luxury (*Against Marcion* 1.29).

The consensus of early Christian writings is that the Nicolaitans were the followers of Nicolaus (Acts 6:5) and thus the founders of libertine gnosticism.

Other scholars use etymological study to posit that the word "Nicolaus" is simply the Greek equivalent of Balaam. This view also proposes that the two words, *Balaam* and *Nicolaitan*, have common meanings. *Balaam*, derived from two Hebrew words *bala' 'am,* means the "destroyer of the people." *Nicolaus,* composed of two Greek words, *nikan laos,* means "conqueror of the people."

The theology of the Nicolaitans can be seen in the description of the evil works of the church at Pergamum (Rev 2:15). What did the Nicolaitans teach? Immorality and idolatry appear to be the heresies that they tried to teach in the churches at Ephesus and Pergamum. Ephesus refused, but Pergamum tolerated a group who believed the Nicolaitans. These pagan practices, contrary to the thought and conduct required in the Christian churches, paralleled the teaching of Balaam in the Old Testament. Balaam "taught Balak to place a stumbling block in front of the Israelites" causing them "to eat meat sacrificed to idols and to commit sexual immorality" (2:14).

The Nicolaitans perhaps had misunderstood Paul's doctrine of freedom from the law when they encouraged eating meat sacrificed to idols and participating in immoral sexual practices. The Nicolaitans also could have been responsible for the teaching that one could "worship Caesar in the flesh and Christ in the Spirit." In order to avoid embarrassment at civic and religious activities, this group may have chosen to assimilate pagan practices into the life of the church. This attempt to accommodate non-Christian practices is condemned by Christ. It was also rejected by the Ephesians. For this the Ephesians are commended by Christ (Glaze, "Nicolaus," 49–53).

The Church Is Criticized for Its Passion
REVELATION 2:4

By all outward appearances this church looked healthy. Its doctrine was spot on, and the lifestyles of its members matched their confession. However—and this is an ever present hazard—they were in danger of becoming "a Pharisee church." They were in danger of a legalism that in time would be their death. They were still doing all the right things, but sometime in the past they had forsaken the right motivation. They didn't have a head problem but a heart problem. Obedience out of duty had replaced obedience out of love for Christ. The difference between the two is massive. It is the difference between "I obey and Jesus accepts me" and "Jesus accepts me and I gladly obey."

Jesus Is Honest with His People

"But I have this against you." What painful and sobering words to hear from our Master. "There is an area of your life where I am in opposition. There is an area that disappoints and offends Me." We are His children, but like our own earthly daughters and sons, we can disappoint our heavenly parent. The Son of God with "eyes like a fiery flame" (1:14) sees something He does not like, and He honestly and straightforwardly tells them so.

Jesus Is Jealous for His People

Specifically, Jesus' honesty reveals His jealous love for His church: "You have abandoned [NIV, "forsaken"] the love you had at first." *The Message* reads, "But you walked away from your first love—why? What's going on with you, anyway?" The Ephesians did not lose their first love. They left it. Could their love for doctrinal and moral purity create a community where love had disappeared?

What is the love they had abandoned? Various views have been proffered: (1) their original love for one another; (2) their love for God; (3) their love for the gospel; (4) their love for Christ. There is a sense in which we need not choose because all four are so interrelated as to prevent separation. The two great commandments would seem to support this (Matt 22:37-40). And yet I think Jesus may have intended, at least as His major focus, to remind them of their love for Him and for the gospel that they had experienced at salvation. Osborne says,

> "They had lost the first flush of enthusiasm and excitement in their Christian life and had settled into a cold orthodoxy with more surface strength than depth." (*Revelation*, 115)

The fervent and passionate love they had for Jesus and His gospel when they first received Him had waned. They were now going through the motions. They could no longer sing, "Every day with Jesus is sweeter than the day before."

Jesus makes clear that He has not lost His passion, His holy jealousy for His people (see Jas 4:5). He wants their obedience, yes. But He also wants their affection. It matters to Jesus not only what we do but why we do what we do.

The Church Is Corrected with a Plan
REVELATION 2:5

All was not well, but all was not lost. It never is with Jesus and His church. Our great physician has diagnosed the illness. Now He offers a threefold remedy with three direct commands or imperatives.

Remember from Where You Have Fallen

Jesus calls the Ephesians to "remember." The present imperative form of this verb beckons them to "keep on remembering." Never forget what you have lost. Go back and note when and where the flame of love grew faint. Take an inventory and evaluate where you are now compared to where you were then. Go back to the time when your love for Jesus was a burning passion and all that mattered. What was it like? What is missing now?

Repent of Your Sin

To repent is to undergo a change of mind resulting in a change of attitude and action. It is to think differently about your sin—sins of indifference, religious formalism, legalistic routine. It requires that we change our minds from thinking that our good deeds are meritorious and earn God's favor. In calling for the Ephesians to repent, Jesus reminds them that *labor* is no substitute for *love, purity* is no substitute for *passion*, and *deeds* are no substitute for *devotion*. Do not pat yourself on the back for doing good things for the wrong reason. God looks on the heart (1 Sam 16:7; Mark 7:6).

Return to Where You First Fell in Love

Finally, Jesus instructs them to "do the works you did at first." The *first works* are the key to restoring their *first love*. When the days with Jesus were so sweet and precious you could think of no one else, what were you doing? What were you thinking? You could not believe He loved someone like you! That He forgave someone like you! That He wanted someone like you! You walked, talked, sang, and thought of Him all day long. You were continually aware of His presence, continually in conversation with Him.

The place where you first fell in love with Christ is the place where you first understood He loved you, not because you deserved it or could even earn it but because He just did. The place where you first fell in love was probably somewhere near the cross. As the hymn writer describes, "At the cross I stood one day. Love and mercy found me. . . . Near the cross! O Lamb of God, bring its scenes before me" (Crosby, "Near the Cross").

Returning and doing the first works will keep a church from losing its witness and eventually its existence. Today Ephesus is a rubble ruin. Did the Ephesians never get their first love back?

The Church Is Challenged with a Promise
REVELATION 2:7

Each of the seven letters in Revelation 2–3 ends with a promise drawn from the end of the book. Each, in some way, is related to the wonderful theme of eternal life and eternal security (Dever, "We Shall Overcome"). And though each letter is written to a specific church, each letter is for every other church as well: "Anyone [that is, us] who has an ear should listen to what the Spirit says to the churches" (note the plural). So, what does the exalted Christ promise to each believer and every church?

We Can Conquer by Perseverance

"The victor" is a reference to the one who "conquers" (ESV; see 1 John 5:4-5) or "overcomes" (NASB). It is the Greek word *nikao* from which we derive the word "Nike." Osborne explains the significance of this image:

> It is an athletic and military metaphor that connotes
> superiority and victory over a vanquished foe. In the NT the
> military overtones are primary. . . . Of the twenty-six NT uses,
> twenty-one are in the Johannine corpus, fifteen in Revelation
> alone. Here it speaks of the eschatological war between the
> beast and the people of God. . . . Ultimate victory is with
> God and God alone. It is the Lamb—the King of Kings and
> Lord of Lords—who finally conquers (17:14). Yet this final
> victory is anchored in the past—as Jesus says in John 16:33,
> "I have conquered the world"—which is reflected in the final
> "overcomer" saying in Rev. 3:21, "To the one who overcomes,

I will give the right to sit with me on my throne, just as I overcame and sat down with my Father on this throne." As made clear in 5:5-6, the true victory was won on the cross, and the final battle in 19:17-21 is only the last act of defiance by an already defeated foe.

Our victory is a participation in his victory. It is critical to realize that in the seven letters the victory is a promise held out to all of them, even the weak churches of Sardis (3:5) and Laodicea (3:21). Yet it must be achieved through perseverance. . . . To be an "overcomer" in the eschatological war demands a day-by-day walk with God and dependence on his strength . . . the overcoming theme in Revelation combines promise (God's blessings on those who persevere) and warning (God's judgment on those who fail to persevere). In short, overcoming in Revelation is analogous to [believing] in Paul, referring to an active trust in God that leads to faithfulness in the difficult situations of life lived for Christ. (*Revelation*, 122–23)

We Will Celebrate in Paradise

We will have the right, through Christ, "to eat from the tree of life, which is in God's paradise." The "tree of life" takes us back to Genesis 2:9; 3:22-24 and forward to Revelation 22:2. What Adam and Eve forfeited through sin we regain in Christ. Heaven is paradise regained and more. The tree of life is a beautiful "symbolic source of eternal life" (Mounce, *Revelation*, 72).

"Paradise" (see Luke 23:43; 2 Cor 12:4) is a Persian word that meant a beautiful garden or park. It is the place where the righteous go to be with God. It is the place where sin is not present and God dwells. It is the place where Jesus is! He is what makes paradise, paradise! There we will live forever. There we will be with Him forever. What a wonderful promise! Will you be there?

Conclusion

Tell me what you think about, and I will tell you what you love. Tell me what you talk about, and I will tell you what you love. Tell me what excites you, and I will tell you what you love. My prayer for you, as well as for myself, is that the answer will be same for all these. May the answer always be Jesus.

Reflect and Discuss

1. Look through the characteristics of the seven churches as presented in the summary chart in this chapter. Where do you see similarities to your own walk with the Lord? Where do you see similarities to your local church?
2. How does the description of Jesus in 2:1 give you comfort for the trials in your life?
3. What good deeds does God have for you to do? How can your church emulate the Ephesians' diligent efforts?
4. Why do you think Jesus was just as concerned with doctrine as He was with good works? What doctrinal tests would you give to those who want to lead and teach in the local church?
5. Why does Jesus use such strong language for His feelings towards the Nicolaitans? How should we reflect Jesus' heart while still loving our neighbor?
6. How does Jesus' holy jealousy for the Ephesians expose religious legalism as inadequate? Do you find that you obey out of love for Christ or simply because it is what you are supposed to do?
7. How can you apply the threefold prescription to remember, repent, and return?
8. Reflect on the place you first fell in love with Christ. What works marked that period of time in your spiritual journey?
9. How would you explain what it means to be a "victor" or overcomer in the Christian life?
10. What makes paradise wonderful, from a biblical perspective, and how does this contrast with popular conceptions of heaven?

Martyrs for Jesus

REVELATION 2:8-11

Main Idea: Though followers of Jesus will face opposition and even martyrdom in this world for the sake of the gospel, the promise of Christ is ultimate deliverance and eternal life.

I. **Christ Is Characterized by His Deity and Resurrection Power (2:8).**
   A. He is the eternal God.
   B. He is the resurrected Lord.
II. **The Church Is Commended for Its Faith and Perseverance (2:9-10).**
   A. We must accept sacrifice (2:9).
   B. We will be attacked by Satan (2:9).
   C. We can anticipate suffering (2:10).
III. **The Church Is Challenged by God's Reward and Promise (2:10-11).**
   A. We will receive a crown for our faith (2:10).
   B. We will overcome the second death (2:11).

There is a famous statement, well known from the early history of the church: "The blood of the martyrs is the seed of the church." It was made by the church father Tertullian in AD 197 in a defense of Christianity to the Roman Empire. The actual quote found in his *Apolegeticus* (Apology) reads, "We multiply whenever we are mowed down by you; the blood of Christians is seed" (Tertullian, *Apology*, 227). There is much truth in this statement.

Suffering, persecution, and martyrdom have indeed been the calling of the church of the Lord Jesus somewhere among the nations throughout her entire history. At one time the book *Foxe's Book of Martyrs* was a perennial best seller, cataloging the stories of men and women who gave their lives for Christ. Today *Voice of the Martyrs* updates us on the persecution and sufferings of our brothers and sisters around the world. *Open Doors* does the same. *Time Magazine* (Alter, "Deaths") reported the number of Christian martyrs doubled between 2012 and 2013. Nigeria led the way in 2012, Syria in 2013, with Iraq, Rwanda, and Sudan not far behind. An estimated 100–150 million Christians have been martyred every year in recent decades. Some estimate that 65 percent of all those martyred took place since the dawn of the twentieth century (*EWTN News*, May 10, 2002). These statistics do not even take into account those imprisoned, tortured, and persecuted by other means. Yes, suffering, persecution, and even martyrdom have often followed in the wake left by the crucified Nazarene as He and His gospel have walked the pages of human history. For some this is the normal Christian life.

We see this in the life of a first-century church located in a city called Smyrna, a church with whom Christ was well pleased (2:8-11). From the outside it did not look like much. It had neither the prestige of Ephesus nor the wealth and prosperity of Laodicea. However, it did have a love and passion for Christ that caught the eye of the One whose "eyes are like a fiery flame" (1:14). As with Philadelphia, our Lord has no word of criticism or correction. This is a church we can learn from. This is a church from whose example many will need to draw strength in the days ahead as they take up their own cross and follow Jesus. John Piper says this is a letter where "things are worse than and better than they seem" ("Things Are Worse").

Christ Is Characterized by His Deity and Resurrection Power
REVELATION 2:8

John is charged to write to the angel, the divine messenger, who watches over the church of Smyrna. Smyrna is modern Izmir and the only one of the seven cities of Revelation 2–3 still in existence. It is 35 miles north of Ephesus. A proud and beautiful city, its coins were inscribed with the words "First of Asia in beauty and size" (Mounce, *Revelation*, 73). Temples of Apollos, Asclepius, Aphrodite, Cybele, and Zeus dotted the landscape of this beautiful pagan city. Politically, the city was close with Rome and the imperial cult, which was marked by emperor worship. The Roman orator Cicero paid Smyrna a great compliment in calling her "the city of our most faithful and most ancient allies." In AD 23, as a reward for her loyalty, Smyrna beat out 11 other cities for the right to build the first temple to honor Tiberius Caesar (AD 14–37), who reigned when Christ was crucified (Johnson, *Revelation*, 1983, 44). Couple this allegiance to Rome with a large and influential Jewish population, and Smyrna had all the ingredients for a hostile environment for the church of the Lord Jesus Christ. While we do not know for certain how the church at

Smyrna began, it is reasonable to suppose that it came about from Paul's ministry in Ephesus. Acts 19:10 tells us, "All the inhabitants of Asia, both Jews and Greeks, heard the message about the Lord."

This was a church that especially needed encouragement. It was persecuted and suffering. And things were going to get worse. Therefore, John takes them back to the vision of the glorified Christ in 1:9-20, specifically to verses 17-18. Here are the words they need to hear and the Christ they need to see.

He Is the Eternal God

Jesus is described as the First and the Last, the *protos* and *eschatos*. This is a title used of God in Isaiah 44:6 and 48:12. The characteristics of deity are appropriately ascribed to Christ. The emphasis is on His eternality and sovereignty. He is the eternal Lord over all of history, and He will have the last word! He has always been aware of the circumstances of His people. He knows their situation right now. He has their future in plain sight. Time is in His hands. This is a God you can trust today and tomorrow. The city Smyrna may claim to be the "first in Asia," but it is Christ who is the "First and Last," and He alone provides "a superior foundation for security" (Graves, "Local References," 25).

He Is the Resurrected Lord

If "the First and the Last" draws attention to His *deity*, "the One who was dead and came to life" speaks to His *humanity*. The former emphasized His authority over *time*. The latter emphasizes His authority over *death and life*. Jesus experienced death for us, a far more horrible death than any human will ever know. He bore the full judgment and wrath of God for the sins of the world (John 1:29). He was subject to slander, persecution, rejection, imprisonment, and death. He walked this road. But He came to life! He conquered! He won! Like their Savior, this church too may walk the road of persecution and suffering. Like Him, they may even walk the road of an unjust death. But they should not lose heart. To live is Christ and to die is gain (Phil 1:21). In Christ believers are in a win-win scenario. He lives and they will live with Him. Because of this guarantee, they have no fear of the death all *should* fear, "the second death" (Rev 2:11).

One of the most powerful examples of this, in my lifetime, occurred in 1999. Here is how *Christianity Today* described it:

Every year for 20 years missionary Graham Staines of Australia conducted five-day open-air "jungle camps" in villages of the eastern Indian state of Orissa. After a meeting on January 23, 1999, the 58-year-old Staines and his two sons, 10-year-old Philip and 7-year-old Timothy, were sleeping in a vehicle parked outside a local church when militant Hindus doused the vehicle with gasoline and set it afire. "My husband and sons tried to get out of the burning vehicle, but were stopped by the attackers," Staines wife, Gladys recounts. As the flames engulfed the vehicle, the mob danced and some shouted, "Justice has been done; the Christians have been cremated in Hindu fashion." The mob kept would-be rescuers at bay for more than an hour until making sure the missionary and his sons had died. Staines, secretary of the Evangelical Missionary Society, an independent missionary organization based in Brisbane, had been operating a hospital and clinic for lepers for 34 years. Two days after the murders, lepers dug the graves for the family while Gladys Staines consoled them as they wept. "God has given me peace, and I have never questioned his wisdom in allowing this tragedy," Gladys Staines said after the tragedy. "These people are my people and I hope to stay here." (Fischer, "Fiery Rise")

Gladys and her 13-year-old daughter, Esther, did stay. *World Magazine* reported that Gladys said, "I am terribly upset but not angry. My husband loved Jesus Christ who has taught us to forgive our enemies" (Belz, "Thugs," 16). Our living resurrected Lord gives us the ability to do this.

The Church Is Commended for Its Faith and Perseverance
REVELATION 2:9-10

The word *Smyrna* means "myrrh," which was a sweet perfume used to embalm dead bodies. As a gift from the wise men (Matt 2:11), it was prophetic of the suffering and death Jesus would experience. This city had a history of suffering (Graves, "Local References," 26). Now that lot was cast on the church. By all outward signs she was weak and poor. But looks can be deceiving. On careful inspection by the Lord, we find a strong and wealthy people, at least as Jesus sees things.

We Must Accept Sacrifice (2:14)

Jesus tells His people at Smyrna, "I know your affliction and poverty." Swindoll puts this statement in a wonderfully descriptive context:

> Imagine yourself sitting among the gathering of God's people in Smyrna on a cold morning before sunrise. A small, lamp-lit room houses the remnant of beaten and beleaguered church members. The once-lively crowd of Christians now displays obvious gaps where men and women once sat. Some have fallen away under the persecution. Others are simply gone— arrested, exiled, or executed. Some of you risked your lives just to meet this morning to pray, to sing hymns to God, and to read from Holy Scripture. All of you are outcasts, desperate for a word of encouragement from the messenger sitting in your midst. In the dim light the pastor unrolls a scroll and begins to read with a calm, quiet confidence. Whispering and shuffling in the room ceases when you hear from whom the message comes—the risen Lord Himself. The entire group seems to hold its breath when Christ begins His commendation: "I know your tribulation and your poverty (but you are rich)" (2:9). (*Insights*, 45)

Christ has firsthand intimate knowledge of their plight. "Affliction" could also be rendered "tribulation" (ESV). He knows the burdens that weigh heavily on you and the daily pressures that affect you. He also knows their "poverty." This church was enduring economic, physical, religious, and social opposition. They were marked out and ostracized. They experienced economic boycott and were misrepresented. And they paid a price. It cost them to take their stand for Jesus. There was real sacrifice in remaining faithful to Jesus. However, Christ saw them not as poor but "rich"! Materially they may have had little, but spiritually they had everything. People on earth mocked them as paupers, but God praised them as wealthy. James 2:5 is helpful here:

> *Listen, my dear brothers: Didn't God choose the poor in this world to be rich in faith and heirs of the kingdom that He has promised to those who love Him?*

There are sacrifices in following Jesus, but He is worth it all.

We Will Be Attacked by Satan (2:9)

This church at Smyrna was particularly attacked by the Jewish population in the city. They were "slandered" by what John vividly describes
as "a synagogue of Satan" (see Rom 2:28-29). This phrase needs to be
carefully explained. First, these were descendants of Abraham by physical birth but not spiritual birth. In John 8:44 we find words quite similar as Jesus said of those unbelieving Jews, "You are of your father the
Devil, and you want to carry out your father's desires." Physical heritage
is no indication of spiritual standing! Hostile, and bent on persecuting
the followers of Christ, these Jews were tools of the evil one. They were
under His influence. Ultimately, Satan was the real enemy. "Satan" is a
Hebrew word and means "adversary." Isaiah 14 and Ezekiel 28 provide
some insight, by way of typology, of his fall. (He is also mentioned in
Rev 2:9-10,13; 3:9; 9:11; 12:9-10,12; 13:4; 20:2,7,10.)

Second, neither this text nor any other text in the Bible gives warrant
for any thought or act of anti-Semitism. In commenting on the reality of
anti-Semitism and a Christian perspective, John Piper is extremely helpful:

> [Anti-Semitism] has seemed amazing to me because Jesus
> was a Jew, and all the 12 apostles were Jews, and the whole of
> our Bible was written by Jews (except for [possibly] Luke),
> and Jesus said, "Salvation is from the Jews" (John 4:22), and
> to be Christian is to be grafted into the covenant made with
> Abraham the first Jew (Romans 11:17-24), and to become a
> Christian is to become "Jewish"—a child of Abraham by faith
> (Galatians 3:7).
>
> And on top of all that, the day is coming when the nation
> of Israel will be brought back to her Messiah and be saved
> and become one with the Christian church in the covenant
> of grace established with Abraham (Romans 11:25-26). . . . So
> how could so much anti-Semitism (hatred and persecution
> and ridicule) rise up in the Christian church? Part of the
> answer is found in texts like this one. It shows that the
> animosity from the Jewish community toward the Christian
> church in the first two or three centuries was immense. And it
> started to go both ways.
>
> I only mention this as a partial explanation not as a
> justification. Hatred and persecution and ridicule toward Jews

as a people is never justified. Our main disposition should be Paul's: "My heart's desire and prayer to God is that they might be saved." And so I exhort you: Don't joke about Jewishness. Don't use cavalier stereotypes. Don't hate. Don't ridicule. If you pray for Jewish people the way Paul and Stephen and Jesus did—with a heart of longing for their salvation and love for them as the estranged people of God—you will find it very difficult to make jokes or speak disparagingly. (Piper, "Things Are Worse")

We Can Anticipate Suffering (2:10)

Verse 10 flows logically and naturally from verse 9. There is a command to trust and a promise of suffering. The admonition "Don't be afraid" calls the believers to stop fearing "what you are about to suffer." They anticipated it and Jesus promises it. "Look, the Devil [Gk *diabolos*, "the accuser," the one active behind his human puppets] will throw some of you into prison to test you." Jesus assures them that their accuser will try to harm them, but Christ will use the Devil's evil intentions to refine and prove them. He will reveal their faith, loyalty, and love for Him. That they "will have affliction for 10 days" is symbolic of a definite but limited period of time. He allows it and will control its duration.

A word about the future of the church, specifically in America, is in order. Those of us in the West must be prepared for the jarring truth that, just as in Revelation 2:9 and Smyrna in the first century, those who oppose and reject Christianity are going to oppose and persecute us. Not only will they say we are wrong; they will say we are bigoted, dangerous, and evil. We will be slandered as antichoice, antidiversity, antigay, anti-inclusion, anti-intolerance. We can anticipate economic boycotts, governmental restrictions, and social ostracism. Eventually more severe persecution and even imprisonment will likely be our experience. Of course this is already true for followers of Christ around the world, and it is coming to America.

What should be our response? Exactly what we see here in Revelation 2: Do not be afraid; expect it. Receive it from the hands of a sovereign God who is testing, pruning, and refining your faith. Remember James again: "Consider it a great joy, my brothers, whenever you experience various trials, knowing that the testing of your faith produces endurance" (Jas 1:2-3).

The Church Is Challenged by God's Reward and Promise
REVELATION 2:10-11

This church now received a much-needed word of encouragement. It is a twofold promise the church can count on because it comes from Jesus. Our Lord does not say tribulation is coming so "suck it up." Hard times are coming so "deal with it." No, men may kill the body, but they cannot destroy the soul (see Matt 10:28). Men may murder our bodies, and that means one thing for the Christian: instant heaven! What do we have to fear?

We Will Receive a Crown for Our Faith (2:10)

"Be faithful until death," Jesus exhorts them. Our King Jesus "will give you the crown of life." The word for "crown" is *stephanos*, meaning a victor's crown. James 1:12 reminds us, "A man who endures trials is blessed, because when he passes the test he will receive the crown of life that God has promised to those who love Him." This crown of life is none other than eternal life. It is the reward for all whose faith is in the crucified and risen Christ.

Crowns are mentioned a number of times in the Bible, and it is instructive to note their occurrences:

- Crown of life (Rev 2:10; also Jas 1:12)
- Crown of righteousness (2 Tim 4:8)
- Crown of glory (1 Pet 5:4)
- Crown of gold (Rev 4:4)
- Crown of rejoicing (1 Thess 2:19)
- Crown of incorruption (1 Cor 9:25)

Each, in some way, draws attention to the blessings of salvation that are ours in Christ.

We Will Overcome the Second Death (2:11)

There is something worse, far worse, than physical death: spiritual and eternal death, what is here called "the second death." In Revelation 20:14 it is called "the lake of fire," another way to describe hell. In Revelation 21:8 we are told who experiences the second death: "But the cowards, unbelievers, vile, murderers, sexually immoral, sorcerers, idolaters, and all liars—their share will be in the lake that burns with fire

and sulfur, which is the second death." It is the second death from which
Christ came to rescue us. Revelation 20:6 tells us because of Christ, this
death "has no power" over us.

John's challenge is, "Are you listening?" The Spirit is speaking this
truth to His churches. There is an eternal reward and an eternal promise. Stay with Jesus no matter what. There is glory on the other side.

Conclusion

Approximately 60 years after John wrote these words to the church
at Smyrna, there would indeed be a man "who would not be afraid of
what you are about to suffer" and who was "faithful until death." He was
their pastor. His name was Polycarp. Irenaeus, who heard him teach,
said he had been a disciple of John. Pastor Polycarp was greatly loved
and respected by his people. However, the citizens of Smyrna and their
governmental official did not share their sentiment. In AD 155 Polycarp
would be arrested, quickly tried, and martyred. He was burned at the
stake and then stabbed to finish the job. Below is the record of his
death—the oldest account of a Christian dying for the Lord Jesus outside the New Testament.

> Polycarp, when he first heard of it, was not perturbed, but
> desired to remain in the city. But the majority induced him
> to withdraw, so he retired to a farm not far from the city and
> there stayed with a few friends, doing nothing else night and
> day but pray for all men and for the churches throughout the
> world, as was his constant habit. . . . Forthwith those searching
> for him arrived. And when they did not find him, they seized
> two young slaves, one of whom confessed under torture. For
> it was really impossible to conceal him, since the very ones
> who betrayed him were of his own household. . . . Late in the
> evening they came up with him and found him in bed in the
> upper room of a small cottage. Even so he could have escaped
> to another farm, but he did not wish to do so, saying, "God's
> will be done." Thus, when he heard of their arrival, he went
> downstairs and talked with them, while those who looked on
> marveled at his age and constancy, and at how there should
> be such zeal over the arrest of so old a man. Straightway he
> ordered food and drink, as much as they wished, to be set
> before them at that hour, and he asked them to give him

an hour so that he might pray undisturbed. And when they consented, he stood and prayed—being so filled with the grace of God that for two hours he could not hold his peace, to the amazement of those who heard. And many repented that they had come to get such a devout old man.

When at last he had finished his prayer, in which he remembered all who had met with him at any time, both small and great, both those with and those without renown, and the whole [universal] church throughout the world, the hour of departure having come, they mounted him on an ass and brought him into the city. . . . There the chief of the police, Herod, and his father, Nicetas, met him and transferred him to their carriage, and tried to persuade him, as they sat beside him, saying, "What harm is there to say 'Lord Caesar,' and to offer incense and all that sort of thing, and to save yourself?"

At first he did not answer them. But when they persisted, he said, "I am not going to do what you advise me."

Then when they failed to persuade him, they uttered dire threats and made him get out with such speed that in dismounting from the carriage he bruised his shin. But without turning around, as though nothing had happened, he proceeded swiftly, and was led into the arena, there being such a tumult in the arena that no one could be heard . . . and when finally he was brought up, there was a great tumult on hearing that Polycarp had been arrested. Therefore, when he was brought before him, the proconsul asked him if he were Polycarp. And when he confessed that he was, he tried to persuade him to deny [the faith], saying, "Have respect to your age"—and other things that customarily follow this, such as, "Swear by the fortune of Caesar; change your mind"; . . . the proconsul was insistent and said: "Take the oath, and I shall release you. Curse Christ."

Polycarp said: "Eighty-six years I have served him, and he never did me any wrong. How can I blaspheme my King who saved me?". . . The proconsul said: "I have wild beasts. I shall throw you to them, if you do not change your mind."

But he said: "Call them. For repentance from the better to the worse is not permitted us; but it is noble to change from what is evil to what is righteous."

And again [he said] to him, "I shall have you consumed with fire, if you despise the wild beasts, unless you change your mind."

But Polycarp said: "The fire you threaten burns but an hour and is quenched after a little; for you do not know the fire of the coming judgment and everlasting punishment that is laid up for the ungodly. But why do you delay? Come, do what you will."

And when he had said these things and many more besides he was inspired with courage and joy, and his face was full of grace, so that not only did it not fall with dismay at the things said to him, but on the contrary, the proconsul was astonished, and sent his own herald into the midst of the arena to proclaim three times: "Polycarp has confessed himself to be a Christian."

When this was said by the herald, the entire crowd of Gentiles and Jews who lived in Smyrna shouted with uncontrollable anger and a great cry: "This one is the teacher of Asia, the father of the Christians, the destroyer of our gods, who teaches many not to sacrifice nor to worship."

Such things they shouted and asked the official Philip that he let loose a lion on Polycarp. But he said it was not possible for him to do so, since he had brought the wild-beast sports to a close. Then they decided to shout with one accord that he burn Polycarp alive. . . . Then these things happened with such dispatch, quicker than can be told—the crowds in so great a hurry to gather wood and kindling from the workshops and the baths, the Jews being especially zealous, as usual, to assist with this. . . . Straightway then, they set about him the material prepared for the pyre. And when they were about to nail him also, he said: "Leave me as I am. For he who grants me to endure the fire will enable me also to remain on the pyre unmoved, without the security you desire from the nails."

So they did not nail him, but tied him. And with his hands put behind him and tied, like a noble ram out of a great flock ready for sacrifice, a burnt offering ready and acceptable to God, he looked up to heaven and said:

"Lord God Almighty, Father of thy beloved and blessed Servant Jesus Christ, through whom we have received full knowledge of thee, 'the God of angels and powers and all creation' and of the whole race of the righteous who live in thy presence: I bless thee, because thou hast deemed me worthy of this day and hour, to take my part in the number of the martyrs, in the cup of thy Christ, for 'resurrection to eternal life' of soul and body in the immortality of the Holy Spirit; among whom may I be received in thy presence this day as a rich and acceptable sacrifice, just as thou hast prepared and revealed beforehand and fulfilled, thou that art the true God without any falsehood. For this and for everything I praise thee, I bless thee, I glorify thee, through the eternal and heavenly High Priest, Jesus Christ, thy beloved Servant, through whom be glory to thee with him and Holy Spirit both now and unto the ages to come. Amen."

And when he had concluded the Amen and finished his prayer, the men attending to the fire lighted it. . . .

But the jealous and malicious evil one . . . pled with the magistrate not to give up his body, "else," said he, "they will abandon the Crucified and begin worshiping this one." This was done at the instigation and insistence of the Jews, who also watched when we were going to take him from the fire, being ignorant that we can never forsake Christ, who suffered for the salvation of the whole world of those who are saved, the faultless for the sinners, nor can we ever worship any other. For we worship this One as Son of God, but we love the martyrs as disciples and imitators of the Lord, deservedly so, because of their unsurpassable devotion to their own King and Teacher. May it be also our lot to be their companions and fellow disciples! ("Martyrdom of Polycarp," *Early Church Fathers*, 150–55)

Jesus said, "If the world hates you, understand that it hated Me before it hated you. . . . Remember the word I spoke to you: 'A slave is not greater than his master'" (John 15:18,20).

Reflect and Discuss

1. What does it mean for the blood of martyrs to be "seed" for the church? Is this always true?

2. Think of a time you experienced discouragement, persecution, or suffering. What encouragement did you need? How do Jesus' words to the church at Smyrna encourage you?

3. How does Jesus' eternality help provide comfort to those who are experiencing persecution or opposition?

4. Read 1 Corinthians 15 and consider how it relates to Revelation 2:8. What are the implications of Jesus' resurrection for the Christian life?

5. Where is the Lord calling you to sacrifice for His kingdom's sake?

6. Does Revelation 2:9 justify anti-Semitism? Why or why not?

7. Is suffering always a bad thing for the church? How can it ever be a blessing?

8. How would you explain the "second death" in your own words?

9. How does Jesus deliver victory over the second death?

10. In what ways is Polycarp's devotion instructive for us today?

The Church That Compromises the Truth

REVELATION 2:12-17

Main Idea: Though believers and churches are constantly tempted to compromise both theologically and ethically, true followers of Christ will remain faithful and receive from the Lord the reward of eternal life.

I.   **Christ Is Characterized by Judgment (2:12).**
    A.   The judgment of Jesus is true.
    B.   The judgment of Jesus is thorough.
II. **The Church Is Commended for Faithfulness (2:13).**
    A.   We must be faithful where we live.
    B.   We must be faithful in our witness.
III. **The Church Is Condemned for Compromise (2:14-15).**
    A.   We must not compromise our morality (2:14).
    B.   We must not compromise our theology (2:15).
IV. **The Church Is Corrected with a Warning (2:16).**
    A.   Christ warns us to repent.
    B.   Christ warns us of rejection.
V.   **The Church Is Challenged by Its Reward (2:17).**
    A.   Christ will nourish us.
    B.   Christ will receive us.
    C.   Christ will acknowledge us.

The church of the Lord Jesus has struggled to understand a valuable lesson throughout her history: Her greatest dangers are almost never from the *outside*. They are always on the *inside*. The enemy really is within. Our greatest threats to spiritual health and life are not opposition or even persecution from unbelieving, evil, and wicked men energized by Satan. Rather, it is when we allow into our community of faith spiritual Trojan horses that will sow seeds of destruction given the opportunity. Now, this toxin is easy to identify with a simple word: *compromise*. Nothing will poison the body of Christ like the poison called compromise. And the church cannot say it has not been warned. Listen to just a few of God's faithful servants:

"Compromise has been a cancer in the church from its inception."—David Levy

"A new Decalogue has been adopted by the neo-Christians of our day, 'Thou shalt not disagree,' and a new set of Beatitudes too, 'Blessed are they that tolerate everything for they shall not be made accountable.'"—A. W. Tozer

"Truth always carries confrontation. Truth demands confrontation; loving confrontation nevertheless. If our reflex action is always accommodation of the centrality of the truth involved, there is something wrong."—Francis Schaeffer

Indeed, something is seriously wrong when Christians begin to compromise the truth to accommodate the culture and world in which they live. Such compromise may be theological or moral. At a church in the city of Pergamum, it was both. If fact, their particular situation was so dire, the glorified Christ of 1:9-20 said that if they did not repent, He would come against them quickly and fight them (2:16). What a striking and painful image: King Jesus fighting His church! Obviously our Lord takes spiritual compromise seriously, and so should we. These six verses are some of the most instructive in the whole Bible for the twenty-first century church, especially in America and the West.

Christ Is Characterized by Judgment
REVELATION 2:12

John receives a charge to write the letter to the third of seven churches. He is to send a message "to the angel of the church in Pergamum." Pergamum was the official capital of the Roman province of Asia Minor. It had a library of 200,000 volumes (second only to Alexandria, Egypt). Pliny called it "by far the most distinguished city in Asia [Minor]" (Mounce, *Revelation*, 78). It had temples dedicated to Dionysus, Athena, Asclepius (the god of healing symbolized by a serpent entwined around a staff), and Demeter. The great altar to Zeus, one of the wonders of the ancient world, was here. It was a city steeped in pagan religion.

It was a city tight with Rome. Pergamum was the official center for worship of the emperor and thus the state. It eventually boasted of three temples dedicated to the emperor, and in 29 BC it was the first city in Asia to receive permission to build a temple dedicated to the worship of a living emperor. So the church in Pergamum faced stiff and zealous opposition from without. However, her vulnerability resided on the inside. In this context the characterization of Christ is instructive.

The Judgment of Jesus Is True

John draws again from the vision of the glorified Christ in chapter 1. There we read that "a sharp double-edged sword came from His mouth" (1:16; see 2:12,16; 19:15,21). The sword is the Word of God. Because it is God's Word, it is true and trustworthy, inerrant and infallible. And here it is coming from the mouth of Christ! His Word is authoritative and sure. This idea is rooted in the messianic prophecy of Isaiah 11:4, where Messiah will judge "with discipline from His mouth." This is a verbal announcement from the exalted Christ. "Anyone who has an ear should listen" (2:17).

The Judgment of Jesus Is Thorough

The sword is sharp and double-edged. It is not dull; it cuts quickly and cleanly. Being double-edged, it hurts and heals. It cuts and cures. This statement recalls Hebrews 4:12, which says,

> For the word of God is living and effective and sharper than any double-edged sword, penetrating as far as the separation of soul and spirit, joints and marrow. It is able to judge the ideas and thoughts of the heart.

This sword of Christ conveys absolute authority, decisive discernment. The Word of God is at once an instrument of life and an instrument of death. Rome had given Pergamum the rare power to exercise capital punishment on its own. The symbol of this authority was the sword (Johnson, *Revelation*, 1983, 47). Rome might wield the sword on earth, but the glorified Christ wielded a mightier sword from heaven. This is the sword the church should fear. This is the sword we should revere.

The Church Is Commended for Faithfulness
REVELATION 2:13

In a culture that is not hospitable to Christianity, opposition and persecution can make living for Christ hard. It can even be deadly. But be assured that Christ knows what we are facing. He is aware of our circumstances in intimate detail. This was the situation at Pergamum, and so our Lord commends them and seeks to comfort them.

We Must Be Faithful Where We Live

Jesus says, "I know. If no one else knows what you are going through, I do. I know where you live, where your home is. I know it is where Satan's throne is" (author's paraphrase). This last phrase is striking and has been variously understood as follows:

1. The acropolis, which is situated on the plateau and from a distance looks like a throne.
2. The idols, altars, shrines, and temples of Pergamum.
3. The altar to Zeus *soter* (meaning "savior") on top of the mountain, a magnificent structure that dominated the city. The legs in the sculpture were serpent's tails, and such a structure epitomized idolatry and paganism.
4. The cult of Asklepios. The symbol of Asklepios was a serpent, aligned with Satan in 12:9 and 20:2. Members of the cult called Asklepios "savior."
5. The imperial cult—worship of the state embodied in the emperor. (Osborne, *Revelation*, 141)

The fifth view is the best, in my judgment. This is the major problem behind Revelation as a whole and was the core of Pergamum religion. Pergamum was obsessed with a love of the state. Patriotism had crossed the line into idolatry. To not line up enthusiastically with the preeminence and politics of the state was to fail to be a good citizen. Those who failed to join in were dangerous and had to be opposed. Only Caesar is Lord, not this so-called Christ. Christians could follow Him if they wanted, but society expected that they would not let their Christian convictions get in the way of their public duty to obey the government. Privatized faith is fine. Faith displayed in the public square is not welcomed.

Jesus knew the peril this placed them in, and He praises them for their faithfulness, that they "were holding on to His name and not denying their faith in Him." They maintained their witness to Jesus. They were faithful in their confession of "Christ is Lord" in Satan's kingdom. (The phrase "where Satan lives" is repeated for emphasis at the end of verse 13, bracketing the verse.)

We Must Be Faithful in Our Witness

Smyrna could be described as a martyr's church (2:8-11). So could Pergamum. Jesus says, "You are holding [present tense] on to My name and did not deny your faith in Me" even in dark days. "Even in the days of Antipas, My faithful witness who was killed among you," this church maintained its fidelity. Their faithful witness had resulted in the martyrdom of one of their own.

We know nothing about Antipas. Some speculate he may have been their pastor. A tradition says he was roasted inside a "brass bull" during the reign of Domitian (Mounce, *Revelation*, 80). Note how Jesus describes Antipas: "my faithful witness" (or "martyr," in the context). This is the same description that is applied to our Lord in Revelation 1:5! Christ was God's faithful witness unto death, and Antipas was Jesus' faithful witness unto death! The Son honored His Father in death, and Antipas honored his Lord in death.

It is happening right now somewhere in the world. Somewhere Christians are dying for Jesus. Christian women are being raped. Christian children are being sold into slavery. Christian brothers and sister are being imprisoned, persecuted, and tortured. In *The Global War on Christians*, respected author and journalist John Allen notes that "80% of all acts of religious discrimination in the world today are directed against Christians" (Allen, *Global War*, 33). These include:

Societal discrimination	Suppression of Christian missions
Institutional discrimination	Suppression of conversion to Christianity
Employment discrimination	Forced conversion from Christianity
Legal discrimination	Suppression of corporate worship
Violence against individual Christians	Community oppression (ibid.)

When it comes to deaths, "90% of all people killed on the basis of religious beliefs in the world today are Christians" (ibid.). Depending on who is counting, there are "100,000 to 150,000 new Christian martyrs every year" (ibid.). We must not forget these! And we must remember what the Scriptures teach us about those who have suffered unto death for the sake of the gospel:

> *The death of His faithful ones is valuable in the LORD's sight.*
> (Ps 116:15)

> *Then I heard a voice from heaven saying, "Write: The dead who die in the Lord from now on are blessed."* (Rev 14:13)

> *For me, living is Christ and dying is gain.* (Phil 1:21)

The Church Is Condemned for Compromise
REVELATION 2:14-15

Many were faithful, some even to death, but this was not true of everyone. Within this church a group of compromisers had appeared, and the health and vitality of the church were at stake. This element of the community said, "Let's go along to get along!" The church was now doing what the world would applaud. They were open-minded, progressive, tolerant. They compromised, and Christ was not pleased. Two areas in particular were infected with this debilitating disease of compromise.

We Must Not Compromise Our Morality (2:14)

Some at Pergamum held the name of Jesus. Some at Pergamum held "to the teaching of Balaam" (used symbolically). The story of Balaam is found in Numbers 22–25 and 31:16 (note especially 25:1-3). Here the Lord says explicitly what sin was instigated by following Balaam: Pagan food and pagan women led to spiritual compromise and adultery on the part of the people of God!

The "stumbling block" (*skandalon*) refers both to immorality and idolatry. They celebrated the idols of the culture and adopted their sexual ethics. The two often go together.

Compromise and accommodation were the identifying markers. They attempted to serve God but in the process allowed the prevailing cultural norms to shape both their thinking and their lifestyles. They had neglected the truth of Romans 12:2, which says, "Do not be conformed to this age, but be transformed by the renewing of your mind, so that you may discern what is the good, pleasing, and perfect will of God." They had forgotten the warning of James 4:4, which says,

> *Adulteresses! Don't you know that friendship with the world is hostility toward God? So whoever wants to be the world's friend becomes God's enemy.*

Pergamum means "thoroughly married." Here was a church thoroughly married to the world. Satan could not defeat this church with a frontal assault from without, so he revised his strategy and fostered friendly accommodation from within and with deadly success. The congregation was welcoming and affirming to the sexually immoral. On the contrary, we must not compromise our morality. It will destroy our witness and invite the judgment of God.

We Must Not Compromise Our Theology

Some at Pergamum hold the name of Jesus. Some at Pergamum hold the name of Balaam. Some at Pergamum hold the name of the Nicolaitans.

We met the Nicolaitans at Ephesus in 2:6. The Ephesian church rejected them. The Pergamum church embraced them. The teaching of Balaam and the Nicolaitans are closely related if not identical. Immorality and idolatry were distinctive characteristics of these false teachers as well. Theologically they were antinomians, libertines. Doctrine mattered little and behavior mattered even less. With each passing day the distinction between this church and the world become more blurred and less clear. The lifestyle of one was barely distinguishable from the other. Worldliness, compromise, and tolerance had rushed into this church like a flood, and she was on the verge of drowning.

What an apt description of the church in the Western world today! What a gross misunderstanding of grace and the gospel we suffer from today.

The Church Is Corrected with a Warning
REVELATION 2:16

Compromise is one of Satan's favorite and most effective weapons. This is so for at least four reasons:

- It never occurs quickly, so you hardly notice the change.
- It always lowers the original standards you once held important.
- It is seldom offensive because it is perceived as loving.
- It eventually leads you to accept what you once rejected and even thought repulsive. It has been well said that what one generation tolerates, the next generation will accept; what that generation accepts, the next generation will celebrate.

What is the antidote, the cure, to such compromise? Jesus provides a twofold remedy that He sets before the church He loves and has set free from their sins by His blood (1:5).

Christ Warns Us to Repent

The words of Christ are clear and direct: "Therefore repent!" This is a word of command from the exalted and glorified Lord Jesus. Exhibit contrition of heart, confess your sin, and change your ways (Levy,

"Church Compromised," 21). It is time for a 180-degree turn. The imperative notes the urgency of the command. Do not delay! Do it now! There is no need or time to debate, dialogue, or declare a moratorium on what God thinks and how we should respond. His Word is not up for discussion.

Swindoll puts it well in what Christ expected of His church:

> In concrete terms, Christ demanded that the Pergamum Christians amend their attitudes regarding the Balaamites and the Nicolaitans, that they take the necessary actions to remove those false teachings from their midst. The compromise had to end. Christ's call for repentance included a warning for those who refused. If the faithful remnant refused to change their lackadaisical policies and if the wicked minority continued their libertine practices, Christ would discipline them. He would come swiftly, waging war against them with the double-edged sword—His just discipline as the righteous Judge. (*Insights*, 54)

These words lead us to our second application:

Christ Warns Us of Rejection

A failure to repent would result in a swift and serious response from Christ. First, "I will come to you quickly" (NIV, "soon"). Second, "I will . . . fight against them with the sword of My mouth" (see 1:16; 2:12). Christ fighting His church: I can think of no sadder image in the whole Bible as it relates to the Christian community. When Jesus addresses the whole church in Revelation 2–3, He says, "You." Here He says He would fight against "them." So this was a group of interlopers within the church that He would deal with in judgment, not those who were faithful.

The weapon of His war would be His Word, "the sword of My mouth." His Word is the one certain source of eternal truth. His Word and only His Word sets the standard for God's people. Antipas, the faithful witness, felt the sword of Rome. The compromisers in Pergamum will feel the sword of Christ! John MacArthur puts it well:

> The church cannot tolerate evil in any form. To the boastful Corinthians, proudly tolerating a man guilty of incest, Paul wrote, "Your boasting is not good. Do you not know that a

little leaven leavens the whole lump of dough? Clean out the
old leaven so that you may be a new lump, just as you are in
fact unleavened" (1 Cor. 5:6-7). Sinning believers should be
made to feel miserable in the fellowship and worship of the
church by being confronted powerfully with the Word of God.
Neither is the goal of the church to provide an environment
where unbelievers feel comfortable; it is to be a place where
they can hear the truth and be convicted of their sins so as to
be saved (Rom. 10:13-17). Gently (cf. 2 Tim. 2:24-26), lovingly,
graciously, yet firmly, unbelievers need to be confronted
with the reality of their sin and God's gracious provision
through the sacrificial death of the Lord Jesus Christ. Error
will never be suppressed by compromising with it. Today's
nonconfrontive church is largely repeating the error of the
Pergamum church on a grand scale, and faces the judgment
of the Lord of the church. (*Revelation 1–11*, 90)

The Church Is Challenged by Its Reward
REVELATION 2:17

A threefold challenge, or promise, is given to this church if they repent
and endure in faithfulness to Christ and observe all that He has "commanded" (Matt 28:20). Now they need ears to "listen." They need to
remember the "Spirit of God" is speaking. This is a word for this church
and every church ("the churches").

Christ Will Nourish Us

To the "victor" He promises "hidden manna." Manna was the food
supernaturally supplied to the Israelites during the exodus and wilderness wanderings. Mounce notes:

> The idea of hidden manna reflects a Jewish tradition that the
> pot of manna that was placed in the ark for a memorial to
> future generations (Exod. 16:32-34; see Heb. 9:4) was taken by
> Jeremiah at the time of the destruction of Solomon's temple
> (sixth century B.C.) and hidden underground in Mt. Nebo
> (2 Macc. 2:4-7). . . . In the context of the letter to Pergamum
> it alludes to the proper and heavenly food of spiritual Israel
> in contrast to the unclean food supplied by the Balaamites.

> While the promise is primarily eschatological, it is not without immediate application for a persecuted people. (*Revelation*, 82)

Jesus, as the Good Shepherd, will graciously feed His people the spiritual food they need for eternal nourishment. After all, He is the true "bread of life" (John 6:35,48-51).

Christ Will Receive Us

Jesus says secondly through the Spirit by the pen of John, "I will also give him a white stone." The exact meaning and significance of the white stone is elusive. Mounce says there are a dozen or more possibilities (*Revelation*, 82). Perhaps John was intentionally vague. Perhaps it was the stone of acquittal at a trial (versus the black stone of guilt and condemnation). Maybe it was the stone of acceptance or entrance when one presented oneself at a banquet. Maybe there is a connection to a stone in the breastplate of the high priest or to the Urim (Exod 28:30). Perhaps it symbolizes the victory of our faith in Christ (Beale, *Revelation*, 252–53; also Mounce, *Revelation*, 82–83). The bottom line is, it points to acceptance and victory in Christ our high priest, Christ our righteousness. He gives us the white stone. It is His gift never to be taken away.

Christ Will Acknowledge Us

On the stone is a "new name . . . that no one knows except the one who receives it." The new name on the stone points to the end-time supper in which intimate fellowship with the risen Lord occurs. This is seen by looking to Revelation 3:12, which suggests that the name in 2:17 refers to "the name of My God and the name of the city of My God—the new Jerusalem, which comes down out of heaven from My God—and My new name." All of these names "refer to the intimate eschatological presence of God and Christ with his people, as expressed most clearly by 22:3-4" (Beale, *Revelation*, 253): "The throne of God and of the Lamb will be in the city, and His slaves will serve Him. They will see His face, and His name will be on their foreheads."

As commentator Greg Beale explains,

> To receive the "new name" (2:17) is to receive Jesus'
> victorious, kingly "name . . . no one knows except himself"
> (19:12-16). Nevertheless, he reveals and imparts it only to his
> people in an escalated manner at the end of each one's life
> and fully at the conclusion of history (so 3:12). 2:17 and 19:12

seem to develop the similar thought from Luke 10:22: "all things have been given to me by my Father, and no one knows who the Son is except the Father, or who the Father is except the Son and to whomever the Son wills to reveal" (see also Luke 10:17). (*Revelation*, 254)

Beale explains the significance of this knowledge as follows:

> In the ancient world and the Old Testament, to know someone's name, especially that of God, often meant to enter into an intimate relationship with that person and to share in the person's character or power. To be given a new name was an indication of a new status. . . . Therefore, believers' reception of this name represents their final reward of consummate identification and unity with the intimate, end-time presence and power of Christ in his kingdom and under his sovereign authority. . . . [T]he "new name" is a mark of genuine membership in the community of the redeemed, without which entry into the eternal "city of God" is impossible. It stands in contrast to the satanic "name" that unbelievers receive, which identifies them with the character of the devil and with the ungodly "city of man." (*Revelation*, 254–55)

Conclusion

There are many points of application in this text. I want to highlight one that is particularly relevant in my own American context.

There is always a grave danger in wedding God to government. The gospel and the government must always be kept distinct and separated. Further, it is lethal to the clarity and purity of the gospel to confuse it with national devotion and pride. Patriotic services may or may not have a place when the bride of Christ gathers to worship her Bridegroom and King. But this much is clear: If we become more moved and teary eyed over our flag and "America the Beautiful" than we do the cross of Christ and "Amazing Grace," something is seriously wrong. Ultimately we must remind ourselves again and again that our hope is in Calvary's hill not Capitol Hill. We must remember that an idol is often a good thing turned into a God thing. There is nothing wrong with loving America (or one's home country). There is everything wrong in worshiping her, even if it is done unintentionally. There is no room for confusion or compromise here. Remember, Christ and only Christ says, "I will be your *food* now and in eternity. I will be your *entrance* into heaven as your home. I will give you *My name* that can never be taken away." What the culture, government, and world offer does not compare. Hold on to His name because He is holding on to you. Do not deny the faith because He will not deny you.

Reflect and Discuss

1. What are some of the external threats to the church? What are some of the internal threats? How are the internal ones often the greater danger?
2. Why is compromise such a deceptive and dangerous temptation for the church?
3. How can we be sure that the Scriptures are true? What evidence does this passage give us that we can believe God's Word?
4. Why is a merely privatized faith not an option for the genuine Christian?
5. How can you support those believers around the world who are being persecuted for their faith? How can you prepare yourself now for persecution if and when it comes to your life?
6. How might Christians be tempted to compromise their moral convictions in the name of open-mindedness and tolerance?
7. Why do you think immorality and idolatry are so closely connected? What are some of the idols that often accompany and fuel the immorality we often see around us?
8. What steps can you take to protect yourself and your church from compromising theologically?
9. Explain the idea of "hidden manna" from Revelation 2:17 in your own words. How is it better than the false supply provided by the teaching of Balaam?
10. What is significant about receiving the stone with the new name on it? Why should believers find hope and strength to persevere in looking forward to receiving this stone?

The Jezebel Church

Main Idea: The church that tolerates false teaching and corrupt morality will receive judgment, while those who hold fast to the true gospel will receive the ultimate reward.

I. **Christ Is Characterized for Us by Penetrating Decisive Judgment (2:18).**
    A. Know that Jesus' judgment is perceptive.
    B. Know that Jesus' judgment is powerful.
II. **Christ Commends Us for Faithful Works (2:19).**
    A. Let us do good works for Jesus.
    B. Let us grow in our good works for Jesus.
III. **Christ Condemns Us for Excessive Tolerance (2:20).**
    A. Guard against a personality problem.
    B. Guard against an authority problem.
    C. Guard against a theology problem.
    D. Guard against a morality problem.
IV. **Christ Corrects Us with Loving Discipline (2:21-25).**
    A. God's discipline is fair (2:21).
    B. God's discipline is full (2:22).
    C. God's discipline is final (2:23).
    D. God's discipline is fearful (2:23).
    E. God's discipline is faithful (2:24-25).
V. **Christ Challenges Us with Future Promises (2:26-29).**
    A. We receive the authority of Christ's power (2:26-27).
    B. We receive the assurance of Christ's presence (2:28-29).

The name *Jezebel* is infamous and rightly so. She was probably the most wicked queen in Israel's history; we find her treacherous behavior described in 1 Kings 16–2 Kings 9. She was "the power behind the throne" as the wife of the weak and wimpish King Ahab. She led her husband to worship pagan gods (1 Kgs 16:31), kill God's prophets (1 Kgs 18:13), and murder a righteous and plain man named Naboth for his vineyard (1 Kgs 21). She was evil personified, and when God chastised a church for allowing false teaching into His body, He said they were "tolerating the woman Jezebel" (Rev 2:20). It has been well said, "We name our sons David and Paul, and our daughters Mary and Rachel, but we name our dogs Goliath and Nero; and we name our cats Jezebel!" A Jezebel church is not a compliment.

Doctrinal and theological compromise is always a danger to the health, vitality, and survival of the church. It can be like "spiritual kudzu" once it is allowed in. It will spread out of control, sucking the life out of every living organism it touches.

Our Lord knew this, so He has a stern word for His people. Here is "tough love" on full display! It may not be easy to hear, but often it is absolutely necessary and for our good.

Christ Is Characterized for Us by Penetrating Judgment
REVELATION 2:18

John for the fourth time is told to write to the angelic watcher, this time to the one over "the church in Thyatira." This is the longest of the seven letters and the most difficult. As Hemer writes, it is also "addressed to the least known, least important, and least remarkable of the cities" (in Mounce, *Revelation*, 84).

Thyatira was an expendable military outpost 40 miles southeast of Pergamos. It was only important through its commerce in wool, linen, leatherwork, bronze work, and especially purple dye. It had an extensive network of trade guilds or labor unions that dominated daily and civic life. Each union had its own patron deity, feasts, and seasonal celebrations that often included sexual immorality. Apollo the sun god and Diana the fertility goddess were the more significant deities. Acts 16:14 teaches us that Lydia, whom Paul led to Christ at Philippi, was from Thyatira and a seller of purple (Johnson, *Revelation*, 1983, 50). She may have been instrumental in evangelizing Thyatira. By all worldly appearances the city was unimportant and its church rather insignificant. This is not the judgment of Jesus. Big or small, well-known or hardly known at all, every church is important to Jesus. Whether you have 10 thousand, one thousand, one hundred, or 10 members makes no difference to Him. He wants you to be pure where you are planted. He wants you to honor Him wherever your home is.

Know that Jesus' Judgment Is Perceptive

Christ is first noted as the "Son of God," a title found only here in Revelation. It stands in contrast to the pagan god Apollo, son of Zeus, who was popular in Thyatira. Jesus is the true Son of God, not Apollo, the son of a lifeless idol (Mounce, *Revelation*, 153). Apollo is a piddly, pathetic, pseudosun god, while Jesus is the eternal and majestic Son of God.

His eyes are like a fiery flame (1:14; 19:12). This speaks of His omniscience—His penetrating, perceptive, and piercing ability to see all that is. He sees all actions, thoughts, and emotions. Nothing escapes His vision. And you can rest assured, He sees through the deceptive appearance and seductive teachings of the Jezebel. Burning indignation and purifying judgment blaze from these divine eyes that continually watch all that is happening.

Know that Jesus' Judgment Is Powerful

That His feet are like fine bronze ("burnished bronze," NIV) speaks of strength and splendor. Thyatira was famous for its bronze work, but their best pales in comparison to that of the Son of God. He is brilliant in appearance, unrivaled in strength, and utterly glorious as a judge. He is the master craftsman and the divine craftsmanship! There is stability and permanence to the judgments He renders. He is "prepared to tread under his feet the enemies of the Christian faith. This stern portrayal prepares us for the equally stern words in verses 26-27" (Ladd, *Commentary*, 50).

Christ Commends Us for Faithful Works
REVELATION 2:19

Jesus graciously praises this church for the good things He sees. Our Lord is always fair in His assessment of His people. Even when He must rebuke and correct them, He will affirm and encourage where He can. Every church would be wise to follow in Thyatira's footsteps in verse 19.

Let Us Do Good Works for Jesus

Jesus praises His church for their works, their godly activity and efforts on His behalf. He notes several things for which He delights in His faithful children.

Jesus commends them for their love and faith (HCSB, "faithfulness"), which refer to their motives for the works they do (Mounce, *Revelation*, 85). Love (*agape*) for Christ and others and faith (*pistin*) in God inspired and moved this church to action. Unlike the church at Ephesus, their love for Christ had not grown cold. Unlike the church at Ephesus, their love for truth had. Ephesians 4:15 teaches us to "speak the truth in love." Second and Third John emphasize the necessity of both for a balanced Christianity. Ephesus lacked love. Thyatira lacked truth. A healthy church needs both.

The Lord also notes their service (*diakonian*, "deacon-acts") and endurance (*upomonen*; NIV, "perseverance"), highlighting the results that naturally follow from love and faith. A person with a servant's heart is one who, with long-suffering and steadfastness, will give himself deliberately, voluntarily, sacrificially, and joyfully to others in order that he may help meet their needs. He will walk away from his own concerns and private interests and give himself—his time, his wisdom, his knowledge, his talents, and his gifts—in order to help others. The qualities of the person with a genuine servant's spirit will exhibit a spirit of humility, willing to stoop to serve another but never asking for recognition. Dependable, loyal, loving, patient—here are things every church should be.

Let Us Grow in Our Good Works for Jesus

Jesus likes these characteristics of His church. He also loves that "your last works are greater than the first." They are not stagnant or satisfied in their service to their King. They had gotten better! They were doing more than ever! "Do good things and grow in good things" is a wonderful goal for any church of Christ, and that goal had been met in the church at Thyatira. Still, there was "a dark spot of cancerous sin eating away from the inside" (Swindoll, *Insights*, 59). Our Lord now moves to address the serious spiritual sickness that impaired the health of this body.

Christ Condemns Us for Excessive Tolerance
REVELATION 2:20

William Hendriksen says,

> Thyatira was indeed a lampstand, a light-bearer. But this does
> not constitute an excuse for failure to exercise discipline with

respect to members who make a compromise with the world."
(*More than Conquerors*, 89)

Now, we should be clear. God does not expect us to be perfect, though perfection is the mark we strive for (see Matt 5:48; Phil 3:12-14). What He does expect is for us to be a community of repenting sinners. What He does expect is for us to call sin what He calls sin. Swimming against the currents of the culture will be hard and almost always unpopular. However, as Peter and the apostles said in Acts 5:29, "We must obey God rather than men" (see Gal 1:10).

Jesus addresses four areas of danger and temptation a church must recognize and confront immediately when they see them—the sooner the better. Delay can be deadly.

Guard Against a Personality Cult

Jesus has something against this church: "You tolerate the woman Jezebel." This is most certainly a descriptive title and not the woman's actual name. It would conjure up images of the evil and vile queen of Israel. However, I do believe our Lord is talking about an actual person. This woman was a powerful personality who had built her own following and kingdom in our Lord's church. She was smart, influential in personality, and powerful in speech. It was easy to join her because she made so much sense. However, like Jezebel of old, she was evil and deceptive, domineering and scheming, idolatrous and sexually immoral. The liberty she promised would actually lead them into slavery and away from God and the lordship of Jesus.

There is such a valuable lesson here, one we must never forget. Anything or anyone that gets your eyes off of Jesus is not of God. Anything or anyone that minimizes or adds to the gospel is not of God. Anything or anyone that compromises on biblical truth is not of God. The impressiveness of their abilities, gifts, and visions makes no difference. Indeed, the greater the gifts, the greater the dangers.

Guard Against an Authority Problem

This danger naturally flows from and is connected to the threat of "personality cults" in a church, denomination, or Christian organization. The Jezebel (a man can be a Jezebel too!) called herself a "prophetess."

Here was a self-proclaimed leader. Who said she was a prophetess? She did. Not God! Now, that there is a legitimate gift of prophecy that may involve women is clearly taught in Scripture (e.g., Anna in Luke 2:36; Philip's daughters in Acts 21:9; see also Joel 2:28-29; Acts 2:17; 1 Cor 11:5). Here, however, was an illegitimate usurpation, an inappropriate seizing of power due to raw ambition. Drawing on parallels to the wicked Jezebel, we can say this woman was cleverly deceptive, manipulatively domineering, viciously scheming, and spiritually idolatrous. She clearly was a leader because people were following her. But leadership can be good or bad, a blessing or a curse. Someone should have stepped up and confronted her, but no one did. Fear paralyzed the good people in the church from dealing with this false teacher.

Guard Against a Theology Problem

A false prophet will mix truth with lies. Not everything they say will be false or wrong. If it were, we would have no problem spotting it. Instead, their message will contain just enough truth to deceive the gullible and shallow, those who for whatever reason cannot think in biblical categories and with a Christian worldview.

The Jezebel "teaches and deceives My slaves" (or "servants," Gk *doulos*). Her doctrine was attractive and seductive. At first blush it seemed insightful, deep, perceptive. She had a way of opening the Scriptures that were new and exciting. Her teachings promised freedom. They promised prosperity. They promised life. They promised to exalt Jesus, but in actuality they dethroned Jesus. She claimed to have the truth, but she peddled a lie. God's standard was perverted, and God's Son removed from His preeminence (Col 1:18). The church must never lose sight of the fact that doctrine matters. Theology matters. Truth matters. We must continually be on guard. Truth is too easily compromised, at which point it is lost.

Guard Against a Morality Problem

The Jezebel taught and deceived God's servants to do two things: commit sexual immorality and participate in pagan idolatry. Robert Mounce is helpful in putting this in historical context. It is striking how twenty-first century it sounds! He writes,

> One thing we can state with a sense of confidence: the
> problem in Thyatira centered on the guilds. For persons
> to maintain their livelihood, some connection, indeed

membership, in the guilds was a virtual necessity. For Christians the problem was that this mandated participation in the guild feasts, which themselves involved "meat offered to idols," since the patron gods of the guilds were always worshiped at the feasts. At times this could also involve immorality. The extent to which these feasts degenerated into debauchery is questionable, and many have argued that "commit adultery" here is an OT metaphor for idolatry. . . . However, it is more likely a reference to immoral practices (though the noun form in 2:21 probably does have this figurative meaning). Whenever Christians refused to participate in the feasts because such participation would compromise their faith, they faced the anger of the pagan populace, and it had economic repercussions if they lost their jobs. Thus while at Pergamum it was a life-threatening situation, at Thyatira the problem was more economic and social. Jezebel probably "taught" that there was nothing wrong with a Christian taking part in the guild feasts and celebrations, for it was merely civil. Since idols were nothing, Christians would not destroy their faith by participating. (*Revelation*, 156–57)

Jezebel said it is fine to compartmentalize your sacred and secular worlds. The thought was, "If you are going to survive in this dog-eat-dog world, you will have to make some allowances. On occasions you will have to compromise your convictions. It won't hurt anything. Jesus understands. He never expected that following Him could be bad for business. And remember, you are free in Christ!" Of course, she was wrong. These compromises in belief and behavior set the Lord Jesus against His own church.

Sexual immorality and acts of idolatry, in any culture, are a big deal to God. God calls us to holiness, not harlotry. He calls us to purity, not spiritual prostitution. God calls us to spiritual fidelity, not spiritual adultery. God calls us to follow Him, not follow the world (see 1 John 2:15-17).

When the church looks like the world, you have a *sick* church. When the church acts like the world, you have an *impotent* church. When the church plays with the world, you have an *unfaithful* church.

God Corrects Us with Loving Discipline
REVELATION 2:21-25

Our God is a good Father. He is a perfect Father. He will not allow His children to walk a path of destruction without intervening. With loving but firm discipline, He will get in our business. He will get involved in our lives and community up close and personal (see Heb 12:5-13). Five aspects of God's discipline for Thyatira are noted. They are instructive.

God's Discipline Is Fair (2:21)

Jesus gave the Jezebel "time to repent." However, "she does not want to repent of her sexual immorality." Our Lord gave her time to change her evil ways. She said no.

The Savior's discipline is always wrapped in grace, love, and mercy. Twice we see the word *repent*, meaning "a change of mind that results in a change of action." Our Lord gave her time, she said no, and now judgment falls. She will have no occasion to question the *justice* of God's judgment. Jeremiah promises it (Jer 17:10). Paul promises it (Rom 2:6). Jesus promises it too (Matt 16:27).

God's Discipline Is Full (2:22)

"Look!" Announcing His sentence, Jesus declares, "I will throw her into a sickbed [along with] those who commit adultery with her." "Great tribulation" will be their lot unless they "repent" (this is the third time He has called them to do so). The imagery is vivid and striking. *Sickbed* may refer to actual disease and illness (see 1 Cor 11:27-29). If so, the suffering will be intense for her and her followers. *The Message* says, "I'm about to lay her low, along with her partners, as they play their sex-and-religion games." MacArthur, however, makes a distinction between the judgment on the Jezebel and her followers. He says,

> In light of the finality of Jezebel's refusal to repent, it is more likely that the bed refers to death and hell—the ultimate resting place for those who refuse to repent. Divine judgment was about to fall not only on Jezebel, but also on those who commit adultery with her. The Lord threatens to cast them into great tribulation—not the eschatological tribulation described in Revelation 4–19, but distress or trouble. Since these were the sinning Christians who had believed her

lies, the Lord does not threaten to send them to hell as He did the false prophetess. He promises to bring them severe chastening—possibly even physical death (see 1 Cor 11:30; 1 John 5:16)—unless they repent of her deeds. (*Revelation 1–11*, 102)

In either case, the Lord's judgment will be certain and sure, intense and painful.

God's Discipline Is Final (2:23)

Jesus declares, "I will kill her children with the plague." *The Message* paraphrases this sentence as, "The bastard offspring of their idol-whoring I'll kill." One hardly knows how to respond to these words. "Her children" speaks of her spiritual offspring, those who share her nature, her DNA. In all likelihood John sees the Jezebel and her children as lost and unregenerate. To kill means to turn them over to the destruction and death they are pursing and deserve. It is to sin away their day of grace and hope. Ladd is helpful in pointing out the difference between "those who commit adultery with her" and "her children":

> The text distinguishes between those who join in adultery with the prophetess and those who are called her children. The punishment of the latter is much more severe than the former: death. Apparently John intends us to distinguish between those who are still struggling with the problem of how to be loyal to Christ and at the same time to adapt fully to the business and social mores about them, and those who have unreservedly committed themselves to the teaching of the false prophetess. (*Commentary*, 52)

God's Discipline Is Fearful (2:23)

When God takes out Jezebel and her children, "all the churches will know." And what will they know? "I am the One who examines minds and hearts, and I will give to each of you according to your works." This statement expounds on the fairness of God's judgment but intensifies it. It echoes Jeremiah 17:10, but also 1 Chronicles 28:9; Psalm 7:9; Proverbs 24:12; Jeremiah 11:20; and 20:12. MacArthur notes the phrase "offers confirmation of Christ's deity, since it is used in the Old Testament in reference to God" (*Revelation 1–11*, 102). Divine discernment peers into their souls seeing them for who they really are. Actions and motives are exposed to His piercing gaze. Jezebel and her clan may fool others, but they do not fool Christ, "whose eyes are like a fiery flame" (2:18).

God's Discipline Is Faithful (2:24-25)

Hope is not lost for this church. There are still some in Thyatira who "do not hold this teaching," who have no knowledge (experiential knowledge is in view) of "the deep things of Satan—as they say." The deep things of Satan may be Jezebel's actual claim, though it is more likely a sarcastic caricature of their libertine claims (see 2:9). Claiming to go deep in the things of God and adding to the simple gospel, they were actually propagating the doctrine of demons and the wisdom of Satan. Mounce, however, believes there may have been something of an actual claim. He says,

> "knowing Satan's deep secrets" is a reference to the view that in order to appreciate fully the grace of God one must plumb the depths of evil. Later Gnosticism [the view that matter is evil and spirit is good] boasted that it was precisely by entering into the stronghold of Satan that believers could learn the limits of his power and emerge victorious. (*Revelation*, 89)

Either way, Jezebel claims she could lead the church into the "deeper life," into greater depths of spiritual understanding and experience. She offered a "Jesus plus" theology. However, what she actually gave them was the deeper lie of Satan, spiritual ignorance, and a "no Jesus" theology. In contrast Jesus says, "Stay with Me and I will put on you no other burden. Stay with Me. Don't follow the seduction of Satan, the doctrine of demons." Jesus says, "Hold on [imperative] to what you have until I come."

Holding on to Jesus, the gospel, and biblical truth would not be easy. Satan, Jezebel, and her children will continue to try to steal those precious things from you. So don't let go. Stay where you are. You have Jesus, and He is all you need.

Christ Challenges Us with Future Promises
REVELATION 2:26-29

We need to "never let go" of Jesus and the gospel. To hold on is to experience true victory; to fail will spell certain defeat. Overcomers, the "victorious," the conquerors, keep Christ's works (NIV, "will") to the end. Perseverance is proof of our profession (Matt 24:13). To those who endure, persevere, Jesus promises a twofold encouragement.

We Receive the Authority of Christ's Power (2:26-27)

Leon Morris says, "The Christian life is not a battle but a campaign" (*St. John*, 74). To the victor Jesus says, "I will give him authority over the nations." Christ honors His faithful disciples by allowing them to co-reign with Him in fulfillment of the messianic Psalm 2. This is a reference to His millennial kingdom (20:1-6) and possibly the eternal state (21:24). Believers will serve under Christ, sitting on thrones (see Matt 19:28; Rev 20:4), jointly exercising His gracious, firm, and sovereign authority. Jesus "received this from [His] Father." He now shares it with His subjects.

We Receive the Assurance of Christ's Presence (2:28-29)

He will give us "the morning star." This is Christ Himself, as 22:16 makes clear (Mounce, *Revelation*, 90–91). In the end we get what we started with: we get Jesus! Our Lord promises us Himself in all His fullness and glory. What more could we dream of or hope for? Listen, those of you who have ears to hear. The Spirit is talking to all the churches. We all need this reminder. We all need to hold on to this hope.

Conclusion

Jesus Christ is the same "yesterday, today, and forever" (Heb 13:8). The gospel is the same yesterday, today, and forever. God's Word is the same yesterday, today, and forever. The Lord's holiness is the same yesterday, today, and forever.

False teachers are always adding to or subtracting from God's truth. John says to stay with the teaching you have in Christ. Adrian Rogers was right to say, "Some may preach the gospel of Jesus Christ better, but no one can preach a better gospel." I believe he is right. So would the apostle John. Stay with Jesus and the gospel.

Reflect and Discuss

1. What does the description of Jesus tell us about His character? How does it prepare the church to hear what He is about to say to them?

2. Discuss the role that both truth and love play in the health of the church. Which of these do you find more difficult to hold on to? Which is easier?
3. What good works has the Lord called you to do in your life? How can you continue to grow in good works such that your "last works are greater than the first" (2:19)?
4. What does it mean for the church to be a community of repenting sinners? How does this play out in the life of the local church?
5. What are some of the warning signs that a personality cult is taking root in the church?
6. If false teachers do teach *some* true things, how can a church be on guard against being led astray by them?
7. In what situations might the decision to follow Christ in holiness and obedience lead to economic and social repercussions? How have you experienced this?
8. How are the mercy and patience of Christ seen in this passage, even in judgment?
9. Why is it that so often claims that promise a deeper and more profound spirituality often end up losing the biblical gospel in the process? How does Revelation 2:24-25 encourage us to respond?
10. How do those who persevere actually receive what the false teachers promise but can't deliver?

Autopsy of a Dead Church

REVELATION 3:1-6

Main Idea: Spiritual lethargy and compromise will bring destruction to a church, but Christ is faithful to graciously call those who will hear back to faithfulness and life.

I. **Christ Is Characterized by His Knowledge and Care (3:1).**

II. **Christ Confronts Those Who Have a Reputation but Are Dead (3:1).**

III. **Christ Corrects Those Who Are Dying but Not Yet Dead (3:2-3).**
   A. Command 1: "Be alert."
   B. Command 2: "Strengthen What Remains."
   C. Command 3: "Remember What You Have Received and Heard."
   D. Command 4: "Keep It."
   E. Command 5: "Repent."

IV. **Christ Commends Those Who Are Holy and Worthy of His Praise (3:4).**

V. **Christ Confesses Those Who Have His Righteousness and Are Written in the Book of Life (3:5-6).**

In 2014 Thom Rainer, president of LifeWay Christian Resources, wrote a highly acclaimed book titled *Autopsy of a Deceased Church*. Its genesis was a popular blog article with the same title. In this book Rainer identifies several fatal causes that put once-alive and vibrant churches in the grave. These include

- treating the past as the hero;
- refusing to adapt to the needs of the present community;
- moving the focus of the budget inward;
- allowing the Great Commission to become the Great Omission;
- letting the church become preference-driven out of selfishness and personal agendas;
- seeing the tenure of the pastors decreasing;
- failing to have regular, corporate prayer;
- having no clear purpose or vision; and
- obsessing over the facilities.

Here I would like to build on Rainer's excellent points with a simple observation. Many a church begins with a *man*, reaches out with a *mission*, becomes a *movement*, but ends up a *monument* or in the *mortuary*. This is a polite way of saying many a church begins with life but ends in death. It has a glorious past, but a glorious past is all it has. It is now a zombie church, a church of the living dead. There are live bodies walking around with dead souls on the inside. Amazingly, astonishingly, sometimes only God notices. Spiritually there is no pulse, no heartbeat. Spiritually they are flat-lined, a dead church.

Another complement to Rainer's precise analysis might be an article titled "When Does My Church Need Revival?" in which Stevan Manley highlights six tell-tale signs of a church standing at death's door:

1. The church is plagued with disagreements.
2. The preaching is ineffective.
3. Few can remember when a person was last saved.
4. God's supernatural power is never seen.
5. God is not praised regularly.
6. No one is being called into God's work. (*Herald*)

Autopsy studies of modern churches are popular and even helpful. However, they are not new, as Revelation 3:1-6 makes clear. Here the exalted and glorified Christ performs an examination of His church at Sardis, and the results are painful: "You are dead." The necrosis was spreading and endangered the whole body, but the situation was not past salvaging if they would listen to the Great Physician's diagnosis and remedies for healing. Hope was fading and time was running out, but it was not yet beyond a cure. Christ is exactly who they need, and His prescription for a possible recovery is what they definitely must hear.

Christ Is Characterized by His Knowledge and Care
REVELATION 3:1

The heavenly watcher, the angel, over the church at Sardis receives a message from Jesus by the pen of the apostle John. Sardis was approximately 30 miles southeast of Thyatira and one of the oldest cities in the province of Asia, having been founded around 1200 BC. It was virtually destroyed by an earthquake in AD 17 but was rebuilt and given new life with the aid of Emperor Tiberius (AD 14–37). The city had fame and wealth, and it took pride in its temple to Cybele, its acropolis, and its famous necropolis, which was known as the "cemetery of a 1,000 hills" because of the hundreds of burial mounds visible on the skyline from some seven miles away (Johnson, "Revelation," 2006, 626). The city, however, had seen its best days and was living on its past reputation. William Ramsay said Sardis "was a relic of the period of barbaric warfare, which lived rather on its ancient prestige than on its suitability to present conditions" (in Mounce, *Revelation*, 91). Indeed, "no city of Asia at that period showed such a melancholy contrast between past splendor and present decay" (Johnson, "Revelation," 2006, 627). It is fascinating to see a church mirroring the history and culture of the city where it is located!

Christ, who is simply described as "the One who has the seven spirits of God and the seven stars," is fully cognizant of the church's condition. What He sees draws His serious concern. The seven spirits of God are not a heavenly angelic entourage or planetary deities (Mounce, *Revelation*, 93). This is the complete or perfect Holy Spirit; the Spirit in all His fullness. I think there is an allusion to Isaiah 11:2-5 and Zechariah 4:1-6. It emphasizes His omnipresence (see Rev 5:6), wisdom, and life-giving power. The Savior has the Spirit but Sardis does not. The Savior has life but Sardis is dead. Sometimes we have no idea of our true spiritual condition. We walk about in a fog of deception, but Christ discerns how things really are. His perfect Spirit sees everything. The seven stars are angels, the "angelic representatives who report to Jesus" (Hamilton, *Revelation*, 105). That He has them is a reminder that they are in His possession and under His protection. They belong to Him and so do the churches they serve. He is responsible for them and they are accountable to Him. He sees; He knows; He cares. Through His life-giving Spirit He has the power to breathe new life, resurrection life, into this church. Church revitalization will always begin in heaven with the glorified Christ who longs to raise to new life a church where "rigor mortis [has] set in" (Swindoll, *Insights*, 64).

Christ Confronts Those Who Have a Reputation but Are Dead
REVELATION 3:1

This church receives no word of commendation or congratulation. There is not a single word of praise. In this regard she is like her sister church at Laodicea (3:14-22). Swindoll says the church at Sardis was "a morgue with a steeple" (ibid.). Vance Havner adds, "She had it all in the show window but nothing in stock" (*Repent*, 63). Jesus confronts them from the beginning: "I know your works; you have a reputation for being alive." Sardis had a reputation as a beehive of activity and vitality. This was most likely a church with size, money, and ministries that caused people to stop and take notice. She appeared to be and claimed to be a healthy fellowship, a successful church. That she had a reputation is an indication of Sardis's past faithfulness and accomplishments. In the past she was something genuine. There had been a time when reputation and reality matched up. There had been a day when she was truly doing great things for God. Now all they had was a name, an outward reputation. Often we can think we are one thing when actually we are altogether something different.

And Jesus reveals exactly that: "but you are dead" (*nekros*). Looks can be deceiving. A body that from all outward appearances seems strong and healthy can, on closer inspection, be found to be racked with cancer or some other terminal disease. Our Lord performs a battery of spiritual tests on the church at Sardis. He subjects her to a divine CAT-scan, MRI, and X-ray. The diagnosis is far worse than any external, superficial examination could have ever revealed: she is dead! They were a zombie church!

What was the cause of her demise? Though we cannot be sure, it may be they had compromised their public witness to Jesus to avoid opposition and persecution. They were trying to blend in with the culture and go along to get along. Jesus promises the victors in verse 5 that He will acknowledge us before His Father and the angels. Is there a hint here that this was a large part of their problem? They were unwilling to confess their allegiance to Christ (Hamilton, *Revelation*, 106)? Osborne succinctly spells out the tragedy of Sardis and those who follow in her deadly footsteps:

> It is a sad thing when the only accomplishment ("deed") of a church is what it names itself, especially if the reality shows that name to be a lie, as here. Their past deeds gave them a reputation among other churches for being alive for Christ, but their present deeds show a quite different picture (in accordance with their city's history). . . . Just outside their city was a famous necropolis, or cemetery, with the graves of long-dead kings. The assembly at Sardis represented that cemetery more than a living church. (*Revelation*, 174)

Christ Corrects Those Who Are Dying but Not Yet Dead
REVELATION 3:2-3

The love our Savior has for His church is utterly amazing! Not only has He redeemed her; He again and again goes out to rescue her from self-inflicted wounds. Even when others would walk away saying, "Let the patient die; she can't be saved," He reaches out in love and compassion to save her yet again.

Our God is in the resurrection business. He is continually active in bringing dead sinners to life (Eph 2:1-7), and He is active in breathing life back into dead churches. When things appear their worst, our Savior is at His best!

An autopsy has been performed. Sardis is dead. What, if anything, can be done? As our Lord looks over the body, His body, He sees a weak beat of the heart, a faint but perceptible pulse. Because this church is *His* church, there is yet hope of recovery, restoration, and revitalization. The condition is critical but not yet terminal, not as long as He is present. In rapid-fire succession our Lord peppers the church at Sardis with five imperatives and steps she must take if she is to once again be the church, the body of Christ, that Jesus saved her to be. There is hope, but she must act quickly. We would all do well to listen in on the treatment He prescribes.

Command 1: "Be Alert"

The first thing Jesus says is, "Wake up" (ESV). Historically the city of Sardis had fallen twice due to military slothfulness. Jesus urges them not to suffer the same fate. They should learn a lesson from their city's history. "Be alert" is an imperative with a durative force. Stay alert! Stay awake! Ladd says,

> This admonition suggests that the church was not yet entirely beyond hope. It was not too late to awaken from spiritual lethargy; there still remained a residuum of life which could be revived. But unless such a revival occurs, this small remainder will also fall subject to spiritual death. (*Commentary*, 56)

I doubt a more needful word could be uttered for and to the twenty-first-century church in the Western world. A lack of faithful vigilance is a certain recipe for disaster. Yesterday's victories are of little value for today's battles.

Command 2: "Strengthen What Remains"

What little that remains must be strengthened, built back up. Why? Because it "is about to die." Specifically, Jesus says, "I have not found your works [which "I know," v. 1] complete before My God." Though the quantity of their works was deficient, it is more likely that it was the quality of their works that was most lacking. They had grown content with a mediocre, halfway, comfortable, and convenient Christianity. Their faith was not radical; it was almost invisible. The lost among whom they lived, worked, and prayed saw nothing different or unique about them. The culture did not oppose them; it simply ignored them as of no real consequence or significance. They were so weak in their confession of Christ that they bothered no one. Like the unfinished temple of Cybele in their city, they too were incomplete in what Christ saved them and called them to be.

Command 3: "Remember What You Have Received and Heard"

Like the church at Ephesus (2:5), our Lord calls those at Sardis to "remember." The idea is that they will continually call something to remembrance. And what are they to remember? The gospel! They need to continually recall the truth of the gospel they had "received and heard." The church "had received the faith as an abiding truth at the moment faith came by hearing" (Mounce, *Revelation*, 94). Again and again, daily, they needed to preach the gospel to themselves. Again and again they needed to remind themselves of what Christ had done for them through His bloody cross and glorious resurrection. He lived the life they should have lived. He died the death they should have died. He experienced the wrath of God that should have been theirs. He paid the penalty for sin that they should have paid. And He gave them the gift of eternal life they do not deserve and wrote their name in the book of life where it can never be erased (3:5). Why hesitate to confess such a Savior? Why compromise gospel truth and shame this King? To do so will be like treason. They must remember!

Command 4: "Keep It"

With the command to "keep it," Jesus encourages the church to hold on, to guard what they received and heard. The truth of the gospel and the truths that flow from it are easily lost. It is a precious treasure that should never be taken for granted. We must never let it slip away.

The fact is, we never *drift* toward anything worthwhile. Never. We never slide into truth, but we can slide into error. You slide and slip into theological liberalism. You slide and slip into moral compromise. No, we never drift anywhere worth going. Furthermore, you do not want to drift and add to the gospel. And you don't want to slip and subtract from the gospel. Stay where you are. Keep it. Hold on. Guard it. Never let it go. Stay with what you received and heard when you put your faith in Jesus.

Command 5: "Repent"

I fear many Christians have an inadequate understanding of biblical repentance. They know they repented from their sin when they were converted, but they fail to understand its ongoing place in a healthy Christian life. Repentance, a change of mind resulting in a change in attitude and action concerning sin, is to be our companion throughout our Christian life and pilgrimage. We never grow out of it or mature beyond it.

It appears the church at Sardis had forgotten the grace of repentance. As a result, they were in danger of receiving an unexpected visit from Christ. This imagery of Jesus coming like a thief is found several times in Revelation (3:3; 16:15) and other places in the Bible (Matt 24:42-44; Luke 12:35-40; 1 Thess 5:2; 2 Pet 3:10). Here it is referring not to His second coming for all but rather a coming in judgment against His church. This is a striking image and a powerful yet grace-filled warning. Jesus is instructing them, "Repent now! There is no promise that you will have time later. My surprise coming in judgment may catch you unprepared."

Christ Commends Those Who Are Holy and Worthy of His Praise

REVELATION 3:4

Our Lord provides an accurate and honest evaluation of His church through the omnipresent and omniscient Holy Spirit, as well as through His own eyes, which "are like a fiery flame" (1:17). He identifies some, not many, "who have not defiled their clothes." The picture is one of spiritual contamination of their Christian witness by accommodating to the current and faddish trends of the pagan culture and its sinful life. A small minority stood strong for Jesus, both in confession and conduct.

They bucked the trends, swam against the current that was engulfing members of their community. Taking this stand most certainly would be costly in the days to come. However, it will be gloriously worth it in the new age that is coming. They will walk in the purity of white clothing provided by Christ, symbolic of their justification and holiness of life. Mounce explains,

> In Revelation 7 the great multitude wearing white robes
> (vv. 9-10) is led by the Lamb to springs of living water (v. 17),
> and in chapter 14 the 144,000 "follow the Lamb wherever he
> goes" (v. 4) . . . it would appear walking "in white" is a way of
> describing those who are justified. (*Revelation*, 95)

They are His, and He knows them by name, one by one.

Christ Confesses Those Who Have His Righteousness and Are Written in the Book of Life
REVELATION 3:5-6

The "victors" are provided a threefold promise for their fidelity to Christ. First, they will be clothed in His perfect righteousness, symbolized by their white clothes (see 4:4; 6:11; 7:9,13; 19:14). This is their justification accomplished, their sanctification in progress, and their glorification that is soon to come. He will dress us, for we could never dress ourselves. Once more He does for us what we do not deserve and cannot do for ourselves!

Second, He promises never to erase their names from the book of life. Jim Hamilton speaks to this issue with clarity and insight:

> To be faithful to confess Jesus' name, whatever it costs, is to
> conquer. Jesus promises white garments, and he promises
> that those who conquer will never have their names blotted
> out of the book of life. There are a number of references to
> the book of life in the Old and New Testaments (cf. Exodus
> 32:32; Psalm 69:28; Isaiah 4:3; Daniel 12:1, 2; Luke 10:20;
> Philippians 4:3; Hebrews 12:23). The value of having one's
> name written in the book of life is seen in what Jesus said to
> his disciples in Luke 10:20: "Nevertheless, do not rejoice in
> this, that the spirits are subject to you, but rejoice that your
> names are written in heaven." In the curse on the Minim
> [Christian "heretics"], the Jews in the synagogue may call for

the names of Christians to be blotted out of the book of life, but Jesus promises the church in Sardis that those who confess his name will never have their names blotted out of that book. (*Revelation*, 109)

Third, Jesus promises to confess these who are clothed in His righteousness before the Father and His angels. He will acknowledge their names as evidence that He knows them and claims them as His own. They were not ashamed of Him, and He is not ashamed of them. Jesus will tell His Father, "Danny belongs to me. He is mine." The angels of God will hear the same message. The promise that our names are permanently affixed signatures in the book of life is a promise that should move us, motivate us, and compel us, out of "grace gratitude," to complete our works, bear our witness, stay clean, and pursue purity that reflects the transforming work of Christ. After all, coupled with the promise of verse 5, we have the wonderful declaration of Matthew 10:32: "Therefore, everyone who will acknowledge Me before men, I will also acknowledge him before My Father in heaven." However, go on and read verses 33-34 for good measure! They provide the warning often neglected that is the companion to the promise:

> *"But whoever denies Me before men, I will also deny him before My Father in heaven. Don't assume that I came to bring peace on the earth. I did not come to bring peace, but a sword."*

Conclusion

I close our study of this letter with the insights of one of my favorite Bible teachers, Chuck Swindoll. He is a fountain of wit and wisdom. So often he is "spot on" in his exposition and application even when there is necessary pain involved. Read carefully what this faithful Bible teacher has to say:

> Finally, a dead church lacks evangelistic and missionary zeal. Turned inward on their own needs, preferences, and comfort, unhealthy churches give halfhearted attention to the conversion of the lost. In contrast, living churches devote time, resources, and energy to both local evangelism and worldwide missions.
>
> In the message to Sardis, we saw Christ revealed as the Life-giver. He alone grants spiritual vitality to those with a

comatose or dying faith. In light of His urgent alarm to Sardis, all of us who tend toward spiritual stupor must turn from stale religious routine and embrace the abundant life only Jesus Christ can provide. He extends a sincere invitation to you right now. If you feel the stiffness of spiritual rigor mortis setting in, take Christ's words to heart: wake up and declare your devotion. (*Insights*, 70)

Swindoll is right. Wake up! Now! Declare your devotion to Christ. Now! Please do not delay. Do not wait until it is too late.

Reflect and Discuss

1. What do you think about the lists provided by Rainer and Manley in the introduction to this chapter? How can your church work to avoid these dangerous trends?
2. How does Jesus' omniscience guide the church to faithfulness? How does it reveal His care for His church?
3. Should a church strive to have a good reputation? How can a reputation actually hide weaknesses in the church?
4. Have you ever been tempted to compromise your convictions to avoid opposition or persecution? What does this temptation reveal about our hearts?
5. What instructions would you give for a dying church? How do they line up with Jesus' instructions in this passage?
6. What does it mean for a church to be mired in spiritual lethargy?
7. What does it mean to remember or preach the gospel to yourself everyday? What tools can you use to help you with this?
8. Do you think the call to keep the gospel is a call to stop growing as a Christian? Does holding to the same gospel from beginning to end mean spiritual stagnation?
9. Why is repentance not merely for the beginning of the Christian life?
10. How do the promises of God encourage us to remain faithful to the gospel and the gospel works He has for us now?

A Great Commission Church

REVELATION 3:7-13

Main Idea: Though she may be of little account by earthly standards, the church that remains faithful to the Savior, the gospel, and the Great Commission will be rewarded by her God.

I. **A Great Commission Church Sees Jesus as Awesome (3:7).**
   A. He is the holy One.
   B. He is the true One.
   C. He is the sovereign One.

II. **A Great Commission Church Is Faithful to the Gospel (3:8-9).**
   A. Be persistent in the work of the gospel (3:8).
   B. Be true to the name of Jesus (3:8).
   C. Be energized by the prospects for evangelism and missions (3:8).
   D. Be encouraged by the hope of vindication (3:9).

III. **A Great Commission Church Lives by the Promises of God (3:10-13).**
   A. Jesus will protect us according to His plans (3:10).
   B. Jesus will come soon, so stay strong (3:11).
   C. Jesus will honor us by giving us a home and His name (3:12-13).

For many years I have taught at a school that aspires to be a Great Commission seminary and college. Throughout our campus you will hear people say things like: "Every classroom a Great Commission classroom," "Every teacher a Great Commission teacher," "Every student a Great Commission student," and "Every graduate a Great Commission graduate sent out to build Great Commission churches." The fact is the churches that please Christ are those Great Commission churches that take seriously His final marching orders given just before He ascended into heaven (Matt 28:16-20; Acts 1:8). Oswald Smith says, "Any church that is not seriously involved in helping fulfill the Great Commission has forfeited its biblical right to exist" (Newell, *Mission Quotes*, 257).

This church in Philadelphia, Asia, was passionate about being a Great Commission church, and the risen and glorified Christ was passionate about enabling it to continue to be a Great Commission church. They were faithful to Jesus, and our Lord promises them, "I have placed before you an open door that no one is able to close" (3:8). What a wonderful promise for any church to receive from the Savior!

Churches may be mighty in their witness even when they look weak in appearance. Who they really are on the inside matters more to God than what they look like on the outside. And when He sees what He likes, there are no limits on what God may do *for* them and *through* them. Chuck Swindoll says it well:

> The size of a congregation, the limitations of its location, or the restrictions of its budget should never determine its vision. Instead, churches should set their vision based on the power of their God. God is infinite, magnificent, awesome, and mighty—beyond description or comprehension! When He chooses to open opportunities, the possibilities are endless. All we need to do is trust and follow Him wherever He leads. (*Insights*, 70)

Certain traits characterize a Great Commission church for which Christ opens doors that no one, not even Satan, can shut. It entails how they see Christ, how they value the power of the gospel, and how they trust in and live by the promises of God. Count Nicolaus Ludwig Von Zinzendorf put it beautifully:

> I have but one passion: it is Christ. It is Christ alone. The world is the field and the field is the world; and henceforth that country shall be my home where I can be most used in winning souls for Christ.

This passion pleases our Savior! Three truths capture well the thrust of that passion in this verse.

A Great Commission Church Sees Jesus as Awesome
REVELATION 3:7

The city of Philadelphia (which means "brotherly love") was 25 miles southeast of Sardis. It was an important high-plateau city on a main highway that connected with Smyrna, which was about one hundred miles due west. In AD 17 the city was devastated by an earthquake and then rebuilt by Tiberius. As a result, it was loyal to Rome. Called "the gateway to the East," it was something of a "missionary city" for the spreading of Greek culture. In this passage Jesus promises the church that it will be a missionary church for the gospel. We do not know how the church was founded. What we do know is that it was a church that pleased Jesus. Like the church at Smyrna (2:8-11), our Lord has no word of criticism or correction (Johnson, "Revelation," 2006, 630; also Mounce, *Revelation,* 98–99). I suspect this was due, in large part, to the exalted view and love they had for Jesus and the gospel. The description of the Savior in verse 7 would support this thesis. Three truths are set forth concerning the Lord who walks among His church (1:12-13).

He Is the Holy One

Jesus is the *ho hagios,* "the Holy One." This title was ascribed to God in the Old Testament (Isa 40:25; Hab 3:3). Here, and elsewhere in the New Testament, it is equally and appropriately ascribed to Jesus (Mark 1:24; Acts 3:14). The idea is one of purity as well as separateness. God is separate from creation as the Creator. He is separate from sin as the Savior. Who God is, Jesus is, because Jesus is God. He is pure, undefiled, spotless, without stain or blemish. Hosea 11:9 says, "For I am God and not man, the Holy One among you." Jesus is this Holy One who walked among us in the flesh (John 1:14) and now walks among us by His Spirit.

He Is the True One

Jesus is the *ho alethinos,* "the True One." Revelation 6:10 combines these two titles, calling Christ there, "the One who is holy and true." Jesus is "the true God," distinct from all others. What He says is "the truth" (John 14:6). What He says is the truth because it flows from the True One. Ideas of trustworthiness, reliability, dependability leap from this title. He is genuine and He is faithful. This would certainly encourage this church with "limited strength." He will sustain them and see them through the commission He had given them. They have His word on it! As 1 John 5:20 declares, they could count on the One who "is the true God and eternal life."

He Is the Sovereign One

Jesus "has the Key of David." That implicitly looks to 1:18 and the fact that Christ "holds the keys of death and Hades." It also looks back to Isaiah 22:22 where the Bible says, "I will place the key of the House of

David on his shoulder; what he opens, no one can close; what he closes, no one can open." Here in Revelation 3:7 the same words appear and are again ascribed to Christ. Jesus is "the Davidic Messiah with absolute power to control entrance to the heavenly kingdom" (Mounce, *Revelation*, 100). He has the authority to admit or exclude who will come into the presence of the King. He alone has the key that lets people into the kingdom of God. No wonder Jesus said in John 10:9, "I am the door. If anyone enters by Me, he will be saved and will come in and go out and find pasture." No wonder Paul says in 1 Timothy 2:5, "For there is one God and one mediator between God and humanity, Christ Jesus, Himself human." Only one is the sovereign Lord who holds the key to the entrance into heaven and eternal life. Only one! His name is Jesus.

A Great Commission Church Is Faithful to the Gospel
REVELATION 3:8-9

Their vision of Christ as exalted and awesome energizes this church for its Great Commission task. Henry Martyn said it well: "The spirit of Christ is the spirit of missions. The nearer we get to [Jesus] the more intensely missionary we become." Unlike the church at Ephesus that "abandoned the love they had at first" (2:4) and were now going through the motions and doing good things as a matter of routine, the Philadelphians were doing good things through proper motivation: love for Christ and the gospel. Jesus commends this church in several important areas that we would be wise to emulate and set as priorities for faithful ministry.

Be Persistent in the Work of the Gospel (3:8)

Jesus says, "I know your works" (see 2:2,19; 3:1,15). The One "who opens and no one will close, and closes and no one opens" (3:7) says, "I know your faithful service on My behalf and the gospel's." Unlike the church at Ephesus, He does not reference their heart; He does not correct them for leaving their "first love" (2:4). Apparently the Philadelphians were doing the right things for the right reasons. Love for Jesus and not ritualism or legalism moved them into action. Osborne notes, "The church was right with the Lord and needed encouragement rather than denunciation" (*Revelation*, 188). To say it another way, they were to keep on doing what they were doing. Their hearts were in the right place. This labor for Christ was exactly what He wanted to see. The gospel was their message and the grace of God their motive.

Be True to the Name of Jesus (3:8)

This church, like many churches, "had limited strength" (ESV, "little power"). They were not large or wealthy. They carried little, if any, influence in the city of Philadelphia. Osborne again says, "The church lacked size and stature in the community and was looked down upon and persecuted. They had 'little authority' or 'influence'" (ibid., 189). But they were hardworking and they were faithful. They had kept Christ's Word and not denied His name. Faced with constant trials, they stayed true to the word of the gospel. Faced with consistent opposition and ridicule, they remained faithful to the only name that saves (Acts 4:12; 1 Tim 2:5). Philadelphia had "only a 'little strength,' but . . . proved successful in standing in that strength" (Keener, *Revelation*, 149). Opposition did not deter them from obedience to the Great Commission and proclamation of the gospel.

Be Encouraged by the Prospects for Evangelism and Missions (3:8)

Jesus makes a promise, a pledge, to this faithful, fledgling community of believers. It is the promise of an open door that no one is able to close. Some believe this is an open door into the kingdom, into heaven (e.g., Keener, Mounce, Osborne). Others believe it is an open door for success in evangelism and missions (e.g., Hamilton, Swindoll). Though an either/or option is not necessary, I believe the primary thrust is indeed a promise for the success of the gospel to go forth and spread. Swindoll puts it well:

> A similar Greek phrase occurs in 2 Corinthians 2:12 in reference to an opportunity for ministry (see also Acts 14:27; 1 Cor 16:9; Col 4:3). If this is the meaning, Christ encouraged the church in Philadelphia with opportunities for ministry in the midst of their trials. That church didn't realize the "open door" they had. As the geographic gateway to the East, Philadelphia sat at the crossroads of several languages, cultures, and people groups. From an evangelistic and missionary perspective, this dynamic, diminutive church had great opportunities for ministry. (*Insights*, 73)

This church had an evangelist and missionary passion, and Christ promised them even greater opportunities to be on mission with God! Mike Stachura gets it: "The mark of a great church is not its seating capacity, but its sending capacity" (Newell, *Mission Quotes*). Philadelphia was a great church, and Christ honors them for their passion for Him, the gospel, and the nations.

Be Encouraged by the Hope of Vindication (3:9)

Jesus is faithful to His people. As the God of all the earth, He promised to make things right. Our exalted Lord's words are bold but appropriate. Here He tells his church,

> *"Take note! I will make those from the synagogue of Satan* [e.g., unbelieving and hostile Jews; see 2:9], *who claim to be Jews* [spiritually] *and are not, but are lying—note this—I will make them come and bow at your feet, and they will know that I have loved you."*

Our Lord has a general love for all but a particular love for His children. Jesus promised His church that He will humble their enemies. The Lord brings about their humiliation. The Lord declares His unique and special love for His church.

The opposition God's people face is often fierce and hostile, but it will not last forever. There is coming a day of judgment, a day of justice, a day of vindication. Graciously, some will come and bow, as they bow to King Jesus as their Messiah (Zech 12:10; Rom 11:25-32). John MacArthur observes, "This imagery derives from the Old Testament, which describes the yet future day when unbelieving Gentiles will bow down to the believing remnant of Israel (see 45:14; 49:23; 60:14)" (*Revelation 1–11*, 123). Here we see unbelieving Jews bowing to Messiah Jesus and His people. And the apostle Paul tells us in Philippians 2:9-11,

> *For this reason God highly exalted Him and gave Him the name that is above every name, so that at the name of Jesus every knee will bow— of those who are in heaven and on earth and under the earth—and every tongue should confess that Jesus Christ is Lord, to the glory of God the Father.*

Bowing to King Jesus either in glad salvation or in bitter submission, they will bow *with* or *to* the people who follow Him as their Lord, Master, and Sovereign King. I wonder if, as he wrote, John thought of the conversion of a brother named Paul and his experience on the Damascus Road (Acts 9).

A Great Commission Church Lives by the Promise of God
REVELATION 3:10-13

A Great Commission church is a church that pleases her Lord. She has, as it is often said, the smile of God upon her. How, then, does Christ specifically smile on a people who do good things for the right reason, keep His word, do not deny His name, and obediently walk through the open doors of evangelism and missions He has placed before them?

Jesus Will Protect Us According to His Plans (3:10)

This is a much disputed verse as to its proper interpretation. Regardless of the position we take, we should hold our view with grace and humility. Good, godly Bible scholars disagree on the exact meaning, and this should give us pause in terms of a dogmatic position. Alan Johnson summarizes well the two hermeneutical challenges before us:

> Related to the promise "I will also keep you from the hour of trial [HCSB, "testing"] that is going to come upon the whole world to test those who live on the earth" are two problems: (1) the identification of the "hour of trial" and (2) the precise sense of His phrase "keep you from the hour of trial." Both involve the ongoing debate among evangelical eschatologists over the tribulation/rapture question. ("Revelation," 2006, 632)

Though I have many dear friends who take different views from mine, here is how I understand what Jesus is saying to His churches in this verse:

When Jesus says, "You have kept my word of endurance" [HCSB marginal reading], he is referring to the "teachings about Christ's endurance (e.g., 2 Thess 3:5; Heb 12:2-3; as well as the Gospel stories of the life of Christ) that became a model for the steadfastness of the Philadelphian church in the midst of their own trials" (Osborne, *Revelation*, 192). In response to their endurance, He promises a remarkable protection from an "hour of testing" that will test "the whole world" and "those who live on the earth."

This last phrase is significant and is repeated several times in Revelation. In every instance it refers to unbelievers exclusively as the objects of God's judgment and wrath (see 6:10; 8:13; 11:10; 12:12; 13:8,12,14). Therefore, several truths should be noted. First, "the hour

of testing" is focused on unbelievers. I think this is primarily a reference to the "tribulation" of chapters 6–19. Second, Christ promises
deliverance or protection to His children not from trial or persecution
in general but from a specific and definite testing that is aimed at rebellious humanity. Now the question arises as to how we best understand
their deliverance, their being kept from the hour of testing. Dr. John
MacArthur summarizes well the pretribulational view with which I am
sympathetic:

> Because the believers in Philadelphia had successfully passed
> so many tests, Jesus promised to spare them from the ultimate
> test. The sweeping nature of the promise extends far beyond
> the Philadelphia congregation to encompass all faithful
> churches throughout history. This verse promises that the
> church will be delivered from the Tribulation, thus supporting
> a pretribulation Rapture. The Rapture is the subject of three
> passages in the New Testament (John 14:1-4; 1 Cor 15:51-54;
> 1 Thess 4:13-17), none of which speak of judgment, but rather
> of the church being taken up to heaven. There are three views
> of the timing of the Rapture in relation to the Tribulation: that
> it comes at the end of the Tribulation (posttribulationism),
> in the middle of the Tribulation (midtribulationism), and the
> view that seems to be supported by this text, that the Rapture
> takes place before the Tribulation (pretribulationism). Several
> aspects of this wonderful promise may be noted. First, the test
> is yet future. Second, the test is for a definite, limited time;
> Jesus described it as the **hour of testing**. Third, it is a test or trial
> that will expose people for what they really are. Fourth, the test
> is worldwide in scope, since it will **come upon the whole world**.
> Finally, and most significantly, its purpose is to test **those who
> dwell on the earth**—a phrase used as a technical term in the
> book of Revelation for unbelievers (cf. 6:10; 8:13; 11:10; 13:8,
> 12, 14; 14:6; 17:2, 8). The **hour of testing** is Daniel's Seventieth
> Week (Dan. 9:25-27), the time of Jacob's trouble (Jer. 30:7),
> the seven-year tribulation period. The Lord promised to keep
> His church out of the future time of testing that will come on
> unbelievers. (*Revelation 1–11*, 124, emphases in original)

While I agree with MacArthur's assessment, I do think hermeneutical restraint is wise at this point; I do not think alternative views are

without merit. Mounce, for example, adds from a posttribulational perspective something we can all affirm, namely that ultimately the most important issue is not physical protection from temporal wrath but spiritual protection from eternal wrath. Our Lord protects us to the end and forever. We are safe from the wicked assaults of Satan and his demons now, in the future, and forever. Might this be the main focus of verse 10 (Mounce, *Revelation*, 103)? When all is said and done on this issue, I appreciate the tempered and reasoned perspective of Alan Johnson:

> [Verse] 10 does not settle the question of the time of the rapture in relation to the tribulation. Rather, it remains ambiguous. One might be on the earth and yet be exempt from the "hour of trial" if (1) the "hour of trial" is an equivalent derived from the briefer term "trial," and (2) this "trial" is directed only at the unbelievers in the world, while the believers are divinely immune not from trial or persecution in general but from a specific type of trial (God's wrath) aimed at the rebellious on the earth. To this writer, the most natural way to understand the expression to be "kept from the hour" of something that is universal in the world is not to be preserved through it but to be kept from being present when it happens. In any event, we have here a marvelous promise of Christ's protection (*tēreō*, "keep") for those who have protected (*tēreō*) his word by their loving obedience. ("Revelation," 2006, 633)

Jesus Will Come Soon, So Stay Strong (3:11)

One of the glorious aspects of biblical eschatology is that we should live in the hope of the any-time, imminent return of Jesus. Titus 2:13 calls it the "the blessed hope." The phrase or idea that "I am coming quickly" (see 2:5,17; 3:3; 22:7,12,20) is not a threat of judgment but a promise of deliverance fast on the heels of verse 10. Because His coming is imminent, any day, any time, they should hold on (see 2:25; 3:3) to what they have—His Word, His name, His promise of deliverance—that no one may take their crown. Loss of salvation is nowhere in view, for that could never be taken. But Satan or evil men could rob them of future reward if they get their eyes off Jesus or if they yield to temptation to deny His name or disobey His word. "Stay with it," Jesus says. "There is a crown waiting at the finish line."

Jesus Will Honor Us by Giving Us a Home and His Name (3:12-13)

Our King concludes this letter with a twofold promise to "the victor." First, our Lord "will make him a pillar in the sanctuary [ESV, "temple"] of My God, and he will never go out again." To a people continually threatened by earthquakes and the need to flee the city when they come, this word would speak powerfully to their hearts. Alan Johnson notes, "Often the only parts of a city left standing after a severe quake were the huge stone temple columns [pillars]" (*Revelation*, 1983, 61).

Revelation 21:22 tells us in the new Jerusalem "the Lord God the Almighty and the Lamb are its temple." To be a pillar of Christ puts the believer in a position of absolute and complete security. No disruption, disturbance, or disaster will ever separate us from our Savior. As Romans 8:38-39 beautifully testifies,

> *For I am persuaded that not even death or life, angels or rulers, things present or things to come, hostile powers, height or depth, or any other created thing will have the power to separate us from the love of God that is in Christ Jesus our Lord!*

The second promise is, "I will write on him the name of My God and the name of the city of My God—the new Jerusalem, which comes down out of heaven from My God—and My new name." The church at Philadelphia had a good name, a wonderful reputation in heaven. Jesus promises them, "It will only get better." Because they had not been ashamed to identify themselves with Jesus, our Lord is not ashamed to identify Himself with them. Three times Jesus promises them a new name of blessing and honor.

They receive the **name of God**, the God of Jesus, the one true God.

They receive the **name of God's city**, the new Jerusalem (see 21:2; Heb 12:22). We discover at the end of this book that the new Jerusalem is both a *place* and a *people*. They will have a citizenship not on earth but in heaven, not earthly Philadelphia but heavenly Jerusalem.

They receive the **new name of Jesus** (see 19:12; 22:4; 2:17). The names signify identification, character, ownership, and recognition. The names signify who *my God* is, where *my home* is and who *my Lord* is! I belong to the Father, heaven is my home, and Jesus is my Lord. I bear *the signature* of my God!

David Platt rightly says,

> This, we remember, is the great reward of the gospel: God himself. When we risk our lives to run after Christ, we discover

the safety that is found only in his sovereignty, the security that is found only in his love, and the satisfaction that is found only in his presence. This is the eternally great reward, and we would be foolish to settle for anything less. (Newell, *Mission Quotes*, 241)

To these marvelous promises the Lord Jesus again gives the challenge, "Anyone [that's you and me!] who has an ear should listen to what the Spirit says [the word from God the Son applied by the Spirit of God] to the churches." This was a word for Philadelphia in the first century and a word for us in the twenty-first century.

Reflect and Discuss

1. How would you describe a church that does not have a heart for the lost? Can that church be a healthy church?
2. What traits would you add that characterize a Great Commission church? How can you pursue those traits in your local church?
3. How can a church cultivate a sense of Jesus' awesomeness?
4. The church at Philadelphia had "limited strength" or influence. What limitations to gospel faithfulness does it seem you have that Christ can use and overcome?
5. What prospects for missions and evangelism has the Lord opened for you? How can you be faithful to take advantage of those opportunities?
6. The Lord promises future vindication for His church, which has suffered for its faith. How does this vision give you strength to remain faithful?
7. How would you explain the difficulties and the best interpretation of verse 10 to a new Christian?
8. What is the main application for our lives of verse 10? How does it provide comfort for all believers?
9. What does it mean that Jesus is "coming quickly"? How do you look forward to that day without getting absorbed in fruitless speculation?
10. In verse 12, what is the reward given to those who persevere? How is it better than any earthly treasure?

The Church That Nauseates God

REVELATION 3:14-22

Main Idea: Churches that lose sight of their dependence on Christ for all things are deceived and useless, but Jesus graciously promises healing to all who will rely on Him for their every need.

I. **Christ Is Characterized by His Dependability (3:14).**
   A. You can trust what He says.
   B. You can trust who He is.
II. **Christ Condemns Those Who Are Deceived (3:15-17).**
   A. Jesus knows what we are doing (3:15-16).
   B. Jesus knows who we think we are (3:17).
III. **Christ Counsels Those Who Are Deficient (3:18-19).**
   A. We need Christ's riches (3:18).
   B. We need Christ's righteousness (3:18).
   C. We need Christ's remedy (3:18).
   D. We need Christ's rebuke (3:19).
IV. **Christ Challenges Those Who Need Direction (3:20-22).**
   A. Jesus will always come in if we invite Him (3:20).
   B. Jesus will allow us to reign with Him if we trust Him (3:21-22).

"You nauseate me!" "You make me sick!" "When I see you, I want to vomit!" These are not exactly words of compliment and praise, yet tragically these are the words spoken by the risen and glorified Christ to His church in the city of Laodicea. Their spiritual condition was nauseating. It made Christ ill. Sadly they were unaware of their true spiritual status. They believed things were fine, but Jesus says, "No. You are like the lukewarm, unfit drinking water that your city is infamous for. You are not like the cold refreshing springs of Colossae or the hot healing waters of Hierapolis. You are lukewarm, and I will not stomach this."

For this kind of church there is not a single word of commendation. Not one. Only censure and condemnation comes from the mouth of "The Amen, the faithful and true Witness" (v. 14).

No church should be satisfied with who or where it thinks it is. I have heard more than once denominational leaders say, "Well, we may not be much, but we are the best God has." The first part of that sentence contains more truth than the latter. It is always dangerous when we think we are something special to God. We should continually remind ourselves that we are nothing apart from Him. We, in our sin, are easily deceived. Our God does not need us. He will not share His glory with another. No, we all desperately need Him. We all need to pursue His glory.

Like the previous six letters in Revelation 2–3, this letter follows a similar pattern, minus any word of praise. Their condition is critical but not terminal. Christ has the spiritual medicine and remedies for their healing if they will listen (v. 22) and act (vv. 18-19) on His counsel.

Christ Is Characterized by His Dependability
REVELATION 3:14

Our Lord addresses the angelic watcher and protector of the church at Laodicea. The historical context of the city will be important for us to understand the imagery our Lord uses in His criticism and correction.

Laodicea was located in the Lycus Valley along with the cities of Hierapolis and Colossae. It was approximately three hundred miles east of Athens and six hundred miles northwest of Jerusalem. Two important imperial trade routes converged here. The city was a wealthy commercial center, the richest in Phrygia (Mounce, *Revelation*, 107). It was known for banking, the manufacturing of clothing (especially black wool), and a famous medical school with ointments for the ears and the eyes. So wealthy was the city that following a devastating earthquake in AD 60, Laodicea rebuilt itself without any assistance from Rome (Johnson, "Revelation," 2006, 634–35). The Roman historian Tacitus said of her, "Laodicea arose from the ruins by the strength of her own resources, and with no help from us" (*Annals* XIV 27). The city and church were alike. They saw themselves as self-sufficient. They did not need the help of anyone, including God. They were just fine all by themselves. The church, for sure, was badly deceived.

Despite its prosperity, the city did have one major weakness: an absence of an adequate and convenient source for good drinking water. By means of aqueducts, it got its water either from the hot springs of Hierapolis that cooled to lukewarm or from a cooler source in Colossae that warmed to lukewarm. For all its wealth the city had very poor drinking water. The water was so distasteful that visitors, not prepared for its tepid flavor, would often vomit after drinking it (Johnson, *Revelation*, 1983, 62; also Swindoll, *Insights*, 78).

The Bible does not reveal when or how the church began here. It is likely it was planted by Epaphras (Col 1:7; 4:12-15), whom Paul may have evangelized on his third missionary journey while ministering at Ephesus (Acts 19). Indeed, all three churches in the Lycus Valley (Laodicea, Hierapolis, and Colossae) were probably established at the same time by this faithful brother (Mounce, *Revelation*, 202). Still, the origin of the church at Laodicea remains a mystery. To this church, and those like it, Christ has significant criticism, but He also has two messages of promise and assurance. Those who have ears should carefully listen.

You Can Trust What He Says

Identifying Jesus as "the Amen, the faithful and true Witness" recognizes in our Lord what is sure and valid, true and trustworthy. It affirms what is certain, reliable, true to reality. "Amen" is a Christological title, and it is always the appropriate human response to divine word and action. The title is unique and reflects Isaiah 65:16 (MacArthur, *Revelation 1–11*). In applying this title to Himself, Christ affirms He is the answer to all the promises of God. As Paul says in 2 Corinthians 1:20, "For every one of God's promises is 'Yes' in Him. Therefore, the 'Amen' is also spoken through Him by us for God's glory." As the Amen, He also is the "faithful and true Witness." This looks back to Rev 1:5. This description stands in stark contrast to the actual condition of the Laodicean church. He is *reliable*, they are not. He is *faithful*, they are not. He is the *true Witness*; but they have no real witness at all. You may not trust the dependability, words, and witness of Laodicean Christians, but you can count on and trust what Jesus says.

You Can Trust What He Starts

That Jesus is "the Originator" (Gk *archē*) of God's creation echoes Colossians 1:15 and 18, which affirm Christ as the chief, the ruler, the originator of both *creation* and the *church*. He is Lord over both the *material* and the *spiritual* realms. Colossae was infected with a Christological heresy. It appears to have denied the full deity and eternality of the Son on one hand and questioned the genuineness of His complete humanity on the other. Like the heresy of Arius in AD 325 and modern Jehovah's Witnesses and Mormons, they said, "There was a time when

the Son was not," and "God was not always a Father." Laodicea, being
in close proximity, no doubt also faced this false teaching. Our Lord
corrects this deviant teaching and asserts He is not a creature or a part
of creation. He is its beginning, its Creator, its Originator. Whether it
be creation or the church, He is Lord, Ruler, Chief. He is first in *time*
and *position*. Laodicean Christians either forgot or ignored the exalted
and preeminent place that belongs only to Jesus. They lost sight of who
He is and what He has done and is doing. What He starts He will complete. What He begins He will finish. The Laodicean Christians may
have stopped before completing their task, but Jesus did not and does
not. What He has *created* and what He has *saved* He will stay with and
sustain to the end. Can the same be said of us?[2]

Christ Condemns Those Who Are Deceived
REVELATION 3:15-17

When Jesus examines the Laodicean church, He sees nothing to praise
or commend—not one single thing. Everything is a stench to His nostrils, an ache to His heart, nauseating to His stomach. How is it that a
church can get into such a deplorable condition and, astonishingly, not
even know it? Our Lord provides two indications that should serve as
warnings to all of us.

Jesus Knows What We Are Doing (3:15-16)

As with every church, Jesus knew the spiritual condition of Laodicea: "I
know your works." What kind of shape were they in? They were "neither
cold nor hot." Instead they were "lukewarm," tepid, moderate.

This text has been misinterpreted more often than not. Many
believe what Jesus means is, "I would rather you be cold and in opposition to Me or hot and on fire for Me." However, it is hardly conceivable
that Jesus would say to His church, "Be cold and oppose Me." It is better to interpret the statement against the historical and geographical
background of Laodicea. Hot, medicinal waters bubbled up at nearby
Hierapolis, while cold, pure waters flowed from Colossae. Our Lord's
point to them is something like this: "You are providing neither healing

---

[2] Beale has a great discussion on the Old Testament background to these titles in
G. K. Beale, *The Book of Revelation: A Commentary on the Greek Text*, The New International
Greek Testament Commentary (Grand Rapids, MI: W. B. Eerdmans, 1999), 297–301. I do
see things a bit differently than he does.

for the spiritually sick nor refreshment for the spiritually thirsty. You are spiritually lukewarm, and I will not tolerate you. If you do not repent (v. 19), I will spew you out, vomit you out of My mouth. You are sickly and insipid. I will not tolerate your condition any longer. You are flat and unsavory. You badly misrepresent the life-changing power of the gospel and the refreshment and healing it brings."

We would be wise to learn the lesson of this lukewarm church. We must not be indifferent or ignorant to our spiritual condition but continually take inventory in the light of God's Word. We must face up to our true spiritual condition. Jesus knows who we are and what we are doing.

Jesus Knows Who We Think We Are (3:17)

Indifference will eventually lead to ignorance concerning where we are spiritually. We may say one thing when the truth is altogether something different. We may fool others, and we may even fool ourselves, but we cannot fool God.

Laodicean Christians are deceived Christians. A comparison of their self-estimation with the Lord's evaluation is tragic and sobering. They could not have been more off base in who they thought they were. They said, "I'm rich; I have become wealthy and in need of nothing." Like their city they boasted about who they were and what they had. They thought every church should be just like them. And it should not escape our eye that the Laodicean Christians claim to have reached this lofty spiritual status on their own. They needed nothing and no one, including the Lord. They had arrived at where they were without the assistance of anyone.

They may have been a great organization, but they were not a great church—not in our Lord's estimation. The Lord Jesus, indeed, has a completely different perspective on this church. His evaluation of their true condition was 180 degrees from theirs—polar opposites. Jesus exposes their deficiencies: "You don't know." He makes clear that they claim one thing, but the truth is another. A cloud of self-deception hovers over them. "Let me set the record straight" says the Lord Christ. Five marks of their true spiritual status are noted:

- *wretched*—miserable, unfortunate; a word used of ravaged lands, devastated countries, pillaging
- *pitiful*—pitiable, the object of extreme pity

- *poor*—extreme poverty, like a beggar or pauper; a slap at a city that bragged of its wealth, commerce, and banking industry
- *blind*—a dig at a city that prided itself on its ophthalmic school and famous Phrygian eye powder
- *naked*—ridicule of a city that boasted of its famous glossy black wool (Rogers and Rienecker, *Exegetical Key,* 622).

Using imagery and illustrations that would hit them right between the eyes and right where they lived, our Lord exposes their spiritual destitution, deception, and desperate condition. In John 9:39 Jesus said, "I came into this world for judgment, in order that those who do not see will see and those who do see will become blind." Jesus has judged the Laodiceans. Now they know who they really are. They can no longer plead ignorance. Action is now called for. And one thing is certain: Things will not stay the same. Our Lord will make sure of that. Vance Havner puts the issue in plain view:

> Smyrna was a rich poor church and Laodicea was a poor rich church. They were blind, shortsighted. They had no vision of God, of their own hearts, of the world's need. I'd rather be a rich poor Christian than a poor rich Christian! (*Repent,* 82–83)

Christ Counsels Those Who Are Deficient
REVELATION 3:18-19

According to Mounce, "Sustained irony runs through verses 17 and 18" (*Revelation,* 111). The arrogant attitude and smug satisfaction of Laodicean Christianity is confronted and countered with counsel that they make specific purchases from Jesus in precisely those areas where they are so certain they have no need. The wisdom our Lord shares is instructive for each and every one of us. Every church should receive this as a personal word. So should every Christian.

We Need Christ's Riches (3:18)

Jesus sternly instructs them: "I advise you to buy from Me gold refined in the fire so that you may be rich." "From Me," from Christ, true and lasting riches can be purchased. The currency of that purchase is always the same: faith, trust, radical dependence on Him and only Him. Because gold is often an emblem of faith, some believe the Laodicean church was filled only with unbelievers (MacArthur, *Revelation 1–11,* 138). This is certainly possible, but I would suspect the church had both believers and unbelievers, and the cure for their spiritual poverty is the same. First comes faith for salvation; then follows faith for sanctification. As Paul said in Romans 1:17, salvation is "from faith to faith." Hebrews 12:2 says that we should keep "our eyes on Jesus, the source and perfecter of our faith." We need the spiritual wealth that comes only by constant and abiding faith in Jesus. Such wealth, unlike earthly riches, will endure forever. Day by day we must renew our faith in the Lord Jesus for everything we need.

We Need Christ's Righteousness (3:18)

Next, Jesus tells the church they need "white clothes so that [they] may be dressed and [their] shameful nakedness not be exposed." In contrast to the beautiful glossy black wool the Laodiceans were so proud of, Jesus offers a garment of white that will cover the shame of their nakedness. White clothes symbolize the imputed righteousness of the Savior and the righteous acts of the saints (see 3:4-5,18; 4:4; 6:11; 7:9,13-14; 19:8,14). That this is a recurring theme in Revelation tells us how important it is. Nakedness in the ancient world was a sign of judgment and humiliation. To receive fine clothing was a symbol of honor and acceptance. Laodicean Christians walk about spiritually naked, completely unaware of their humiliation and need for the pure white righteousness that is available only in Jesus (Mounce, *Revelation*, 111). Before the One whose "eyes are a flame of fire" (1:14), we are stripped naked and exposed for who we really are. We dare not stand in the filthy rags of our own righteousness and good deeds. We desperately need the righteousness of Jesus.

We Need Christ's Remedy (3:18)

We also need to buy from Christ "ointment to spread on [our] eyes so that [we] may see." Laodicea was famous for its eye salve called "Phrygian Powder." But ironically, the Laodicean church was blind to its spiritual condition. Only the great physician had a cure for their sightlessness. The blindness of their self-deception could only be remedied by the healing ointment made available by Jesus (Mounce, *Revelation*, 111). Such healing comes from looking to Him in the gospel and into His Word for instruction and wisdom (see 2 Tim 3:16-17).

Honest evaluation is essential for spiritual restoration. Spiritual compromise and complacency are "spiritual cataracts" that shut out the light of spiritual sight. Regularly, daily, we need to ask the Lord—in prayer and by the Word—"Show me my true spiritual condition. Reveal to me my spiritual *blind spots* and areas of sin where I no longer see. Help me, Lord, to see myself as You see me!"

We Need Christ's Rebuke (3:19)

Next comes a somewhat encouraging part of Christ's discipline: "As many as I love . . ." Amazingly Christ loves Laodicean Christians and churches. Their sin does not quench His love. ". . . I rebuke and discipline," says the Lord Jesus. Christ corrects and disciplines, as with a child, those He loves.

This echoes Proverbs 3:11-12 and Hebrews 12:5-11 (see also 1 Cor 11:32). Love is never cruel, but it can be tough. Discipline that educates and brings about repentance and change is what our Lord extends to Laodicean churches. If we reject His discipline, He will spit us out. If we receive it, He will come in and stay with us as the next verse beautifully promises.

Our expected response is crystal clear: "Be committed [ESV, "zealous"] and repent." Be fervent, and turn now and daily. Keep on, with fire in your soul, turning from sin. Turning from sin once is not enough. It must become the daily practice and habit of our life. A community of daily repenting sinners characterizes a healthy church and healthy Christians.

Christ Challenges Those Who Need Direction
REVELATION 3:20-22

These verses are an appropriate conclusion not only to the letter for the church at Laodicea but to the letters for all the seven churches. Yet it is specifically and definitely right for this church. What does Jesus say? How does He challenge them?

Jesus Will Always Come In if We Invite Him (3:20)

"Listen," Jesus says. It is a simple imperative: Look! See! Take note! Wake up! "I stand at the door and knock." Jesus has taken a position outside the door of the church and will remain there knocking and knocking; graciously and patiently waiting. "If anyone"—what an amazing promise! Just one, anyone—"hears My voice and opens the door, I will come in to him and have dinner with him, and he with Me." It appears only one humble, receptive, repentant sinner is necessary to spark revival within a local church. The Master is calling. Are we listening? Are we willing to welcome Him back into His church?

The debate over whether this verse is to be exclusively applied to a local church and not an individual sinner is really unnecessary when the verse is taken as a whole. It should be recognized that the church and its individual members are being addressed. I doubt, however, it is inappropriate imagery in application to any sinner with whom Christ seeks table fellowship.

In the Middle Eastern world, an invitation to share a meal was characteristic of hospitality and the occasion for intimate fellowship with family and close friends. For believers, enjoying table fellowship in communion (Matt 26; Mark 14; Luke 22; 1 Cor 11) with Jesus and spiritual brothers and sisters is a foretaste of a future table fellowship in the messianic kingdom and the marriage supper of the Lamb (Rev 19:1-10). It is hard to imagine any follower of the Lamb rejecting this magnificent invitation to dine at the table of the King (Mounce, *Revelation*, 113–14).

Jesus Will Allow Us to Reign with Him if We Trust Him (3:21-22)

Jesus promises the one who is a "victor," an overcomer, a conqueror, the privilege of sitting with Him on His throne, just as He has sat down with His Father on His throne (v. 21). To sit "with" Jesus means any and every blessing we receive in kingdom life we receive by virtue of our union with Christ. Our joint reign with King Jesus rings throughout Revelation (1:6,9; 2:25-27; 5:10; 20:4-6) as well as the whole New Testament (Matt 19:28; Luke 22:28-30; Rom 8:17; 2 Tim 2:12). And we are victors because of the victory He won. As the Son shares the throne of His Father, we share the throne of the Son (Johnson, *Revelation*, 1983, 65). It is astonishing! Because of our union with the victorious Lamb, we not only get heaven; we also get a throne.

"Anyone who has an ear"—individuals and churches—"should listen to what the Spirit says to the churches." This is a word for all of us. Are we listening?

Conclusion

A church (or a Christian) must be careful not to lose its first love (Ephesus). It must trust God in the midst of suffering (Smyrna). It must not compromise its doctrine (Pergamum). It must not waffle on its morality (Thyatira). It must be on guard against spiritual deadness

(Sardis). It must walk through open doors for sharing the gospel (Philadelphia). It must avoid at all costs becoming lukewarm in its passion for Jesus (Laodicea).

Revival is both an individual and a church matter. God deals with people one person at a time. He deals with churches one church at a time. Sometimes, like Laodicea, we have everything in our life and in our church except the Lord Jesus. God forbid that that would be true of us, of you, or of me! Dr. Havner puts it all in context: "The big question today is not 'Is God speaking?' The really big question is, 'Are you listening?'" (*Repent*, 102).

Reflect and Discuss

1. How do you think you would feel if you heard the Lord Jesus say, "You make Me sick!"? What would you say in response?
2. How have you been able to see that Jesus' words are trustworthy in your life?
3. How would you explain the eternality of the Son? How would you defend it from Scripture?
4. Briefly research Jehovah's Witness and Mormon teaching. What errors concerning the person of Christ do you see?
5. What does Jesus mean when He says the church at Laodicea was "lukewarm," and how can we receive instruction from His rebuke?
6. Have you ever been mistaken or deceived about your spiritual condition or maturity? How did you come to learn of your mistake?
7. What is the proper response when the Lord exposes spiritual immaturity or disobedience in our lives?
8. What does it mean that sanctification, like justification, comes through faith?
9. Why is discipline actually a sign of love? How does this conflict with the conception of love in contemporary culture?
10. How is that we as believers benefit from Jesus' victory and reign?

Praise to the Almighty, the King of Creation

REVELATION 4:1-11

Main Idea: In both His person (holiness and goodness) and His work (creation and redemption), God alone is worthy of all worship and honor and praise, and He will receive it.

I. **Praise God Because He Is the King over All Things (4:1-5).**
   A. The plan of God demands our praise (4:1).
   B. The person of God demands our praise (4:2-3).
   C. The privileges of God demand our praise (4:4).
   D. The power of God demands our praise (4:5).
II. **Praise God Because He Is Holy in His Nature (4:6-8).**
   A. His creatures show His holiness (4:6-8).
   B. His creatures tell of His holiness (4:8).
III. **Praise God Because He Created Everything That Exists (4:9-11).**
   A. Show Him you believe He is worthy of your worship (4:9-10).
   B. Tell Him you believe He is worthy of your worship (4:10-11).

The great preacher of London, England, Charles Spurgeon (1834–1892), simply but profoundly said, "Beloved Friends, we may well continue to praise God, for our God continues to give us causes for praise" ("Saints Guarded"). Such a simple theology is profoundly missing in our culture, and even in our churches, today. Few talk of a God who is "too big," as if that were even possible. Timothy George is certainly correct: "In much contemporary theology today, the note of God's grandeur, greatness, and glory that so fills the Bible is noticeably missing. Such theology suffers from a *doxological deficit*" ("Nature of God," 158, emphasis added). *Such doxological deficiency can be corrected, however, when we realize the God of the Bible is*

> "a consuming fire" (Deut 4:24), the living God into whose
> hand to fall is "a dreadful thing" (Heb 10:31). This God cannot
> be relegated to the safety of the seminar room or scrutinized
> like a butterfly under a microscope. The God of the Bible is
> the God with whom we have to do in life and death, in time
> and eternity, the God to whom we must all give an account and

whom no one can escape. Every human being, Calvin says, has *negotium cum deo*, "business with God." (Ibid., 160)

The God with whom we have business is majestically addressed in Revelation 4. He is praised as the King of creation who is eternal, holy, and glorious, a God who alone is worthy of praise and worship. Actually chapters 4–5 constitute one vision of two parts:

Chapter 4   →   God the **Father** and **Creation**
Chapter 5   →   God the **Son** and **Redemption**

The two chapters are immersed in Old Testament texts like Isaiah 6; Ezekiel 1–2; and especially Daniel 7. Greg Beale notes that Revelation 4–5 parallel Daniel 7:9-27 at 14 specific points (*Revelation*, 314–15). The thrust of the two chapters is that both by creation and by redemption God is sovereign over His world. He created it and He redeemed it. He may do business with it as He wills.

Chapter 4, then, focuses on God the Father and the throne room in heaven. He is the King. He is holy. He is the Creator. These three truths provide the expositional outline of our study.

Praise God Because He Is the King over All Things
REVELATION 4:1-5

The Lord Jesus has been walking among His seven churches in chapters 2–3, giving us a view from below, from earth. Now the scene shifts to heaven, giving us the view from above. All that is taking place on earth is under the sovereign control of the one who sits on the throne in heaven. Corrie ten Boom, who hid Jews from the Nazis and went to prison for her efforts, says it well: "There is no panic in Heaven! God has no problems, only plans." She is right. This is the first thing John draws our attention to.

The Plan of God Demands Our Praise (4:1)

"After this" refers to the vision of the exalted and glorified Christ in 1:9-20 and the seven letters to the seven churches in chapters 2–3. John is suddenly given a vision in "heaven" (mentioned 50 times in Revelation) and "an open door." He then hears "the first voice [he] had heard speaking to [him] like a trumpet" in 1:10. It is the voice of Jesus. Our Lord tells him, "Come up here, and I will show you what must take place after this." This statement looks back to 1:19, which provides an outline for the book in terms of both structure and chronology. John is instructed to write

- what you have seen (ch. 1),
- what is (ESV, "those that are," chs. 2–3),
- and what will take place after this (chs. 4–22).

Robert Mounce captures well the plan of God that is about to unfold:

> John is about to see "what must take place after this." This definitely assigns the content of the following chapters to a period of time yet future (although embedded in the material are sections that refer to times already past, e.g., 12:1-6). In 1:19 Christ had commanded John to write "what will take place later"; now he will show him those things. Since events on earth have their origin in heaven, the heavenly ascent is not unexpected. A true insight into history is gained only when we view all things from the vantage point of the heavenly throne. (*Revelation*, 118–19)

When my four sons were small, they saw something on TV that discussed the potential of nuclear holocaust and the annihilation of the earth by the push of a button. That night Paul asked me if I was afraid someone might push that button and we would be wiped out. I confidently told him no, that I had no worries. Jesus has the whole world in His hands! God is in control, and He has a plan to make a perfect new heaven and new earth (Rev 21–22), and no one can stop God's plan from happening. "God has no problems, only plans."

The Person of God Demands Our Praise (4:2-3)

"Immediately," John tells us, "I was in the Spirit" (see 1:10; 17:13; 21:10). Four times this phrase appears in Revelation, each time taking John into an ecstatic, revelatory experience. In the tradition of the prophets, he is seized by the Spirit! What a gift for this lonely old man exiled as a prisoner to the island of Patmos (Mounce, *Revelation*, 118).

Like Paul in 2 Corinthians 12:2-4, he was taken into "the third heaven," what the Bible also calls "paradise." This is the presence of God. And like Paul, whether this was "in the body" or an "out of the body" experience we do not know. And further still, "John does not attempt to describe the 'someone sitting on' the throne (cf. 1 Ki 22:19; 2 Ch 18:18;

Ps 47:8; Isa 6:1-5; Eze 1:26-28; Sir 1:8)" (Johnson, "Revelation," 2006, 641). He can only tell us what He is "like"! After all, 1 Timothy 1:17 tells us our King is "eternal, immortal, invisible." And 1 Timothy 6:16 tells us He dwells "in unapproachable light; no one has seen or can see Him." In our sinful, fallen state, no human can gaze on this God in His undiminishable glory and majesty and live. No one!

Still, John does his best. He saw "a throne," which appears more than 40 times in Revelation (making up three-quarters of all New Testament occurrences), "set there in heaven." This throne has appeared before in Scripture. Isaiah 6:1 says, "I saw the Lord seated on a high and lofty throne." Psalm 47:8 adds, "God reigns over the nations; God is seated on His holy throne."

Drawing from Ezekiel's vision (1:26-28), John says, "The One seated looked like jasper and carnelian stone" (Rev 4:3). Gordon Fee notes that in Exodus 28:17-20 "these are the first and last of the twelve stones mentioned in the description of the breastplate of the high priest" and that "both of them are red" (*Revelation*, 69). The jasper stone may represent majesty, holiness, or purity. The carnelian stone signifies wrath or judgment (Mounce, *Revelation*, 120). John also says, "A rainbow that looked like an emerald surrounded the throne," a reminder of God's covenant to Noah and His faithfulness (Gen 9:16-17). Put them all together and you have a vision of God's majesty, splendor, glory, and faithfulness. He is beyond description in appearance and utterly reliable in His promises. He is awesome, magnificent, transcendent, and spectacular. There is no God like our God!

The Privileges of God Demand Our Praise (4:4)

John sees 24 thrones with 24 elders sitting on them dressed in white with 24 crowns (Gk *stephanous*) on their heads. The identity of these 24 elders has been much debated. Beale informs us of the various options and then strikes something of a compromise understanding between the two most popular views:

> Now a heavenly entourage around the throne is pictured.
> The elders have been variously identified as (1) stars
> (from an astrological background), (2) angels, (3) OT
> saints, (4) angelic, heavenly representatives of all saints,
> (5) patriarchs and apostles representing the OT and NT saints
> together, and (6) representatives of the prophetic revelation
> of the twenty-four books of the Old Testament.

> The elders certainly include reference to OT and NT
> saints. They are either angels representing all saints or the
> heads of the twelve tribes together with the twelve apostles,
> representing thus all the people of God. Identification of them
> as angels is consonant with some of our earlier observations
> that many of the traits and functions characteristic of angels
> are likewise applicable to humans. . . . Probably the elders
> are angels who are identified with the twelve tribes and the
> twelve apostles, thus representing the entire community of the
> redeemed of both testaments (the songs in 15:3-4 may also
> point to the inclusion of OT and NT saints). (*Revelation*, 322)

Though I appreciate this treatment, I am of the judgment the redeemed are in view for a few reasons. First, angels are never called elders. Second, believers are granted to sit on thrones as coheirs with Christ (Matt 19:28; Rev 3:21; 20:4). Third, white clothes, though applied to both angels and humans in Scripture, are particularly the apparel of the redeemed in Revelation (3:4-5,18; 6:11; 7:9,13-14; 19:8). Finally, the *stephanos*, the victors' "crown" (2:10), is appropriate more for the redeemed than it is for angels.

What an honor this is for followers of this great God and the crucified Galilean. He created us and He has redeemed us in order that we might reign with Him! No wonder in verse 10 the elders surrender their crowns as they worship the One seated on the throne. We gladly return in worship what our God has given us, for we readily acknowledge that all we have was first given to us by Him.

The Power of God Demands Our Praise (4:5)

John now sees "flashes of lightning and rumblings of thunder . . . from the throne." This reminds the people of God's descent at Mount Sinai in Exodus 19:16-20. Symbolic of awesome power and strength, lightning and thunder appear four times in Revelation (4:5; 8:5; 11:19; 16:18). It is likely that John is drawing again from Ezekiel 1. Mounce notes, "In Revelation the symbols of thunder and lightning are always connected with a temple scene and mark an event of unusual import" (*Revelation*, 122). In Revelation 10, "thunder judgments" are about to be unleashed on the earth, but God in mercy seals them up (10:4).

John also sees "seven fiery torches . . . burning before the throne, which are the seven spirits of God" (see 1:4; 5:6). Here again we see the perfect light-bearing Spirit. The Spirit who convicts us of sin and changes our heart in regeneration (Titus 3:5) is the same Holy Spirit who is forever ablaze before the throne of God in heaven. Perfect in His *person*, perfect in His *position*, perfect in His *purity*, and perfect in His *power*. "This is the Spirit's only appearance in heaven in this book . . . this is rightly understood as 'the sevenfold Spirit,' imagery taken from Isaiah 11:2" (Fee, *Revelation*, 70).

What a vision! What a King! As one commentator has noted,

> Our affairs rest in the hands not of men but of *God*! Hence, when the world is enkindling the flames of hatred and slaughter and when the earth is drenched with blood, may our tear-dimmed eye catch a vision of *The Throne* which rules the universe. In the midst of trial and tribulation may our gaze be riveted upon the One who is King of kings and Lord of lords. (Hendriksen, *More than Conquerors*, 99–100)

Praise God Because He Is Holy in His Nature
REVELATION 4:6-8

> Holiness so defines the character of God that it can be said to include all of the other divine moral perfections as well. . . . Holiness in [the] absolute sense belongs only to God, since only God is untouched by evil. (George, "Nature of God," 191–92)

John continues to unfold the throne-room vision given to him by Jesus. What we now see is both magnificent and strange. However, the point made is as crystal clear as the sea of glass John now beholds.

His Creatures Show His Holiness (4:6-8)

John sees something "like a sea of glass, similar to crystal . . . before the throne." This adds to the splendor and brilliance of the vision. Maybe this represents purity and the lack of any need for cleansing in heaven. Maybe it stands for God's transcendence and holiness. That it is a sea of glass may pick up on the fact that "the sea is usually negative imagery in Scripture, as a place that is wild and untamed. But here it has clearly been tamed, appearing like 'glass, clear as crystal'" (Fee, *Revelation*, 71).

John then sees "four living creatures covered with eyes." One was like a lion, another a calf, a third had the face of a man, and the fourth was like an eagle. In addition to being covered with eyes, they each had

six wings. These are angelic beings of worship, who have the charac-
teristics both of Isaiah's seraphim (Isa 6:2-3) and Ezekiel's cherubim
(Ezek 1:5-25; 10:1-22). That they are full of eyes emphasizes God's
omniscience, His exhaustive knowledge of all that is or ever could be.
The wings "suggest swiftness to carry out the will of God" (Mounce,
Revelation, 125).

Dogmatism on their fourfold appearance is unwarranted. However,
we can suggest a few truths our God may be communicating to us
through this image. First, **God is perfect in His authority**. The lion
is king of the animal world. It emphasizes strength and honor—that
which is noble, respected. Second, **God is perfect in His activity**. The
calf or ox is a servant. It exercises great power for the benefit of others.
It was the mightiest among the domesticated animals. Third, **God is
perfect in His majesty**. Man is the pinnacle of creation, and only man
has a "face" in this vision. He is intelligent, rational, and spiritual. He is
the apex of all God made. He is God's vice-regent on earth. And finally,
God is perfect in His deity. The eagle soars in the heavens and often
represented deity. It is the mightiest among the birds and the swiftest of
God's creatures. These creatures are strong like a lion, serve like an ox,
see like a man, and are swift like an eagle. Each in its particular appearance gives witness to the greatness and glory of our God. No creature is
as strong as He. No creature serves as does He. No creature sees as does
He. No creature is as swift as is He! (Mounce, *Revelation*, 124–25; also
Osborne, *Revelation*, 233–34).

His Creatures Tell of His Holiness (4:8)

Adrian Rogers called the four living creatures "God's cheerleaders!"
While the meaning of their appearance may be unclear, their activity
is not. "Day and night they never stop." These angels never sleep. And
what is their message, their chant, their song? Echoing the words of
Isaiah 6, they say,

> Holy, holy, holy,
> Lord God, the Almighty,
> Who was, who is, and who is coming.

I appreciate the insights of Alan Johnson on this verse:

> The four living creatures ceaselessly proclaim the holiness of
> God: "Holy, holy, holy" (cf. Isa. 6:3). In Hebrew, the double
> repetition of a word adds emphasis, while the rare threefold

repetition designates the superlative and calls attention to the infinite holiness of God—the quality of God felt by creatures in his presence as awesomeness or fearfulness (cf. Ps. 111:9: "Holy and awesome is his name"). The living creatures celebrate God's holiness and power as manifested in his past, present, and future activity. Such holiness cannot tolerate the presence of evil (21:27). . . . This hymn is the first not only of the five sung by the heavenly choirs in chs. 4–5 but also of a number of others in Revelation (4:8,11; 5:9-10,12,13; 7:12,15-17; 11:15,17-18; 12:10-12; 15:3-4; 16:5-7; 18:2-8; 19:2-6). These hymns relate to the interpretation of the visions and provide a clue to the literary structure of Revelation. In these two chapters, the sequence of hymns shows that the first two are addressed to God, the next two to the Lamb, and the last one to both ("Revelation," 2006, 642).

Yes, His creature continually and forever tells of His holiness.

Praise God Because He Created Everything That Exists
REVELATION 4:9-11

Our King is the "Lord God, the Almighty," a title found 10 times in our New Testament, nine in Revelation (see 2 Cor 6:18). He is possessed of unlimited power and might. He is the great "I AM" of Exodus 3:14, the One "who was, who is, and who is coming." Indeed, "The future is characterized by His coming" (Beasley-Murray, *Revelation*, 118). Because our God is eternal, infinite, and omnipotent, the worshiping creatures in heaven acknowledge that their existence and being are completely dependent on the One who sits on the throne in heaven. In witness and word they testify to His greatness, to His worthiness. Wonderfully, we can join them in their worship.

Show Him You Believe He Is Worthy of Your Worship (4:9-10)

Whenever the living creatures "give glory, honor, and thanks to the One seated on the throne," which is always and forever, the redeemed (the 24 elders) worship! And how do they worship? They fall down and cast their crowns before the throne. What He gave they joyfully give back. They acknowledge that all they have is His gift to them. They did not earn it. They did not merit it. Nothing they have would they withhold from the One on the throne who is majestic, awesome, and holy.

This brings deep conviction and raises a question: Am I withholding anything from my God, even good things? Money? Time? Mind? Service? Heart? Chuck Swindoll is right: "We miss it when our focus becomes horizontal—riveted on people and things—rather than vertical—centered on God and God alone" (*Insights*, 98).

Tell Him You Believe He Is Worthy of Your Worship (4:10-11)

Our passage ends with a glorious and majestic hymn praising God as the Creator. Falling down and casting their crowns before the throne in worship, the 24 elders now sing to our Almighty Creator: "Our Lord and God, You are worthy." Mounce notes:

> the first words of the hymn are taken from the political language of the day: "You are worthy" greeted the entrance of the emperor in triumphal procession, and "our Lord and God" was introduced into the cult of emperor worship by Domitian. For the Christian only the One who sits on the heavenly throne is worthy: the claims of all others are blasphemous. (*Revelation*, 127)

This singularly worthy One is worthy to receive glory (Gk *doxa*), honor (Gk *timen*), and power (Gk *dunamin*). Why? First, "because You have created all things." Only God is eternal; the universe is not. Only God is eternal; matter is not. This God spoke into existence all that exist (Gen 1). Second, He is worthy "because of [His] will they exist and were created." God willed it and creation happened. God wills it and creation continues. Had He not willed it there would be nothing. If He does not continue to will it, there will be nothing. You are still here because He willed it. Adrian Rogers is right: "If you woke up this morning and you are still here, then God still has a plan for your life." That alone is worth praising Him for!

Conclusion

Written in 1826 for Trinity Sunday by Reginald Heber (1783–1826), a bishop in the Church of England, the hymn finds its inspiration in Revelation 4:1-11. Its title: "Holy, Holy, Holy, Lord God Almighty," and its words provide a fitting conclusion to this chapter:

> Holy, holy, holy! Lord God Almighty!
> Early in the morning our song shall rise to thee.

Holy, holy, holy! Merciful and mighty,
    God in three persons, blessed Trinity!

Holy, holy, holy! All the saints adore thee,
    casting down their golden crowns around the glassy sea;
    cherubim and seraphim falling down before thee,
    which wert, and art, and evermore shalt be.

Holy, holy, holy! Though the darkness hide thee,
    though the eye of sinful man thy glory may not see,
    only thou art holy; there is none beside thee,
    perfect in power, in love and purity.

Holy, holy, holy! Lord God Almighty!
    All thy works shall praise thy name, in earth and sky and sea.
    Holy, holy, holy! Merciful and mighty,
    God in three persons, blessed Trinity.

A. W. Tozer said worship is "the missing jewel in modern evangelicalism" (Swindoll, *Discoveries*, 29). Might a glimpse of the God of Revelation 4 help us rediscover that jewel?

Reflect and Discuss

1. How have you seen a "doxological deficit" in your own life? What can you do to cultivate a doxological heart?
2. How does God's providential plan for creation give us comfort in uncertain times?
3. What aspects of God's character and splendor draw you to praise and worship Him? Where do you see these attributes in the Scriptures?
4. God's power drives us to praise, even as if instills awe and fear. How do these go together in Christian worship?
5. What is shown about God's character by the creatures in Revelation 4:7? Why is it significant that they are worshiping the One on the throne?
6. This passage implicitly invites us to worship the One who is on the throne. The elders do so by bowing down. How do you express your worship to the King of kings?
7. Why is it noteworthy that the elders cast their crowns, which the Lord gave them, before the throne? What has the Lord given you that you can use to worship Him?

8. What are you tempted to withhold from God that He is worthy of?
9. Reflect on the truth that our existence depends on the will of God to sustain it. How does it make you feel? How does it lead you to worship?
10. Read through the words to the hymn at the end of this chapter. How do they reflect the truths of Revelation 4?

The Lion, the Lamb, and the World

REVELATION 5:1-14

Main Idea: Jesus Christ is the Savior of the world who stands victorious over sin and death in His resurrection; therefore, He deserves to be worshiped and revered by all creation.

I. **Jesus Christ Is the Lord of History (5:1-5).**
   A. He is Lord because of God's plan (5:1).
   B. He is Lord because of heaven's problem (5:2-4).
   C. He is Lord because of His power (5:5).
II. **Jesus Christ Is the Lord of Victory (5:6-7).**
   A. He is victorious because He was slaughtered (5:6).
   B. He is victorious because He is standing (5:6).
   C. He is victorious because He is strong (5:6).
   D. He is victorious because He is searching (5:6).
   E. He is victorious because He is sovereign (5:7).
III. **Jesus Christ Is the Lord of Glory (5:8-14).**
   A. He is praised by the saints (5:8-10).
   B. He is praised by the angels (5:11-12).
   C. He is praised by all creation (5:13-14).

When I was in graduate school at the University of Texas at Arlington, I encountered a kaleidoscope of worldviews and perspectives on life.

- Some were persons like myself—Bible-believing, evangelical Christians who operated out of a supernatural worldview.
- Others saw themselves as neoorthodox Christians. They did not believe the Bible *is* the Word of God but that the Bible *can become* the Word of God to you in a personal encounter and experience.
- Others referred to themselves as liberal Christians. They were skeptical, at best, concerning the supernatural parts of the Bible, but they were fond of the moral teachings of the Bible, especially passages like the Sermon on the Mount (Matt 5–7).

It could be said that they tended toward the view that the Bible *contains* the Word of God.

- Still others approached life from a religious but non-Christian perspective. At the university there were Hindus, Buddhists, Muslims, and Jewish persons.
- Finally, there were also agnostics and atheists. Many of my professors fell into this last category.

I remember on one occasion one of my classmates asking an atheist professor an important question: "What do you believe the future holds for mankind?" He thought for a moment, and then his answer was quick, forthright, and surprising. "I'm not very optimistic," he said. "When I look at history, I discover man has not treated man very well. When I look at the contemporary world, I discover not much has changed. I'm not hopeful about the future." He then concluded by saying, "I believe the future holds for mankind *certain destruction* and *potential annihilation*. I have no reason to be encouraged about the future." In a related vein, the German liberal Rudolf Bultmann said, "We cannot claim to know the end and goal of history. Therefore, the question of meaning in history has become meaningless" (*Presence of Eternity*, 120).

If I held to the same worldview as my atheist professor, I would agree with his prediction 100 percent. If man can hope only in himself, and if man must save himself as both Humanist Manifestos I and II affirm, then I too believe the future holds for humanity certain destruction and potential annihilation.[3] But that is where Revelation 5 enters the scene with a word of hope and certainty. I might summarize the theme of this chapter by the words of a little chorus I was taught as a small boy in my Baptist church in Atlanta, Georgia: "He's got the whole world in His hands!" This world is not out of control rushing headlong toward destruction and annihilation. All things are under the sovereign and secure control of our great God because in heaven there is a Lion, who is also a Lamb, and He has the whole world on His heart and in His hands!

Revelation 5 teaches us the Lamb of God is a missionary Lamb who is in control and who is supremely worthy. We saw a glorious vision of

---

[3] Humanist Manifesto I can be found at http://americanhumanist.org/humanism/humanist_manifesto_i. Humanist Manifesto II can be found at http://americanhumanist.org/humanism/humanist_manifesto_ii. Both accessed April 5, 2016.

Him in 1:13-16. Now we see a second one that beautifully complements it. In the Old Testament we see the Lamb on an altar and His blood on the Passover doorpost. In the Gospels, He is on the cross. In the Revelation, He is on the throne (Woods, "The Lamb," 27). The theme of His worthiness is preeminent, and three reasons in particular are noted and developed in this fifth chapter.

Jesus Christ Is the Lord of History
REVELATION 5:1-5

Revelation 4–5 is actually one vision of two parts. Chapter 4 focuses on **God the Father** and **creation**. Chapter 5 focuses on **God the Son** and **redemption** (but note the Trinitarianism of 5:6-7). God has the authority and the right to do with this world as He pleases. He created it. He redeemed it. David Levy says the vision in these chapters "provides a fitting introduction to the revelation of God's program to be unfolded in chapters 6–22" ("The Scrolls," 20).

He Is the Lord Because of God's Plan (5:1)

John sees God the Father on His "throne," a word appearing more than 40 times in Revelation. Some even call it a "throne book." This is the place of sovereignty and authority. In His "right hand," the hand of authority, John sees "a scroll with writing on the inside and on the back, sealed with seven seals." The scroll is filled to the edges with information, and it is perfectly or completely sealed up (Johnson, *Revelation*, 1983, 73). The scroll is mentioned eight times in this chapter.

Of course the question is, what is the scroll? Many different answers have been given: (1) a title deed to the earth; (2) a last will and testament; (3) Ezekiel's book of lamentation, mourning, and woe (2:9-10); (4) the sealed book of the end time in Daniel 12:4. I am sympathetic to both options 3 and 4. However, there may be a much simpler answer: it is the remainder of the book of Revelation (chs. 6–22). Don Carson says it is a book of "blessing and cursing" ("Rev. 5"). I like that but would expand it to three categories: it is a book of judgment, salvation, and restoration:

Judgment—seals (v. 6), trumpets (vv. 8-9), bowls (vv. 15-16), lake of fire (20:11-15)

Salvation—Jew and Gentile (vv. 7,14; 19:1-10)

Restoration—new heaven, new earth, new Jerusalem (vv. 21-22).

God has a definite plan for history and its consummation. It is mapped out. It is set. It will not fail (Johnson, *Revelation*, 1983, 74–75).

He Is Lord Because of Heaven's Problem (5:2-4)

John now sees a second thing: "a mighty angel" who with a "loud voice" (Gk *phone megale*, a "megavoice") demands, "Who is worthy to open the scroll and break its seals?" The response of verse 3 is disheartening to say the least: "But no one in heaven or on earth or under the earth was able to open the scroll or," for that matter, "even to look in it." John's response in verse 4 is understandable: "I cried and cried because no one was found worthy." The word *worthy* is crucial, appearing four times in our text (vv. 2,4,9,12). For a brief moment a survey of heaven reveals no one possesses the merit to approach God, take the scroll, and usher in the eschaton. Not Abraham or Moses. Not Joshua or Caleb. Not Elijah or Elisha. Not Jeremiah, Ezekiel, or Daniel. Not James, Peter, or Paul. Not an angel or even an archangel. A universal search is made. No one is worthy. Heaven has a problem.

He Is Lord Because of His Power (5:5)

An elder, one of the redeemed (4:4), chastens John, telling him, "Stop crying. Look! The Lion from the tribe of Judah, the Root of David, has been victorious so that He may open the scroll and its seven seals."

"The Lion from the tribe of Judah" is a messianic title drawn from Genesis 49:9-10. Messiah will come from Judah, and He will be a king. It speaks of authority, power, strength. "The Root of David" is also messianic and draws from Isaiah 11:1,10 and Jeremiah 23:5. Messiah will be a descendant of David (2 Sam 7:12-16), and as "the Root" He is the source and genesis of all the blessings bestowed on God's people. Are His humanity and deity both in view with the use of these two messianic titles?

John says He is "victorious," using the Greek *nike*. It means to conquer (ESV), triumph (NIV), prevail (NKJV), or "overcome" (NASB). Later in 12:11 it will be said of the saints that they "conquered [Satan] by the blood of the Lamb." This statement prepares us for two of the most awesome verses in the whole Bible.

Jesus Christ Is the Lord of Victory
REVELATION 5:6-7

When we come to verse 6, we encounter an enigma in the drama of redemption. We are not prepared for what we see. We have been told to look for the Lion from the tribe of Judah and the Root of David. We are looking for a great and mighty King. This, however, is not what we see in the surprising story of salvation. John is slow and dramatic in his presentation. He builds suspense! We are not disappointed in what unfolds.

He Is Victorious Because He Was Slaughtered (5:6)

The ordering of the Greek text creates anticipation. A literal reading might go something like this: "Then I saw One like a slaughtered lamb standing between the throne and the four living creatures [angelic beings of worship; see 4:6-8] and among the elders." Both the Lamb and His death are pushed back for effect and emphasis.

The word *Lamb* (Gk *arnion*) is a special word used 29 times in Revelation and only one time outside the book (see John 21:15). Mounce notes it is used exclusively of the resurrected and victorious Christ (*Revelation*, 132n18). However, 28 times it refers to Jesus in Revelation. One time it does not, and that is in 13:11, where it speaks of the false prophet who "had two horns like a lamb, but he sounded like a dragon" (i.e., Satan). He looks like a friend, but his words reveal his true allegiance and character. He is actually God's and the true Lamb's enemy.

The theme of the lamb is a rich one in the grand redemptive story line of the Bible:

Genesis 22:8 (Abraham and Isaac)—"God Himself will provide the lamb for the burnt offering."

Exodus 12:5 (Passover)—"Your lamb shall be without blemish" (NKJV).

Isaiah 53:7 (The suffering servant of the Lord)—"Like a lamb led to the slaughter."

John 1:29 (The declaration of John the Baptist)—"Here is the Lamb of God, who takes away the sin of the world!"

All of these types, prophecies, and proclamations find their fulfillment in the victorious warrior Lamb (see *1 Enoch* 90), the Lord Jesus Christ. "Slaughtered" is in the perfect tense. There is permanence about the scars of His sacrifice. There is also a once-and-for-all nature with abiding results to His sacrifice. He was slaughtered as a sacrifice, taking our place and bearing our sin.

He Is Victorious Because He Is Standing (5:6)

"Slaughtered" speaks of His death. "Standing" speaks of His resurrection. This word is also in the perfect tense. There is permanence to the resurrection. There was a day when His dead body got up and left the tomb, and it will never die again! Jesus of Nazareth began to stand in resurrection life at a point and time in history, He stands today, and He will stand forever.

He Is Victorious Because He Is Strong (5:6)

That "He had seven horns" will confuse and terrify (especially children!) if we forget this is apocalyptic literature filled with images that must be interpreted symbolically. Seven is the number of perfection. Horns in this context represent power and strength. Put together He has perfect strength; He is all-powerful; He is omnipotent.

He Is Victorious Because He Is Searching (5:6)

He also has "seven eyes." Eyes represent wisdom and knowledge. Seven again means perfect. In tandem they inform us He has perfect knowledge, He is all knowing, He is omniscient. And these "are the seven spirits of God sent out in all the earth" (see 1:4). Now we know there is only one Holy Spirit of God, but the number seven again speaks of the perfection, completeness, and fullness of the Spirit (note Isa 11:2) who goes out over the whole of the earth. The emphasis is on His omnipresence.

This description is nothing less than a full affirmation of the Lamb's deity, for only God is all-powerful, all knowing, and everywhere present. So, in light of what the Lamb has done (His work of atonement) and in light of who He is (God), He can do in verse 7 what no one else in all of creation can do.

He Is Victorious Because He Is Sovereign (5:7)

"He [the Lamb] came and took the scroll out of the right hand of the One [the Father] seated on the throne." No one else can do this. No one else even attempts to do this. John Piper notes,

> The Lion gets the victory through the tactics of the Lamb. . . . Because Jesus is a Lion-like Lamb and a Lamb-like Lion, he has the right to bring the world to an end for the glory of his name and the good of his people." ("Lion and the Lamb")

One man, reflecting on this truth, put it in a familiar rhyme like this:

God's Perfect Lamb
Mary had a little Lamb,
His soul was white as snow.
And anywhere His Father sent,
the Lamb was sure to go.
He came to earth to die one day,
the sin of man to atone.
And now He reigns in heaven alone.
He's the Lamb upon the throne!

Jesus Christ Is the Lord of Glory
REVELATION 5:8-14

The redeeming blood of the Lamb is no embarrassment in heaven. Not only are they not ashamed to talk about it; they love to sing about it. Verses 8-14 introduce three beautiful hymns sung in heaven. The first is sung by **the saints** (8-10). The second is sung by **the angels** (11-12). And the third is sung by **all creation** (13-14). The first choir is the smallest, the second larger, and the third the largest of all. The first song is the longest, the second shorter, and the third the shortest by far. In heaven they sing about Jesus, the Lamb of God. How they sing and what they sing is inspiring and instructive for our worship when we gather to praise our Savior.

He Is Praised by the Saints (5:8-10)

Jesus takes the scroll (5:8), and all heaven breaks loose! "The four living creatures and the 24 elders" fall down in adoration, praise, and worship. They have in their possession "harps," the instrument of praise. They have in their possession "gold bowls full of incense, which are the prayers of the saints" (see 8:3-5). In praise and in prayer, they bend their knees and put their faces to the "sea of glass, like crystal" (4:6).

Their praise is voiced in a new (Gk *kainos*, indicating a newness of kind or quality) song, the "Song of Redemption." The Lamb is declared to be worthy to take the scroll and to open its seals. Why? Four reasons are given:

1. "Because You were slaughtered."
2. "You redeemed [ransomed, purchased] people for God by Your blood."
3. And from where? The missionary Lamb who is a Lion has ransomed people "from every tribe and language and people and nation" (see 7:9-17). No one is barred from the cross. All the barriers have been shattered and destroyed (Eph 2:11-22).
4. "You made them [the saints] a kingdom and priests to our God." As kings we *reign with* Him, "coheirs with Christ" (Rom 8:17). As priests we *serve for* Him, "a holy priesthood to offer spiritual sacrifices acceptable to God through Jesus Christ" (1 Pet 2:5). We "will reign on the earth" looks to the millennium reign in 20:4-6 and possibly also to the eternal reign in chapters 21–22. It is no wonder He is so loved, adored, and praised by the saints.

He Is Praised by the Angels (5:11-12)

The angelic host will not sit on the sideline and watch this glorious worship. They must get involved too! Suddenly, John sees and hears from around the throne the living creatures and the elders, "the voice of many angels." The text says they numbered literally "myriads of myriads" (NIV, "thousands upon thousands"; HCSB, "countless thousands"), "plus thousands of thousands." Their number, however, is not what is important. Speculation on the number of angels is wasted time. What they do, on the other hand, is worth paying attention to. They praise the Lamb with a magnificent sevenfold (again signifying perfection) blessing. The Lamb who was slaughtered is worthy (see 5:9) to receive (1) power, (2) riches, (3) wisdom, (4) strength, (5) honor, (6) glory, and (7) blessing. Neither we nor the angels can give Him the first four things. We can only acknowledge He has them in all their fullness and perfection. However, we can give Him honor, glory, and blessing.

The word *blessing* is the Greek word (*eulogia*) from which we get our word *eulogy*. Etymologically (and I know there is a potential fallacy here!) it breaks down to mean "a good word." In other words, as long as we have breath, we can say a good word about Jesus. We can witness to others about Jesus. We can brag on Jesus. We can take the gospel to the nations for Jesus. We do talk about what we love, do we not? Are we talking a lot and saying good gospel things about our Lord and King (19:16)?

He Is Praised by All Creation (5:13-14)

The redeeming work of the Lamb now draws the praise of all creation. After all, creation itself longs for the day when it "will also be set free from the bondage of corruption" (Rom 8:21). In a doxological affirmation John hears "every creature in heaven, on earth, under the earth, on the sea, and everything in them." A. T. Robertson called these "the four great fields of life" (*Word Pictures*, 6:336). In words similar to but shorter than the previous hymn, all creation ascribes "blessing and honor and glory and dominion [ESV, "might"] to the One seated on the throne [i.e., God the Father] and to the Lamb [i.e., God the Son] forever and ever [lit., unto the ages of the ages]." The four living creatures who day and night never stop worshiping (4:8) say, "Amen!" We agree! So be it! "Oh, Yes!" (*The Message*). The elders once more (see 5:8) "fell down and worshiped," and some translations like the NKJV add, they "worshiped Him who lives forever and ever." Although not in the best manuscripts, the latter phrase certainly captures the spirit of the vision we have had the blessing of eavesdropping in on for a few verses. Imagine what it will be like when we are there!

Conclusion

If we were all gathered together and the state governor were to walk in, it would be appropriate for us to stand in honor of his office, whether we agreed with his politics or not. And if the president were to walk in, it would be right both to stand and to applaud, regardless of his politics. But if the Lord Jesus, the Lamb who is a Lion, were suddenly to walk in, to stand would be inadequate, and to stand and applaud would almost be arrogant. No, in light of who He is and what He has done, the only rightful response is to do what we see in verse 14: they "fell down and worshiped Him who lives forever and ever."

Reflect and Discuss

1. Go back and read Exodus 12. What does this tell you about how the lamb imagery would have been communicated to Jewish believers?
2. How do chapters 4–5 introduce the rest of the book of Revelation? What common themes do they share?
3. What is so sad about the scene in verses 2-4? Why do you think the scroll needs to be opened?
4. What do the messianic titles for the Lamb reveal about His character and His work?
5. What is significant about the fact that the Lamb is slaughtered? How does this show Christ's work?
6. What is significant about the fact that the Lamb is standing? What significance does Jesus' resurrection have for our lives?
7. The people around the throne are from every tribe and people and language. What does this tell us about the nature of the church?
8. How should Revelation 5:9-10 shape our missionary activity?
9. Why will worshiping God for eternity be a delight and not a chore?
10. This vision involves a great deal of anticipation. Do you look forward to the revelation of Jesus? How can you keep His future unveiling as a present hope and expectation in your life?

The Four Horsemen of the Apocalypse

REVELATION 6:1-8

Main Idea: Though judgment will come on all the earth through deception, war, famine, and death, Christ is sovereign over every step and is working through the trials.

I. **Be Aware of God's Weapon of Deception (the White Horse) (6:1-2).**
   A. Deception is under God's control (6:1).
   B. Deception will come to conquer (6:2).
II. **Be Aware of God's Weapon of War (the Red Horse) (6:3-4).**
   A. Destruction is inevitable (6:3).
   B. Destruction is immense (6:4).
III. **Be Aware of God's Weapon of Famine (the Black Horse) (6:5-6).**
   A. Famine is unstoppable (6:5).
   B. Famine will be unbearable (6:6).
IV. **Be Aware of God's Weapon of Death (the Pale Horse) (6:7-8).**
   A. Death is controlled (6:7).
   B. Death will be comprehensive (6:8).

The fury and thunder of their hoofbeats has been anticipated for centuries. Harbingers of deception, destruction, deprivation, and death—the world has feared and resisted their coming. Yet come they will. God guarantees it! In 1983 Billy Graham addressed their coming in his book *Approaching Hoofbeats: The Four Horsemen of the Apocalypse.* There he wrote, "The shadows of all four horsemen can already be seen galloping throughout the world at this moment" (9). Dr. Graham is right. Their shadow looms large, and they could appear at any time.

The mass murderer Charles Manson identified the musical quartet "The Beatles" as the four horsemen. No one questions their popularity and influence, but it will pale in comparison to what the world will experience when the real four horsemen come riding into town.

Revelation 6–19 contains the heart of the end time called the "Day of the Lord." It is also referred to as the "time of Jacob's trouble" (Jer 30:7), Daniel's seventieth week (Dan 9:27), and the tribulation. Though the rapture of believers is never specifically addressed in Revelation, it is my judgment that it occurs sometime before Revelation 6. First Thessalonians 5:9 says we are not destined for the wrath of the Day of the Lord. And the rapture is discussed in 1 Thessalonians 4:13-18 before the Day of the Lord is addressed in 1 Thessalonians 5:1-11. This, and the doctrine of imminence, supports a pretribulational eschatology.

The four horsemen introduce us to the first of God's three series of judgments in Revelation: the seal judgments of chapter 6, the trumpet judgments in chapters 8 and 9, and the bowl judgments in chapters 15 and 16. I believe there is a telescopic relationship to the judgments, with each successive series coming out of the last of the former. In other words, the **seventh seal is the seven trumpets** and the **seventh trumpet is the seven bowls**. This would indicate an increase both in *rapidity* and *intensity* as the judgments unfold (Patterson, *Revelation*, 176–77). It will be a time of great sorrow and suffering.

As we investigate the four horsemen, it is important to note their Old Testament background and imagery from Zechariah 1:7-17; 6:1-8; Ezekiel 14:12-23 (esp. v. 21); and even Leviticus 26:14-33. But the words of Jesus are also imperative, as recorded in Matthew 24:5-8; Mark 13:7-9; and Luke 21:9-12. What we discover is a remarkable parallelism between Jesus' teaching and this passage. And the fact that in Matthew 24:8 Jesus says, "All these events are the beginning of birth pains" must be carefully considered. There is a real sense in which the three series of judgments give us patterns of divine judgment and spiritual conflict that have occurred throughout history. Yet there has been something of a spiraling nature to these judgments as they move us toward the "omega point" of history. Eventually, these judgments come in their final and climactic fullness just before the return of King Jesus (Rev 19:11-21) to establish His earthly kingdom of a thousand years (Rev 20:1-6).

Now, some see the seal judgments as prior to and preparatory for the great tribulation (6:17). This is why Jesus refers to them as "the beginning of birth pains" (Matt 24:8) and why He also says, when these things happen, "the end is not yet" (Matt 24:6). Others believe the four horsemen will come and inflict judgments that fit into the first half of the tribulation, usually understood to be the initial three and one-half years of a seven-year period of tribulation. Dogmatism is unwarranted on these kinds of details. What is clear beyond question is those who "deny that God will judge anybody for anything" are dead wrong (Swindoll, *Insights*, 109). A day of reckoning is coming. The Four Horsemen of the

Apocalypse are the first harbingers of this judgment that is unparalleled in human history (Matt 24:21). As they ride forth in all their fury, what spiritual insights and lessons does our God have for every generation of His people to learn and embrace?

Be Aware of God's Weapon of Deception (The White Horse)
REVELATION 6:1-2

The heavenly throne-room vision of chapters 4–5 sets the stage for the judgments of chapters 6 and following. By virtue of His act of creation (ch. 4) and His act of redemption (ch. 5), our sovereign God has the authority and the right to judge His world. He initiates that judgment by sending forth His four horsemen. The Lamb, King Jesus, opens the seals (6:1). All that unfolds is under His command.

Deception Is Under God's Control (6:1)

John sees the Lamb of chapter 5 begin to open the seven seals of the scroll He took from God the Father in 5:7. Then he hears "one of the four living creatures [see 4:6-8; 5:6,8,11] say with a voice like thunder, 'Come!'" The voice emanates from heaven's throne with power. The thunder warns of an impending storm of divine wrath and judgment. The command to the first rider is simple and direct: "Come!" Warren Wiersbe notes, "Events will now take place because of God's sovereign direction in heaven" (*Be Victorious*, 62). The riders come because God sends them.

Deception Will Come to Conquer (6:2)

John sees a white horse whose rider has a bow and is wearing a crown (Gk *stephanos*). He goes out "as a victor to conquer." Exactly who this rider is has generated much discussion and disagreement. Opinions include (1) Jesus Christ (see Rev 19:11-16), (2) the advance of the gospel, (3) Apollo (representing false religion), (4) the antichrist, (5) the spirit of conquest, (6) government persecuting Christians, and (7) Satan's servants in general.

The rider cannot be Jesus, even though this view goes back at least to the time of the church father Irenaeus (late second century). The riders of 6:1-2 and 19:11-21 have little in common other than being on a white horse. Further, The Lamb opens the seals, and no angel would command Christ to do anything! The better view is that this is the spirit of deception and conquest that will be embodied in the counterfeit Christ, the antichrist (2 Thess 2:3-4), the beast of 13:1-10. This deceptive, conquering rider keeps company with war, famine, and death—the next three riders. This rider fulfills the warning of Jesus in Matthew 24:4-5 where He tells us to be on guard against deception and false christs.

Beale provides helpful commentary:

> The first rider represents a satanic force attempting to defeat and oppress believers spiritually through deception, persecution, or both (so 11:7; 13:7). The image of the rider may include reference to (1) the antichrist, (2) governments that persecute Christians, or (3) the devil's servants in general. An allusion to forces symbolized by the beasts later in the book could be uppermost in mind (see below on 6:8). "White" elsewhere in the book does not primarily connote victory but the persevering righteousness of Christ and the saints (see on 3:4-5). Here white may refer to the forces of evil as they try to appear righteous and thus deceive by imitating Christ (cf. 2 Cor. 11:13-15). The portrayal is intended by John as a parody of Christ's righteousness and victory in 19:11-16: Satan's attempts to be victorious are but feeble imitations of Christ, worthy only for ridicule (as in, e.g., 11:7; 13:1-13). Such attempts are doomed to failure from the beginning because they are ultimately decreed by God to contribute to the establishment of his kingdom and glory (cf. 17:17). (*Revelation*, 377)

God sends this rider to reveal that which is true and that which is false, the real from the inauthentic. There is great deception today. It will increase as the final chapter of history is written.

Be Aware of God's Weapon of War
(The Red Horse)
REVELATION 6:3-4

Some believe the rider on the white horse promises a deceptive peace. If so, it will be temporary and short-lived. He may have carried a bow but no arrows, but the red horse of war brings a rider who possesses a "large sword" of destruction and death. He too comes only at God's command.

Destruction Is Inevitable (6:3)

Christ is in control as the second seal is opened. What He opens no one can shut or stop. The second living creature, in response to Christ's sovereign action, beckons the second rider: "Come." The red horse of war inevitably follows the white horse of conquest.

Destruction Is Immense (6:4)

The color of the second horse is "fiery red" and rightly depicts his mission of bloodshed and slaughter (Mounce, *Revelation*, 143). But while he takes peace from the earth, the people slaughter one another. The idea seems to convey civil strife within and between peoples and nations. Assassination and civil unrest, riots in the streets, and rebellion against authority will run rampant. No one will be safe. One will live in constant fear of life not knowing whom to trust. Jesus said in Matthew 24:10, "Many will take offense, betray one another, and hate one another." No one will be excluded. This rider takes peace from the earth. Anarchy and worldwide bloodshed are signatures of the last days.

World War II General Omar N. Bradley once delivered "An Armistice Day Address" in Boston. He said,

> With the monstrous weapons man already has, humanity is in danger of being trapped in this world by its moral adolescents. Our knowledge of science has clearly outstripped our capacity to control it. *We have many men of science; too few men of God. We have grasped the mystery of the atom and rejected the Sermon on the Mount.* Man is stumbling blindly through a spiritual darkness while toying with the precarious secrets of life and death. The world has achieved brilliance without wisdom, power without conscience. Ours is a world of nuclear giants and ethical infants. We know more about war than we know about peace, more about killing than we know about living. This is our 20th century's claim to distinction and to progress. (*Collected Writings*, 1:588–89, emphasis in original)

During World War II, Albert Einstein helped bring a German photographer to the United States. They became friends, and the photographer took a number of pictures of Einstein. One day he looked into the camera and started talking. He spoke about his despair that his formula $E=mc^2$ and his letter to President Roosevelt had made the atomic bomb possible, and his scientific research had resulted in the death of so many human beings. He grew silent. His eyes had a look of immense sadness. There was a question and a reproach in them. At that moment the cameraman released the shutter. Einstein looked up and the cameraman asked him, "So, you don't believe there will ever be peace?" "No," he answered. "As long as there will be man, there will be wars."

God has used man as His instrument of judgment. He will do it again as the red horse of war rides and time, as we know it, comes to an end.

Be Aware of God's Weapon of Famine
(The Black Horse)
REVELATION 6:5-6

War has a close companion, an ever-present partner: famine. Conquest, war, famine: these three tend to show up at the same time together. William and Paul Paddock warned in their book *Famine—1975*, "Today hungry nations, tomorrow starving nations" (40). Some may accuse them of being alarmist. Revelation teaches us tomorrow could come any day.

Famine Is Unstoppable (6:5)

Christ opens the third seal, and the third living creature commands the rider, "Come." John looks and sees the black horse of famine with its rider holding "a set of scales" or balances in his hand as he rides onto the stage of history. John MacArthur notes that "the color black is associated with famine in Lamentations 5:10 (KJV). Famine is a logical consequence of worldwide war as food supplies are destroyed and those involved in food production are killed" (*Revelation 1–11*, 182). Christ has released the black horse of famine and starvation, and no one and nothing can deter it. It is coming. It is unstoppable.

Famine Will Be Unbearable (6:6)

From among the four living creatures John hears "something like a voice" saying, "A quart of wheat for a denarius, and three quarts of barley for a denarius." A quart of wheat was approximately the amount necessary to sustain one person for one day. Barley was the poor man's wheat, and it was normally fed to animals. It was low in nutritional value and occasionally mixed with wheat to increase the feeding amount. A denarius was basically a day's wage. In other words, a man will work all day for just enough wheat to sustain himself or enough barley to barely keep his family alive. This means that inflation prices would be 10–16 times above normal according to prices cited by Cicero for wheat sold in Sicily (Beasley-Murray, *Revelation*, 133; see also Mounce, *Revelation*, 145).

The phrase "do not harm the olive oil and the wine" is less clear as to its meaning. Some see the phrase as setting a limit on the deprivation caused by the horse of famine. Others argue that oil and wine were the commodities of the wealthy. The former understanding is more likely. Food for the poor will be scarce and in short supply. Still, there are limits, at least for now. However, once the trumpet and bowl judgments are finished, nothing will be left. Nothing.

Today we know that famine and hunger kill more people every year than AIDS, malaria, and tuberculosis combined. Some 805 million people in the world do not have enough food to lead a healthy active life. That's about one in nine people on earth. The vast majority of the world's hungry people live in developing countries, where 13.5 percent of the population is undernourished. Sub-Saharan Africa is the region with the highest prevalence of hunger by percentage of population, where one person in four is undernourished. Poor nutrition causes nearly half (45%) of deaths in children under five—3.1 million children each year. One out of six children—roughly 100 million in developing countries—is underweight. This is what hunger and famine are like today. It will get much worse when the black horse rides.

Be Aware of God's Weapon of Death
(The Pale Horse)
REVELATION 6:7-8

B. F. Skinner was a famous behavioral psychologist who for much of his life was an optimist. However, at the age of 78, his optimism began to fade. At the American Psychological Association Convention on September 25, 1982, Skinner said,

> Why are we not acting to save the world? The world is fatally ill
> . . . it is a very depressing way to end one's life. The argument
> that we have always solved our problems in the past, and shall
> solve this one, is like reassuring a dying man by pointing out
> that he has always recovered from his illnesses. . . . When I
> wrote *Beyond Freedom and Dignity*, I was optimistic about the

future. . . . A decade ago there was hope. . . . Today the world is fatally flawed. (White, "Hope")

While I would disagree with B. F. Skinner on many things, his diagnosis of the condition of the world was spot on. The world is fatally flawed. The pale horse of death with the grim reaper riding saddle is just around the corner with nothing less than a global agenda.

Death Is Controlled (6:7)

Thankfully death cannot act apart from the plans and purposes of the sovereign Christ. As with the three previous riders, this horse comes forth at the permission of the Lamb of God and with the command of one of the living creatures. Jesus reminds us in Matthew 10:28, "Don't fear those who kill the body but are not able to kill the soul; rather, fear Him who is able to destroy both soul and body in hell." Death is God's prerogative. He and He alone decides when it will come and how it will come.

Death Will Be Comprehensive (6:8)

John looks and sees a pale horse, the ashen-green color of a decomposing corpse. Its rider is Death, that which claims the body. Following close behind is its ever-present companion Hades, that which claims the soul. The death visited on the earth is massive and comprehensive in its numbers: one-quarter of the earth. It is also comprehensive in its nature: it kills by the sword (see v. 4), by famine (see v. 6), by plague, and by the wild animals of the earth.

> In 1800 the world reached 1 billion in population.
> In 1930 the world reached 2 billion in population.
> In 1960 the world reached 3 billion in population.
> In 1974 the world reached 4 billion in population.
> In 1987 the world reached 5 billion in population.
> In 1999 the world reached 6 billion in population.
> In 2011 the world reached 7 billion in population.

By 2044, the projection is 9 billion. Think about it. If the Lord were to come back today, in all too brief a time over 1.75 billion people will depart planet Earth not by rapture but by death. Later in Revelation 8:18, because of the sixth trumpet, one-third of those remaining will die. In less than seven years, half of the world's population will be taken in death (see Ezek 14:21). In a world decimated by war and famine, even the wild beasts will join in the carnage. Does this sound far-fetched and beyond reality? Not really.

Conclusion

In his book *Death in the City*, Francis Schaeffer said of our modern world, "the dust of death" is on everything (21). His diagnosis is correct, and the dust will only grow thicker until our great God has accomplished His purposes. However, we should not fear or fret. He is in absolute control. The Lamb holds history in His hand. Are you trusting Him? He will determine, to the last detail, history's consummation. He will orchestrate each and every event according to His perfect plan. God has such a plan for the world. God has such a plan for you. Let Him who is taking the world to its appropriate end do the same for you. The way may not be easy, but I promise you: you will not be disappointed.

Literary Construction: 6:1-17; 8:1–9:21; 11:15-19; 15:1–16:12; 16:17–21:27

	Seals			Trumpets			Bowls		
	1–6	( )	7	1–6	( )	7	1–6	( )	7
A parenthesis between sixth and seventh judgments in each series		7:1-17			10:4–11:14			16:13-16	
A parenthesis between the trumpet judgment and the bowl series						12:1–14:20			
A parenthesis between the bowl series and the description of the second coming of Jesus									17:1–19:10

Suggested Interrelationships of the Seals, Trumpets, and Bowls

Judgments are seen as occurring simultaneously, with repetition showing the intensification of the judgments.	7 Seals 7 Trumpets 7 Bowls
The consecutive arrangement envisions a total of 21 judgments, each following directly after the other.	7 Seals → 7 Trumpets → 7 Bowls
This telescopic arrangement has the seventh seal introducing the trumpet series and being explained by it, and the seventh trumpet introduces the bowl series and is explained by it. So the seven bowls equal the seventh trumpet, and the seven trumpets are the seventh seal. This is the best view based on the book itself.	7th Seal → [1 2 3 4 5 6 Seals] ; 7th Trumpet → [1 2 3 4 5 6 Trumpets] ; 1 2 3 4 5 6 7 Bowls

REVELATION 6–19

Content and Correlation of the Judgments of
Seals, Trumpets, and Bowls

NUMBER	SEALS Opened by the Lamb	TRUMPETS Blown by seven angels	BOWLS Poured by seven angels
1	White horse: conqueror	Hail and fire: 1/3 of vegetation burnt	Sores
2	Red horse: war	Mountain of fire: 1/3 of creatures in sea destroyed	Sea becomes blood: all marine life dies
3	Black horse: famine	Star called wormwood falls: 1/3 of fresh water poisoned	Fresh water turned to blood
4	Pale horse: death	Partial darkness: 1/3 of sun, moon, and stars	Scorching sun burns men
		HIATUS: Last three trumpets announced as woes	
5	Martyrs reassured	Woe 1: Angel releases locusts from abyss.	Darkness on beast's kingdom
6	Great day of wrath: earthquake, signs in heaven	Woe 2: Four angels loosed at Euphrates; they slay 1/3 of earth's population.	Euphrates dries up: kings assemble for war at Armageddon
	HIATUS: Sealing of 144,000	HIATUS: Mystery of God to be concluded with seventh trumpet.	
7	1/2 hour of silence: Introduction of trumpets	Announcement of the Lord's victory and the introduction of the bowls	Severe earthquake and great hail

SEVEN YEARS OF TRIBULATION / Daniel's 70th Week

Battle of Armageddon
2nd Coming of Christ
Rev 19:11-21 see Matt 24:27-31

The Present Age	Tribulation — The Beginning of Sorrows Matt 24:5-8 — 3½ years →			← THE GREAT TRIBULATION Matt 24: 9-26 →		Satan's Final Rebellion Rev 20:7-10 The Great White Throne Judgment—Rev 20:11-15
The Rapture of the church takes place before the opening of the seal judgments in chapter 6 (see 1 Thess 5:9; Rev 3:10).	Year 1	Year 2	Year 3	Year 4	Years 5–7	The Millennium Christ's 1,000 year reign on the earth. Rev 20:1-6 — Eternity Revelation 21–22
The Seals	1 The White Horse	2 The Red Horse	3 The Black Horse	4 The Pale Horse	5 The Cry of the Martyrs	6 Cosmic Disturbances	7 The Seven Trumpets 8:1-6
	Revelation 6:1-8				Revelation 6:9-17	

Daniel 9:27a

3½ years — Daniel 9:27b

The Seven Bowls
Revelation 16

Reflect and Discuss

1. What does it mean that the "shadows of all four horsemen" are readily seen on the earth today?

2. Read 1 Thessalonians 4:13-18 and 5:1-11. How do these passages fit into the messages and teaching of Revelation?

3. Read Matthew 24:1-8. What parallels do you see between Jesus' teaching and Revelation 6:1-8?

4. Why is dogmatism about the precise interpretation of this passage unhelpful? What are the most important lessons that are the clearest?

5. Why is it significant that the Lamb is the One who opens the scroll? Why would God unleash these judgments on the world?

6. How have you seen the Lord use evils like the ones in this passage for His purposes?

7. How can you see elements of the red horse already at play today?

8. What other biblical passages speak of famine? How has God used famine throughout Scripture?

9. How should Christians respond to the numbers of those who will die at the hand of the fourth judgment?

10. These verses reveal God's mysterious providence, even through judgment and trial. Are there any trials that God is leading you through? How are you trusting in Him?

The Wrath of the Lamb

REVELATION 6:9-17

Main Idea: A day is coming when the Lord's wrath will be poured out on His enemies, and until then believers are called to be faithful even unto death.

I. **Those Who Are Faithful to Jesus Can Anticipate They Will Suffer (6:9).**
   A. Be faithful to the Word of God.
   B. Be faithful in the witness you bear.

II. **We Should Trust Our Sovereign God to Do Right According to His Time, Not Ours (6:10-11).**
   A. Pour out your heart in prayer (6:10).
   B. Rest in the providence of His plan (6:11).

III. **When the Lamb Comes Again, the Signs Will Be Clear for All to See (6:12-14).**
   A. Judgment is initiated by Christ (6:12).
   B. Judgment is cosmic in scope (6:12-14).

IV. **The Nature of God's Judgment Is Comprehensive (6:15).**
   A. One's position in life will not matter.
   B. One's social status in life will not matter.

V. **The Horror of God's Wrath Is Even Greater than Death (6:15-17).**
   A. No one can hide from divine judgment (6:15-16).
   B. No one can stand before divine judgment (6:17).

It is one of the most ironic and unexpected phrases in the whole Bible. It sounds contradictory, paradoxical, incredible: "the wrath of the Lamb" (6:16). A lamb, by its nature, is gentle, meek, passive. Few animals are less threatening. And yet there it is in Holy Scripture for us to consider and contemplate: "the wrath of the Lamb."

In chapter 5 we were introduced to this Lamb—a Lamb that was slaughtered but now standing (5:6). There we also discovered that this Lamb is also a Lion, "the Lion from the tribe of Judah" (5:5; see Gen 49:9-10). So this Lamb is lion-like and this Lion is lamb-like. But in judgment He pours out His wrath and fury on a sinful and rebellious humanity that has defiantly rejected His offers of forgiveness, grace, and salvation.

Liberal and modernist theologians have been quick to extol and embrace the portrait of the meek and lowly Jesus, the gentle and compassionate man from Galilee. Now to be sure, He is all of these things: meek and humble, gentle and compassionate. However, this portrait is only a partial picture of the Savior revealed in the Bible. Scripture also reveals a Jesus who twice cleanses the temple (Matt 21:12-17; John 2:13-22), who angrily condemns the hypocrisy of the scribes and Pharisees (Matt 23:13-36), calling them "serpents" and "a brood of vipers," and who says more about the eternal fire and judgment of *gehenna* (hell) than anyone else in the Bible. A balanced view of the Savior portrayed in the Bible must hold in tension His love and His holiness, His compassion and His justice, His grace and His righteousness, His mercy and His wrath.

In Revelation the wrath of the Lamb, the wrath of God, is a recurring theme (11:18; 14:10; 16:19; 19:15). Warren Wiersbe, former pastor of the Moody Church in Chicago, puts this theme in perspective: "If men and women will not yield to the *love* of God, and be changed by the *grace* of God, then there is no way for them to escape the *wrath* of God" (*Be Victorious*, 67). As those days approach, and then ultimately and climactically arrive, how should God's children prepare to respond?

Those Who Are Faithful to Jesus Can Anticipate They Will Suffer
REVELATION 6:9

The apostle Paul tells us in 2 Timothy 3:12, "All those who want to live a godly life in Christ Jesus will be persecuted." We see this truth lived out especially in those who are martyred for the Lamb, the Lord Jesus. Knowing we could find ourselves in this chosen company, what is the posture, the mind-set, we must adopt?

Be Faithful to the Word of God

The Four Horsemen of the Apocalypse have come forth leaving destruction, devastation, and death in their path (6:1-8). John now sees the Lord Jesus opening the fifth seal. He sees "under the altar the people slaughtered [see 5:6,9] because of God's word and the testimony they had." He sees martyred saints for the Savior. Why were they killed?

Because they remained true to the Word of God. They did not compromise the truth of God's Word even though it cost them their lives.

They are "under the altar." Whether this is the altar of burnt offering (Exod 29:12; Lev 4:7; 17:11) or the altar of incense is not important. Mounce notes, "The theme of sacrifice would suggest the former, but the prayers that rise (6:10) seem to indicate the latter. There is no reason why in John's vision the two should not blend together as one" (*Revelation*, 146). Faithfulness to God's Word may involve sacrifice, but such sacrifice is a sweet aroma in the nostrils of our God.

Be Faithful in the Witness You Bear

Their testimony, their witness, was also the cause of their martyrdom. They maintained their witness to Jesus regardless of the consequences. Ladd points out,

> One of the repeated emphases of the entire New Testament is that it is the very nature of the church to be a martyr people. When Jesus taught that a man to be his disciple must deny himself and take up his cross (Matt 10:38; 16:24), he was not speaking of self-denial or the bearing of heavy burdens; he was speaking of willingness to suffer martyrdom. The cross is nothing else than an instrument of death. Every disciple of Jesus is in essence a martyr; and John has in view all believers who have so suffered. (*Commentary*, 104)

On December 2, 2014, the *Christian Post* carried a story titled, "Vicar of Baghdad: Four Iraqi Christian Kids Beheaded After Refusing to Convert to Islam, Telling ISIS Militants 'No, We Love Jesus.'" That story contained the following:

> Four Iraqi Christian children, who were all beheaded by the Islamic State, refused to betray Jesus and graciously died in his name when the ISIS militants gave them one last chance to say the Islamic words of conversion, the Rev. Canon Andrew White revealed in a recent interview. . . . White recounted the recent incident when ISIS militants beheaded four kids, all of who were under the age of 15, when the kids refused to say that they would follow the Prophet Muhammad and told the ISIS fighters that they will always "love" and "follow" Jesus.

"ISIS turned up and they said to the children, 'You say the words that you will follow Muhammad.' The children, all under 15, four of them, they said, 'No, we love Yasua [Jesus]. We have always loved Yasua. We have always followed Yasua. Yasua has always been with us,'" White said. "[The Militants] said, 'Say the words!' [The Children] said, 'No, we can't do that.' They chopped all their heads off." ("Beheaded," Dec. 2, 2014)

Martyrs for Jesus appear repeatedly in Revelation (7:9-14; 13:15; 18:24; 20:4). They are an ever-occurring presence in the church's history. Faithful to the Word and in their witness, many seal their testimony to Jesus with their blood.

We Should Trust Our Sovereign God to Do Right According to His Time
REVELATION 6:10-11

Pastor Adrian Rogers used to say, "God is never early and He is never late. He is always right on time." We know this is true. However, there are times when we struggle to believe it. This is especially the case when injustice and suffering are involved. When those occasions arise, and they will, what should we do?

Pour Out Your Heart in Prayer (6:10)

They martyrs of verse 9 now "cry out with a loud voice," a *phonē megalē*. They call to "Lord," *despotes*, a term used for the master of slaves; it emphasizes absolute authority and power and is used only here in Revelation. They cry, "Lord, the One who is holy and true [see 3:7], how long until You judge and avenge our blood from those who live on the earth?" (3:10; 8:13; 11:10; 13:8,12; 17:2,8).

This is the only prayer of supplication in the Apocalypse. It is short and simple. It begins with a reverential address that leads to a plea for justice (Mounce, *Revelation*, 284–85). The pattern of the imprecatory psalms is evident (Pss 6:3; 74:10; 79:5; 80:4; 89:46; 90:13). This has caused some to question the appropriateness of this prayer when considered in light of the words of Jesus on the cross (Luke 23:34) and Stephen at his stoning (Acts 7:60). Thomas Glasson is straightforward in his assessment: "It should be frankly recognized that this is not a

Christian prayer" (quoted in ibid., 147). To this charge two things can be said. First, divine retribution and vindication are a prominent Old Testament theme (see Deut 32:35; Pss 64:7-9; 79:10; 94:1-2,23; Mal 4:1-2). And second, divine retribution and vindication are an important New Testament theme (Luke 21:22; Rom 1:18; 12:19-20; Heb 10:30).

The prayer of these martyrs is heartfelt, sincere, and biblically grounded. They do not cry out for personal revenge or vengeance but for divine justice. Further, they trust all of this into the hands of our sovereign Master and Lord: "This is how I feel! I will leave the rest up to You, my God."

Rest in the Providence of His Plan (6:11)

God's care for these martyred saints is made clear in verse 11: "A white robe was given to each of them." The white robe symbolizes blessedness, dignity, honor, purity, victory, and most of all the imputed righteousness of Christ. They are then "told to rest a little while longer until the number would be completed . . . who were going to be killed just as they had been." More "fellow slaves" of Christ and "brothers" of Christ are yet to shed their blood for Jesus. Until then, rest, be patient, trust in the Lord of all the earth who will do right (Gen 18:25). Osborne is helpful here: "The emphasis is on divine sovereignty. God knows each one who is to be martyred, and will vindicate them all at the proper time, which will be soon" (*Revelation*, 289). God's delay does not mean He does not know. It does not mean He does not care. He knows and He cares. So rest. Justice has been determined and justice will be done. "Those who have died for the faith (and those who will yet die), have not suffered in vain. They are secure because they have the robe of Christ's righteousness" (Goldsworthy, *Lamb and the Lion,* 51). Yes, we have His righteousness, and we can trust in His judgment.

When the Lamb Comes Again, the Signs Will Be Clear for All to See
REVELATION 6:12-14

In verse 11 the martyrs for Jesus are told to wait, "to rest a little while longer." They are not told to wait forever. The great day of the wrath of the Lamb is coming. Indeed, it is coming much sooner than most expect. Far too many will not be ready.

Judgment Is Initiated by Christ (6:12)

"Then I saw Him open the sixth seal." John sees Jesus break this seal just as He had broken seals one through five. All that has happened and is about to happen is under His sovereign control and direction. This is a divine doing. "He's got the whole world in His hands." What follows leaves no one in doubt.

Judgment Is Cosmic in Scope (6:12-14)

The Lamb opens the sixth seal, and cosmic upheaval is the result. The Bible repeatedly promises such happenings when our Lord draws history to a close (see Isa 13:9-10; Joel 2:10-11; 2:28-32; 3:14-16; Matt 24:29-30; Mark 13:24-37; Luke 21:25-28). Some fine Bible scholars view these judgments as only symbolic, perhaps signifying political and social upheaval. I believe, however, it is better to understand these end-time events as genuine descriptions, in apocalyptic terms, of God's direct intervention in eschatological judgment. The imminent end of history has come.

"A violent earthquake occurs." Earthquakes often accompany a divine visitation in Scripture (Exod 19:18; Isa 2:19; Hag 2:6; Matt 24:7; 27:51). Zechariah 14:4 tells us when Messiah comes again, "On that day His feet will stand on the Mount of Olives, which faces Jerusalem on the east. The Mount of Olives will be split in half from east to west, forming a huge valley, so that half the mountain will move to the north and half to the south." Cosmic upheaval also impairs the light of the sun so that it is darkened like a dark cloth made from goat's hair and worn in times of mourning. The moon likewise is affected and appears like the deep, red color of blood. Some speculate that worldwide earthquakes will produce catastrophic volcanic activity spewing ash and smoke throughout the atmosphere, and that this causes the darkening of the sun and the reddening of the moon. Whatever the cause, all of this is a sign of God visiting His world in judgment. But there is more.

"The stars of heaven fell." The word translated "stars" simply refers to any celestial body, large or small, having the appearance of a star. A meteor or asteroid shower is possibly in view and they fall "as a fig tree drops its unripe figs when shaken by a high wind."

John then writes in verse 14, "The sky separated like a scroll being rolled up; and every mountain and island was moved from its place." Precisely what this describes we can only guess. What we do know is there is a total cosmic meltdown. The Day of the Lord has arrived in its climactic and eschatological reality. The wrath of the Lamb is here! On that day no one will be in doubt as to what is happening and who is bringing all of this about.

The Nature of God's Judgment Is Comprehensive
REVELATION 6:15

In Acts 10:34 Peter says, "God doesn't show favoritism." James 2:1-9 is even more direct, concluding with, "If you show favoritism, you commit sin and are convicted by the law as transgressors." Just as God's salvation shows no favoritism among the nations, neither will His judgment.

One's Position in Life Will Not Matter

When the day of judgment arrives, no one will be excluded or excused. Those who normally get special treatment will get none. "Kings of the earth, the nobles, the military commanders, the rich, the powerful" will not escape the wrath of the Lamb. Their sense of status and privilege will vanish in an instant when they stand before the Lord Jesus Christ (v. 17). Untouchable in this life, they are totally vulnerable to the One whose piercing gaze is "like a fiery flame" (1:14; 2:18; 19:12). On that day all earthly status and privilege will count for nothing.

One's Social Status in Life Will Not Matter

"Every slave and free person" will have to do business with the Lamb on that great day. No one gets a pass. All must and will give an account. Divine judgment is the great equalizer. The free person will be held accountable by God. The slave will be held accountable by God. From the Roman emperor to the lowest slave, all social distinctions evaporate before the judgment bar of God. Gordon Fee notes, "Following these various forms of 'the mighty,' John finally includes everyone else, both slave and free; and with this he has simply included all of the known human race that made up the Roman Empire" (*Revelation*, 101). The nature of God's judgment is comprehensive. We all must give an account.

The Horror of God's Wrath Is Even Greater than Death
REVELATION 6:15-17

You would think all of this would drive people to God in brokenness, confession, and repentance. Tragically, that is not what happens. Here, as well as in 9:20-21 and 16:11, there is no repentance or sorrow over sin. Faced with the awesomeness of God's wrath, people "plead for a violent death (cf. Isa 2:10, 19–21; Hos 10:8; Luke 23:20)" (Duvall, *Revelation*, 109). Death is more desired, foolishly I might add, than a relationship with the Lamb who was slaughtered on their behalf.

No One Can Hide from Divine Judgment (6:15-16)

Like their primordial parents, Adam and Eve, human persons become fearful and irrational fugitives. They "hid in the caves and among the rocks of the mountains." They even talk to the mountains and rocks asking them to be their executioners: "Fall on us and hide us . . . from the wrath of the Lamb." This is utterly amazing. "The sacrificial Lamb has now become their Judge. . . . They hide from his face, whereas believers are comforted by the promise that one day they will see God's face (22:4)" (Duvall, *Revelation*, 109) However, no one can hide from the omnipresent and omniscient God. No one can escape, as we see repeatedly in Revelation, the fiery gaze of the Lamb (1:14; 2:18; 19:12). Can we hide from Him who sees all things? Sin truly makes us stupid. It turns us into fools.

No One Can Stand Before Divine Judgment (6:17)

The time of Jacob's trouble is here (Jer 30:7). Daniel's seventieth week is on us (Dan 9:24-27). The great tribulation has come (Rev 7:14). The Day of the Lord has arrived. The great day of the wrath of the Lamb visits planet Earth. Only one question remains: "Who can stand?" The answer, of course, is, "No one!" No one can stand! Rather than turn to Christ in faith, they hide in fear. And according to verse 16, *they know from whom they are hiding!* They know who has come and what has come. Knowing it is the Lord and His judgment, they run rather than repent. They flee rather than turn to Christ in faith. The great and awesome Day of the Lord is here. The end has finally arrived. What will men do? What can they do? No one can stand before divine judgment. No one. Craig Keener is right:

> The impact on the reader is . . . complete: There is no
> security, no firm ground to stand on, nothing in the universe
> to depend on except God himself. The rest of creation will
> collapse. (*Revelation*, 225)

Conclusion

A great day is coming for every one of us when we will come face-to-face with the Lamb. We will either stand with Him in His salvation or stand before Him at His judgment. We will either rejoice in His glorious grace or be terrified before His righteous wrath. Grace or wrath? Forgiveness or condemnation? Where will you stand? Take your stand for the Lamb, King Jesus, now. A day is coming when it will be too late.

Reflect and Discuss

1. What comes to your mind when you think of a lamb? a lion? How does Jesus embody characteristics of both of these animals?
2. Why is the stereotypical picture of Jesus as simply "meek and mild" inadequate to understand who He is? What images and scenes from Scripture fail to line up with this simplistic portrayal?
3. Why does faithfulness to the Word and to the testimony of Christ so often lead to suffering and persecution? How does God view this suffering?
4. Why is it acceptable for the martyrs to call for God to avenge their death?
5. What are some burdens on your heart that need to be poured out to the Lord in prayer?
6. What comfort does God's sovereignty give to believers as they experience persecution? When have you faced opposition because of your faith and had to trust in the Lord's perfect plan?
7. Why do we not have to wonder if Jesus has returned? What does this text tell us about "the Day of the Lord"?
8. Why will social and economic statuses not matter at the time of judgment?
9. In this passage those faced with judgment try to avoid it by seeking death. What is your natural response when faced with judgment and accountability for your sins and failures?
10. If people know Christ is bringing judgment, why do they still flee rather than repent?

The Lamb Will Shepherd the Nations

REVELATION 7:1-17

Main Idea: Jesus is the sacrificial Lamb who will also shepherd the nations and receive worship from all the peoples of the world.

I. **We Are Sealed and Protected by the Lamb (7:1-8).**
   A.   In wrath the Lord shows mercy (7:1-3).
   B.   Seeing unfaithfulness, the Lord still keeps His promise (7:4-8).
II. **We Are Saved and Made Pure Through the Lamb (7:9-12).**
   A.   The scope of His salvation is global (7:9-10).
   B.   The scope of His salvation is glorious (7:11-12).
III. **We Are Satisfied and Provided For in the Lamb (7:13-17).**
   A.   He makes us clean (7:13-14).
   B.   He lets us serve (7:15).
   C.   He gives us His presence (7:15).
   D.   He provides us our needs (7:16).
   E.   He promises us to be our shepherd (7:17).

First Peter 2:24-25 reads, "You have been healed by His wounds. For you were like sheep going astray, but you have now returned to the Shepherd and Guardian of your souls." *The Message* says it like this: "His wounds became your healing. You were lost sheep with no idea who you were or where you were going. Now you're named and kept for good by the shepherd of your souls."

We all desperately need a Shepherd for our souls, don't we? The nations need a Shepherd for their souls who will, as Revelation 7:17 promises, "guide them to springs of living water, and . . . wipe away every tear from their eyes." How can He do this? He can do it because He washed us clean and made our robes "white in the blood of the Lamb" (7:14). The Lamb, who is a Lion (Rev 5), is also the one who is our Shepherd.

Revelation 7 has been the subject of much discussion and disagreement, especially verses 1-8. Is the "144,000 sealed from every tribe of the Israelites" (1) 144,000 Jehovah's Witnesses who will reign in heaven? (2) selected Sabbatarians who honor and worship on the seventh day of the week? (3) the church as the "new Israel" and thus the redeemed of all the ages symbolically represented? Or are they (4) Jewish believers who are saved and sealed for service during what John calls "the great tribulation" (7:14) and "the great day of Their wrath" (6:17)? While I do have my own view and will briefly explain it, to wrestle excessively over this is to miss the fact that Jew and Gentile alike will be gathered around the throne and the Lamb in heaven (7:9) and that the focus of this text is the worship of this Lamb who will shepherd all the nations. In other words, this is one of the greatest texts in the whole Bible to encourage a passionate, radical, and sacrificial missionary agenda because the Lord Jesus has promised us that every *ethne*, every nation, will be there!

Revelation 7 is an interlude, parenthesis, or complementary perspective between the sixth and seventh seals. It consists of two visions (vv. 1-8 and 9-17), and it provides an answer to the ominous question that concludes chapter 6: Who can stand in the day of the Lamb's wrath? The answer is, those who have "the seal of the living God" (7:2). Robert Mounce says it well: "The vision contrasts the security and blessedness that await the faithful with the panic of a pagan world fleeing from judgment" (*Revelation*, 154).

We Are Sealed and Protected by the Lamb
REVELATION 7:1-8

In chapter 6 the Lamb begins to unfold the eschatological scroll introduced in chapter 5. He breaks six of the seven seals, and we are introduced to the Four Horsemen of the Apocalypse. Massive destruction sweeps across the earth (6:1-8), martyred saints in heaven cry for justice (6:9-12), and those on the earth seek to hide from Him who is seated on the throne (God the Father) and from the Lamb (God the Son; 6:16). It appears no one will survive, much less stand against the righteous wrath of God. But then we see two wonderful truths emerge: In wrath the Lord shows mercy (see Hab 3:2), and the Lord keeps His promise.

In Wrath the Lord Shows Mercy (7:1-3)

"After this," after the six seals of chapter 6, John saw "four angels standing at the four corners of the earth," a figure of speech implying the four directional points of the compass. They are said to be holding back four winds of judgment that have the power "to harm earth and sea"

(7:2), "the earth or the sea or the trees" (7:3). They are agents of righteous judgment and destruction, and they are ready to act.

However, their hand of judgment is stayed, or at least delayed. In this apocalyptic vision John sees "another angel . . . rise up from the east" (7:2). A number of Bible teachers have pointed out that some good things in Scripture come from or are in the east (Gen 2:8; Ezek 43:2; Matt 2:1; Luke 1:78; Rev 22:16). This angel is not a messenger of destruction and death but one of grace and mercy. He has with him "the seal of the living God" (7:2), a seal with which he will mark "the slaves of our God on their foreheads." Revelation 14:1 informs us this seal is the name of the Lamb and the name of the Father (see 22:4). This sealing—with Old Testament roots in Ezekiel 9:4—is a sign, a promise of divine *possession* and *protection*. Gordon Fee notes,

> The "seal" in this case is the stamp of divine ownership and authenticity; thus it functions as a divine commitment that God's own people will not experience the divine wrath when it is poured out. . . . At the same time . . . this marking of the foreheads of God's servants stands in deliberate contrast to the later marking on the foreheads of followers of the "beast out of the earth" in chapter 13:16-17. (*Revelation*, 107)

In wrath our God shows mercy.

Seeing Unfaithfulness, the Lord Still Keeps His Promise (7:4-8)

"The seal of the living God" (used 14 times in the New Testament; see also Josh 3:10; Ps 42:2; Hos 1:10), the one true God who stands in contrast to all false gods and idols of this world, is now applied to 144,000 "from every tribe of the Israelites" (7:4). The number is carefully catalogued in verses 5-8. My own dogmatism over the correct interpretation of these verses has softened over the years. I have good friends and I know respected evangelicals who understand the verses differently than I do. And they make good arguments. They understand the 144,000 to be the church, the whole people of God.

Still, I remain convinced the 144,000 sons of Israel represents Jewish believers who are included in the one people of God and the great multitude of Revelation 7:9. I find this view to be consistent with and supported by seven important passages:

- The Abrahamic covenant of Genesis 12:1-3
- The Davidic covenant of 2 Samuel 7:12-16

- The new covenant of Jeremiah 31:31-34 (and vv. 35-37)
- The promise of Jesus to the apostles in Matthew 19:28
- The answer of Jesus to the kingdom question in Acts 1:6-8
- The prophecy and promise of Paul in Romans 11:25-29
- The depiction of the new Jerusalem in Revelation 21:12-14

Some would object and ask, What about the peculiarities in the list, specifically (1) Judah appearing first, (2) Levi being included, and (3) the absence of Dan and Ephraim? To these I would simply respond as follows:

- There are 19 different arrangements of the names of the tribes in the Old Testament, and this list is different from all of them.
- Judah is listed first because Messiah, our Lord Jesus, comes from Judah (see Gen 49:9-10; Rev 5:5).
- Levi, though not allotted a portion of land, is rightly involved in this sealing for security and service.
- Ephraim is replaced by Joseph possibly because of its history of idolatry and its allying with the enemies of Judah (Isa 7:2,5; Hos 5:3). Yet the inclusion of Joseph allows for the inclusion of Ephraim but without the mention of his name.
- Dan is omitted, replaced by Levi, because of its practice of gross idolatry. Further, Irenaeus (a second-century church father) noted the pre-Christian Jewish tradition that antichrist would come from Dan, and Hippolytus wrote, "As the Christ was born from the tribe of Judah, so will the Antichrist be born from the tribe of Dan" (Mounce, *Revelation*, 159–60). And Genesis 49:17 says, "Dan shall be a serpent in the way, a horned snake in the path, that bites the horse's heels, so that his rider falls backward." Finally, the *Testament of Dan* (5:6) says Satan is the prince of Dan.

Still, it seems that Ezekiel 48 and Mathew 19:28 make clear that all the tribes will be honored and share in the millennial reign of Christ. During this time Hebrew Christians will receive the Lamb's name and the Father's name as their seal (14:1) and for their service, again standing in stark contrast to those who receive the mark of the beast and follow antichrist (13:17; 14:11; 16:2; 19:20).

However, we miss the main point if we fail to see that our God in this day, in that day, and in every day, has His faithful servants who are His possession and have His protection. As unfaithful as Israel has been, and as unfaithful as we have been, our God, on the other hand, is completely and utterly faithful. Having sealed us with the Holy Spirit (2 Cor 1:22; Eph 1:13; 4:30), He maintains His covenant promises to His people. We find ourselves saved, safe, and secure. In the Lamb we have His stamp of approval!

We Are Saved and Made Pure Through the Lamb
REVELATION 7:9-12

John now sees a second vision. It complements the first, but it is significantly different. The first is on earth, while the second is in heaven. The first concerns "144,000 sons of Israel," but the second concerns "a great multitude no one could number" (7:9). I love what Craig Keener says of these verses: "Here the promised multitude is gathered from all nations; the hope of the gospel has touched all people" (*Revelation*, 243). Keener is right on target. Two wonderful aspects of this "gospel of the Lamb" have indeed touched all peoples.

The Scope of His Salvation Is Global (7:9-10)

After seeing the 144,000, John sees a vast multitude that is innumerable "from every nation, tribe, people, and language" (see 5:9; 11:9; 13:7; 14:6). Echoing God's promise to Abraham in Genesis 15:5 and 32:12, their number is like the stars of heaven and the sand of the sea. In this massive throng of the redeemed in heaven, there is not the slightest hint of bigotry, ethnocentrism, prejudice, or racism. Of the 11,243 people groups in the world, each is present and represented. Of the 3,056 people groups currently unengaged, each is represented (IMB, Mar. 7, 2014). Of the 3.7 billion persons still not having an adequate opportunity to hear the gospel, the Lamb is reaching out and calling them unto Himself by the Spirit and through His people. The gospel is going to be heard and believed among all the peoples of the earth. The nations will rejoice! The nations will worship!

Four things are said about these people in heaven:

- *Their location*—They stand before the throne (of God) and before the Lamb. Now the question of 6:17 is answered as to who can stand. It is the redeemed!
- *Their clothing*—They are clothed permanently in white robes of victory and purity; they stand before God in the imputed, perfect righteousness of the Lamb (7:14).

- *Their instruments of worship*—They have palm branches of joy, celebration, and praise.
- *Their confession*—They are crying out (continually) in a loud voice (see 7:2), "Salvation belongs to our God, who is seated on the throne, and to the Lamb!" Deliverance from sin and victory over Satan are ours because of the Father on the throne and the Son (Lamb) at His side.

Indeed, the scope of His salvation is global!

The Scope of His Salvation Is Glorious (7:11-12)

Once more the angels join in the worship of heaven (see 5:11-14). "All" the angels were standing around the throne. This looks back to the "thousands of thousands" in 5:11. Like the elders in 5:14 the angels fell on their faces before the Lord. This scene is holy; this time is sacred. Like the saints in verse 10, they speak not of *what God has done* but to *who God is.* Sandwiching a sevenfold blessing is the word "Amen." And in their sevenfold blessing they affirm what the saints have said and then add their own words of adoration, praise, and worship:

- *blessing (eulogia)*—a good word, a praise
- *glory (doxa)*—honor derived from one's character and a good reputation; it is the radiance or outshining of the divine person
- *wisdom (sophia)*—divine knowledge and perspective on all things, especially in the outworking of God's plan of salvation
- *thanksgiving (eucharistia)*—we get our word *eucharist* from it
- *honor (timē)*—esteem; public and deserved recognition (see 4:11; 5:12-13)
- *power (dunamis)*—God's omnipotence; His ability to act as He wills
- *strength (ischus)*—often related to God's mighty acts in salvation history

All of this has one focus, one direction, one and only one deserving object: "to our God forever and ever" (7:12). This word of worship is not temporary; it is eternal. It is not for a moment but forever. This is the praise of all nations and angels that is ringing through the corridors of heaven.

Once again, as we saw in chapter 5, the theme of the Lamb is prominent (7:9,10,14,17), as it is throughout Scripture, beginning in Genesis and culminating in Revelation. In Genesis 22 God tells Abraham to sacrifice his only son, Isaac. When the boy asks his father, "Where is the lamb for the burnt offering?" Abraham answers, "God Himself will provide the lamb for the burnt offering, my son" (22:7-8). On that occasion God would provide a ram (22:13). Two thousand years later He would provide the Lamb.

In Exodus 12:5 we are told that the Passover must be sacrificed and that the lamb must be without blemish. In Isaiah 53 we meet the messianic Suffering Servant of the Lord. We are told in verse 7 that He was led as a lamb to slaughter. We then come to the New Testament and the ministry of John the Baptist, who seeing the Lord Jesus declares, "Here is the Lamb of God who takes away the sin of the world" (John 1:29). Now, in Revelation, we see the eschatological warrior Lamb on the throne with His Father. He had been slaughtered, but now He stands as the omnipotent, omniscient, omnipresent resurrected Lamb—a Lamb who is a Lion and also, as we now see, a Shepherd.

We Are Satisfied and Provided For in the Lamb
REVELATION 7:13-17

This glorious vision of all nations gathered around the throne and the Lamb now reaches a crescendo, but it also takes a surprising turn. As it does, blessings flow in our direction that are too great to imagine. These blessings must be shared with the nations that the Lamb will shepherd. That is His intention. That gives us our mission.

He Made Us Clean (7:13-14)

One of the elders (see 4:4,10-11; 5:5-6,8,11), one of the redeemed, speaks to John, asking him the identity of the great multitude clothed in white robes (7:13). John bats the ball back, no doubt out of ignorance or at least uncertainty, and says to the elder, "Sir, you know" their identity. The elder responds (7:14) directly and to the point, "These are the ones coming out of the great tribulation. They washed their robes and made them white in the blood of the Lamb."

I am in basic agreement with Mounce:

> The use of the definite article in the phrase "the great tribulation" indicated that the angel is referring primarily to that final series of woes which will immediately precede the end. It is the hour of trial that is to come upon the whole world (3:10). It is not "the awesome totality of tribulation

which from century to century has been the experience of the
people of God" nor does it correspond to "the entire history
of the church—past, present, and future." It is that specific
period of distress and cruel persecution which will take place
prior to the return of Christ. Prophesied by Daniel (12:1)
and reflected on the screen of history at the fall of Jerusalem
(Mark 13:19 and parallels), it finds its fulfillment in that final
persecution which supplies the full complement of Christian
martyrs (6:11). . . . Their robes are white by virtue of the
redemptive death of the Lamb. Their rewards are those of
all the faithful. Persecution has always been the lot of those
who follow the Lamb (John 16:33; 2 Tim 3:12). The intensity
of the final conflict of righteousness and evil will rise to such
a pitch as to become *the great tribulation.* (*Revelation*, 164,
emphasis in original)

While I do think this is the best understanding of the text, what we
all can agree and focus on is the wonderful truth, "They washed their
robes and made them white in the blood of the Lamb." The metaphor
is striking and even paradoxical, perhaps drawn from Isaiah 1:18. The
Lamb took our filthy, soiled, ugly garments of sin and plunged them
into His red, pure blood (His death), and miraculously and supernaturally they come out white, pure, clean.

Corrie ten Boom, Christian Holocaust survivor and protector of
Jewish persons, said of the cleansing and redeeming blood of the Lord
Jesus,

The blood of Jesus Christ has great power! There is perhaps
not a phrase in the Bible that is so full of secret truth as is
"the blood of Jesus." It is the secret of His incarnation, when
Jesus took on flesh and blood; the secret of His obedience
unto death, when He gave His life at the cross of Calvary; the
secret of His love that went beyond all understanding when
He bought us with His blood; the secret of the enemy and
the secret of our eternal salvation. (Quoted in Simcox, "The
Greatest Sacrifice," 14–15)

So it is that these saints have experienced the truth sung by many
Christians:

There is a fountain filled with blood,
drawn from Immanuel's veins.
And sinners plunged beneath that flood
lose all their guilty stains.

He Lets Us Serve (7:15)

Verses 15-17 "form a poetic stanza. . . . They depict the eternal blessings of God shared inclusively by the redeemed" (Smalley, *Revelation*,
198). Once again the redeemed are located "before the throne of God,"
granted access by virtue of the fact "they washed their robes and made
them white in the blood of the Lamb" (7:14).

Here they serve in priestly and worshipful service day and night
(i.e., continually) in His temple. Later (21:22), John says, "I did not see
a sanctuary in it [i.e., in the new Jerusalem], because the Lord God the
Almighty and the Lamb are its sanctuary."

In Luke 2:37 it is said of the prophetess Anna, "She did not leave the
temple complex, serving [this is the same Greek word] God night and
day with fasting and prayers." Any thought of heaven being a boring and
dull place is banished forever by the beautiful simplicity of this verse.
For all of eternity it will be our delightful and joyful privilege to serve
in the worship of Him who saved us by washing us clean by His blood.

He Gives Us His Presence (7:15)

"The One seated on the throne will shelter them" and us. Literally, "He
will spread His tent [tabernacle] over them." This calls to mind the tabernacle in the wilderness (Exod 26–30), the pillar of cloud and of fire
(Exod 13:21-22), the *shekinah* glory of God's radiant presence in the
midst of His people (Exod 40:34-38), and the incarnation of the Son
(John 1:14). God is with them, right there in their midst. Never again
will they feel forsaken; never again will they be tortured and tormented.
They will enjoy the supreme presence and protection of the Lord God
Himself forever and ever.

He Provides Us Our Needs (7:16)

Hunger and thirst were constant obstacles and threats in the ancient
world. They remain so for much of our world today, but not so in heaven.
Starvation, thirst, and the burning heat of the sun will find no place in
heaven. This is almost a direct contrast with what the Four Horsemen

bring in 6:1-8. They curse but God blesses. They bring suffering and sorrow, but God gives us satisfaction.

The language here draws on Isaiah 49:10 and Isaiah's description of returning exiles from Babylon. It also recalls the words of Jesus in Matthew 5:6; John 4:14; 6:35; and 7:37. Every need is met by the Lamb who is, as we now see, our Shepherd.

He Promises Us to Be Our Shepherd (7:17)

In chapter 5 we saw a Lamb who is also a Lion. Now we see a Lamb who is also a Shepherd. And what a Shepherd He is! He is a Shepherd-King in the midst of the throne. He is like the Shepherd-King in the Song of Songs. He is like the Lord our Shepherd in Psalm 23, one who "will guide them to springs of living waters." He is the Good Shepherd of John 10 who "will wipe away every tear from their eyes."

The Shepherd image is one of the richest and most beloved in all of Scripture. Everyone needs a Shepherd of their soul. We find this image taking shape when God called a little shepherd boy named David to be Israel's king. It is said of that shepherd he was a man after God's own heart (1 Sam 13:14; Acts 13:22). Later that shepherd-king would pen the most beloved song in the entire Psalter, where we are taught, "The LORD is my shepherd," and because He is, I have all I need (Ps 23:1). Then, when the nation is in exile, having been abused by those who should have been "shepherds of Israel" (Ezek 34:2), God makes a promise to His people:

> "I will appoint over them a single shepherd, My servant David, and he will shepherd them. He will tend them himself and will be their shepherd." (Ezek 34:23)

And in Micah 5:2-4, His promised shepherd is said to come out of Bethlehem, which means "the house of bread." Of Him it is promised, "He will stand and shepherd them in the strength of Yahweh, in the majestic name of Yahweh His God. They will live securely, for then His greatness will extend to the ends of the earth." Micah 5:5 adds, "He will be their peace."

We then arrive to the New Testament where all of these Old Testament promises and themes find their fulfillment in the "good shepherd" of John 10, the "great Shepherd" of Hebrews 13:20, the "chief Shepherd" of 1 Peter 5:4, the Shepherd of souls of 1 Peter 2:25, and the Shepherd-King of Revelation 7:17. What a Shepherd He is!

Conclusion

Several years ago I came across an article titled "The Room." Only recently did I discover it was written by my friend Joshua Harris (it first appeared in *New Attitude*, 1995 and is used here by permission). It is a real dream that Joshua had, and it beautifully illustrates why we—why the nations—need to hear about and know this Lamb who is a Shepherd, a Shepherd of our souls.

In that place between wakefulness and dreams, I found myself in "the room." There were no distinguishing features save for the one wall covered with small index card files. They were like the ones in libraries that list titles by author or subject in alphabetical order. But these files, which stretched from floor to ceiling and seemingly endlessly in either direction, had very different headings. As I drew near the wall of files, the first to catch my attention was one that read "Girls I Have Liked." I opened it and began flipping through the cards. I quickly shut it, shocked to realize that I recognized the names written on each one.

And then without being told, I knew exactly where I was. This lifeless room and its small files was a crude catalog system for my life. Here were written the thoughts and actions of my every moment, big and small, in detail my memory couldn't match.

A sense of wonder and curiosity, coupled with horror, stirred within me and I began randomly opening files and exploring their content. Some brought joy and sweet memories, others a sense of shame and regret so intense that I would look over my shoulder to see if anyone was watching. A file named "Friends" was next to one marked "Friends I Have Betrayed."

The titles ranged from the mundane to the outright weird. "Books I Have Read," "Lies I Have Told," "Comfort I Have Given," "Jokes I Have Laughed At." Some were almost hilarious in their exactness: "Things I've Yelled at My Brother." Others I couldn't laugh at: "Things I Have Done in My Anger," "Things I Have Muttered under My Breath at My Parents." I never ceased to be surprised by the contents. Often there were many more cards than I expected. Sometimes fewer than I hoped.

I was overwhelmed by the sheer volume of the life I had lived. Could it be possible that I had the time in my [brief life] to write each of these thousands or even millions of cards? But each card confirmed the truth. Each was written in my own handwriting. Each signed with my signature.

When I pulled out the file marked "Songs I Have Listened To," I realized the files grew to contain their contents. The cards were packed tightly, and yet after two or three yards, I hadn't found the end of the file. I shut it, shamed, not so much by the quality of music, but more by the vast amount of time I knew that file represented.

When I came to a file marked "Lustful Thoughts," I felt a chill run through my body. I pulled the file out only an inch, not willing to test its size, and drew out a card. I shuddered at its content. I felt sick to think that such a moment had been recorded.

An almost animal rage broke on me. One thought dominated my mind: "No one must ever see these cards! No one must ever see this room! I have to destroy them!" In an insane frenzy I yanked the file out. Its size didn't matter now. I had to empty it and burn the cards. But as I took it at one end and began pounding it on the floor, I could not dislodge a single card. I became desperate and pulled out a card, only to find it as strong as steel when I tried to tear it.

Defeated and utterly helpless, I returned the file to its slot. Leaning my forehead against the wall, I let out a long, self-pitying sigh. And then I saw it. The title card bore "People I Have Shared the Gospel With." The handle was brighter than those around it, newer, almost unused. I pulled on its handle and a small box not more than three inches long fell into my hands. I could count the cards it contained on one hand.

And then the tears came. I began to weep. Sobs so deep that the hurt started in my stomach and shook through me. I fell on my knees and cried. I cried out of shame, from the overwhelming shame of it all. The rows of file shelves swirled in my tear-filled eyes. No one must ever, ever know of this room. I must lock it up and hide the key.

But then as I pushed away the tears, I saw Him. No, please not Him. Oh, anyone but Jesus.

I watched helplessly as He began to open the files and read the cards. I couldn't bear to watch His response. And in the moments I could bring myself to look at His face, I saw a sorrow deeper than my own. He seemed to intuitively go to the worst boxes. Why did He have to read every one?

Finally, He turned and looked at me from across the room. He looked at me with pity in His eyes. But this was a pity that didn't anger me. I dropped my head, covered my face with my hands, and began to cry again. He walked over and put His arm around me. He could have said so many things. But He didn't say a word. He just cried with me.

Then He got up and walked back to the wall of files. Starting at one end of the room, He took out a file and, one by one, began to sign His name over mine on each card.

"No!" I shouted rushing to Him. All I could find to say was "No, no," as I tried to pull the card from Him. His name shouldn't be on these cards. But there it was, written in red so rich, so dark, so alive. The name of Jesus covered mine. It was written with His blood.

He gently took the card back. He smiled a gentle smile and began to sign the cards. I don't think I'll ever understand how He did it so quickly, but the next instant it seemed I heard Him close the last file and walk back to my side. He placed His hand on my shoulder and said, "It is finished."

I stood up, and He led me out of the room. There was no lock on its door. There were still cards to be written. (*New Attitude*).

Yes, there are still cards to be written. But praise His name, each and every one has been covered with His name and by His blood. Hallelujah! What a Shepherd! Hallelujah! What a Savior!

Reflect and Discuss

1. What does it mean for Jesus to be the "Shepherd of our souls"?
2. How does the Lord show mercy, even in wrath? Does this mean God is indecisive?
3. How should we understand the 144,000? What are the options? What is the main point we need to gather from these worshipers in this passage?

4. When has the Lord proved Himself faithful in your life despite your own unfaithfulness?
5. How might the vision of Revelation 7:9 inform and shape out missionary efforts?
6. What does it mean to ascribe to the Lord the characteristics of Revelation 7:12? How do you honor the Lord with each of these praises in your own life?
7. How does the blood of Jesus make us clean?
8. Why do you think some think of heaven as a boring and monotonous place? How do these verses provide an alternative picture?
9. In these verses the Lord provides for His people's every need and counteracts their greatest threats (see 7:16). How have you seen the Lord provide for your needs, and what threats do you long to see Him address?
10. Do a word search of *shepherd* in the Bible. How does Jesus fulfill or give new meaning to each of these images as He relates to His redeemed bride?

Prayers in Heaven / Judgment on Earth

REVELATION 8:1-12

Main Idea: God responds to the prayers of His people by bringing judgment on the earth that vindicates their faithfulness and demonstrates His sovereignty.

I. **Jesus Christ Has All Authority (8:1-2).**
   A. His authority is awesome to contemplate (8:1).
   B. His authority is delegated to angels (8:2).
II. **The Prayers of the Saints Are Gathered in Heaven (8:3-6).**
   A. Our prayers rise before God in heaven (8:3-4).
   B. Our prayers return in judgment to the earth (8:5-6).
III. **Judgment on Earth Follows from Our Pleas to God (8:7-12).**
   A. God is sovereign in judgment over the earth (8: 7).
   B. God is sovereign in judgment over the seas (8:8-9).
   C. God is sovereign in judgment over the rivers and springs (8:10-11).
   D. God is sovereign in judgment over the starry heavens (8:12).

Few spiritual disciplines are more difficult to cultivate than the discipline of prayer. One reason is that it is hard work. Another is that we fail to see the immediate benefits. It seems to be wasted effort. However, that latter opinion is misguided and misinformed. Oswald Chambers got it right when he said, "Prayer does not fit us for the greater work; prayer is the greater work" (*My Utmost for His Highest,* October 17). If you doubt this, you need only look to Revelation 8 to see what God does with our prayers in the context of future and climactic spiritual warfare.

Revelation 8–9 contains the second great series of judgments: the seven trumpets. Revelation began with a greeting from the Trinity (1:1-8) and a glorious vision of the exalted Lord Jesus who walks among His churches (1:9-20). Seven letters to seven specific historical churches make up chapters 2–3, and then a significant turn takes place in 4:1. There John is told, "Come up here, and I will show you what must take place after this." John is taken in the Spirit both to *heaven* and into the *future* as God shows to His servant His plan for the consummation of

167

167

history. Chapters 4–5 are a glorious vision of two parts: chapter 4 focuses on God the Father, the Lord of *creation*, while chapter 5 focuses on God the Son, the Lord of *redemption*. Thus by creation and redemption God has the right to do with this earth and its inhabitants as He pleases. Chapter 6 begins the divine account of the tribulation, the Day of the Lord, Daniel's seventieth week. The nineteenth chapter will bring it to its rightful conclusion with the second coming of Jesus Christ to the earth to establish His earthly millennial kingdom. Chapter 6 contains the seal judgments and introduces us to the Four Horsemen of the Apocalypse. Chapter 7 is something of an interlude or parenthesis, a break in the action, that teaches us that in the midst of great judgment there is still mercy, God is not through with the Jews, and the tribulation will also be a time of great revival as "a vast multitude . . . which no one could number" (7:9) will "[wash] their robes and [make] them white in the blood of the Lamb" (7:14). Now, however, the judgment of God on planet Earth resumes with the blowing of the trumpets. The seventh seal contains the seven trumpets.

What unfolds is an amazing truth: our prayers ascend to heaven and unleash the power of God in judgment on evil. They matter! They work for God's glory and our good. Alfred Lord Tennyson said, "More things are wrought by prayer than this world dreams of." I suspect, in light of Revelation, he had no idea how true his words were!

Jesus Christ Has All Authority
REVELATION 8:1-2

It is well said, "It is often quietest before the storm." The stillness and silence can almost take your breath away in anticipation of what may come. Those words are appropriate when they are applied to the trumpet judgments of Revelation 8. Revelation 8:1 speaks of silence in heaven but only for half an hour, a short time. Judgment almost too great to imagine will quickly follow, and when it is finished, one-third of God's glorious creation will be gone, destroyed by the God who made it.

These judgments recall the plagues God poured out on Egypt and the story of Joshua and the battle of Jericho. In both of those scenes God moved in response to the cries of His people. Now God will do it again as the sovereign Lord Jesus acts in response to the prayers of His people. The prayers of God's people are an important theme in Revelation. They were first mentioned in 5:8. In 6:10 we saw martyred believers crying with loud voices for justice. Now in chapter 8 the prayers of the saints are noted again (8:3-4). In light of the judgments that have preceded (Rev 6) and those that will follow (Rev 8–9; 15–16), the response of King Jesus to the prayers of His people takes on an even greater significance.

His Authority Is Awesome to Contemplate (8:1)

"Prayer lays hold of God's plan and becomes the link between His will and its accomplishment on earth."—Marvin J. Newell

The Lamb who took the scroll from the Father in 5:7 and began to open the seals in 6:1 now breaks the seventh seal. All of heaven is suddenly silent "for about half an hour," which is symbolic of a short period of time. The heavenly hosts wait with anticipation to see what the Lord Jesus, the warrior Lion/Lamb will do next as He judges the earth for its idolatries, immorality, and rebellion against His rightful authority.

Why is heaven silent? Some believe it allows time for God to hear the prayers of the saints in verses 3-4. That is certainly possible. What is more certain is, "It is a dramatic pause that makes even more impressive the judgments about to fall upon the earth" (Mounce, *Revelation*, 170). A similar idea can be seen in several Old Testament passages:

The Lord is in His holy temple; let everyone on earth be silent in His presence. (Hab 2:20)

Be silent in the presence of the Lord God, for the Day of the Lord is near. (Zeph 1:7)

Let all people be silent before the Lord, for He is coming from His holy dwelling. (Zech 2:13)

John MacArthur summarizes the situation succinctly when he says, "The hour of God's final judgment had come—the hour when the saints will be vindicated, sin punished, Satan vanquished, and Christ exalted" (*Revelation 1–11*, 238).

His Authority Is Delegated to Angels (8:2)

"We should wrestle in prayer and fasting for the things we know are God's will in our lives and families and our church and our city and our world. But by and

> large we should probably leave it to God how he will
> use angels to get his work done."—John Piper

God does indeed use His angels to carry out His will. Some of the time it is in specific response to our prayers. Daniel 10 and an angel's response to Daniel's prayer makes this clear (see vv. 12-14). Angels and demons are engaged in warfare in the spiritual realm in a manner we could never truly imagine. Now, in Revelation 8:2, our sovereign Lord gives seven trumpets to "the seven angels who stand in the presence of God." The nonbiblical Jewish book *1 Enoch* 20:2-8 makes reference to seven angels who stand before God and names them: Uriel, Raphael, Raquel, Michael, Saraqael, Gabriel, and Remeil. Trumpets, according to Numbers 10, called the people together, announced war, and proclaimed special times and events. They were sounded at Mount Sinai when the law was given (Exod 19:16-19), when Jericho fell (Jos 6:13-16), and when the king was enthroned (1 Kgs 1:34,39). A trumpet will sound at the rapture (1 Thess 4:13-18) and when Christ returns (Matt 24:31). These in chapter 8 are eschatological trumpets of judgment. Christ, with all authority in heaven and on earth (Matt 28:18-20), summons His angels to carry out His will on earth.

The Prayers of the Saints Are Gathered in Heaven
REVELATION 8:3-6

> "When there is no hope on the horizontal level, there's
> always hope on the vertical level." —Adrian Rogers

Prayer activates us and engages us in spiritual warfare in the present and also the future. And it is not a battle, a war, lightly to be entered. Ephesians 6:18 tells us that prayer is essential as we engage in spiritual battle, and must be constant, alert, and persevering. We should offer these prayers and supplications for ourselves and "for all the saints."

David Platt notes several aspects of the spiritual conflict we are to engage. Looking at warfare prayer in the context of Revelation 8–11, he says,

1. Our battle is fierce!—There are demons who are fighting you and want to destroy you.
2. Our prayers are effective!—Our cries go up and His kingdom comes down.

3. Our God is faithful!—He will demonstrate His power, vindicate His people, extend His mercy, and uphold His justice. ("Life of the Christian")

Most Christians do not consider prayer to be anything at all like this. But it is! Look now at the presence of our prayers in heaven and the power they unleash.

Our Prayers Rise Before God in Heaven (8:3-4)

> "It is a good fall when a man falls on his
> knees." —Charles Spurgeon

"Another angel," separate from the seven trumpeters, comes before the altar of God "with a gold incense burner" (see Exod 30:1-10; 2 Kgs 6:22; Heb 9:4). We know this is the altar of incense because "He was given a large amount of incense to offer." However, something unique and unusual is to be mixed with the incense as he offers it before "the gold altar in front of the throne." It is "the prayers of all the saints"! Mixed, both the incense and the prayers of the saints rise as a sweet aroma and fragrance "in the presence of God." Mounce again is helpful: "The scene in heaven suggests that there is something sacrificial about genuine prayer. Both the believer and his prayer enter the presence of God by way of the altar" (*Revelation*, 175).

For centuries the saints of God have talked to God in prayer, praying for His kingdom, asking for His will to be done, for His kingdom to come on earth. Those prayers have not been in vain. Those prayers have been heard. Those prayers that Satan sought to thwart and block by his demonic host got through to heaven. Now they ascend before God, and He delights in their fragrance. In some inexplicable, mysterious providence, they become the means whereby God moves into action and brings His kingdom. William Hendriksen says,

> The Throne-Occupant sees the sighs and sufferings, he hears
> the request and the thanksgiving of his children who are
> in the midst of tribulation. The angel understands this: he
> realizes that the prayers are heard. Hence, he takes the censer,
> now emptied of its incense, and fills it with fire of the altar,
> and empties it upon the earth; that is *God has heard the prayers
> of the saints, and the judgments upon earth are his answer to them.*
> (*More than Conquerors*, 142, emphasis in original)

Our Prayers Return in Judgment to the Earth (8:5-6)

> "Prayer is not getting man's will done in heaven,
> but getting God's will done on earth. It is not
> overcoming God's reluctance but laying hold
> of God's willingness."—Richard Trench

The angel takes the incense burner filled with fire from the altar and hurls it to the earth. There follows "rumblings of thunder, flashes of lightning, and an earthquake." A storm is coming, flowing out of the prayers of verses 3-4. The language of these verses is reminiscent of Sinai with its thunder, lightning, and earthquake (Exod 19:16-19), and the vision of Ezekiel 10:2-7 where a man clothed in linen fills his hands with coals and scatters them over the city. Intercession has turned to judgment not according to man's timetable but God's! The angel priest casts fire onto the earth followed by harbingers of impending storm and disaster. The cosmos trembles before the presence and power of its Creator. A day of reckoning has arrived: "The seven angels are prepared to blow" (8:7).

Romans 12:19 reminds us, "Friends, do not avenge yourselves; instead, leave room for His wrath. For it is written, 'Vengeance belongs to Me; I will repay,' says the Lord" (see Deut 32:35; Heb 10:30). A day is coming when God will make things right. The trumpet judgments are a portion of that day. We need to wait on Him. He hears our prayers. He will not be late. He will be right on time.

Judgment on Earth Follows from Our Pleas to God
REVELATION 8:7-12

> "God's delays aren't God's denials."—Adrian Rogers

In Matthew 6:9-13 we find what we call "the model prayer." There Jesus tells us in verse 10 to pray, "Your kingdom come. Your will be done on earth as it is in heaven." That prayer is once more being answered in the trumpet judgments of Revelation 8–9. The seal judgments of chapter 6 saw the destruction of a fourth of the earth (6:8). The trumpet judgments will see the destruction and devastation of a third of the earth. The word *third* occurs thirteen times in chapter 8, and each is like the tolling of a bell with the knell of judgment.

The precise nature of each trumpet is not altogether clear, though the end results are plain and tragic. The judgments recall the plagues of Exodus, which God visited on Pharaoh and the Egyptians. The first four trumpets of chapter 8 are natural in that they affect the land, salt water, freshwater, and stellar bodies. The fifth and sixth trumpets of chapter 9 unleash demonic forces that torment and then kill. The seventh trumpet (11:15-19) will constitute the seven bowls of chapter 16. In the blowing of the first four, facets of God's sovereignty over His creation are revealed as He acts in response to the pleas of His people.

God Is Sovereign in Judgment over the Earth (8:7)

> "When we depend on our organizations, we get what
> organizations can do; when we depend on education,
> we get what education can do; when we depend on
> man, we get what man can do; but when we depend
> on God, we get what God can do."—A. C. Dixon

The first of the angels "prepared to blow." He blew and "hail and fire, mixed with blood, were hurled to the earth. So a third of the earth was burned up, a third of the trees were burned up, and all the green grass was burned up." The imagery is that of the seventh plague God brought on Egypt in Exodus 9:13-35, with allusion also to Joel's prophecy (Joel 2:31; Acts 2:19). "Burned up" occurs three times in just one verse. Blood is probably symbolic of terrible judgment. Whatever this is, great devastation follows this cosmic storm that had its genesis in heaven (Mounce, *Revelation*, 178). That it is a third indicates that,

> although God is bringing punishment on the earth, it is not as
> yet complete and final. The purpose of the visitation is to warn
> people of the full wrath of God yet to fall, and in so doing to
> bring them to repentance. (Ibid.)

Tragically, most will not repent, as 9:20-21 painfully reveals. These words fulfill what Jesus promised and prophesized in Luke 21:25-28. Patterns of this judgment have occurred throughout history. However, in the Day of the Lord, it reaches a crescendo. As Osborne says, "Nothing will escape this terrible judgment" (*Revelation*, 351). Whatever these images represent, the impact should rattle our bones in awe of this God.

God Is Sovereign in Judgment over the Seas (8:8-9)

> "Prayer releases the grip of Satan's power;
> prayerlessness increases it. That is why prayer is
> so exhausting and so vital."—Alan Redpath

Romans 8:22 reminds us that all creation has been groaning since Adam and Eve were defeated by Satan in the garden of Eden (Gen 3). One can only imagine its pain during this time of horrific and cataclysmic judgment. However, in response to the prayers of the saints, these judgments are actually Satan's defeat and a prelude to creation's redemption.

John sees "something like a great mountain ablaze with fire was hurled into the sea." The apocalyptic vision cannot be fully captured with human language. The results, however, are "a third of the sea became blood, a third of the living creatures in the sea died, and a third of the ships were destroyed." The judgment recalls the first Egyptian plague where "the rivers were turned to blood, killing the fish and making the water undrinkable" (Exod 7:20-21) (Mounce, *Revelation*, 180). Osborne notes:

> The sea lanes were called the lifeblood of Rome because the
> Romans were so dependent on the sea for both food and
> commerce (see also Rev 18:17-19). Thus, this is even more
> devastating than the first plague. It is difficult to imagine such
> an extensive apocalyptic judgment. (*Revelation*, 353–54)

However, the judgment is partial not total. Time is running out for the defiant and idolatrous earth dwellers, but it is not completely gone. Not yet.

God Is Sovereign in Judgment over the Rivers and Springs (8:10-11)

> "No one is a firmer believer in the power of
> prayer than the devil; not that he practices
> it, but he suffers from it."—Guy King

Now the third trumpet blows and a great, blazing star named "Wormwood" falls from heaven on a third of the rivers and springs. The waters become wormwood, and many people die from its bitter poison. This judgment is both a parallel to the first Egyptian plague that contaminated the fresh water supply (Exod 7:20) and a reversal of the experience of the children of Israel in the wilderness at Marah, where the Lord made bitter water drinkable (Exod 15:22-25). The word "wormwood" appears only here in the New Testament. It "is mentioned eight times in the Old Testament, where it is associated with bitterness, poison, and death (Deut 29:18; Prov 5:4; Jer 9:15; 23:15; Lam 3:15,19; Amos 5:7; 6:12)" (MacArthur, *Revelation 1–11*, 249).

That it is a "third" again tells us it is partial. That it comes from heaven tells us it is a sovereign act of God in response to the pleas of His people in 8:3-4. It is not clear whether John intends the star to be understood naturally or supernaturally, as an angel (see 9:1) or possibly an asteroid. Again, its end result is indisputable. The springs and the rivers that provide our drinking water are poisoned, and many die as a result. The water becomes bitter and poisonous, and the inhabitants of the earth become even more familiar with the bitterness and death of God's just judgment.

God Is Sovereign in Judgment over the Starry Heavens (8:12)

> "God does nothing but by prayer, and
> everything with it."—John Wesley

The fourth trumpet sounds, and a third of the starry heavens are darkened with an accompanying effect of darkness on the earth. This plague looks back to the ninth plague in Egypt (Exod 10:21-23). Amos 5:18 teaches us that the Day of the Lord will be darkness, not light. Joel 2 says the Day of the Lord will be "a day of darkness and gloom, a day of clouds and dense overcast." The darkness of the fourth trumpet anticipates the demonic activity of chapter 9 and even greater sorrow.

We would be foolish to press the details of what we read in a crassly literal way. We would be equally foolish to simply symbolize these images away. They are symbols, but they represent real and catastrophic eschatological realities. The bottom line, as David Platt well says, is this: "Do not put your ultimate hope in created things. All things—even the most secure things like the light of the sun—all things in heaven and on earth are passing away" ("Life of the Christian"). Osborne summarizes well the impact God intended to make on finite humans who too often wish to shake their fist in God's face and scream, "I'll live my life my way!" He says,

> The purpose of the first four trumpet judgments is primarily
> to disprove the earthly gods and to show that Yahweh alone
> is on the throne. By recapitulating the Egyptian plagues,

God wants to make his omnipotence known to the world
and to show the futility of turning against him. Each of these
judgments addresses a different aspect of life in the ancient
world and in the modern world as well. The first shows that
the material world is no answer; the second and third address
the sea trade, including food supplies; and the fourth focuses
on life itself in the heat and light of the celestial bodies. The
four together prove that those who live only for this world
have chosen foolishly, for only in God is there true life.
Earthly things turn on us, and we dare not depend on them.
(*Revelation*, 357)

Conclusion

Prayer is an action of finite sinful humans that in some amazing and
mysterious way moves into action a sovereign and omnipotent God. I
cannot explain it, but I do believe it. Spurgeon said,

> Prayer is a gift from God as well as *appeal* to God. Every prayer
> for mercy is not a cause, but a result! Divine grace is at the
> back of prayer and at the base of prayer. ("Song for the Free")

This is true on the cosmic level. It is also true on the personal level.
Prayer is what moves God to judge the world and vindicate His saints.
Prayer is also what moves God to save souls and bring them into His
kingdom. A day is coming when you will either have the mark of the
beast (13:16-18) or the mark (the name) of the Lamb (2:17; 14:1). Time
is short. Judgment is coming. Salvation is as near as a prayer: "Everyone
who calls on the name of the Lord will be saved" (Rom 10:13).

Reflect and Discuss

1. Do you struggle to pray? How would you encourage another believer
   to see the importance of prayer?
2. What role does silence play in your prayer life? Spend some time in
   silence before the Lord simply contemplating His glory and power.
3. What role do angels play in carrying out God's will?
4. Look at the characteristics of "warfare prayer" listed in this chapter.
   How do your prayers line up with these? What element will you add
   to your prayer life this week?

5. Spiritual conflict is real, but many believers fail to consider it in their own lives. How have you seen each of Platt's characteristics of spiritual warfare in your own life? How can these truths shape your prayer life?

6. Why do you think God receives Christians' prayers as a sweet aroma? How does this encourage you in your prayer life?

7. How should we pray for God's judgment? Should we seek to carry out that judgment ourselves?

8. How is God's mercy shown even in His judgment as seen in Revelation 8?

9. How would you summarize the main purpose of these trumpet judgments? What evidence would you use to support your view?

10. What material or earthly things are you tempted to trust in? How is Jesus better than each of these things?

When God Uses Evil to Judge Evil

REVELATION 9:1-21

Main Idea: In carrying out judgment on unrepentant humanity, the sovereign Lord will use Satan and his forces, but He will always remain in control over them.

I. **Spiritual Warfare Is Real and Intense (9:1-12).**
  A. God is sovereign in what He allows (9:1-5).
  B. Humans may suffer and even seek death (9:5-6).
  C. Demons are powerful and love to harm us (9:7-12).
II. **When God's Restraining Grace Is Removed, Hell Comes to Earth (9:13-19).**
  A. God again directs what evil does (9:13-16).
  B. God again determines what evil does (9:15-19).
III. **God's Judgments Reveal the Utter Depravity of the Human Heart (9:20-21).**
  A. Humans love their idols (9:20).
  B. Humans love their immorality (9:21).

The great reformer Martin Luther is credited with saying, "The Devil is still God's Devil." His point is that clearly Satan is both evil and powerful, but he is still under the authority of the sovereign Lord. There is only one sovereign God, and the Devil is not that God. The important truth is this: Ultimately nothing happens apart from the sovereign determination of God. Nothing! And when it comes to evil and the wicked, destructive devices of Satan, demons, and even human persons, God is not the author of evil even as He, for His good purposes, allows evil (Jas 1:13). In Revelation 9, we even see our great God turning evil on itself. We see God using evil to judge evil, and He is rightly glorified in doing so.

Revelation 8:13 serves as a transition into chapter 9. The flying eagle mentioned in that verse should be understood symbolically and may have a connection with the eagle-like living creature of 4:7-8. Before the last three angels sound their trumpet, a threefold woe is pronounced on the earth "in a loud voice." The first woe is to be identified with the fifth trumpet. The second woe is to be identified with the sixth trumpet. The third woe is to be identified with the seventh trumpet, which constitutes the final series of judgments: the seven bowls of chapter 16.

The phrase "those who live on the earth" is used throughout Revelation to designate those who live in rebellion and unbelief before the true and living God. It occurs 12 times in this book. These are persons who live not only *on* the earth but *for* the earth. The things of God count for nothing. The issues of heaven matter nothing. What a tragic way to live! What a terrible way to die.

Chapter 9 naturally divides into three parts: (1) The fifth trumpet comprises verses 1-12 as demons are released from the bottomless pit or the abyss. (2) The sixth trumpet is sounded in verses 13-19, recording the death of one-third of humanity through demonic destruction. (3) The refusal of humanity to repent of its idolatries and immoralities is recorded in verses 20-21, summarizing man's response to the trumpet judgments of 8:7–9:19. In all that unfolds, the absolute and awesome sovereignty of God is on full display. Even Satan and demons ultimately do His bidding. How amazing that in the face of all of this, humanity still shakes its fist in God's face and refuses to repent of all the evils of its heart and hands. John only needed six verses to set forth the first four trumpets in chapter 8. Now he devotes an entire chapter of 21 verses to the blowing of trumpets five and six—what the Bible calls the first and second woes (9:12).

Spiritual Warfare Is Real and Intense
REVELATION 9:1-12

Chapter 9 addresses real war in a real (spiritual) world that eventually invades our world (spiritual and physical). The imagery is terrifying as the spiritual world invades the physical world and demons are unleashed to bring devastation, destruction, and death. Revelation 8:13 warned us that the last three trumpets would bring three woes to the earth. That day is here, and what takes place is again hard to put into human words. Chuck Swindoll is so helpful when he says, "As we study John's vision and observe the armies of darkness battling in the future, we can better understand how similar spirits of wickedness try to torment us today" (*Insights*, 133).

80 Christ-Centered Exposition Commentary

God Is Sovereign in What He Allows (9:1-5)

The most important thing for us to understand is that all that takes place is under the control of our God. He tells the angels to blow their trumpets, and they blow (9:1). He gives Satan "the key to the shaft of the abyss" (v. 1). He tells the demons what they can do (v. 4). He puts a limit on the torment they can inflict (v. 5).

The fifth angel blew, and John saw a star that had fallen from heaven to the earth. "Had fallen" is a perfect tense participle emphasizing an event in past time with continuing results. This star, unlike the star of 8:10, is a person (personal pronouns are applied throughout). The statement is reminiscent of Luke 10:18 where Jesus said, "I watched Satan fall from heaven like a lightning flash." Though dogmatism again is unwarranted, I believe the best interpretation is to see this as a reference to Satan (MacArthur, *Revelation 1–11*, 254–57). It is neither a good angel nor a chief demon under the Devil's direction. It is Satan, the Devil himself, who is in view. He "had fallen"—it had already occurred prior to the blowing of the fifth trumpet. The exact time is not specified. Lucifer, the star of the morning, son of the dawn (Isa 14:12), the anointed cherub (Ezek 28:14), was cast out of God's presence and heaven's glory when sin was found in his heart. Now as we move toward history's climax, he is allowed a diabolical freedom on the earth that he was previously denied. The key and thus the authority "to the shaft of the abyss"—a prison house for demons (see Luke 8:31; 2 Pet 2:4; Jude 6) and the abode of the dead (Rom 10:7)—is given to him by God. Immediately he opens it, and smoke, dark and hot, fills the air and darkens the sun. The beast, the antichrist, also will arise from the abyss (see 11:7). But the Devil will not always have authority over it. He will be imprisoned there for a thousand years following the second coming of Jesus (see 20:1-3).

When the shaft to the abyss is opened, demons in the form of locusts flood the earth. Power and authority are given them like scorpions. This is reminiscent of the eighth plague on Egypt (Exod 10:1-20) and the locust vision of Joel 1–2 (Duvall, *Revelation*, 131). These are not literal locusts, however. These are demons, released to torment mankind spiritually, physically, and in every other way conceivable.

Verses 4-6 make clear their mission: Torment all persons "who do not have God's seal [which denotes possession and protection] on their foreheads" (see 7:2-8). Believers will not be touched by these ambassadors from the abyss. And there is a limitation to what they can do:

They can torment, yes, but not kill. Verse 5 places a further limitation in terms of time. They are given five months. The normal life span of a locust was approximately from May to September, or five months. This verse would also seem to indicate the torment they inflict is primarily physical—stinging and striking like that of a scorpion. However, we should not place limitations on exactly how they will torment mankind. Remember, this is apocalyptic language. What is certain is what they do to humanity is horrible, and what they do is only what God allows.

Humans May Suffer and Even Seek Death (9:5-6)

These demonic locust-like creatures torment human persons in a painful and severe manner. I am certain they take delight in their activity. They would like nothing better than to kill off the human race. God, however, in grace, limits what they can do. They can sting and strike mankind, but they are not permitted to slay him, not at this point in the judgments (see 9:15).

Verse 6 is both amazing and heartbreaking. While death will be the lot of Christian martyrs at the hands of evil men (6:9), these evil people will seek death. They will look for the same fate they inflict on others, but they will not find it. They will long for death, but it will run from them, and they will be unable to catch it. For thousands of years men have run from the grim reaper only to find him too swift to evade. Now men chase him but find they are too slow of foot. What irony! What tragedy!

John MacArthur captures well the magnitude of what is unfolding before us. His words are painful to contemplate:

> So intense will be the torment inflicted on unbelievers that
> in those days (the five months of v. 5) men will seek death
> and will not find it; they will long to die, and death flees
> from them. All hope is gone; there will be no tomorrow.
> The earth people have loved and worshiped will have been
> utterly devastated, the land ravaged by earthquakes, fires,
> and volcanoes, the sea filled with the putrefying bodies of
> billions of dead creatures, much of the fresh water supply
> turned into bitter poison, the atmosphere polluted with gases
> and showers of heavenly debris. Then, worst of all, will come
> foul smoke from the pit of hell as the demons are released to
> spiritually and physically torment wicked people. The dream

of a worldwide utopia under the leadership of Antichrist (the beast of 13:1ff.) will have died. Driven mad by the filth and vileness of the demon infestation, people will seek relief in death—only to find that death has taken a holiday. There will be no escape from the agony inflicted by the demons, no escape from divine judgment. All attempts at suicide, whether by gunshot, poison, drowning or leaping from buildings will fail. (*Revelation 1–11*, 261–62)

Demons Are Powerful and Love to Harm Us (9:7-12)

These verses provide a detailed description of these demons who have been confined, perhaps since Satan's fall. John is probably more concerned with the overall impression made by this vision than he is with the details (Duvall, *Revelation*, 132; also Mounce, *Revelation*, 188–89). Still, without pressing the particulars beyond reason, we learn something about these maniacal monsters from the pit. The composite picture is that of unnatural and uninhibited evil and wickedness.

"Horses equipped for battle" informs us they are an army prepared to wage war against God and His people (9:7). Further, they are considerable in size and terrifying in appearance. "Gold crowns" point to authority and power. Faces "like men's faces" speaks of intelligence. They are cunning and cruel, wise and wicked. There is a method to their madness. They have a leader, and they follow a well-orchestrated game plan. "Hair like women's hair" (9:8) is perhaps an indication of the long antennae of locusts or to the seductiveness of their strategies. That they are alluring and enticing could be the idea. Teeth "like lions' teeth" denotes fierceness and lethal power in their attack. "Chests like iron breastplates" (9:9) tells us they are virtually invulnerable. They are strong and well protected. It would take a supernatural power greater than their own to defeat them. Their wings are "like the sound of chariots with many horses rushing into battle." They are intimidating in their coming. The sound of their attack and approach would strike fear in the heart of any opponent who attempted to face them. "Tails with stingers like scorpions" (9:10) communicates they possess a painful sting that causes great agony and great suffering. Finally, John notes again that they can "harm people for five months," which adds emphasis and intensity to their mission of misery.

All of this takes place *ultimately* under God's authority. But *directly* and *immediately* it takes place under the direction of "their king the angel of the abyss" (9:11). And this king has a name: "In Hebrew [it] is Abaddon, and in Greek he has the name Apollyon." Both, I believe, are again references to Satan.

The Hebrew word *Abaddon* appears six times in the Old Testament and is derived from a verb that can mean "to become lost," "to perish," or "to destroy, kill." Abaddon has a similar meaning to Hades as used in Revelation 1:18 and 6:8. A similar usage is found in Psalm 88:11 where it is paralleled with the grave. Job 31:12 used the word to imply an unquenchable appetite. Abaddon is not only a place but also a person. Abaddon is an appropriate name for the angel of the underworld and the king of the locusts in Revelation 9:11. Though Abaddon is under God's sovereign power, it (and he) has an insatiable appetite and represents not only a destruction that takes life but a destruction that reaches beyond the grave to the afterlife. Abaddon would have conjured images of doom and despair for John's readers and would have made them even more fearful of the torture coming at the hand of the angel of the underworld and his army of destroyers.

Apollyon, the Greek counterpart to Abaddon, is used as a proper name only here in the Bible. The word also carries the connotation of "one who destroys." Something more subtle, however, may have been in John's use of *Apollyon* to translate *Abaddon*. John may have intended an indirect attack on the Greek/Roman god Apollo, and thus on the reigning emperor, Domitian, who thought of himself as Apollo incarnate. Apollyon and Apollo (*Apollon* in Greek) look and sound similar. Furthermore, worshipers of Apollo had as one of their symbols for him the locust. In John's Apocalypse the Greek reader could not have missed the echo of the name Apollo, the god, and Apollyon, the destroyer. The well-known pagan god, a favorite of the emperor whose persecution of Christians lies behind the Revelation, is identified with hell and destruction (Beale, *Revelation*, 502–4; also Mounce, *Revelation*, 191).

The horror of this judgment—which God allows—is unspeakable, and yet something worse is yet to come. Verse 12 simply and straightforwardly says, "The first woe [the fifth trumpet] has passed. There are still two more woes [the sixth and seventh trumpets] to come after this." The first disaster has passed, but we see two more on the way, just around the corner.

When God's Restraining Grace Is Removed, Hell Comes to Earth
REVELATION 9:13-19

Consider these challenging words from J. Boyd Nicholson:

> The gospel is not a tranquilizer for worried weaklings to help them sleep at night. It is not a mass of dead dogmas, deep frozen in some ancient cathedral to be carried as a burden through life and thawed out five minutes before death. The gospel is not a list of religious rules and regulations to be strung around the soul like a lucky charm in case of accidents. No, the gospel of our Lord Jesus Christ is a message—and what a message! It is a living message from the living God for living people, just like us, for people with sins just like us, for people with sorrows and heartaches just like us. It is the only message on the face of the earth with concrete promises and absolute assurances of an eternal inheritance that will withstand the impact of death and the collapse of the universe. (*Uplook*, 11)

Such a gospel is especially "good news" as we consider the seven angels with seven trumpets of Revelation. That is especially true when hell comes to earth at the sovereign direction and determination of God.

God Again Directs What Evil Does (9:13-16)

The sixth angel sounds its trumpet, and an unspecified voice speaks from the golden altar before God (9:13). Possibly this is the angel-priest of 8:3-5. He speaks to the sixth angel with a clear and precise word. The angel is told to "release the four angels bound at the great river Euphrates." These angels, I believe, are demons. Good angels are never said to be bound. The Euphrates marked the boundary separating Rome from her primary enemies to the east. Historically these were the Parthians (Keener, *Revelation*, 270).

Verse 15 reveals that they had been prepared for the hour, day, month, and year. This is a precise time. There is also a precise purpose: to kill a third of mankind. Combined with Revelation 6:8, we discover that half of the earth's population will die as a result of the seal and trumpet judgments. The carnage is unfathomable. Verse 16 tells us the enormity of the army bringing about this carnage: 200 million warriors. John says, "I heard their number."

The 200 million-member army—is it composed of demons or humans? An either/or decision may not be necessary or even best. Some connect the army with the kings of the east in 16:12 and identify them with a human army. *Time Magazine* noted more than 50 years ago that China claimed an army of 200 million (May 21, 1965). It is certainly possible, even reasonable, to believe demons will work through human instrumentality in this day. Still the primary description before us is that of a massive number of demons. God directs this mind-boggling demonic activity. They can only do what He permits.

God Again Determines What Evil Does (9:15-19)

Verse 15 informs us the demons bring about the death of "a third of the human race" (see again 6:8, where "over a fourth of the earth" is killed). Verses 17-19 provide a vivid description of the demonic army that will arrive in the last days and carry out this destruction.

Only here in Revelation does John directly indicate the visionary nature of what he experienced (Mounce, *Revelation*, 196). Again the overall impression of the horses and their riders is more important than the details. What did John see in the vision? He saw riders with breast-plates of fire and hyacinth (a dark blue) and sulfur yellow. According to Mounce, "The red, blue and yellow of the protective breastplates matches the fire, smoke and brimstone that comes out of the mouth of the horses" in verse 18 (ibid.). The heads of the horses are like the heads of lions, speaking to their ferocity, cruelty, and destructive strength and power.

The destructive forces of fire, smoke, and brimstone proceed from the mouths of these demons, and by these three plagues, one-third of mankind is killed. Verse 19 provides an additional descriptive word: there is also power in the horses' tails, for they "resemble snakes, have heads, and they inflict injury with them." With their mouths they kill and with their tails they harm. From either direction or both ends, they have the capacity to damage and destroy. Such a description supports the view that these are demonic hordes that are causing havoc on the earth. Fire-breathing monsters were common in ancient mythology. Fire-breathing demons will be a reality during the great tribulation. One cannot help but think back to Genesis 19 when fire and burning sulfur rained on Sodom and Gomorrah. Then it affected two cities. In the future much of the world will suffer (ibid., 197).

God's Judgment Reveals the Utter Depravity of the Human Heart
REVELATION 9:20-21

W. A. Criswell, the famous and faithful pastor of the FBC Dallas for more than 50 years, wisely noted,

> One of the strangest things about human nature is that man has not changed because of punishment. . . . He may desist from evil because he is afraid, but his heart is still evil. He would do evil if he could get by with it. A man is really changed only by the Gospel of the grace of the Son of God. (*Sermons*, 3:192).

Criswell was right, and Revelation 9:20-21 makes this tragically clear.

Humans Love Their Idols (9:20)

John Calvin said, "The mind begets an idol; the hand gives it birth" (*Institutes*, 1.11.8). His words ring true to Scripture. In both verses 20 and 21 we are informed that humanity does not repent in the face of God's judgment. Verse 20 drives home the truth that idolatry is at the core of an unrepentant heart. "The rest of mankind" refers to unrepentant unbelievers who did not die from the seal (Rev 6) and trumpet judgments. They refuse to worship the God who created and made them, but they gladly worshiped the gods "of their hands" (Rom 1:18-25). And we must take note: idol worship and demon worship are close companions. Worshiping "idols of gold, silver, bronze, stone, and wood, which are not able to see, hear, or walk" is in concert with "worshiping demons." To worship stuff is akin to worshiping Satan. Dead sinners worship dead gods of their own making. No wonder Romans 1:22 says, "Claiming to be wise, they became fools." Idolatry robs God of His glory and rightful place in your life as demons take His place. Do not think such idolatry is reserved for faraway places around the world. It is down the street. It is next door. It is in your own home.

Humans Love Their Immorality (9:21)

Four particular sins are additionally noted in verse 21. These sins, like those in verse 20, have afflicted humanity throughout history. It is possible they will be especially prevalent in the last days. "Murders" is the wanton taking of innocent human life. "Sorceries" is witchcraft, magic arts, occultic activity. It is the Greek word *pharmakon* and could indicate the use of drugs in divination practices. "Sexual immorality" is the Greek word *porneia* and refers to all forms of sexual sin that occurs outside the marriage relationship between a man and woman. "Thefts" is simply another word for stealing, taking what is not yours.

The sins of verses 20-21 involve a basic violation of the Ten Commandments (Exod 20; Deut 5). Idolatry violates commandments one and two. Murder violates the sixth, immorality the seventh, and theft the eighth. As it was in the days of the judges, it will be a time of unbridled and unrepentant evil, when "everyone did whatever he wanted" (Judg 21:25). Mounce makes a remarkable observation: "Once the heart is set in its hostility toward God, not even the scourge of death will lead people to repentance" (*Revelation*, 198). Amazingly, it appears it will only spur sinful humanity to sin even more. What an indictment of the depraved human heart!

Conclusion

Satan, demons, and evil are real. They are often powerfully real. But—and this is so critically important for us to understand—they are all on a divine leash! There are heavenly imposed limits on what they are allowed to do. Pastor-theologian Helmut Thielicke put it well in his book *Man in God's World*:

> But however great may be the leeway that the satanic power possesses in history [and who is not conscious of this today!], however strong may be the rebellion and the opposition, the fact still remains that in the ultimate reckoning even this opposition is included in God's plan for the world and is being guided by God to a goal which the demons themselves never sought. Luther summed up this experience in the rather startling phrase that even the devil is still "God's devil" and must be subservient to his higher goals because God is

his Lord, too. When the apocalyptic horsemen storm across the earth, and the earth and the world shake beneath their hoof beats . . . and terror lays waste mankind, then we must remember that it is God who allows even those powers of destruction to ride [and the trumpets blow], that it is he who waves them on and he who can check them with a flick of his sovereign hand.

This is the hidden structure of providence and God's government of the world, and it is there even when God has abandoned men to their own self-destruction and seems to be doing nothing but "letting things happen." This is the ultimate comfort of the Christian faith in providence when God is silent and history grows murky and dark. (*Man*, 149)

Our God is there and He is working. The question for all of us is, are we listening? Will we repent? Will we worship the God who made us, or will we worship the gods we make?

Reflect and Discuss

1. When have you seen God use evil to accomplish His purposes?
2. How do you see God's authority over agents of evil in this passage?
3. Why will people be looking for death, as in Revelation 9:5-6? Why is it unavailable to them?
4. What strikes you as most terrible about the description of the demonic locusts?
5. John's description of Apollyon may have been an indirect attack on one of the false gods of his day. How does this judgment counter the idols of our day?
6. Why will people not repent, even after seeing the judgment of God?
7. Has there ever been a time when you were slow to repent? Why did you not immediately turn from sin?
8. What does it mean that "idolatry is at the core of an unrepentant heart"? How would you explain this to someone who does not worship wood, metal, or stone idols?
9. How are idol worship and demon worship related?
10. Why does punishment spur sinful humanity toward greater rebellion?

The Bittersweet Book:
A Mighty Angel and His Little Scroll

REVELATION 10:1-11

Main Idea: Despite the opposition of God's enemies, He has given His people His authoritative and trustworthy Word and commissioned them to proclaim it to the nations.

I. **God's Word Comes with Authority (10:1-4).**
   A. It is authoritative and comprehensive (10:1-3).
   B. It is sovereign and mysterious (10:4).
II. **God's Word Is Certain (10:5-7).**
   A. Trust God to confirm His Word (10:5-6).
   B. Trust God to complete His work (10:6-7).
III. **God's Word Must Be Assimilated (10:8-11).**
   A. Take the Word (10:8).
   B. Feed on the Word (10:9-10).
   C. Proclaim the Word (10:11).

In 2 Corinthians 2:14-17 the apostle Paul speaks of the Christian ministry of the gospel as a ministry of life and a ministry of death. He writes in verses 14-16,

> But thanks be to God, who always puts us on display in Christ and through us spreads the aroma of the knowledge of Him in every place. For to God we are the fragrance of Christ among those who are being saved and among those who are perishing. To some we are an aroma of death leading to death, but to others, an aroma of life leading to life.

The ministry of the Word is a ministry of life and death, or as the apostle John records in Revelation 10:9-10, it is bitter and sweet. It is a bittersweet message we are commanded to proclaim again among the nations (10:11).

Revelation 10:1–11:14 is an interlude, or parenthesis, between the sixth and seventh trumpets. We saw an earlier interlude in 7:1-17 between the sixth and seventh seals. There is no parallel interlude between the sixth and seventh bowl judgments in chapter 16 (Duvall, *Revelation*, 142). The reason is clear: When the bowl judgments are poured out, "it is done!" (16:17).

Chapter 10 revolves around a mighty angel, a little scroll, and a recommissioning for John to "prophesy again about many peoples, nations, languages, and kings" (10:11). The idea of prophecy, proclamation of the word given by God, concludes the argument of this passage. There is certainly a change of subject matter from chapters 8–9. There we witnessed the outpouring of God's wrath on unbelieving humanity— what Revelation repeatedly calls "those who live on the earth" (8:13) or those who lack the seal of God's protection on their foreheads (9:4). Now we see a word of encouragement for believers. God's hidden plan will be completed (10:8). You can trust Him to finish things in His time and in His way. You can be confident in His purposes, so keep on proclaiming the gospel among "many peoples, nations, languages, and kings" (10:11). There will be a price to pay (11:1-10), but God will honor and vindicate His people (11:11-19). You can count on it. Chapter 10 begins with a word from heaven. It is both instructive and timely.

God's Word Comes with Authority
REVELATION 10:1-4

Devastating and horrific judgment is interrupted for a moment. The interruption provides "additional information bearing on the previous events and ... prepare[s] the reader for further developments" (Johnson, *Revelation*, 1983, 102). The interlude comes in a glorious and powerful manner as God addresses His servant. Indeed, God speaks with majestic authority. The overused word "awesome" is appropriate on this occasion.

It Is Authoritative and Comprehensive (10:1-3)

John says, "Then I saw," an important and recurring phrase in Revelation (4:1; 7:1,9; 15:5; 18:1; 19:1,11,17,19; 20:1,4,11; 21:1). Here he saw "another mighty angel." Angels are mentioned more than 60 times in Revelation, mighty or strong angels three times (5:2; 10:1; 18:21). The angel, coming down from heaven, is described as "mighty," perhaps because he is both majestic (10:1) and mammoth (10:2,5,8). Demons ascend out of the abyss in chapter 9, but this angel, as God's servant, descends from above. He comes to earth with great authority as God's ambassador.

The description of the angel recalls the vision of the exalted Christ 1:12-16. However, this is not Christ but His heavenly representative. Some think it could possibly be "Michael, the great prince" (Johnson, "Revelation," 2006, 677). Regardless, the fourfold description is the most detailed and majestic of any angel in Scripture (Osborne, *Revelation*, 393). "Surrounded [ESV, "wrapped"] by a cloud" symbolizes glory, majesty, and power. It recalls the coming of the Son of Man in Daniel 7:13-14. God led Israel by a cloud (Exod 16:10). Dark clouds covered Sinai when the law was given (Exod 19:9). God appeared to Moses in a cloud of glory (Exod 24:15; 34:5). Indeed the Bible says in Psalm 104:3, "[He makes] the clouds His chariot, walking on the wings of the wind." Nine of the twenty occurrences of clouds in the New Testament are connected with judgment (Matt 24:30; 26:64; Mark 13:26; 14:62; Luke 21:27; Rev 1:7; 14:14,15,16) (Levy, "Angel," 21).

"A rainbow over his head" is a sign of God's covenant faithfulness. It echoes the story of Noah and the flood. It adorned his head like a crown (Gen 9:12-16; Ezek 1:26-28; Rev 4:3). MacArthur notes, "While the cloud symbolizes judgment, the rainbow represents God's covenant mercy in the midst of judgment (as it did in 4:3)" (MacArthur, *Revelation 1–11*, 280).

The angel's "face was like the sun," brilliant and radiant, for he had been in the presence of God. As a result, he is an awesome reflection of the Lord. "His legs were like fiery pillars," a picture of stability and uncompromising holiness. And with a possible background in the exodus wanderings, ideas of guidance, protection, and deliverance are lurking about (Osborne, *Revelation*, 394).

In verse 2 we are told the angel "had a little scroll" (mentioned four times in ch. 10). This, I believe, is a different book from the sealed book of chapter 5 (Mounce, *Revelation*, 202). So massive is this angel that he lays claim for his message on all the earth, setting his right foot on the sea and his left on the land (mentioned three times). Furthermore, his message is to warn all and be heard by all. He "cried out with a loud voice, like a roaring lion" (10:3). Hosea 11:10 similarly says the Lord "will roar like a lion." And Joel 3:16 says, "The LORD will roar from Zion and raise His voice from Jerusalem; heaven and earth will shake."

His cry is accompanied by seven thunders, which spoke. In the little scroll is the Word of God. In the seven thunders there is additional judgment from God, a judgment that comprehensively will impact the whole world.

It Is Sovereign and Mysterious (10:4)

Seven seals have afflicted the earth. Six of seven trumpets have blown in cataclysmic judgment. Seven thunders are now ready to vent their judgment as well. They have already sounded. They are ready to act; John is ready to write. Then something amazing occurs: John hears a voice from heaven, which I believe is the voice of our God. John is told, "Seal up what the seven thunders said, and do not write it down!"

These are the only words in the Revelation that are sealed up. Revelation 22:10 says, "Don't seal the prophetic words of this book, because the time is near." But here, this one time, John is commanded not to write what the "thunders said." We cannot be certain as to why. We can only make educated guesses. God did something similar to the prophet Daniel (see 8:26; 12:4,9). And Deuteronomy 29:29 tells us the secret things belong to the Lord, so it may be best simply to admit that we do not know. But there is a second consideration to contemplate. The seven thunders no doubt would be another horrible series of judgments unleashed on planet Earth. But God says no. They will not act. He speaks and they are stilled. Is God silencing them as an act of grace and mercy? Is it an evidence of God's long-suffering and patience? How could it be if there will "be no more delay" in God's judgment (10:6 ESV)? We must remember, as bad as the seal, trumpets, and bowls are, it could have been worse.

Exactly why John was not allowed to write further about the thunders remains a mystery, at least for now. Maybe someday we will know. Then again, maybe not. Osborne wisely notes,

> John is being told to affirm God's sovereign control over the judgments proclaimed in the thunders and then is prohibited from revealing the contents to his readers. The major message is one of sovereignty. God is in control, and the saints do not need to know all the details. (*Revelation*, 397)

Osborne is right. So in the meantime, we will trust in the plans of our sovereign God and marvel at His mysterious ways. After all, He is God and we are not—a lesson we mere mortals too often struggle to remember.

God's Word Is Certain
REVELATION 10:5-7

In Isaiah 55:11 our God promises us, "So my word that comes from My mouth will not return to Me empty, but it will accomplish what I please and will prosper in what I send it to do." When our Lord speaks, His word is certain, sure, and trustworthy. It will come to pass. You and I can count on it. In a powerful and sovereign declaration, the mighty angel swears that which God "announced to His servants the prophets" (10:7) "would be fulfilled" (ESV). Indeed, "there would be no more delay" (10:6 ESV). I believe the drama of Daniel 12 finds its fulfillment in these verses.

Trust God to Confirm His Word (10:5-6)

In an act of solemn oath taking, the angel of 10:1 raises his right hand to heaven. This is the only time an oath is taken in Revelation. In Matthew 5:34-35 Jesus spoke against frivolous and deceitful swearing. His brother James taught the same lesson (Jas 5:12). However, throughout Scripture godly men and women such as Abraham (Gen 21:25-31), Isaac (Gen 26:26-31), David (1 Sam 20:12-17), and Paul (Acts 18:18), along with Jesus (Matt 26:63-64) and God Himself (Heb 6:13), took oaths as a witness of confirmation to speak the truth (MacArthur, *Revelation 1–11*, 284). This angel swears an oath, and he takes it in the name of the living God "who lives forever and ever" (10:6). This acknowledges His eternity (see 1:18; 4:9-10; 15:7). Furthermore, He is the God who created heaven, the earth, and the sea and "what is in it" (spoken three times for emphasis). He is the sovereign Creator. He alone is the uncaused Cause, Aristotle's "Unmoved Mover," the Source and ultimate Cause of all that is. This angel could not have sworn by any greater. God will confirm His Word.

Trust God to Complete His Work (10:6-7)

The message of God's servant angel is twofold: First, "there would be no delay" (ESV), literally, "there will no longer be a period of time." This answers the question of the martyrs in 6:10. God will not stop or delay the remaining judgments. Evil will now run its course quickly as antichrist rises from the abyss (11:7) and emerges as a world ruler (see 2 Thess 2:3-12; Rev 13:1-18). God and evil, the Lamb and the dragon, are headed for cosmic conflict, a global showdown. It will happen soon.

Second, when the seventh angel sounds to send forth the seven bowls (ch. 16), the mystery or "hidden plan" (Gk *musterion*) of God will be fulfilled, completed, finished, as He declared to His servants the prophets. In the New Testament a *mystery* is a truth previously concealed but now revealed (e.g., Eph 3:2-11). God's plan and purpose in creation and redemption, made possible through the blood of the Lamb, is now revealed plainly. It is nothing less than the answer to the prayers of the saints throughout history, "Your kingdom come . . . on earth as it is in heaven" (Matt 6:10). The time is now. The kingdom will come. God has willed from eternity past the complete and final defeat of evil. That day is coming. You can trust God to complete His work. We may fail Him, but He will never fail us! His word is certain: "God has instigated the final events of world history, and nothing can delay them" (Mounce, *Revelation*, 399).

God's Word Must Be Assimilated
REVELATION 10:8-11

These verses are the most applicable and practical in this passage of Scripture. They have a clear relevance for every generation of believers and followers of the Lamb. The imagery is striking, and the meaning is self-evident. The "little scroll" of verse 2 reappears and takes center stage. It is mentioned three times in verses 8-10. God's Word comes with authority. Its promises and prophecies are certain to be fulfilled. However, it is of little or no value to us personally if we do not take it, read it, feed on it, and then proclaim it. It is a bittersweet book to be sure. It is a book that will change us. It is a book that leaves no one the same. Life and death are in its words. How then do we respond to this word?

Take the Word (10:8)

The voice from heaven speaks again (10:4). The voice is almost certainly the voice of God. This voice commands authority and demands obedience. John is told to "go" and "take the scroll that lies open in the hand of the angel." Both "go" and "take" are imperatives of command. No doubt John needed such a word to approach such a mighty angel (10:1). Interestingly, the scroll lies open. For you and me, we also have an open book God has prepared for us to read. It is called the Bible. As John is commanded to go and take this little scroll for his spiritual edification, God commands us to go and take His big book and explore its truths. For us there is no intimidating angel to approach. There is an open book ready for the taking. All you have to do is go and get it.

Feed on the Word (10:9-10)

John approaches the angel and requests the scroll. The angel responds by telling him to "take" it and to "eat it." Both verbs are imperatives. John is to take the scroll and devour it, to completely eat it up. The Old Testament background is plainly Jeremiah 15:16 and Ezekiel 2:9–3:3.

What a powerful image for how we should approach the Word of God! This book is honey (Pss 19:10; 119:103; Prov 24:13), better than bread (Matt 4:4), meat (1 Cor 3:1-2), and milk (1 Pet 2:2). Here is a diet for spiritual health and nourishment. However, we can expect a twofold reaction when eating and digesting this book. It will be sweet in our mouths, but it can be bitter to our stomachs (10:9-10). It is sweet in our mouths because it reveals the gospel—God's goodness and grace, His love and mercy, His plans and purposes, His will and His ways. It is bitter to our stomachs because it is a word of judgment to unbelievers and a word of persecution and suffering for believers (Beale, *Revelation*, 552–53; also Osborne, *Revelation*, 404, and Mounce, *Revelation*, 210). To my mind, MacArthur puts it well:

> All who love Jesus Christ can relate to John's ambivalence. Believers long for Christ to return in glory, for Satan to be destroyed, and the glorious kingdom of our Lord to be set up on earth, in which He will rule in universal sovereignty and glory while establishing in the world righteousness, truth, and peace. But they, like Paul (Rom. 9:1-3), mourn bitterly over the judgment of the ungodly. (*Revelation 1–11*, 288)

There is joy and sorrow, sweetness and bitterness, gladness and sadness when God's Word does its perfect saving and sanctifying work in our lives.

Proclaim the Word (10:11)

God, by means of His angel, has a commission (or recommission) for John. Though it is not identical, the commission is similar to the Great Commission the Lord Jesus gave the church (Matt 28:18-20; Acts 1:8). These are words of important application for all of us. "You must" sounds a moral imperative, a moral and spiritual obligation. You must prophesy, preach, and proclaim again (see 1:11,19). He is to prophesy "about many peoples, nations, languages, and kings." Fourfold classifications are common in Revelation, occurring seven times. The inclusion of "kings" occurs only here. Osborne says, "This is probably added due to the presence of the 'kings of the earth' in 6:15; 16:14; 17:10-11 as rulers of the nations and persecutors of the saints" (*Revelation*, 405). Like the book itself, proclaiming God's Word to the nations is bittersweet. It is a positive word of redemption to those who believe, and it is a bitter word of judgment to those who refuse to repent (9:20-21) and who persecute God's people (11:1-14). Our assignment is to go. Our calling is to proclaim the good news of the gospel. In the midst of judgment, God is announcing through His prophets the good news of His grace revealed in the gospel of His Son. The sweetness of faithful obedience cannot be soured by the bitterness of persecution, rejection, suffering, and even death.

Conclusion

Chuck Swindoll is a faithful Bible teacher God has used to bless many lives. I count myself as one of those lives. His insight on applying Revelation 10 is just about perfect and is a wonderful way to conclude our study:

> Just like John, we have roles to play in God's ultimate plan. We can't call ourselves "apostles," and we don't receive literal visions and revelations from God. We're not required to swallow prophetic books to utter inspired words. But each of us has been given a crucial mission to share the good news of salvation with the world (Matt 28:19-20). Yet just like John, we must first internalize the message, allowing it to become a part of our own lives.
>
> It's true that the gospel of Jesus Christ involves both bad news and good news—bad news about lost humans subject to divine judgment but good news about the righteous Redeemer, Jesus Christ, who paid the complete penalty for us and saves us when we simply trust in Him. As ambassadors for Christ in this age, we must not only understand and accept the gospel ourselves, but we must also be able to communicate that message to others.
>
> Have you accepted God's commission on your life?
>
> Or, like John, are you ready for a recommissioning from God? (*Insights*, 151)

Reflect and Discuss

1. When have you experienced some of the bitter times of gospel ministry? Do these times necessarily indicate failure?
2. When have you experienced some of the sweet times of gospel ministry?

3. The destruction in the previous several chapters may be discouraging for Christians. What confidence and encouragement does this text give Christians to continue working among the lost?
4. Read through the story of the flood in Genesis 6–9 and reflect on God's covenant faithfulness as symbolized in the rainbow.
5. Why is John not allowed to write the words from the thunders? Why does this not distract from the main message of the book?
6. How do the events of Daniel 12 relate to this passage?
7. The oath of verse 6 is made in God's name. How does this speak to the trustworthiness of God's Word?
8. How does the justice of God in judgment fulfill the plan God revealed to His prophets?
9. How can you "feed on" the Word of God? Why are the words of Scripture bittersweet?
10. Though John's commission is specific to him, it is similar to the Great Commission given to all of God's people. Where and how has God called you to speak the good news of the gospel to those who currently reject Him?

Happy Dead Witnesses Day

REVELATION 11:1-19

Main Idea: Though Christians will be persecuted for their faithfulness to Christ, God promises to vindicate His people and that His kingdom will stand forever.

I.   God's Plan Marches On in Spite of Opposition (11:1-2).
II. We Have God's Promise of Protection to Complete Our Ministry (11:3-6).
III. We Can Expect Persecution and Even Death for Telling the Truth (11:7-10).
IV. We Can Be Assured God Will Honor Our Faithful Service (11:11-14).
V.   We Can Be Certain God's Kingdom Will Come and He Will Be Glorified (11:15-19).

Two of my heroes in church history are Michael and Margaretha Sattler. They were husband and wife evangelical Anabaptists in the early sixteenth century. Devoted followers of and witnesses to Christ, their lives were cut short by martyrdom in their 20s. The record of their death has been providentially preserved as a testimony of their faithfulness:

> The torture, a prelude to the execution, began at the market place where a piece was cut from Sattler's tongue. Pieces of flesh were torn from his body twice with red-hot tongs. He was then forged to a cart. On the way to the scene of the execution the tongs were applied five times again. In the market place and at the site of the execution, still able to speak, the unshakable Sattler prayed for his persecutors. After being bound to a ladder with ropes and pushed into the fire, he admonished the people, the judges, and the mayor to repent and be converted. Then he prayed, "Almighty, eternal God, Thou are the way and the truth: because I have not been shown to be in error, I will with thy help to this day testify to the truth and seal it with my blood."

As soon as the ropes on his wrists were burned, Sattler
raised the two forefingers of his hands giving the promised
signal to the brethren that a martyr's death was bearable.
Then the assembled crowd heard coming from his seared lips,
"Father, I comment my spirit into Thy hands."

Three others were executed. After every attempt to secure
a recantation from Sattler's faithful wife had failed, she was
drowned eight days later in the Neckar. (Estep, *The Anabaptist
Story*, 47)

Today there is a memorial plaque at the site of Michael Sattler's
execution. It reads,

The Baptist Michael Sattler was executed by burning after
severe torture on 20 May 1527 here on the "Gallows Hill."
He died as a true witness of Jesus Christ. His wife Margaretha
and other members of the congregation were drowned and
burned. They acted for the baptism of those who want to
follow Christ, for an independent congregation of the faithful,
for the peaceful message of the Sermon on the Mount.

The Baptist historian William Estep says, "Perhaps no other execution of an Anabaptist had such far-reaching influence" (*The Anabaptist
Story*, 47).

God has had many superlative witnesses throughout history like
Michael and Margaretha who have sealed their witness with their blood.
His Word promises there will be many more. And He also promises that
it is by their witness that His kingdom will come. The world may celebrate their death, but our God will honor their death and use it for the
advancement of His kingdom and glory.

Revelation 11 is universally viewed as a challenging and difficult
text to interpret in terms of the details. It is a continuation of an interlude or parenthesis that runs from 10:1 to 14:20. It provides additional
insight as to what takes place during the three series of judgments God
unleashes on planet Earth: the seals (ch. 6), the trumpets (chs. 8–9),
and the bowls (ch. 16). However, particular spiritual lessons stand out,
on which most students of the Apocalypse can agree. Duvall provides a
good summary of these lessons:

- Although God's people are protected spiritually, they are still
  vulnerable to persecution.

- God's people are called to speak prophetically.
- The world will often react with hostility to the church's pro-phetic witness.
- God promises to raise His people from the dead, reversing their temporary defeat at the hands of evil powers.
- The witnessing church possesses tremendous power and author-ity to carry out its mission. (*Revelation*, 149)

Our verse-by-verse study of this chapter will explore and unwrap these theological themes. Humility is again the order of the day as we encoun-ter numerous hermeneutical landmines.

God's Plan Marches On in Spite of Opposition
REVELATION 11:1-2

Following his recommissioning to "prophesy again about many peoples, nations, languages, and kings" (10:11), John is "given a measuring reed like a rod" (11:1). He is given the equivalent of a modern yardstick. He is then told to "go and measure God's sanctuary and the altar, and count those who worship there." The Old Testament background is Ezekiel 40–42 and perhaps Zechariah 2:1-5. The idea is one of ownership and protection (Osborne, *Revelation*, 409). However, in verse 2 John is told, "But exclude the courtyard outside the sanctuary. Don't measure it, because it is given to the nations, and they will trample the holy city for 42 months" (11:2). This recalls Luke 21:24 where our Lord says, "And Jerusalem will be trampled by the Gentiles until the times of the Gentiles are fulfilled." Three issues immediately confront us: What is God's sanc-tuary? What is the holy city? And how do we understand 42 months?

Working backwards, I take the 42 months to be 3½ years, though those who take it to mean simply a short period of time are tracking in the right direction (see Dan 9:24-27; Matt 24:22). I also believe John's first-century audience would have understood the holy city to be Jerusalem, though I understand why some believe it represents the church (Mounce, *Revelation*, 215) or even "the earthly, 'not yet' aspect of the future heav-enly Jerusalem (see 3:12; 21:2, 10; 22:19)" (Duvall, *Revelation*, 149).

The big question, however, is the identity of God's sanctuary or temple. Here we must consider both historical and spiritual reali-ties. Historically two temples have been built on the Temple Mount in Jerusalem. First was the temple built by King Solomon that was destroyed by Nebuchadnezzar in 587–586 BC. The second was Zerubbabel's temple that was later magnificently enlarged by Herod the Great only to be destroyed by the Romans in AD 70. Spiritually the idea of the temple or temple theology is multifaceted and developing. Jesus used the image of the temple to refer to Himself in John 2:19-22. The church is called the sanctuary of God in 1 Corinthians 3:16 and Ephesians 2:21-22. Believers in Jesus are a sanctuary of the Holy Spirit (1 Cor 6:19-20). The sanctuary in Revelation is referred to as both the place where God is present and even as God Himself (3:12; 7:15; 11:19; 14:15,17; 15:5-6,8; 16:1,17; 21:22).

So, how are we to understand the sanctuary in 11:1-2? Many fine scholars believe it represents the church, the Christian community. They see no reason for us to expect a rebuilt temple in Jerusalem. However, based on what Jesus says in Matthew 24:15, and Paul in 2 Thessalonians 2:4, I believe a future temple will be built during the last days. I believe there may also be a millennial temple as described in Ezekiel 40–47.

Now, who are those who worship in this sanctuary? Are these Jews who worship in belief in Jesus as Messiah, or is it Jews who worship there in unbelief? We cannot be sure. However, Ladd, who does not anticipate the rebuilding of a literal temple, has a perspective concerning the future of Jewish persons I find compelling and heartily endorse:

> [Another] interpretation sees here a prophecy of the preservation and ultimate salvation of the Jewish people. In the day when John wrote, Jerusalem had been long destroyed and the temple laid waste. Just before the conflagration of AD 66–70, the Jewish Christian community had fled from Jerusalem to the city of Pella in Transjordan. This had augmented the hostility of the Jews toward the Jewish Christian community and hastened the complete break between the synagogue and church. The burning question among Jewish Christians was, "Has God rejected his people?" (Rom. 11:1). Paul devoted three whole chapters to this problem and concluded that finally the natural branches (Jews) which had been broken off the olive tree (the people of God) would be grafted back onto the tree; "and so all Israel will be saved" (Rom. 11:26). It is difficult to interpret these three chapters symbolically of the church—the spiritual Israel. They teach that literal Israel is yet to be included in spiritual Israel.
>
> Our Lord himself had anticipated this. After his lament over Jerusalem, he asserted, "For I tell you, you will not see me again, until you say, 'Blessed be he who comes in the name of

the Lord'" (Matt. 23:39). Again, he implied the salvation of Israel when he said, "Jerusalem will be trodden down by the Gentiles until the times of the Gentiles are fulfilled" (Luke 21:24). . . . The prophecy in Revelation 11 is John's way of predicting the preservation of the Jewish people and their final salvation. (*Commentary*, 150–51)

Regardless of the exact and precise details, one thing is certain: God's plan marches on. Sinful humanity has its say for a day. The Lord God, the Almighty, has His say for all eternity.

We Have God's Promise of Protection to Complete Our Ministry
REVELATION 11:3-6

God in sovereign power gives the holy city over to the nations to be trampled for 42 months. His place and His people are the objects of intense opposition (11:1). However, at the same time God will raise up His two witnesses who come in power and spirit of Moses and Elijah. They will proclaim His word and display His power (11:3-6). No one will be able to harm them until "they finish their testimony" (11:7).

To navigate these verses let's ask and answer basic questions of interpretation. First, we should ask, **Who are the two witnesses?** Numerous suggestions have been given, including the following:

Old Testament and New Testament
The witnessing church
Witnesses in general
Elijah and Enoch
Elijah and Moses
Zerubbabel and Joshua
Elijah and Elisha
James and John
Peter and Paul
Law and Prophets
Law and gospel
Israel and the church
Israel and the Word
Churches of Smyrna and Philadelphia
Spirit of Elijah and Moses

Though each of these suggestions may have its own merit, it seems best to see the two witnesses as individuals or a group who come in the spirit of Moses and Elijah to fulfill a specific ministry given to them by God.

Second, we need to ask, **What will these witnesses do?** The text tells us they will prophesy for 1,260 days (3½ years) in sackcloth, the garments of grief, humility, mourning, and repentance.

Third, we should ask, **How will they carry out their ministry?** They will do their ministry as two olive trees and two lampstands that represent God on the earth. This draws from a vision in Zechariah 4 where there are two men named Joshua (the high priest) and Zerubbabel (the governor under the Persian King Darius) (Mounce, *Revelation*, 218). Olive trees provide oil for lamps. Lamps provide light. Mounce, therefore, concludes, "They are the bearers of divine light (Matt 5:15-16)" (ibid.). These light bearers are also olive trees in that "the oil of the Spirit . . . keeps alive the light of life" (ibid.). Their power clearly is reminiscent of the ministry of Moses and Elijah (vv. 5-6; see Exod 7:14-18; 8:12; 1 Kgs 17:1; 2 Kgs 1:10-14). There is no reason to deny their supernatural abilities and actions. God worked in these ways in the past, and He will do so again in the future.

Finally we ask, **When do they come?** According to this text, they minister during the great tribulation, or Daniel's seventieth week. It was expected that Moses (Deut 18:18) and Elijah (Mal 4:5; see Matt 11:14) would come at the end of history, and here they are. They stand before the God of the earth and on the earth of God preaching His Word and revealing His power. And they are untouchable until their work is done. The Baptist missionary to China, Lottie Moon, said, "I have a firm conviction that I am immortal 'til my work is done" (Akin, *10 Who Changed the World*, 64). She was right, and that is a truth every servant of God can claim.

We Can Expect Persecution and Even Death for Telling the Truth
REVELATION 11:7-10

The faithful missionary to the Auca Indians, Jim Elliott, had the same conviction as Lottie Moon. In a letter to his parents, he wrote,

> Remember you are immortal until your work is done. But don't let the sands of time get into the eyes of your vision to reach those who still sit in darkness. They simply must hear. (Akin, *10 Who Changed the World*, 81)

Will these two witnesses know they only have a short time? I think so. They certainly will not let the sands of time get into their eyes. "When they finish their testimony," they are attacked and killed by someone called "the beast." Actually he "will make war" against them until he murders them. This beast rises from the abyss, the bottomless pit, the realm of the demonic. This is the first of 36 references to the beast in Revelation. A more detailed description of him is found in chapters 13 and 17. He is clearly the one John calls in his epistles "the antichrist" (1 John 2:18,22; 4:3; 2 John 7) and Paul calls the man of sin or "the lawless one" (2 Thess 2:8-9). He is a Satan-possessed and demonically inspired person who will rule the world for a brief time as a counterfeit Christ. He will murder God's prophets and then disgrace them by denying them burial (11:7). This will take place in what John describes symbolically as "Sodom and Egypt," the place where our Lord was crucified (11:8). Sodom, a city, represents that which is abominable, immoral, and wicked. Egypt, a nation, symbolizes idolatry, oppression, slavery, and suffering. John appears to separate Jerusalem from Sodom and Egypt in terms of symbolism. The phrase "where also their Lord was crucified" makes more sense if the identification is literal Jerusalem, though all the evil cities and nations of the world had their hand in the death of King Jesus (see Babylon in Rev 17–18). Jerusalem in this day will be no better than Sodom or Egypt. A Jew hearing this would be shocked, scandalized, angered. Yet her wickedness in that day will approach her wickedness when she crucified the sinless Son of God. These two superlative witnesses will be treated in the same shameful fashion as their Lord. The words of Jesus come to mind at this point: "A slave is not greater than his master" (John 15:20).

Peoples, tribes, languages, and nations (note again the all-encompassing fourfold division) will first see their dead bodies left in the street and exposed in shameful humiliation for 3½ days (11:9). Second, they will gloat and celebrate and send gifts (11:10)! A new holiday will be established in order to celebrate the deaths of the two men of God. We can call it "Dead Witnesses Day." What a stunning indictment of human depravity, wickedness, sinfulness, and evil.

Remarkably, this is the only mention of rejoicing in the book of Revelation. Men and women will hate God so much that only in the killing of His precious servants are they made happy. They hated Him. They will hate us (John 15:18).

We Can Be Assured God Will Honor Our Faithful Service
REVELATION 11:11-14

In Romans 12:19, Paul cites Deuteronomy 32:35 and writes, "Friends, do not avenge yourselves; instead, leave room for His wrath. For it is written: Vengeance belongs to Me; I will repay, says the Lord." "Payday someday," as R. G. Lee famously preached, is "today" for the earth dwellers (11:10). After 3½ days, "the breath of life from God entered them, and they stood on their feet." The 3½ days recalls the entombment of our Lord. The breath of life harks back to Ezekiel 37 where God revives the valley of dry bones by His Spirit. This is resurrection language!

Not surprisingly, "great fear fell on those who saw them" (11:11), those from among the various "tribes, languages, and nations" (11:9). This is certainly one of the great understatements of the Bible! But for the earth dwellers it gets worse (though better for some). Having been resurrected, the two witnesses now ascend into heaven with their enemies watching them (11:12). This is no secret or hidden rapture. This is a historical and visible moment for the eyes of sinful humanity. Some believe this is the resurrection of the church (Mounce, *Revelation,* 223). Some believe this is a reference to the conversion of Israel (Ladd, *Commentary,* 158). While I still believe it is best to see two historical persons, the bottom line is clear: God honors His faithful saints.

Verse 13a records God's judgment on evil Jerusalem: Seven thousand people are killed. Verse 13b records man's response: Those who remained in Jerusalem were terrified, and they gave glory to the God of heaven. I believe this speaks of a genuine conversion of a great multitude of Jews in Jerusalem. John MacArthur points out that giving glory to the God of heaven is a mark of genuine worship in Revelation and elsewhere in Scripture (see 4:9; 14:7; 16:9; 19:7; see also Luke 17:18-19; Rom 4:20): "This passage, then, described the reality of the salvation of Jews in Jerusalem, as God fulfills His pledge of blessings for Israel (Romans 11:4-5,26)" (MacArthur, *Revelation 1–11,* 305).

God vindicates His saints who serve Him, and He deals with sinners who reject Him. The first group receives grace and mercy. The second group receives judgment and wrath. Verse 14 sums up the situation: "The second woe [the sixth trumpet] has passed. Take note: The third woe [the seventh trumpet, which contains the seven bowls of Revelation 16] is coming quickly." For those saying "Happy Dead Witnesses Day," turn out the lights. The party is over.

We Can Be Certain God's Kingdom Will Come and He Will Be Glorified
REVELATION 11:15-19

For almost two thousand years Christians have prayed a prayer taught to us by Jesus: "Your kingdom come. Your will be done on earth as it is in heaven" (Matt 6:10). In Revelation 11:15-19 that day has come. In words immortalized by George Frederick Handel (1685–1759) in his *Messiah* (1741), "The kingdom of the world has become the kingdom of our Lord and of His Christ, and He shall reign forever and ever."

Remember: the seventh seal contains the seven trumpets, and the seventh trumpet contains the seven bowls. Thus there is a sense in that the seventh seal, seventh trumpet, and the seventh bowl all bring us to the end. We might say it like this: The seventh seal brings us to "the end," the seventh trumpet to "the very end," and the seventh bowl to "the very, very end."

In verse 15 the seventh trumpet sounds, accompanied by loud voices in heaven and the glorious declaration that the kingdom of God has come to this world, and our God and His Christ will reign forever. Psalm 2 now finds its eschatological fulfillment! Verse 16 finds the redeemed (represented by the 24 elders) once more falling on their faces in a posture of praise and worship (see 5:8,14; 7:11; and later 19:4).

Verses 17-18 are the song they sing. In 4:10-11 they celebrated the God who created and sustains all things. In 5:8-14 they worshiped the Lamb who was slaughtered and who redeems the nations by His blood. Now they give thanks to the God who brings history to its climactic end and who begins His cosmic and eternal reign. The song begins by focusing on the person of our God. He is the "Lord God, the Almighty" (1:8; 4:8; 11:17; 15:3; 16:7,14; 19:6,15; 21:22). There is no god as powerful and omnipotent as our God. And He is the One "who is and who was." The phrase "and who is to come" is omitted because He has come and His reign is inaugurated. In other words, "You have taken Your great power and have begun to reign."

Verse 18 reflects Psalm 2 and is a declaration of God's righteous judgment and wrath on a defiant and rebellious world. The nations were angry, and they received God's righteous anger in return. "The dead," those spiritually separated from God, face their judgment at His great white throne (Rev 20:15), judged according to their works. In stark contrast, there will be rewards for those who love and follow the Lord and the Lamb. Five different categories are used to identify the people of God: (1) servants (lit. "slaves"), (2) prophets, (3) saints, (4) those who fear Your name, and (5) small and great. The song concludes by simply noting that the "Lord God, the Almighty" will "destroy those who destroy the earth." MacArthur again points out,

> This is not a reference to those who pollute the environment, but to those who pollute the earth with their sin. That includes all unbelievers, especially in the context of Revelation the false economic and religious system called Babylon (cf. 19:2), Antichrist and his followers, and Satan himself, the ultimate destroyer. (*Revelation 1–11*, 320).

Verse 19 closes the chapter with heaven's response to the song of verses 17-18. The temple of God in heaven, in contrast to the temple of God on earth (11:1-2), is opened with the ark of the covenant visible for all to see. Because of the redemptive work of the Lamb, access to the ark of the covenant is no longer restricted only to the high priest. As a kingdom of priests redeemed by the Lamb (5:9-10), all believers enjoy the fullness of God's presence and His covenant promises (21:2-7,22-27) (Duvall, *Revelation*, 156). Such a glorious vision is accompanied by the harbingers of judgment: "Flashes of lightning, rumblings of thunder, an earthquake, and severe hail." God is faithful to show grace and mercy (e.g., the ark). He is also faithful to send judgment and wrath. To know and love Jesus is to receive grace. To reject the Savior is to receive wrath. Are you God's friend or are you God's enemy? It is hard to imagine a more important question.

Conclusion

There is a humorous but insightful story about the sixteenth-century Reformer Martin Luther (1483–1546) and his wonderful wife Katie. In *Reformation's Rib: Celebrating Katherine von Bora*, James Cobb recounts the event:

> Katie: Doctor Luther had been in a despondent, sad mood for much too long. I don't recall if there was a reason for such a mood but I decided on a course of action. I dressed in black . . . and met him at the door.
>
> Martin: Katie, you are in the color of mourning. Who died?

Katie: I spoke what I felt: "Your God died. At least so you act!" I suppose it was dramatic for me, but the shock of my words and actions did succeed. We did get him back and that was the point. (12)

God has not died. An empty tomb stands as a perpetual monument that "the kingdom of the world has become the kingdom of our Lord and of His Messiah, and He will reign forever and ever!" (11:15). Yes, we will be opposed and rejected by this world. Satan will raise up enemies who will persecute us and kill us. There will be people who will celebrate and rejoice over our deaths and apparent defeat. But never forget: there is a resurrection day that awaits, a kingdom that is coming, and a reward for the servants who revere the name of Jesus. In the end our God wins! So keep on and press on as you proclaim His gospel and pursue His glory. It is worth it all.

Reflect and Discuss

1. God has often used the death of His people to advance His kingdom. Where do we see examples of this in Scripture?
2. How does the world view martyrs? How does this line up with or differ from the way God views them?
3. How do the two witnesses of Revelation 11 fit into the overall plan of God?
4. Do you share Lottie Moon's and Jim Elliott's confidence in their immortality? How does this truth spur you on toward faithfulness?
5. Should every Christian expect to be persecuted? Should every Christian expect to be martyred?
6. Why does the world rejoice at the death of the two witnesses? Do you see the same spirit today?
7. How does God promise to vindicate those who serve Him unto death?
8. How does the certainty of the coming of God's kingdom shape the way we live now?
9. What is the significance of the full visibility of the ark of the covenant? How does this compare with the ark in the Old Testament?
10. How is God's faithfulness shown in both mercy and wrath? Are these contradictory?

An Apocalyptic Christmas Story

REVELATION 12:1-17

Main Idea: God has always been faithful to keep His promises, and through Christ He will bring to completion the final salvation of His people, despite Satan's opposition.

I.   **God Sent a Savior Just as He Promised (12:1-6).**
   A. Trust God to keep His Word (12:1-2).
   B. Trust God to honor His Son (12:3-5).
   C. Trust God to care for His people (12:6).

II. **God Has Accomplished a Salvation That Is Certain (12:7-12).**
   A. Remember our enemy is a defeated foe (12:7-9).
   B. Remember our salvation is a settled reality (12:10).
   C. Remember our victory is through the blood of Christ and the gospel (12:11-12).

III. **God Will Provide for His Servants in His War Against Satan (12:13-17).**
   A. Satan seeks the destruction of God's people (12:13).
   B. God is a rescuer of those who are His (12:14-17).

Concerning our text, Eugene Peterson says, "This is not the nativity story we grew up with, but it is the nativity story all the same" (Mounce, *Revelation*, 234n15). Peterson is right. There is no baby in a manger, shepherds rejoicing, or wise men bringing gifts and worshiping. There are angels, but they are not singing. Rather, they are engaged in a heavenly war of eschatological proportions. No, in this Christmas story there is a beautifully clothed woman, a male child ("Son"), and a great fiery red dragon who stands ready to devour, to eat, the Son "who is going to shepherd all nations" (12:5). This is an apocalyptic Christmas story.

Revelation 12:1-17 tells us, in part and in summary fashion, the grand redemptive story of the Bible. It is something of a panorama of salvation history. It tells us in fantastic imagery and vision the true story of the whole world. It looks to the past, addresses the present, and points to the future. It naturally divides into three sections: (1) Verses 1-6 tell the story of the woman, the male child, and the dragon. (2) Verses 7-12 show a war in heaven and a song of redemption. (3) Verses 13-17 chronicle the satanic attempt to destroy the people of God and its failed project. This is a Christmas story unlike any you have probably ever heard!

God Sent a Savior Just as He Promised
REVELATION 12:1-6

The story of Christmas does not begin in a city called Bethlehem. It begins in a garden called Eden. There, immediately following the fall when Adam and Eve yielded to the temptation of "the ancient serpent" (12:9), God made a promise to send a Savior. In Genesis 3:15 he said to Satan, "I will put hostility between you and the woman, and between your seed and her seed. He will strike [or crush] your head, and you will strike [or bruise] his heel." This promise, made in the presence of Adam and Eve, often called the "proto-evangelium" or first gospel, would be further developed in God's promise to Abraham (i.e., the Abrahamic covenant of Gen 12) and God's promise to David (the Davidic covenant of 2 Sam 7). The fulfillment of those promises is now explained in our text.

Trust God to Keep His Word (12:1-2)

John says, "A great sign appeared in heaven: a woman clothed with the sun, with the moon under her feet and a crown of 12 stars on her head." This is the first of seven signs that appear in the remainder of the Revelation (see 12:3; 13:13,14: 15:1; 16:14; 19:20). This is also the second of four symbolic women in Revelation. There is the Jezebel in 2:20, the prostitute of chapter 17, and the bride of the Lamb in chapter 19 (MacArthur, *Revelation 1–11*, 3–4).

The identity of this woman has been variously understood. The Catholic Church has identified her as Mary. Others have said it is Israel, the church, or the "the messianic community, the ideal Israel" (Mounce, *Revelation*, 231). Her marvelous description draws directly from the dream of the patriarch Joseph in Genesis 37:9-11. There the sun represents Jacob, the moon Rachel, and the stars the tribes of Israel. Perhaps it is best to see her representing the righteous remnant of Israel, the people of God. I believe Romans 11 would lend support to this understanding.

Verse 2 informs us she is "pregnant . . . in labor and agony . . . about to give birth." Crying out in labor and in pain to give birth is reflective of Old Testament imagery that is often applied to the nation of Israel as a mother giving birth (Isa 26:17-18; 54:1; 66:7-12; Hos 13:13; Mic 4:10; 5:2-3; Matt 24:8). Indeed, the nation agonized and suffered throughout the centuries as she longed for her Messiah to come. "It is out of faithful Israel that Messiah will come" (ibid., 232). God promised us He would send a rescuer, a deliverer, a Savior. We can trust Him to keep His word.

Trust God to Honor His Son (12:3-5)

John now sees a second sign in heaven. It is "a great fiery red dragon." In verse 9 he is identified as "the ancient serpent . . . the Devil and Satan." Thirteen times in Revelation Satan is described as a dragon. As a dragon he strikes fear in our hearts. As fiery red his murderous character is revealed. The description of seven heads, ten horns, and seven diadems recalls the fourth beast of Daniel 7 and speaks of his great power and authority. We will see this again in chapters 13 and 17.

Verse 4 informs us that the tail of the dragon "swept away a third of the stars in heaven and hurled them to the earth." I believe this refers to the primordial war in heaven when Satan rebelled against God and a third of the angelic host chose to follow him in his rebellion (Osborne, *Revelation*, 461). Isaiah 14:12-15 may typify this tragic event where the prophet says,

> Shining morning star, how you have fallen from the heavens! You destroyer of nations, you have been cut down to the ground. You said to yourself: "I will ascend to the heavens; I will set up my throne above the stars of God. I will sit on the mount of the gods' assembly, in the remotest parts of the North. I will ascend above the highest clouds; I will make myself like the Most High." But you will be brought down to Sheol into the deepest regions of the Pit.

The dragon takes his stand in front of the woman to devour, consume, eat up her child. This action, on the part of the dragon, is not new. Since God's declaration in Genesis 3:15, Satan has sought to prevent this male child from coming. He moved Cain to kill Abel (1 John 3:12). He moved Pharaoh to kill Hebrew baby boys (Exod 1–2). He moved Saul to kill David (1 Sam 18:10-11). He moved wicked Athaliah to destroy all the royal heirs of the house of Judah (2 Chron 22:10). He moved Haman to plot genocide against the Jews (Esther). He moved Herod to kill Jesus (Matt 2). But in all of this, he failed! Verse 5 tells us, "But she gave birth to a Son—a male who is going to shepherd all nations with an iron scepter." David Platt says,

> The birth of Christ on that day in Bethlehem inaugurated the
> death of this ancient serpent, just as it had been promised
> back in Genesis 3. The birth of Christ declared the death
> of the ancient serpent; the death of Christ defanged the
> adversary. ("Fighting," 2012)

Shepherding the nations reflects the messianic Psalm 2: "In Psalm 2 the
messianic Son is to receive the nations as an inheritance and 'rule . . .
with an iron scepter' (v. 9). As a shepherd defends his flock against wild
beasts of prey, so Christ will strike the nations that oppress and persecute his church" (Mounce, *Revelation*, 234).

Suddenly and unexpectedly, John writes, "And her child was caught
up to God and to His throne." What are we to make of this? Verse 5 summarizes the "first-coming career" of the Lord Jesus Christ. It includes
His birth, His destiny to rule all the nations (see Ps 2:9), and His ascension. The reason the ascension is highlighted rather than the crucifixion and resurrection is twofold: First, the crucifixion and resurrection
were beautifully expounded in chapter 5. Second, the ascension is the
unquestionable proof that Satan was defeated in that he could not prevent Christ from rising from the dead and ascending back to His Father,
where He now is seated at the right hand of the throne of God, perhaps
the place Satan coveted when he fell. Satan disgraced and dishonored
himself with his idolatrous ambition. God exalted and honored His Son
in His incarnation and humiliation. The way *up* really is found in a will-
ingness to go *down*.

Trust God to Care for His People (12:6)

Verse 6 anticipates the dragon's rage in verses 13-17. Here the wilderness symbolizes a place and promise of protection and provision, just
as God cared for Israel following the exodus. God has specifically prepared a place for the woman, a place where He will feed her for 1,260
days, or 3½ years. The place will be one of spiritual refuge. She may be
persecuted and suffer, but she will also be provided for and sustained.
Everything the righteous remnant needs to honor her God and experience the victory provided by the male child, the babe of Bethlehem, she
will have. God has preserved and taken care of His people in the past.
He continues to meet our needs in the present. He will not fail us in the
future. We have His word. You can trust Him.

God Has Accomplished a Salvation That Is Certain
REVELATION 12:7-12

The incarnation of the Son (12:5) was nothing less than a declaration of war on Satan and his demonic forces. It was God keeping His promise to "ransom captive Israel" with the coming of Immanuel. It was indeed His promise kept to "fill the whole world with heaven's peace." However, heaven was anything but peaceful when the Son was born, lived, died, rose, and was caught up to heaven in ascension and exaltation. Heaven's "Battle of the Bulge" ensued, but an empty cross and an empty tomb sealed the Devil's fate!

Remember Our Enemy Is a Defeated Foe (12:7-9)

"War broke out in heaven." The time is not specified. Some believe it looks back to the time of Satan's original, primordial fall. Others believe it looks to the time of the crucifixion and his climactic defeat. Still others believe it looks to the future and possibly the midpoint of the great tribulation. Dogmatism is unwarranted. What is certain are the results of the cosmic conflict.

Michael is named in Scripture as the archangel (Dan 10:13,21; 12:1; Jude 9). The name *Michael* means, "Who is like God?" The rhetorical question stands in stark contrast to Lucifer's egocentric attack on the Lord, in which he said, "I will be like the Most High" (Isa 14:14). Michael is the guardian and protector of God's people. He has a particular role with respect to Israel, as Daniel 12:1 makes clear.

Satan and his angels (i.e., demons) fight and are defeated. They are cast out of heaven, and, as verse 13 notes, they are "thrown to the earth." Satan and his demons were cast out of heaven as their home at the time of their original rebellion. The Bible seems to indicate that they still had some degree of access to heaven for a time (see Job 1:6; 2:1), but now having been beat down in this great battle, they are cast out permanently and denied any access to heaven at all. In other words, they are banished and barred from the presence of God and heaven forever.

Revelation 12:9 contains a mini seminar in Satanology by means of four instructive titles of our archenemy: (1) "The great dragon" emphasizes his ferocity and terror. (2) That "ancient serpent" identifies him with the beguiling snake of Genesis 3 who seduced Adam and Eve into committing sin. (3) "The Devil," literally *diabolos,* means "the accuser" or "the slanderer." And (4) "Satan" is a proper name that means "the adversary" or "the enemy." He is the "one who deceives the whole world," the one Jesus says is "a murderer from the beginning and has not stood in the truth, because there is no truth in him. . . . he is a liar and the father of liars" (John 8:44). He is defeated, humiliated in this war, along with his angels. The critical and crucial battle is done. The end of the war is soon to follow. Remember: our enemy is a defeated foe.

Remember Our Salvation Is a Settled Reality (12:10)

Verses 10-12 constitute another beautiful hymn in the Apocalypse. John hears a loud and unspecified voice in heaven, declaring the victory of the saints by virtue of the redemptive work of the Lamb. Verse 10 addresses four wonderful realities that have come and now are ours "because the accuser of our brothers has been thrown out; the one who accuses them before our God day and night." The perpetual spiritual tattletale has been kicked out of the heavenly house. In his place come salvation, power, the kingdom of God, and the authority of Messiah Jesus.

Brothers and sisters, when Satan accuses you of being a grievous sinner, you look him in the eye and say, "You are right I am. But I have a Savior greater than my sin, and He has given me salvation, power, a kingdom, and the authority of my Messiah. I have been delivered, and I am safe from your accusations now and forever." Yes, our salvation is a signed, sealed, and settled reality!

Remember Our Victory Is Through the Blood of Christ and the Gospel (12:11-12)

Revelation 12:11 provides the basis or ground of our salvation through a beautiful and magnificent declaration. Those who follow the Lamb, the Christ of God, have conquered, become victorious, over the dragon. And how did we overcome? Two grounds for our victory are noted: the blood of the Lamb and the word of our testimony (i.e., our faithfulness to the gospel of King Jesus). The power of the blood of Jesus is indeed sufficient for our sin. It is also sufficient for a martyr's death. Indeed, the loyalty of the child of God to the Lamb who shed His blood is witnessed by their faithfulness even unto death. This verse beautifully states that their love for the Lamb was greater than their love for their own life. Amazingly, the blood of the martyrs shows not the triumph of Satan but rather the triumph of the saints as their acceptance of Jesus and His work on the cross provides victory over sin as well as Satan. Because our sins have been washed in the blood of the Lamb of God, no accusation by the Devil can stand against us. We have not been forgiven because of who we are; we have been forgiven because of who He is and what He has done for us. He washed our sins away in His precious blood. For such a great salvation, we gladly and willingly put our lives on the line. He is worth it.

In verse 12 those in heaven and those on the earth who know the Lamb are called to rejoice. In contrast, there is a woe pronounced on the inhabitants of the earth—unbelieving humanity that stands in opposition to God. The basis for the woe is the fact that the Devil has come down and he has great wrath. He knows he has a short time. Indeed, he has no more than three and one-half years before he will find his new home for a thousand years in the abyss (Rev 20:1-6). Satan has raged against humanity ever since we were placed in the garden of Eden. He is not letting up one wit in our day. As his time draws to a close, his fury will increase to proportions beyond our wildest imagination. Truly hell will come to earth during these horrible final days of the tribulation. Sinners can only expect destruction, disaster, and death at the hands of the great fiery red dragon. But it does not have to be that way. God has accomplished a certain salvation that is available and offered to all who will trust in the Lamb, in His Son.

God Will Provide for His Servants in His War Against Satan
REVELATION 12:13-17

Christmas was indeed a declaration of the war that was promised in Genesis 3:15. Calvary was the decisive battle where the final outcome of this war was settled and made clear. There is no question as to how it is going to end. However, our enemy, the dragon, Satan, fights on. And "because he knows he has a short time" (he does know his Bible), his hostility and rage is only going to intensify as the end draws near. His rage against the people of God will be a special focus of his attention. But as he failed to destroy the male child, he will fail in destroying His children too!

Satan Seeks the Destruction of God's People (12:13)

In verse 6 the woman, the righteous remnant, fled into the wilderness to be cared for by God. Verses 13-17 further develop that verse and reveal the wrath of the dragon who has "been thrown to the earth." Indeed, he "persecuted the woman who gave birth to the male child." Clearly the woman was righteous Israel in verses 1-2. Here she is not only that remnant but the eschatological remnant, the church, the true vine of Jew and Gentile as Paul makes clear in Romans 11. Mounce is helpful when he writes,

> It is out of faithful Israel that the Messiah will come [ultimately embodied in a particular woman named Mary]. It should cause no trouble that within the same chapter the woman comes to signify the church (v. 17). The people of God are one throughout redemptive history. The early church did not view itself as discontinuous with faithful Israel. (*Revelation*, 232)

The Devil rages against this woman. He always has and he always will. The rage will only grow more intense as the end approaches.

God Is a Rescuer of Those Who Are His (12:14-17)

Exodus imagery and typology dominate these final verses of chapter 12. The dragon seeks the destruction of the Son's children, but God comes to the rescue: "The woman was given two wings of a great eagle, so that she could fly from the serpent's presence to her place in the wilderness, where she was fed for a time, times, and half a time" (i.e., 3½ years).

The phrase "two wings of a great eagle" should not be taken literally. Neither should this be viewed as some type of Boeing 747! It is simply a picture of God's providential protection of His people. Wings often appear in the Bible as a sign of God's protection (see Exod 19:4; Deut 32:9-12; Pss 17:8; 18:10; 36:7; 57:1; 61:4; 63:7; 91:4; Isa 40:31). Indeed, Exodus 19:4 says, "You have seen what I did to the Egyptians and how I carried you on eagles' wings and brought you to Me." The length of her time in the wilderness is again specified as 3½ years. Furthermore, she is said to be in a place that is separated from the presence of the serpent. Some have identified this wilderness place as Petra. Others believe it simply indicates a scattering of the people of God through-out the nations for protection. One cannot specify with any certainty exactly where this place will be. What we do know is that God will make a way for His people during this great wave of persecution. That anti-Semitism may be a component of this persecution should not be ruled out. I believe it is almost certain.

In verse 16 the serpent spews water out of his mouth like a flood. It is an indication of his desire to destroy the woman. Some believe this refers to an army because often an army is pictured as a great flood of water (see Jer 46:8; 47:2). Others believe the flood from his mouth refers to his arrogant and blasphemous words (see the activity of the beast in Rev 13:5). However that Satan comes at the woman, his efforts will utterly fail.

Verse 16 also indicates that the earth will help the woman, opening its mouth and swallowing up the flood that comes from the dragon. If this is a reference to a literal physical miracle, we can think back to when the Lord had the earth open up to swallow Korah (Num 16:31-32). It is possible that even one of the great earthquakes that visit the earth during the great tribulation will be the avenue whereby God will provide a physical miracle to spare His people. The dragon-inspired Egyptians of old were swallowed up by the earth. Exodus 15:12 reminds us, "You stretched out your hand, and the earth swallowed them."

Having failed to destroy the woman, the fury of the dragon is fanned to even greater heat. Not being able to defeat her, he chooses now to go off to make war with the "rest of her offspring." This is probably simply a reference to all the other followers of the Lamb that he can find throughout the earth, Jew and Gentile alike. The rest of her offspring are clearly believers, for they are referred to as those who keep the commandments of God and have the testimony or witness of Jesus. The phrase "to wage war" is the same expression used of the beast's attack on the two witnesses in 11:7 and also his attack against the saints in 13:7.

Although the Devil will be unable to totally exterminate Israel, Zechariah 13:8 sorrowfully informs us that two-thirds of the Jewish population will be killed during the tribulation. Satan will not utterly succeed in wiping God's people from the face of the earth, but he will succeed in plunging many to their death. Satan indeed hates the righteous remnant of God.

Conclusion

Penned by the wonderful Methodist hymn writer Charles Wesley, the following hymn provides the appropriate conclusion to this passage. It is only two simple verses. However, they powerfully capture the drama that has unfolded in our "Apocalyptic Christmas Story."

Come, Thou long expected Jesus,
Born to set Thy people free;
From our fears and sins release us;
Let us find our rest in Thee.
Israel's strength and consolation,

Hope of all the earth Thou art;
Dear desire of ev'ry nation,
Joy of ev'ry longing heart.

Born Thy people to deliver,
Born a child, and yet a King,
Born to reign in us forever,
Now Thy gracious kingdom bring.
By Thine own eternal Spirit
Rule in all our hearts alone;
By Thine all sufficient merit,
Raise us to Thy glorious throne.

Reflect and Discuss

1. How does Revelation 12 provide a summary of the grand narrative of the Bible?
2. Read the covenants God makes with Adam (Gen 3), Abraham (Gen 12), and David (2 Sam 7). What are the similarities? What are the differences? Are there other similar promises God makes to His people?
3. This passage shows that God is faithful to fulfill His promises. What word of promise from God do you need to trust today?
4. Satan was cast down because he coveted a place of authority and honor. How are you tempted to covet places of honor, and how can you work to humble yourself in those areas?
5. Consider each of the descriptors for Satan in 12:9. What do these tell us about his character and his goals for humanity?
6. This passage shows that our salvation is secure and our enemy is defeated. How do Christians sometimes fail to rest in these realities? How can we learn to rest in them?
7. What does it mean to have victory as described in Revelation 12:11-12? How can believers walk in this victory?
8. Why does Satan want to destroy the people of God?
9. This passage shows God's provision of means for the woman's escape. Read 1 Corinthians 10:13 and discuss how these passages relate to one another.
10. What parallels does this passage have to the traditional Christmas story found in the Gospels?

Antichrist: The Beast from the Sea

REVELATION 13:1-10

Main Idea: The Devil will imitate Christ in his rage against God, but Christ will be victorious in the end and vindicate those who resist Satan's lies.

I. **Satan Works Through Evil Individuals and Governments to Advance His Kingdom (13:1-2).**

II. **Satan Desires to Be Worshiped and Treated like God (13:3-4).**

III. **Satan and His Minions Will Be Given Great Power but Only for a Short Time (13:5-8).**

IV. **Satan's Deceptive Devices Will Not Fool the Followers of Jesus Who Will Persevere Even as They Suffer (13:8-10).**

Antichrist. The word itself conjures up images of supreme evil, ultimate deception, and eschatological holocaust. Called the "beast coming up out of the sea" in Revelation (13:1), his origin is the abyss or bottomless pit (11:7). It speaks of one who is coming at the end of history, though he has been preceded by many forerunners (1 John 2:18; 4:3; 2 John 7). The word identifies one who will be given power, a throne, and a great authority from Satan himself (13:2). He will be worshiped as a god, and the whole world will marvel as they follow him (13:3). But his reign of terror will not last. Actually it will be quite brief (13:5-7).

The word *antichrist* does not appear a single time in Revelation. In the Apocalypse he is called "the beast." Elsewhere in Scripture he is called

- the little horn (Dan 7:8)
- the prince (ruler) who is to come (Dan 9:26)
- the lawless one or man of sin (2 Thess 2:3-8)
- the antichrist (1 John 2:18,22; 4:3; 2 John 7)

The word *antichrist* (Gk *antichristos*) means "one who is *against* Christ" or "one who is *in the place of* Christ." Both are true. The beast is an antimessiah. He is in war against Christ even as he attempts to replace the true Christ.

Now it is important to understand that the concept or idea of *antichrist* is multifaceted. It is used in at least four ways in the Bible:

1. An evil empire or political power (Rev 13; 17)
2. A past and present impersonal force, presence, or spirit; the evil spirit of this age (1 John 4:3)
3. Literal persons who are forerunners of the final antichrist (1 John 2:18)
4. The final and climactic embodiment of satanic power and opposition to God in a person (2 Thess 2:3-8; Rev 13:1-10)

There is a fluidity and even overlap, especially in Revelation 13:1-10, where the beast, the antichrist, at times seems to be both a political empire and at the same time a person. This is not all that unusual. When you think of evil Nazi Germany, you think of Hitler. When you think of the founding of America, you think of George Washington.

Throughout history many candidates have been proffered as the coming antichrist. Bernard McGinn in *Antichrist: Two Thousand Years of the Human Fascination with Evil* catalogs much of the history. He notes, "The mythological background of the picture of two beasts is apparently Jewish speculation about Leviathan and Behemoth . . . (Isa. 27:1, and especially Job 40:15–41:26)" (54). There are also Old Testament types in men like the Pharaoh, Nebuchadnezzar, Cyrus, and the intertestamental Antiochus Epiphanes (Riddlebarger, *Man of Sin,* 40). Then the parade begins. Notable suggestions include Nero, Domitian, Constantine, Charlemagne, Napoleon, Martin Luther, Mussolini, Stalin, Hitler, Gorbachev, Jimmy Carter, Henry Kissinger, Ronald Reagan, Anwar Sadat, Saddam Hussein, Barack Obama, Pat Robertson, and numerous popes (McGinn, *Antichrist,* 260–61). In fact Luther, Calvin, Cotton Mather, John Knox, Cranmer, John Wesley, and Roger Williams all identified the pope as the antichrist.

On November 1, 1999, *Newsweek* magazine's cover story was "Prophecy." It reported that 40 percent of US adults believe the world will end in a battle of Armageddon between Jesus Christ and the antichrist. It also reported that 19 percent of Americans believed the antichrist was alive on the earth right now. One thing is certain: everyone in the past who has made a specific identification of the antichrist has been wrong! That fact alone should give us pause in following in their footsteps.

I believe Revelation 13 and the Bible's teaching on the antichrist is not intended to provoke our speculation as to who he is. Rather, I think God's design is to instruct us now and in every generation concerning what antichrists do and how they work as they are empowered and deployed by the dragon (13:2), Satan himself. The text seeks to enlighten us to the devices of the Devil, the strategies of Satan.

Chapter 13 is a part of a long parenthesis or interlude (10:1–14:20). Here we are introduced to two beasts. The antichrist or beast from the sea is the focus of 13:1-10. The false prophet (16:13; 19:20; 20:10) or the beast from the earth is the focus of 13:11-18. Joined at the hip with the dragon, they constitute nothing less than a counterfeit trinity! Satan counterfeits God the Father. Antichrist counterfeits God the Son. The false prophet counterfeits God the Holy Spirit.

Satan Works Through Evil Individuals and Governments to Advance His Kingdom

REVELATION 13:1-2

Satan, the dragon of chapter 12, stands on the sand of the sea in 12:17. The sea was often associated with evil in the ancient world, as "the reservoir of chaos" (Mounce, *Revelation*, 244). In the Apocalypse it may even "symbolize the Abyss, the source of demonic powers that are opposed to God" (Johnson, "Revelation," 1981, 705). Others think it could represent also the nations of the world with all its ethnic, national, political, and social chaos and wickedness (see 17:15) (MacArthur, *Revelation 12–22*, 41). From the sea John sees "a beast coming up out of the sea. He had 10 horns and seven heads. On his horns were 10 diadems, and on his heads were blasphemous names." The word *beast* appears 16 times in chapter 13. Fifteen refer to the antichrist and one to the false prophet (13:11).

This begins the biography of the beast. The 10 horns speak of great power. "Seven heads" may draw from seven-headed monster mythology in ancient Near Eastern texts. It also speaks of great power but with the added connotations of ferocity and intelligence. The 10 diadems convey great authority and political influence. Additionally, though we must be cautious at this point, 17:9-12 speaks of the seven heads as both seven mountains or hills (the city of Rome) and also seven kings or kingdoms. There the 10 horns are a future political alliance in consort with the beast who will enjoy a short reign. The same symbolism is applied to

Satan here in 12:3. On these heads are blasphemous names, mentioned four times in our text (13:1,5,6 [2x]). MacArthur well notes,

> In addition to his ten horns, the beast is described by John as having seven heads. As will be seen in Revelation 17 . . . , those seven heads represent seven successive world empires: Egypt, Assyria, Babylon, Medo-Persia, Greece, Rome, and Antichrist's final world kingdom. The ten diadems (royal crowns) indicate the horns' regal authority and victorious power. John also noted that on the beast's heads were blasphemous names. Like many of the Roman emperors and other monarchs before them, these rulers will blasphemously arrogate divine names and titles to themselves that dishonor the true and living God. They will follow the pattern of their master, Antichrist, "who opposes and exalts himself above every so-called god or object of worship, so that he takes his seat in the temple of God, displaying himself as being God" (2 Thess. 2:4). (*Revelation 12–22*, 43)

Verse 2 draws on the vision of Daniel 7:3-8 but in reverse order, perhaps because John is looking at it in the past. Here, three terrifying elements of three great empires of the ancient world are said to characterize the beast. The leopard represented the Greek empire under Alexander the Great. It speaks of the swiftness of its destructive power. The bear represented Medo-Persia and symbolized its great strength and devouring power. The lion was Babylon, with its majesty, power, and fierceness. This awesome political entity and person is empowered by the dragon, who will give to it and him three things: his power, his throne, and great authority. The great Greek scholar A. T. Robertson wrote, "The dragon works through this beast. This beast is simply Satan's agent. Satan claimed this power to Christ (Matt 4:9; Luke 4:6) and Christ called Satan the prince of this world (John 12:31; 14:30; 16:11). So the war is on" (*Word Pictures*, 6:398–99).

Satan Desires to Be Worshiped and Treated like God
REVELATION 13:3-4

Satan is the great counterfeiter, the great imposter. He is a wannabe god who will never be God. Still he delights in aping the one true triune God. In verse 3 we see him counterfeiting the resurrection of the Son. In verse 4 we see him counterfeiting the worship of God.

Verse 3 tells us that one of the heads of the beast "appeared to be fatally wounded, but his fatal wound was healed," leading the whole world to be amazed and to follow the beast. The word *wounded* is the same word in Greek translated "slaughtered" in 5:6,9. There it addresses the vicarious death of the Lamb. Chapter 13 verse 14 adds that the beast "had the sword wound and yet lived." The word *lived* is "the very term used for Jesus' resurrection in 2:8" (Osborne, *Revelation,* 495). What we have here is nothing less than a counterfeit death and resurrection taking place at the end of the age. Some believe it is the resurrection of a political entity (e.g., the Roman Empire that is dead and will be revived), others of the personal antichrist, and others a combination of both. I am sympathetic to this last view. Walvoord well notes, "The identification of a head with the government over which he has authority is not a strange situation. The person is often the symbol of the government, and what can be said of the government can be said of him" (*Revelation,* 199). Many believed in a *Nero redividus* myth, in which Nero returns from the dead as the antichrist. In fact, in Armenian "the word Nero became and remains the equivalent for the Antichrist" (Beasley-Murray, *Revelation,* 211).

Amazed at the apparent resurrection of the beast, the whole earth begins to submit to his authority: "They worshiped the dragon because he gave authority to the beast" (13:4). In addition, they also worshiped the beast, declaring, "Who is like the beast? Who is able to wage war against him?" Wonder turns to worship. Divine worship is substituted by Devil worship. Idolatry of the most terrible sort imaginable now blankets the earth. "Who is like the beast?" is a parody of the acclamation of Yahweh (Exod 8:10; 15:11; Pss 71:19; 89:8; Isa 44:7; 46:5; Mic 7:18). "God alone is incomparable, and the beast once more is usurping what belongs only to God" (Osborne, *Revelation,* 498). Swindoll is insightful as usual at this point:

> How like Satan! The one who "disguises himself as an angel of light" (2 Cor. 11:14) will provide the world with a copycat "christ" to match all their man-centered ideals of personality, politics, and power. No wonder the whole world will be swept off its feet by this attractive, persuasive figure (13:3)! In fact, we are told the world will worship the dragon through their worship of the Beast. In this rabid fit of hypernationalism that will make Hitler's Third Reich look like a high school sporting

event, the world will cry out, "Who is like the beast, and who is able to wage war with him?" (13:4). (*Insights*, 181)

Satan desires to be worshiped and treated like God. He always has. He always will.

Satan and His Minions Will Be Given Great Power but Only for a Short Time
REVELATION 13:5-8

Satan's reign of terror with the beast will have definite and specific characteristics. These are carefully logged in verses 5-8. The beast is given a mouth "to speak boasts and blasphemies." He is given this mouth *directly* by the dragon, but *ultimately* he is permitted to speak by God. He, like the Devil, is God's beast and on God's leash. With this mouth he will utter haughty, boastful, proud words of arrogance. He will also speak "blasphemies," a word appearing three times in verses 5-6. The objects of his slanders are noted in verse 6: God, His name, His dwelling, and His people ("those who dwell in heaven"). Mounce provides helpful commentary at this point:

> The beast opens his mouth to blaspheme God. This activity of the Antichrist is clearly portrayed in 2 Thess. 2:4: "He will oppose and will exalt himself over everything that is called God . . . proclaiming himself to be God." The blasphemy of Antiochus (Dan. 7:25; 11:36) and the use of divine titles by the Roman emperors would for John identify the Antichrist as the one in whom secular authority had assumed the mantle of deity. The expression, "to open the mouth," is frequently used at the beginning of a prolonged discourse (cf. Matt. 5:2; Acts 8:35) and suggests that the blasphemies of the beast against God were sustained. (*Revelation*, 250)

These blasphemies, these slanders, indeed will go on for a sustained period of time. John says it will be for 42 months, or 3½ years (13:5). But not only will he *speak* against God and His people; he will also *act* against God and His people. In a story all too familiar for those who know the history of the church, the beast will be "permitted to wage war against the saints and to conquer them." He will persecute God's people, and many will perish as they take their faithful stand for the Lamb. Conquering the people of God will not satisfy the insatiable appetite of Satan and his antichrist. Again, by divine permission, he will be given authority over the people the Lamb came to redeem: "every tribe, people, language, and nation" (13:7). Indeed "all those who live on the earth will worship him" (13:8). Unbelieving humanity on a world-wide scale will worship the beast as god. Mocking the authentic worship rightly given to the Son of Man in Daniel 7:14, the beast "imitates the glory, authority, and worship of which only Christ is worthy" (Osborne, *Revelation,* 502). All of this and more will Satan, the beast, and the earth dwellers do. But it will only be for a short time.

Everybody worships somebody. Whom do you worship? Here are two possibilities: Christ or antichrist!

Satan's Deceptive Devices Will Not Fool the Followers of Jesus Who Will Persevere Even as They Suffer
REVELATION 13:8-10

Verse 8 says, "All those who live on the earth will worship [the beast]." But there is a second group on this planet who are not "earth-dwellers" and devotees of the dragon and beast. They follow a different Leader, march to the beat of a different Drummer, pledge allegiance to a different Master. And unlike the earth dweller "whose name was not written from the foundation of the world in the book of life of the Lamb who was slaughtered" (13:8), their name has been. The book of life is the book containing the names of the redeemed, the saved (see Phil 4:3); those who follow the Lamb have their name in this book. We should note in this the security of our salvation. Our name was written in this book in eternity past. Further, this is a book that belongs to the Lamb who was slaughtered (5:6,9). I love what MacArthur says about this verse:

> Seven times in the New Testament, believers are identified as those whose names are written in the book of life (cf. 3:5; 17:8; 20:12,15; 21:27; Phil. 4:3). The book of life belonging to the Lamb, the Lord Jesus, is the registry in which God inscribed the names of those chosen for salvation before the foundation of the world. (This phrase is used as a synonym for eternity past in 17:8; Matt. 13:35; 25:34; Luke 11:50; Eph. 1:4; Heb. 9:26; 1 Pet. 1:20; cf. 2 Thess. 2:13; and 2 Tim. 1:9.) Unlike unbelievers, the elect will not be deceived by Antichrist (Matt. 24:24), nor will they worship him ([Rev] 20:4). Antichrist will not be able to destroy believers' saving faith, for the Lord Jesus

Christ promised, "He who overcomes will thus be clothed in
white garments; and I will not erase his name from the book of
life, and I will confess his name before My Father and before
His angels" (Rev 3:5; cf. 1 John 5:4). Believers have been in the
keeping power of God since before creation, and they will be
there after the destruction of this order and the establishment
of the new heaven and the new earth (21:1ff.).

Believers are doubly secure, because the book of life
belongs to the Lamb who has been slain. Not only the decree
of election, but also the atoning work of Christ seals the
redemption of the elect forever. (*Revelation 12–22*, 50)

Verse 9 is a simple invitation to pay attention and be spiritually discerning. This is an invitation every generation needs to heed, but how
much more as we edge toward the end of history. Verse 10 is somewhat
enigmatic to be sure. I believe it best to understand it as a proverb of
destiny for those whose name is in the book of life. You can expect to
be captured and imprisoned. Your earthly destiny may be to be slaughtered. However, endure and remain faithful. David Platt puts it well:

It is, and it will be, costly to follow Christ in this world, but
don't compromise! Even if it means you're being slain, hold
fast to your faith. Even if it means you lose your job and all
your money, hold fast to your faith. Even if it means ridicule
and oppression and isolation or imprisonment or death,
follow the Lamb! And one day you will stand with him, you
will sing with him, and you will be satisfied completely in him.
("Fighting," 2012)

Conclusion

Satan's antichrist is coming. But so is God's Christ, the Lord Jesus. What
will you do? Will you be pro-Christ or anti-Christ? Will you worship God
and the Lamb, or will you worship the dragon and the beast? The choice
is that clear. And the choice is yours. Your eternal destiny hangs in the
balance. Your eternal home is at stake. You must take a stand. You are
taking a stand right now. Jesus said in Matthew 12:30, "Anyone who is
not with Me is against Me." There is no neutral ground. You are either
with Him or against Him. So, what will you do? John Piper is right:

The main point of the book of Revelation is that Christ wins in the end. And that to have your name written in the Lamb's Book of Life, so that you don't get any mark of belonging to any beastly power, is absolutely essential.

Those who have their names written in the Lamb's Book of Life are enabled not to give in to any beastly, antichrist power that comes along.

And that's the most important thing for us individually: that we love Christ so much that we defeat Satan by the word of our testimony and by the blood of the Lamb, and thus find ourselves on the right side of the Lamb when he comes when others are going to say, "O rocks, fall upon me!" because they can't bear to look upon the wrath that will stream forth from the face of the Lamb of God when he comes the second time. ("United States")

Reflect and Discuss

1. Read 1 and 2 John. What do these books teach us about antichrist?
2. What are the dangers of too much speculation regarding the exact identity of the antichrist?
3. If the point is not to speculate about the precise identity of the antichrist, why does John give us this description?
4. This passage shows that Satan can work through both individuals and governments or institutions. How have you seen this to be the case in your life and in the world today?
5. Why does the beast imitate Christ in this passage? How is all sin ultimately a perversion of God's goodness?
6. Why do you think God allows the beast to reign and even blaspheme His name? How does this evil fit into God's ultimate plan?
7. What does it mean that "everybody worships somebody"?
8. How can believers have confidence amid persecution like that which comes from the beast?
9. What does it mean to be "spiritually discerning"? How can we cultivate spiritual discernment?
10. Why is it impossible to take a neutral position between Christ and antichrist? How do some try to do so?

The False Prophet

Main Idea: Satan sends false prophets to deceive and coerce worship for himself, but at best he can only imitate the glory of the true Savior, Jesus Christ.

I.   The False Prophet Will Be a Deceiver (13:11).
II. The False Prophet Will Speak the Words of Satan (13:11).
III. The False Prophet Will Promote False Worship of Antichrist (13:12).
IV. The False Prophet Will Use Miracles to Deceive the World (13:13-14).
V.   The False Prophet Will Persecute Those Who Follow the Lamb (13:15).
VI. The False Prophet Will Mark Those Who Worship Antichrist (13:16-17).
VII. The False Prophet Will Lead the World to Worship a Mere Man (13:18).

If I had to pick one word to describe the most effective device of the Devil in building his empire, I would pick the word *deception*. Our Lord Himself tells us in John 8:44, "He is a liar and the father of liars," and in Revelation 13 we see his masterpiece of deception put on full display through the antichrist (the sea beast) and the false prophet (the earth beast).

In his excellent study of the Apocalypse, Grant Osborne helps us get a handle on just what this thirteenth chapter is all about as Satan seeks to usurp God's kingdom with his own:

> Satan's final rebellion will be waged relentlessly. To fight
> this great battle against God and his people, he parodies the
> Holy Trinity and establishes his own false trinity: the dragon
> (himself), the beast from the sea (the Antichrist), and the
> beast from the earth or false prophet (the religious leader
> of the movement). The dragon uses these creatures to gain
> control of both the governmental and religious apparatus,
> creating both a one-world government (with the Antichrist as
> "king of kings") and a one-world religion (with the Antichrist

228

as idol of the world). This combination of political and religious control is the core of the absolute power of the false trinity over the nations. This has always been Satan's method, from the Egyptians in Moses' time to the Babylonians and Persians of Daniel's day to the Romans of John's day to the Nazis and Stalin in the twentieth century. The people of God have always been both persecuted and led astray into idolatry and immorality by the same evil forces (Rev 2:14,20). In other words, the material here about the final Antichrist also fits the many "antichrists" that have preceded, of both the political and the religious variety.

The first beast gains control by parodying Christ's death and resurrection but in a far more public forum. When he returns from the dead, his associate, the false prophet, will use the event to forge a new world religion with the beast, and behind him the dragon (13:3-4,12), as its focus. . . . Again, this tendency for world leaders to arrogate to themselves divine powers and to pretend that their actions are answerable to no one (note the "lawless one" of 2 Thess. 2:3-4) is seen everywhere today as well. The message of 13:5-8,14-15 is critical. Though the beast and his followers believed their "authority" had been given by Satan (13:2), it is clear that the ultimate authority had come from God. The blasphemous names (13:5-6), the worship of the nations (13:7b-8), the power to perform miracles and deceive (13:14-15), and even the persecution of the saints (13:7a) happened only because God allowed it. There is no true power in evil. God is in firm control, and it can do no more than its part of the divine will. Nothing in the world, from Croatia to Rwanda to the moral wasteland that is modern America, escapes his notice, and it will end at his predetermined time. At the end of history, the Antichrist will control the economics of the world. Nothing will be bought or sold without his "mark," and many "Christians" will capitulate to the pressure (the "great apostasy" of Matt. 24:4-5 and 2 Thess. 2:3). But that also is seen today, where the idol of too many Christians is the dollar sign and so many in our churches put economic success ahead of following God. . . .

The passage describes [then] the final "tribulation period" of history, when the beast/antichrist comes to power and the second beast/false prophet becomes the prime minister, or high priest, of the evil empire, forcing the world to make a choice between Christ and the beast. After the Antichrist is assassinated and comes back to life, the false prophet will erect a statue and bring it to life, thus inaugurating the period when every person will either accept the "mark" or die. It will become a capital crime to refuse to participate in the universal worship of the beast. While at the present period in history it seems unthinkable that such a state of affairs could occur, we must remember that we are only seventy years removed from the rise of Hitler and Stalin, and it is pure arrogance to think something similar could not happen again. If anyone could solve the terrorist crisis, the Palestinian-Israeli conflict, and the unrest in Africa and bring peace to our troubled world, people would rush to worship such a person. (*Revelation*, 507–8, 522)

The second beast of Revelation 13:11-18 is correctly identified as the false prophet (see 16:13; 19:20; 20:10). Though they are distinct persons, there are similarities and differences between him and the first beast, the antichrist of 13:1-10.

Comparison of the Two Beasts in Revelation 13	
First Beast Antichrist	Second Beast False Prophet
Rises from the sea (13:1)	Rises from the earth (13:11)
Seven heads with blasphemous names (13:1,3)	One head (13:11)
Ten horns with crowns (13:1)	Two horns like a lamb (13:11)
Authority given to him by the dragon (13:2)	Exercises authority of the first beast (13:12)
The whole earth worships the dragon because of the beast (13:3-4)	Causes people to worship the first beast (13:12)
Speaks blasphemies against God for 42 months or 3½ years (13:5-6)	Performs amazing signs to deceive the whole world into worshiping the first beast's image (13:13-15)
Makes war with the saints and for a time overcomes them (13:7)	Forces the world to receive the mark of the beast or suffer severe persecution (13:16-17)
(Swindoll, *Insights*, 183)	

So as we navigate verses 11-18, we will discover that it will be through the instrumentality of this second beast empowered by Satan that a one-world government, one-world religion, and one-world economy will come to fruition. Humanity will willingly submit to it. This individual called the false prophet will be given power by Satan to perform miracles (13:12-15). He will apparently duplicate the miracles of that one who comes in the spirit of Elijah (13:13; see 11:5-6), perhaps deceiving the world into believing that he is the one who fulfills the prophecy of Malachi 4:5. Further, he apparently will cause some type of lifeless image of the beast to come alive and to speak, and he will force the world to worship it.

Paul pointed out in 2 Thessalonians 2:11 that during the tribulation, the Day of the Lord, God will send the world a powerful delusion so that they should believe the lie. I believe the lie is that antichrist, who will rule over a one-world government, one-world religion, and one-world economy, is actually the world's messiah, the world's god.

Walking through these eight verses, we discover seven defining characteristics of the antichrist's "minister of propaganda." These are valuable lessons for every generation of Christians who encounter false messiahs and false prophets and false teachings.

The False Prophet Will Be a Deceiver
REVELATION 13:11

John sees another beast of the same sort as the first. He comes up out of the earth. Some believe this refers to the land of Israel and means the false prophet will be a Jew. Others say the earth is a reference to the abyss. The difference in origin from the first beast may be intended to help us distinguish the two beasts from each other. It is also possible that the earth, in contrast to the turmoil of the sea, implies the false prophet is calmer, more peaceful, and subtler than the antichrist. Like a lamb, he has the appearance of a friend.

He has "two horns like a lamb." The two horns signify strength but not great strength. The antichrist is powerful with 10 horns (13:1). The false prophet is one with much less strength. And he has the appearance of a lamb. The word "lamb" appears 29 times in Revelation. Twenty-eight of those times it refers to Jesus. This is the one time it refers to someone or something else. There is deceptiveness in this person, and once more we are reminded of the truth, "Looks can be deceiving!"

The False Prophet Will Speak the Words of Satan
REVELATION 13:11

With the appearance of a lamb, this beast gives the impression of being harmless and gentle. However, Jesus warned us in Matthew 7:15, "Beware of false prophets who come to you in sheep's clothing but inwardly are ravaging wolves." Here is the most ravenous wolf of all who is nothing less than a mouthpiece, a megaphone, for Satan. "He sounded like a dragon." This is not the roar of an intimidating dragon but the beguiling, deceitful, and deceptive speech of the serpent who deceived Adam and Eve in the garden (Mounce, *Revelation*, 256). Jim Hamilton rightly affirms,

> This beast speaks like Satan, and Satan speaks against God's word, blasphemes Jesus, and tells lies meant to result in the death of Jesus and his people. Christians do not tell lies to get other people killed. . . . Watch out for lambs who talk like dragons. (*Revelation*, 270–71)

The False Prophet Will Promote False Worship of Antichrist
REVELATION 13:12

Two affirmations are made about the false prophet in verse 12. First, "He exercises all the authority of the first beast on his behalf." Second, he "compels the earth and those who live on it to worship the first beast, whose fatal wound was healed." The false prophet is empowered by Satan and loyal to the antichrist. With delegated authority, he is the representative of the beast. He is his witness and advocate. Further, he is the promoter of gross idolatry. He causes earth dwellers to worship the first beast who parodied our Lord's sufferings, death, and resurrection. As Kistemaker says, "These two anti-Christian forces are united in their effort to overthrow the rule of Christ" (*Exposition*, 389).

Here is the establishment of false religion on a worldwide scale. Christians, Muslims, Jews, Buddhists, Hindus, Animists, etc.—all persons of faith will join hands and heart in worship, praise, and adoration of the antichrist. No doubt each faith will retain certain particular emphases that characterize their faith, but they will—they must—unite in their devotion and dedication to the beast. This will be the most dishonoring form of idolatry the world will ever know. Its seeds are continuing to be sown today. The fruit it will bear will multiply as the world as we know it draws to a close.

In an article titled "U.N. Faithful Eye Global Religion," James Harder writes,

> The secretary-general of the United Nation's Millennium Peace summit thinks that all religious apples fall from the same tree and are equally delicious. At a recent international meeting, he told 1,000 delegates that religions need to accept the validity of all religions or else it will be difficult to attain world peace. Recently, the notion has emerged that the pathway to peace necessitates the unification of religions. The Universal Religion Initiative (URI) recently convened with 300 people present representing 39 religions and signed a charter, which officially launched the movement. The goal is that there will come a day in which "religious people will no longer insist on a single truth." Episcopal Bishop Swing, a leader in the movement, goes even further: "There will have to be a godly cease-fire, a temporary truce where the absolute exclusive claims of each [religion] will be honored but an agreed upon neutrality will be exercised in terms of proselytizing, condemning, murdering, or dominating. These will not be tolerated in the United Religions Zone." (22–23)

I am not suggesting that the United Nations is in league with the antichrist, but I am saying that the impulse to unify the world in a single religion is already alive and well in our day. We must be on guard and realize that the true gospel necessarily makes exclusive claims about God, Christ, salvation, and eternity, and to minimize those claims is neither loving nor wise. As the North Carolina evangelist Vance Havner well said, "A house big enough for all of us is too big."

The False Prophet Will Use Miracles to Deceive the World
REVELATION 13:13-14

Not everything that appears to be a miracle is a miracle. And not everything that is a miracle is a miracle from God. That is true today, and it will clearly be true during the reign of the antichrist. Our text tells us that the false prophet "performs great signs." This same phrase is used for the miracles of Jesus in John 2:11,23 and 6:21. The false prophet is also something of a false Christ.

One specific sign miracle he performs is "causing fire to come down from heaven to earth in front of people." Here he duplicates the miracle of Elijah (1 Kgs 18:28; see Mal 3:5-6) and the two witnesses (Rev 11:5). The spectacular nature of these miracles mesmerizes and deceives the earth dwellers. Amazingly, they reject the true fire of 11:5 for a false fire in 13:14. But their deception and seduction do not stop here.

The false prophet tells them to make an image, an idol, to "the beast who had the sword wound and yet lived," and that is exactly what they do. Like Nebuchadnezzar in Daniel 2, a great idol will be erected, this time to honor and worship antichrist. This will take place probably near the midpoint of the tribulation, possibly in a rebuilt temple in Jerusalem (Matt 24:15; 2 Thess 2:2-12).

Swindoll says,

> Blinded by unbelief and sin, the world will easily fall prey to the second Beast's deceptive message and methods. Intellectually attracted to him, emotionally drawn by his appealing style and convinced by his amazing signs, they will voluntarily submit and obey [and worship]. (*Insights,* 184)

The False Prophet Will Persecute Those Who Follow the Lamb
REVELATION 13:15

Verse 15 is a mixed bag in terms of interpretation. The first part is extremely difficult as to the meaning, whereas the second half is straightforward and transparent. The false prophet is allowed (by God) to "give a spirit," or breathe life, into the image, the idol, of the antichrist. The image is even said to speak. The miraculous and the mysterious merge. Some believe this is trickery that uses ventriloquism to make it seem like the image comes to life. Others believe that through Satanic and demonic enablement, the statue will come to life and speak (Osborne, *Revelation,* 515–16). Alan Johnson makes a sound observation when he says,

> In speaking about giving "breath" (*pneuma*) to the image, John implies the activity of the false prophets in reviving idolatrous worship, giving it the appearance of vitality, reality, and power (cf. Jer. 10:14). Curiously, the two witnesses were also said to receive "breath" (11:11). ("Revelation," 2006, 713)

Idols normally cannot hear or speak, walk or see. They also do not murder. However, this is not a normal idol. Breathing and talking, it goes on a vicious campaign, a Christian holocaust, a Christian pogrom. Duvall is on target:

> The demonic idol demands worship on penalty of death (cf. 16:14; 19:20). Christians may either give allegiance to false gods and 'live' or stay faithful to Christ with the real possibility of physical death. (*Revelation*, 186)

No doubt the temptation to compromise and give in will be great. The power of the gospel to endure and persevere will never be more needed.

The False Prophet Will Mark Those Who Worship Antichrist
REVELATION 13:16-17

Determined to coerce and enforce worship of the antichrist, the false prophet will engage in a global movement, a plan and program, to bring everyone into submission. All the various categories of humanity (13:16) will receive some type of mark, some form of identification on their right hand or their forehead. Without it they will not be able to buy or sell. While we do not know exactly what the mark is, we know its design is to mark people as belonging to the antichrist so they might be able to do the things necessary to live. It is clear from this passage that no one will receive it unknowingly. All will know exactly what they are doing. Believers will face economic boycott and social alienation in that day. The beast counterfeits the mark, the seal, of God in 7:3 and 14:1. God marks His people and Satan marks his too!

John MacArthur tells us the mark

> will consist of either the name of the beast or the number of his name. Antichrist will have a universal designation, his name within a numbering system. The exact identification of that phrase is unclear. What is clear is that everyone will be required to have the identifying mark or suffer the consequences. (*Revelation 12–22*, 63)

David Platt is right: "Mark it down: there will always be a price to pay for believers who do not worship the idols of this world. Life will not be easy in this world when you fight the idolatry of this world, plain and simple" ("Fighting").

The False Prophet Will Lead the World to Worship a Mere Man
REVELATION 13:18

More paper, ink, and worry have been wasted on this verse than perhaps any other verse in the Bible. What is "the mark of the beast" and the "number of his name"? The ancient Hebrew game called *Gematria* recognized that letters could also stand for numbers. Hence a series of letters could form a word and at the same time indicate a number. Hence the 666 of verse 18 has given us various identifications of the antichrist:

- From ancient times it was said to be the Roman emperor, Nero Caesar particularly, and his priest who enforced caesar worship.
- From modern times some say Ronald Wilson Reagan.
- Some saw the mark in Social Security cards; others in credit cards.
- Still others identified it with the coming of computers.
- Some have noted that taxi license plates in Israel begin with 666.
- Of course many during the time of the Reformation were certain the "mark of the beast" involved being a follower of the pope and the Roman Catholic Church.
- Still others spiritualize both beasts seeing the first as representing evil political power and the second representing evil religious power wedded to the first.

Speculation has not been helpful, and in many instances it has been rather harmful.

Verse 18 issues a call for wisdom. Perhaps the wise person would avoid this hermeneutical quicksand altogether. But an important statement in the verse might lead us to make a cautious suggestion. The statement is, "It is the number of a man. His number is 666." I think the number is more of a description than an identification. Six is the number of man. He was created on the sixth day. He is to work six days. In contrast, the number of perfection is seven, and the superlative of seven is 777.

The beast is the greatest man but still a man. He is a six, not a seven. He, along with Satan and the false prophet, is a 666, a trinity of imperfection. Not now or ever will they be a 777! He is the best man can produce, but he is still just a man! He is "the completeness of sinful incompleteness," the ultimate in "coming up short." He is good enough to deceive many, but he is nowhere close to good enough to displace Jesus (Beale, "Number of the Beast").

Conclusion

Some people put their trust in government. Some people put their trust in money and the economy. Many people put their trust in religion. The Bible teaches that none of these will meet your expectations. None of these is the answer. Rather, our faith and confidence should be put in the kingdom of God, a bloody cross, and an empty tomb. We should put our trust in King Jesus and His gospel. Tragically, the world would rather believe a lie than the truth. They would rather align with antichrist than Jesus Christ. They are quicker to follow a false prophet than a true prophet of God. Do not be deceived! Follow Him who is the way, the truth, and the life (John 14:6). Do not seek the mark of the beast. Seek to have the seal of the Savior of all men. Seek to bear the true mark, the mark of Jesus Christ. The decision is yours, and it is an important one.

Reflect and Discuss

1. Why is "deception" the best way to describe the work of Satan? Where do you see this in Scripture?
2. What other words could be used to describe Satan's tactics?
3. What parallels do you see between the description of the false prophet in this chapter and false teaching that is spread today?
4. The false prophet looks like a lamb but talks like a dragon. What role does speech play in revealing what's in our hearts?
5. How does a unified world religion help Satan accomplish his goals? What is required of religious truth claims for all faiths to unite?
6. What passages of Scripture point to the exclusive claims of Christianity? How would you explain to someone why biblical Christianity cannot endorse the validity and equality of all faiths?
7. Why aren't miracles alone enough to prove the validity of a person or event? From the biblical perspective, what else must be present to confirm that something is of God?
8. In this passage the image seems to come alive, giving apparent validity to the idolatry. Discuss how sin often gives the appearance of validity and reality that it cannot deliver.
9. Discuss some of the bad ways to interpret the number of the beast. What do these miss about what John is trying to tell us?
10. In contrast to the mark of the beast, what is the mark God places on His people?

My Eyes Have Seen the Coming of the Glory of the Lord

REVELATION 14:1-20

Main Idea: At the return of the Lamb, the enemies of Christ will be eternally punished while eternal rest and reward are promised for those who have their faith in Jesus.

I. **Faithful Followers of Jesus Have a Glorious Future (14:1-5).**
  A. The redeemed will stand with Him securely (14:1).
  B. The redeemed will sing to Him loudly (14:2-3).
  C. The redeemed will be sanctified through Him completely (14:4-5).

II. **God Will Be Just in His Treatment of All Persons (14:6-13).**
  A. All peoples are called to fear, glorify, and worship their Creator God (14:6-7).
  B. Unbelievers can anticipate defeat, wrath, and eternal torment (14:8-11).
  C. Believers will endure, obey, find rest, and be rewarded (14:12-13).

III. **Jesus Will Pour Out His Wrath on the Earth in Righteous Judgment (14:14-20).**
  A. The judgment will be in glory and on time (14:14-16).
  B. The judgment will be universal and horrific (14:17-20).

There is an old song called "The Battle Hymn of the Republic," which begins with words that reflect the text before us: "Mine eyes have seen the glory of the coming of the Lord; He is trampling out the vintage where the grapes of wrath are stored." The idea of God trampling out sinners in wrath is not a popular idea in our culture. One denomination recently refused to include the popular hymn "In Christ Alone" because it found offensive the line "When on the cross as Jesus died, the wrath of God was satisfied." They preferred to change the latter phrase to "the love of God was magnified." The idea of wrath offends modern sensibilities. However, the wrath of God is a thoroughly biblical concept we neglect or deny at our peril.

In Psalm 94:1-2 we read, "LORD, God of vengeance—God of vengeance, appear. Rise up, Judge of the earth; repay the proud what they deserve." The prayer of the psalmist is answered in Revelation 14, a text that stands in amazing contrast to chapter 13. There the beast, the antichrist, rises to power. He wars against the saints and overcomes them (13:7), takes authority over the whole earth (13:7), and puts to death those who will not worship him or bear his mark (13:15-18). Now in three separate visions (see "I looked" or "I saw" in 14:1,6,14) we see the warrior Lamb standing on Mount Zion with his army of saints (14:1). They sing the song of redemption (14:2-3) and follow after the Lamb in holiness and purity (14:4-5). They have the promise of heaven and glory whereas the followers of the beast have the certainty of judgment and hell (14:6-20). This chapter is a preview of coming attractions. The one you follow is crucial. The one you worship is decisive.

Faithful Followers of Jesus Have a Glorious Future

REVELATION 14:1-5

Warren Wiersbe is certainly correct: "Better to reign with Christ forever, than to reign with Antichrist for a few years" (*Be Victorious*, 112). To this I would add, "Better to worship the Lamb who redeems and rewards than the beast who deceives and destroys." John begins this chapter with his attention turned to the Lamb, the Lord Jesus, and His followers. Three glorious promises are ours to enjoy forever and ever.

The Redeemed Will Stand with Him Securely (14:1)

The Lamb is now standing on Mount Zion and with Him 144,000. This is the same 144,000 of Revelation 7:1-8. As there, I believe these are Jewish believers who belong to God and are protected by God. Both His name and the Father's name are written, permanently inscribed, on their foreheads. These followers of Christ are dependent on God, loyal to God, owned by God, safe and secure in God.

They stand with the Lamb on Mount Zion. Some believe this is heavenly Zion, based on Hebrews 12:22-24. That is certainly possible. However, I believe it is better to see this as earthly Jerusalem and a reflection of the beautiful messianic hymn of Psalm 2. There in verse 6 we read, "I have consecrated My King on Zion, My holy mountain." Psalm 48:2 says that God's holy mountain, "rising splendidly, is the joy

of the whole earth. Mount Zion on the slopes of the north is the city of
the great King." Isaiah 24:33 adds,

> *The moon will be put to shame and the sun disgraced, because the
> Lord of Hosts will reign as king on Mount Zion in Jerusalem, and He
> will display His glory in the presence of His elders.*

This is the mountain of the great King, and there He stands in triumphant victory. By glorious grace those who follow Him stand with
Him.

The reign of terror of the dragon, antichrist, and false prophet is
already passing away. Their doom is certain. There is a new King on the
scene! The beast is going down as the Lamb stands up (see 5:6-7; see
also Ps 76).

The Redeemed Will Sing to Him Loudly (14:2-3)

In verse 1, John sees the glory of God. Now he hears singing to the glory
of God. Once more he hears "a sound from heaven" (see 4:1; 10:4,8;
11:12; 12:10,13; 18:14; 19:1). This recalls the vision of 1:15 (see Ezek
43:2). Here the voice is not one but many. Duvall says John hears "a
resounding heavenly anthem. The sound is both booming and beautiful" (*Revelation*, 191). Indeed, the sound of the waters and thunders are
impressive and powerful. The song, John says, is "like harpists harping
with their harps" (my translation).

To these instruments is added "a new song," the song of the
redeemed (see 5:9). They sing before the throne, angels ("the four living creatures"), and the representatives of the redeemed ("the elders").
Only the redeemed (the 144,000) can learn and sing this song. If I am
correct that the 144,000 represent Jewish believers, it may also be correct
that here they represent all believers as they sing the song of redemption and salvation. Such joy and celebration is the natural response of
all who have been purchased for God by the blood of the Lamb. Saved
by a salvation we do not deserve or could ever earn, we rejoice in the
Lamb who was slaughtered but is now standing (5:6). Christianity has
always been a singing faith. It will remain so for all eternity!

The Redeemed Will Be Sanctified Through Him Completely (14:4-5)

Verse 4 can be a bit tricky if we forget Revelation is apocalyptic, symbolic
language. We are introduced to virgins who have not defiled themselves

with women. This, without question, is symbolic of their fidelity and allegiance to the Lamb whom they follow wherever He goes. In other words, they are spiritually faithful to their God in a world awash in idolatry and immorality (see 9:20-21; see also Jas 4:5). They have remained morally and spiritually pure in their devotion of and love for the Lamb. No other God would they consider. No other lover would they entertain. They follow Christ and only Christ, for He redeemed them. He set them free from slavery to sin. He purchased them from the enslavement and bondage to sin. They continually follow the Lamb as "firstfruits." This could indicate they are the beginning of a greater harvest to follow. Based on Revelation 7:9-14, we know that many will come to Christ during the great tribulation even as God pours out His judgment and wrath on unrepentant humanity.

Verse 5 informs us that as they follow the Lamb, there is no lie in their mouth, and they are blameless. "They are ambassadors of truth and enemies of falsehood in what they say and how they live" (Duvall, *Revelation*, 192). Believers hold fast to Christ (14:4-5) because He holds fast to them (14:1). He is truly glorified in us because we are fully and totally satisfied in Him. He is all we could ever want!

God Will Be Just in His Treatment of All Persons

REVELATION 14:6-13

Beginning with verse 6, we are introduced to six angelic messengers who appear in the remainder of the chapter (14:6,8,9,15,17,18). Their messages contain both blessing and cursing. There are words of gospel (14:6). There are also words of judgment. What is made crystal clear is there is no place in a biblical, orthodox theology for universalism (i.e., the belief that eventually all persons will be saved). A biblical portrait of hell and eternal torment is painted for us in verses 10-11 that are simply too plain to be denied. Revelation 14:6-20 could not be more politically incorrect for an age that tolerates anything and everything. However, one thing is certain: the God of all the earth will do right (Gen 18:25). A day of reckoning is coming for all of us. We will not all be treated the same though we will all be treated justly and righteously. No one will stand before God at judgment and say, "You did me wrong. You were unfair." Such a day will never come.

All Peoples Are Called to Fear, Glorify, and Worship Their Creator God (14:6-7)

Flying "high overhead" (ESV, "directly overhead") is actually mid-heaven. It refers to that point in the sky where the sun reaches its apex or highest point. This angel will be at the highest point, and verse 7 informs us that he will speak with the loudest voice. All will see him and all will hear him.

He preaches the everlasting gospel. This is the only time an angel is said to preach the gospel! Generally this is our assignment. The "eternal" gospel is the same gospel proclaimed throughout all of history. It is the good news of forgiveness and eternal life made possible through the death of Jesus Christ for sinners. Old Testament saints looked forward to this day. All New Testament believers look back to what Christ accomplished.

The gospel is identified in various ways in the Bible:

- "the good news of the kingdom" (Matt 4:23)
- "the gospel of Jesus Christ" (Mark 1:1)
- "the good news of God" (Mark 1:14)
- "the gospel of God's grace" (Acts 20:24)
- "the gospel of the glory of Christ" (2 Cor 4:4)
- "the gospel of salvation" (Eph 1:13)
- "the gospel of peace" (Eph 6:15)
- "the glorious gospel" (1 Tim 1:11) (MacArthur, *Revelation 12–22*, 86)

The gospel truly is great and multifaceted!

Jesus promised that this gospel would be preached throughout the whole world before the end (Matt 24:14). The preaching of this angel will in some sense assure that this promise is indeed fulfilled (MacArthur, *Revelation 12–22*, 86).

The audience of this message is said again to be "the inhabitants of the earth." This is the phrase used throughout Revelation to refer to unbelievers. Furthermore, they are described as "every nation, tribe, language, and people." The nature of this angel's ministry is comprehensive and worldwide in the truest sense. He will indeed preach the gospel to all creation. To preach the gospel to all creation was the last command our Lord gave to His disciples (Matt 28:18-20; Acts 1:8). We are never more faithful to the heart and will of our Lord than when we, like this faithful angel, preach the gospel to all creation. There is still time, but it will not last forever.

Verse 7 contains the rightful response of every person to the God who made them and the gospel that can redeem them. This particular verse is steeped both in imperatives and in natural revelation. The words *fear*, *give*, and *worship* are all imperatives of command.

God is the sovereign Lord; therefore, we should fear Him. Complete awe and reverence are His rightful due.

God is the awesome Judge; therefore, we should give Him glory. The text says, "The hour of His judgment has come." The time for salvation is almost gone. The opportunity to receive Christ is fading quickly. The bowl judgments of chapter 16 are fast approaching. Armageddon is just around the corner. The Second Coming (19:11-21) could happen at any moment.

God is the marvelous Creator; therefore, we should worship Him. Our text emphasizes the magnitude of God's creative work. He is the One who made heaven and earth, the sea and springs of water. God has therefore revealed Himself both in Scripture (special revelation) and in nature (general revelation). Romans 1 and 2 remind us that because of this general revelation, no one has an excuse. In nature God has made Himself known to all persons both in creation and in conscience.

When Paul evangelized Jews, he almost always started with the Old Testament Scriptures, since he shared with them the belief that the Scriptures are God's Word. However, when he evangelized Greeks and pagan Gentiles, his starting point was almost always creation (see Acts 14 and 17) (MacArthur, *Revelation 12–22*, 89). In secular America today, creation is often the best, even a necessary, starting point when it comes to evangelizing those who need to know Jesus. Before you introduce someone to the Redeemer, you must first help them understand there is a Creator. As Creator, God made everything and everyone. Knowing such a truth is a starting point for my understanding that I have a responsibility to rightly relate to that One who made me. This is the heart of Paul's theology in Romans 1. This is the heart of John's argument here in Revelation 14:7.

Unbelievers Can Anticipate Defeat, Wrath, and Eternal Torment (14:8-11)

Verses 8-13 reveal a tremendous contrast between those who follow the Lamb and those who follow the beast, between the saved and the lost.

We see first the destiny of the unsaved. Their end can only be described as heartbreaking, sorrowful, and tragic. Their future is unimaginably dark and hopeless.

"A second angel" appears announcing the fall of "Babylon the Great." Babylon is introduced here for the first time in Revelation, though a more full description will be provided in chapters 17 and 18. Babylon the Great is referenced six times (14:8; 16:19; 17:5; 18:2,10,21; see also Dan 4:30). Ancient Babylon in Mesopotamia, modern-day Iraq, had been a political, commercial, and religious powerhouse. It was once a great empire and known for its decadence, gross immorality, and idolatry.

In Revelation, Babylon stands for that system that stands religiously, politically, and economically in opposition to all that is of God. It is the antichrist's worldwide political, economic, and religious empire. Founded by Nimrod (Gen 10:9), Babylon was the site of the first organized system of idolatrous and false worship (Gen 11:1-4). The tower of Babel was its most pronounced expression. So certain is its demise that the word *fallen* is repeated. It is certain to be destroyed (MacArthur, *Revelation 12–22*, 90).

All nations have been intoxicated, deceived, and seduced by this false system headed by the antichrist. Like a seductive prostitute, the Babylonian system leads men into passionate maddening adultery with a god who is no god at all.

Those who drink Babylon's wine and experience her passion will also drink another wine and experience another passion. Tragically, it will be the wine of the wrath of God. As the 144,000 follow the Lamb, so those on the earth follow Babylon and the beast (14:9). The result is that they will now drink the wine of the wrath of God in full strength and in full measure.

In the Old Testament, God's wrath is often pictured as a cup of wine to be drunk (Ps 75:8; Isa 51:17; Jer 25:15). Such wrath is the personal and proper response of a holy and righteous God to rebellious sinners who have said no to His love and grace revealed in Jesus Christ.

Verses 10 and 11 provide a terrifying picture of hell and eternal damnation. It is impossible to read these verses and come up with any kind of doctrine of universalism, annihilationism, or conditional immortality. The picture is one of conscious, eternal, and everlasting torment before the angels and the Lamb. Those in hell will have a constant awareness and knowledge of the God they rejected. This will only enhance the horror and torment they will experience. Fire and brimstone are often used in Scripture with respect to divine judgment. God used it to destroy Sodom and Gomorrah (Gen 19:24-25; Luke 17:29) (MacArthur, *Revelation 12–22*, 91). Our Lord spoke of hell as a place of "eternal fire" (Matt 18:8; 25:41), "unquenchable fire" (Mark 9:43), and where "the fire is not quenched" (Mark 9:48). In Matthew 25:41 Jesus taught that the everlasting fire or hell was "prepared for the Devil and his angels." God does not desire that anyone would go to hell, but that all would come to repentance (2 Pet 3:9). Those who go to hell choose their destiny, saying no to the grace of God made available to all through His Son, the Lamb, Jesus Christ.

Believers Will Endure, Obey, Find Rest, and Be Rewarded (14:12-13)

The destiny of those who know Christ is radically different from those who die without Him. In verse 12 we are called to endurance, patience, steadfastness, or perseverance. Duvall notes, "The term 'endurance' (*hypomonē*), perhaps 'the key ethical term in the Apocalypse,' appears seven times in Revelation (1:9; 2:2,3,19; 3:10; 13:10; 14:12)" (*Revelation*, 198). While our salvation is a signed, sealed, and settled issue rooted in the keeping power of God (Jude 24-25), we are indeed challenged to persevere, and the means of our perseverance is noted here in verse 12: those who keep the commandments of God and their faith in Jesus. Jesus reminded us in John 8:31, "If you continue in My word, you really are My disciples." John also wrote in his first epistle, "For this is what love for God is: to keep His commands" (1 John 5:3). Those who follow the Lamb have faith in Jesus, and those who have faith in Jesus follow the Lamb. The two concepts cannot be separated from each other. In the midst of horrible tribulation and great wickedness, we cannot help but wonder, *Is our devotion to the Lamb truly worth it?* Verse 13 provides a resounding "Yes!" to that question.

John again hears a voice from heaven telling him to write—to write words that will be permanent and lasting. Here we encounter the second of seven beatitudes in the book of Revelation (1:3; 16:15; 19:9; 20:6; 22:7,14). "The dead who die in the Lord from now on are blessed" is a remarkable statement. It can only be understood when taken as a whole. If we were to say, "Blessed are the dead," that would certainly make no sense and seem blatantly absurd. However, when you add the phrase "who die in the Lord," everything takes on a new perspective.

Paul taught us that "to be out of the body" is to be "at home with the Lord" (2 Cor 5:8). He also said in Philippians 1:21, "For me, living is Christ and dying is gain." Psalm 116:15 teaches us that "the death of His faithful ones is valuable in the LORD's sight." So certain is this truth that the Holy Spirit gives His hearty affirmation, "Yes." This is the only time the Holy Spirit is quoted in the whole Revelation except in 22:17. His emphatic "yes" reveals His absolute agreement with the voice from heaven that states that those who die in the Lord are indeed blessed.

Those who die in the Lord have their final rest. Sorrow and suffering are at an end. Those who die in the Lord find their works following them. In other words, rest and reward is the promise of eternity for those who have followed the Lamb and have kept their faith in Jesus.

Jesus Will Pour Out His Wrath on the Earth in Righteous Judgment
REVELATION 14:14-20

I once heard a Jewish evangelist named Hyman Appleman say, "If I could scare you out of hell, I would." I have to agree with him, knowing how terrible and eternal hell will be. Revelation 14:9-11 makes this clear. Now verses 14-20 demonstrate its future horror by the images of two harvests: grain in 14-16 and grapes in 17-20. While some students of Scripture believe the first depicts the harvest of the righteous and the second the unrighteous, it is best to see both as harvests of judgment on the wicked. The Old Testament background is Joel 3:12-13, where the Bible says,

> Let the nations be roused and come to the Valley of Jehoshaphat, for there I will sit down to judge all the surrounding nations. Swing the sickle because the harvest is ripe. Come and trample the grapes because the winepress is full; the wine vats overflow because the wickedness of the nations is great.

The Judgment Will Be in Glory and on Time (14:14-16)

John looks (see vv. 1,6) and sees the Son of Man on a white cloud with a golden victor's crown on His head. This is the Lord Jesus (see 1:13-16; Dan 7:13-14). Here is our Lord in dazzling brilliance and majesty, awesome authority and power. Revelation 1:7 is coming to fruition.

He has a sharp sickle in his hand (14:14) and an angel coming out of the temple in heaven says the time to harvest the earth has come because "the earth is ripe" (14:15). Jesus Himself "likens the final judgment to the harvest of the earth (Matt. 13:30, 39)" (Johnson, *Revelation*, 1983,143).

Verse 16 is brief and simple: "So the One seated on the cloud swung His sickle over the earth, and the earth was harvested." The divine, heavenly "terminator" has come. Judgment day has arrived and it cannot be delayed. God's wrath comes via the Lamb. God's wrath comes on time. The ministry of mercy is over. Sowing the seed of the gospel is at an end. Tomorrow or "someday" is now today.

The Judgment Will Be Universal and Horrific (14:17-20)

The vision shifts from the "grain harvest" to the "grape harvest." I believe this is also our first glimpse of the battle or campaign of Armageddon (see 16:12-16; 19:17-21). The fifth and sixth angels of chapter 14 appear in verses 17-18. The fifth, like the fourth, comes from the sanctuary. Like our Lord, he has a sharp sickle for reaping. The sixth angel comes from the altar, the altar of incense (6:9-11; 8:3-5). There is once more a connection between the prayers of the saints and judgment on earth. God hears and answers our prayers. The fifth angel commands the sixth to harvest the grapes "from earth's vineyard, because its grapes have ripened." *Fully* ripened is the idea. The time is now.

The angel responds immediately and decisively (14:19). There is no delay, no hesitation. In the ancient Near East in John's time, grapes were trampled or stomped by foot in a trough that had a duct leading to a lower trough or basin where the juice was collected. "The splattering of the juice as the grapes are stomped vividly pictures the splattered blood of those who will be destroyed" (MacArthur, *Revelation 12–22*, 117).Treading grapes in a winepress was a familiar figure of divine wrath and judgment.

> *I trampled the winepress alone, and no one from the nations was with Me. I trampled them in My anger and ground them underfoot in My fury; their blood spattered My garments, and all My clothes were stained. For I planned the day of vengeance, and the year of My redemption came.* (Isa 63:3-4)

> *The Lord has rejected all the mighty men within me. He has summoned an army against me to crush my young warriors. The*

Lord has trampled Virgin Daughter Judah like grapes in a winepress. (Lam 1:15)

Swing the sickle because the harvest is ripe. Come and trample the grapes because the winepress is full; the wine vats overflow because the wickedness of the nations is great. (Joel 3:13)

A sharp sword came from His mouth, so that He might strike the nations with it. He will shepherd them with an iron scepter. He will also trample the winepress of the fierce anger of God, the Almighty. (Rev 19:15)

Jerusalem will be spared the terrible judgment at the second coming of Christ according to God's Word. She will be damaged but not destroyed. This is in keeping with God's prediction and promise in Zechariah 14:1-5:

A day of the LORD is coming when your plunder will be divided in your presence. I will gather all the nations against Jerusalem for battle. The city will be captured, the houses looted, and the women raped. Half the city will go into exile, but the rest of the people will not be removed from the city.

Then the LORD will go out to fight against those nations as He fights on a day of battle. On that day His feet will stand on the Mount of Olives, which faces Jerusalem on the east. The Mount of Olives will be split in half from east to west, forming a huge valley, so that half the mountain will move to the north and half to the south. You will flee by My mountain valley, for the valley of the mountains will extend to Azal. You will flee as you fled from the earthquake in the days of Uzziah king of Judah. Then the LORD my God will come and all the holy ones with Him.

The war that will truly end all wars will no doubt be worldwide, yet its focal point will be on the Plain of Esdraelon near Mount Megiddo (about 60 miles north of Jerusalem). This is what we know as Armageddon. Here will take place the most horrific and destructive battle the world will ever know.

Armageddon is also noted in 16:12-16 and 19:17-21. It is more a slaughter than a battle. Blood will flow or be splattered up to a horse's bridle, or about four feet high. It will run for 1,600 furlongs or stadia—184 miles. This is hyperbole suggesting massive, unimaginable slaughter and destruction (MacArthur, *Revelation 12–22,* 117). Josephus tells us that when Jerusalem was destroyed in AD 70 by the Roman general Titus, he killed so many Jews that the whole city ran with blood so much that the fires of many houses were quenched with their blood (*Wars of the Jews,* 6.8.5). In the coming battle, the blood will fill the troughs and streambeds throughout the valley of Megiddo and beyond. It will truly be a just and terrible day of vengeance and judgment.

Conclusion

The faithful Baptist preacher of London, Charles Spurgeon, understood the gravity of what it means to stand either with Jesus or against Jesus. He understood, as many do not, what was at stake. Bringing his own sermon from this chapter to a conclusion, he pled with conviction and passion in words I simply cannot ignore. I urge you to heed his warning and his counsel lest you are thrown into the great winepress of the wrath of God.

> I beseech you, do not risk that doom for yourselves. Escape for your lives; look not behind you but fly to the only refuge which God has provided. Whoever will entrust his soul to Jesus Christ shall be eternally saved. Look unto him who wore the thorn-crown, and repose your soul's entire confidence in Him, and then, in that last great day, you shall see Him seated on the white cloud, wearing the golden crown, and you shall be gathered. . . . But if you reject Him, do not think it wrong that you should be cast with the grapes into the winepress of the wrath of God, and be trodden with the rest of "the clusters of the vine of the earth." I beg you to take Christ as your Saviour, this very hour lest this night you should die unsaved. Lay hold of Jesus, lest you never hear another gospel invitation or warning. If I have seemed to speak terribly, God knoweth that I have done it out of love to your souls; and, believe me, that I do not speak as strongly as the truth might well permit me to do, for there is something far more terrible about the doom of the lost than language can ever express or thought conceive. God save all of you from ever suffering that doom, for Jesus Christ's sake! Amen. ("Harvest")

Reflect and Discuss

1. Why do you think the concept of divine wrath has fallen out of favor with many who consider themselves to be Christians?
2. What is significant about the 144,000 having God's name written permanently on their heads?
3. Why has Christianity always been (and always will be, based on this passage) a faith that sings?
4. Read the passages listed in this chapter that describe the gospel being preached by the angel. Discuss what aspect of the gospel each of these descriptions emphasizes. How do they all fit together?
5. Discuss the difference between special and natural revelation. How are they similar? How are they different?
6. Why is creation often the best starting point in sharing the gospel with unbelievers today?
7. What would you say to someone who believes that, in the end, everyone goes to heaven? How does this passage correct that belief?
8. Why are those who die "in the Lord" blessed? How does this differ from many prevailing notions of death by Christians and non-Christians alike?
9. Read Matthew 26:39 and Revelation 14:9-10. How does Jesus' work relate to the wrath of God?
10. Whom has God placed in your life with whom you need to plead, as Spurgeon did, to flee the wrath and judgment of God?

Judgment Day Comes to Planet Earth: Armageddon Has Arrived

REVELATION 15–16

Main Idea: God is directing history toward the day when He will finally pour out His wrath on His enemies, where His glory and majesty will be on full display.

I. **God Will Make Preparation for Judgment Day (15:1-8).**
  A. God's wrath will be finished (15:1).
  B. The nations will worship (15:2-4).
  C. God's glory and power will be displayed (15:5-8).

II. **God Will Pour Out His Wrath on Judgment Day (16:1-21).**
  A. God will send disease (16:1-2).
  B. God will destroy the seas (16:3).
  C. God will pollute the waters (16:4-7).
  D. God will torment unrepentant humans (16:8-9).
  E. God will destroy the kingdom of the antichrist (16:10-11).
  F. God will gather His enemies for a final battle (16:12-16).
  G. God will conclude His judgment giving sinners what they deserve (16:17-21).

Throughout the Bible we are warned that judgment day is coming. The eschatological Day of the Lord is inevitable. It will happen. Joel 1; Zephaniah 1; Malachi 4; Matthew 24; 1 Thessalonians 5; and 2 Thessalonians 2 are just a sampling of the passages that guarantee its arrival. Here in Revelation 15–16, that day has arrived. The context is significant. Revelation records three series of judgments as follows:

Tribulation Judgments in the Book Revelation (Swindoll, *Insights*, 216)		
"Seal" Series (Rev 6:1–8:5)	"Trumpet" Series (Rev 8:6-9:21)	"Bowl" Series (Rev 16:1-21)
1. Conquest	1. Hail and Fire (⅓ of vegetation ruined)	1. Malignant Sores
2. Warfare	2. Meteor Shower (⅓ of sea life killed)	2. Poisoned Seas (death of all sea life)
3. Famine and Poverty	3. Water Pollution (⅓ of water supply poisoned)	3. Poisoned Fresh Water
4. Death (¼ population)	4. Darkness	4. Humanity Scorched
5. Martyrdom	5. Demonic Locust Attack	5. Widespread Darkness/ Misery
6. Earthquake	6. Demonic Hordes (⅓ of humanity killed)	6. Vast Military Invasion
7. Introduction of "Trumpet" Judgments	7. Introduction of "Bowl" Judgments	7. Most Destructive Earthquake/Hail

There is a spiraling and intensifying nature to these judgments as the seven trumpets emerge from the seventh seal and the seven bowls emerge from the seventh trumpet. In a sense the seventh always takes us to the end.

A lengthy interlude (Rev 10–14) precedes the final series of judgments. Chapter 15 serves as a prelude to the bowl judgments of chapter 16. There we learn that there is glory in God's wrath. In fact, we should worship God in His wrath because He is holy, just, and righteous in all His ways. Sinners, apart from Christ, will receive "what they deserve" (16:6). No one will call God unfair or unjust at the judgment. The evidence is too great. It is overwhelming. He is the just Judge of the universe.

God Will Make Preparation for Judgment Day
REVELATION 15:1-8

Chapter 15 is easily structured around the phrase "I saw/looked" in verses 1, 2, and 5. Suffering Christians in the first century and in every century would be encouraged and given hope to remain faithful by this chapter. God is in control. He hears our cries, He sees our tears, and He knows all about our hurting hearts. The Lord God, the Almighty (15:3; 16:7,14), is advancing His kingdom. It will be established.

God's Wrath Will Be Finished (15:1)

John sees another "sign in heaven." This looks back and connects to the vision in 12:1. This sign is "great and awe-inspiring" as he sees "seven angels with the seven last plagues"—plagues that will finish or complete "God's wrath." History is at its end, and horrible judgments will come. Judgment patterns in history reach a climax in the tribulation. That they are called the last plagues sets them apart from the seals and trumpets. There are similarities, to be sure, but there are also differences. Now God's wrath is brought to its appropriate and climactic conclusion (see Lev 26:21). Mounce says, "These are the last of the plagues in that they complete the warnings of God to an impenitent world. All that remains is final judgment itself" (*Revelation*, 284).

The Nations Will Worship (15:2-4)

Before judgments falls, the redeemed appear beside "a sea of glass mixed with fire" (a sign of judgment) to sing a victory song. They have conquered the beast (i.e., antichrist), and now they take harps to sing what is called the song of Moses and of the Lamb. The themes of God's redemptive work for the Hebrews now resounds in the redemptive work of the Lamb. Exodus 15:1-8 and Revelation 5:8-14 provide source material for this song of worship.

The God who is praised is great and amazing in His deeds, ways, and righteous acts. He is the "Lord God, the Almighty" and the "King of the Nations." This is a God we should "fear" and "glorify" because He alone is holy—pure, undefiled, separate from His creation. There is no God like our God.

And who will come and worship this great, amazing, just, true, holy, and righteous God? "All the nations will come and worship before You" (see 5:9; 7:9). Every tribe, language, people, and nation will gather to sing and worship this awesome God. What a great missionary promise!

The saints do not sing of their victory over the beast (15:2). They sing about the sovereignty, glory, justice, and righteousness of their Almighty God and King. As all the nations come together to worship, the focus is as it should be: on our God. David Platt well notes that there is a high view of God in heaven ("How Do We Worship God in

His Wrath?"). If that is true, and it is, then there should be a high view of God on earth. There should be a high view of God in our churches. There should be a high view of God in my life.

God's Glory and Power Will Be Displayed (15:5-8)

For the third time John sees something. This time it is "the heavenly sanctuary—the tabernacle of testimony," another Exodus theme (15:5). This is the place where God manifests His presence. From here the seven angels with the seven plagues emerge. They have the appearance of holy priests with their "clean, bright linen" and "gold sashes" (15:6). One of the living creatures (i.e., the angelic beings introduced in ch. 4) gives them seven bowls full of the wrath of the eternal God (15:7). Immediately "the sanctuary was filled with smoke from God's glory and from His power" (15:8). So great was this display of glory and power that no one could enter the sanctuary until judgment was finished.

This imagery is familiar to students of the Old Testament. When God made a covenant with Abraham, He passed through the divided pieces of the sacrifice in the smoking fire pot and burning torch (Gen 15:17). When Moses received God's law on Mount Sinai, God revealed His holiness with fire and smoke (Exod 19:18). After Israel placed the ark of the covenant in the tabernacle, God's presence was symbolized with smoke and fire (Exod 40:34-35). In Solomon's temple the glory of the Lord filled the holy place in the form of a cloud (1 Kgs 8:10-11). This is an ongoing reminder of God's holiness. God's glory is always manifest during the time of His judgment. Smoke from God's glory made entering the temple impossible until His seething indignation was poured out. What a sign to the ungodly people on the earth who chose to shun the worship of a holy God and to follow the beast.

God Will Pour Out His Wrath on Judgment Day
REVELATION 16:1-21

Human beings should have a high view of God and a humble view of man. Instead we have a low view of God and a high view of ourselves. We have invited justly the wrath of God in our lives and on our world. These last seven plagues, the bowl judgments, are similar to both the exodus plagues (Exod 7–12) and the trumpet judgments (Rev 8–9). However, their worldwide scope and intensity are of such a nature that they are said to be "like no other since man has been on the earth" (16:18).

Precursors have appeared throughout history, but they have been less spectacular. The final and climactic manifestation is now poured out (16:1), never again to be repeated. Do not miss the fact that all of this is God's doing (Mounce, *Revelation*, 291–305).

God Will Send Disease (16:1-2)

John hears "a loud voice," a phrase occurring 20 times in Revelation. It is certainly the voice of God. He commands the angels to "go and pour out the seven bowls of God's wrath on the earth" (see 15:1,7; 16:19). The fierce anger of God and His righteous judgment are to be poured out in full measure on an unrepentant world, a rebellious world.

The angel pours out his bowl, and harmful and painful sores appear on those who follow and worship the beast (16:2). This recalls the sixth Egyptian plague (Exod 9:9-11) and the stories of Job (Job 2:7) and Lazarus (Luke 16:21). Only unbelievers experience this foul and loathsome plague. Zechariah 14:12 teaches,

> This will be the plague the LORD strikes all the peoples with, who have warred against Jerusalem: their flesh will rot while they stand on their feet, their eyes will rot in their sockets, and their tongues will rot in their mouths.

God Will Destroy the Seas (16:3)

The second angel pours his bowl, and the sea becomes like the blood of a corpse. There are parallels to the first Egyptian plague in Exodus 7:19 and the second trumpet of 8:8-9. Every living thing dies in the seas of the earth. The oceans, which occupy 70 percent of the earth's surface, become a pool of death, a toxic wasteland of water. The term *watery grave* will take on a whole new and tragic meaning.

God Will Pollute the Waters (16:4-7)

Blood follows blood. What God did through His angel to the seas He now does to the fresh waters. All turns to blood. This recalls also the first Egyptian plague, the third trumpet (8:10-11), and the drought brought on by the two witnesses (11:7). Water is already scarce. It now becomes even more so.

Suddenly the third angel breaks into a song that sounds much like the Song of Moses and the Lamb in 15:3-4. The eternal God ("who is and who was") is just in bringing these judgments because He is the

Holy One. The earth dwellers "poured out the blood of the saints and the prophets" so He gives them "blood to drink" in return. Indeed, He gives them what they deserve (16:6). Verse 7 provides a word of confirmation: the judgments of the "Lord God, the Almighty" are "true and righteous." Genesis 18:25 teaches, "Won't the Judge of all the earth do what is just?" Psalm 19:9 says, "The ordinances of the Lord are reliable and altogether righteous." The Apocalypse is fully in agreement: God is never arbitrary, capricious, or vengeful in His judgment. He is always fair, just, and true. His is the only bar of perfect justice. There is a logic and rightness in His judgment. We glorify Him in His righteous wrath.

God Will Torment Unrepentant Sinners (16:8-9)

In contrast to the first three bowls, which were poured out on the earth, the fourth angel pours out his bowl on the sun. People are scorched with fire, "by the intense heat." This is in contrast to the fourth trumpet (the judgments are not concurrent), which darkened the sun, moon, and stars (8:12). MacArthur says, "Searing heat exceeding anything in human experience will scorch men so severely that it will seem that the atmosphere is on fire" (*Revelation 12–22*, 155).

The specifics of exactly what will happen are not revealed to us. We need not speculate. However, the human response is crystal clear: they cursed God and "they did not repent and give Him glory." What an undeniable and sad commentary on the depravity and wickedness of Adam's sons and daughters. Knowing full well from whom these plagues come and why they come, they do not repent; they revile. They do not bless God; they blaspheme God (see also 16:11,21). God has been long-suffering and patient with sinful man (2 Pet 3:9). Multiple opportunities have been given for people to repent and run to the redeeming Lamb. Repeatedly and with willful disregard for the grace of God, men and women refuse to repent (see 6:16-17; 9:20-21). They refuse to give glory to the only God deserving of glory. They turn away from Him. He rightly brings divine, retributive torment to them.

God Will Destroy the Kingdom of the Antichrist (16:10-11)

The fifth bowl judgment is reminiscent of the ninth Egyptian plague (Exod 10:21-29). It starts locally but extends worldwide. The throne of the beast, the antichrist, is the object of this judgment. He and his kingdom are "plunged into darkness." We do not know precisely in what way this happens. It could be economic, physical, political, spiritual, or any and all of these (but see Mark 13:24-27). What we do know once again are the results: "People gnawed their tongues because of their pain," they "blasphemed the God of heaven because of their pains and their sores" (16:2), and "they did not repent of their works."

The phrase "God of heaven" is from Daniel 2:44. It speaks of the God who sovereignly destroys the false kingdoms of this world and establishes His own rightful kingdom. Daniel 7:13-14 tells us this kingdom is given to the Son of Man! We know this refers to Jesus.

This is the final time we are told that mankind would not repent. The day of grace is at an end. God's deadline is now past. Neither mercy nor judgment changed the heart of sinful humanity. They loved their idols too much. They loved their sin more than the Savior who would have set them free from their bondage and slavery. It is hard not to weep.

God Will Gather His Enemies for a Final Battle (16:12-16)

The sixth angel pours his bowl out "on the great river Euphrates," a river designated this way five times in the Bible (Gen 15:18; Deut 1:7; Josh 1:4; Rev 9:14; 16:12). It runs 1,800 miles from Mount Ararat to the Persian Gulf and was seen as the eastern boundary of the land God promised to Israel. It continues as the lifeblood of what is called the Fertile Crescent. The river is dried up to prepare for the coming of an army, "the kings from the east" (16:12). Who they are and why they come is not revealed, but there certainly seems to be a relationship to the army from the east when the sixth angel blew his trumpet in 9:13-19. Ultimately, they come as God allows and directs.

Coupled with the coming of these kings are three unclean spirits, or demons, who spring from the mouth of the unholy, counterfeit trinity of the dragon, beast, and false prophet (16:13). These demons are said to be like frogs, an unclean animal (Lev 11:10,41). Once more they act with spiritual deception via the miraculous, which reminds us again that not every miracle is a miracle from God. Their goal is for "the kings of the whole world to assemble them for the battle of the great day of God, the Almighty" (16:14). I believe they think they are gathering to battle earthly powers, perhaps Israel (Ezek 38–39; Zech 14), or the people of God as a whole. Actually God is the One who has bought them there to do battle with Him (see 19:11-21).

Almost parenthetically, verse 15 interjects the third of seven beatitudes in Revelation:

"Look, I am coming like a thief. The one who is alert and remains clothed so that he may not go around naked and people see his shame is blessed."

Christ can come any moment on any day. "Coming like a thief" means many will be caught by surprise, unprepared, not ready (see 1 Thess 5:2). Do not find yourself in that camp. Be alert; "stay awake." There is a blessing for those who do! Have your spiritual clothes on at all times (see 3:18). Do not allow your spiritual vigilance to flag or wane so that you are found naked or exposed. On this day everything will be made plain. The "deceptive propaganda" of the false trinity will be fully exposed.

That day, verse 16 tells us, will happen "at the place called in Hebrew, Armageddon." Har-Magedon is probably a reference to the hill of Megiddo, "the ancient city lying on the north side of the Carmel ridge . . . between the coastal plain and the valley of Esdraelon" (Mounce, *Revelation,* 301). It is a famous battlefield with many strategic conflicts having occurred there. Armageddon has taken on the idea of the place and time of the war that ends all wars as history draws to a close. I believe history will end in cataclysmic world war. I think Armageddon will serve as the focal point (14:14-20; 16:10; 19:17-21; see Joel 3:2; Zech 14). Still I am in full agreement with Mounce, who clarifies that

> geography is not the major concern. Wherever it takes place, Armageddon is symbolic of the final overthrow of all the forces of evil by the might and power of God. The great conflict between God and Satan, Christ and antichrist, good and evil, that lies behind the perplexing course of history will in the end issue in a final struggle in which God will emerge victorious and take with him all who have placed their faith in him. This is Har-Magedon. (Ibid., 302)

God Will Conclude His Judgment Giving Sinners What They Deserve (16:17-21)

There are similarities between the seventh trumpet and the seventh bowl, even the seventh seal, because in a telescopic and spiraling manner each brings history to a close. The seventh angel pours out his bowl in the air, the space encompassing the earth. Again a "loud voice" comes from "the sanctuary," and specifically from "the throne." God speaks, saying, "It is done!" "It is completed" (see 15:1). Like the seventh seal

(8:5) and the seventh trumpet (11:19), there is lightning, rumblings (sounds or voices), and thunder. There is also an earthquake that is unprecedented in human history (16:18).

Verse 19 says, "[T]he great city split into three parts." Good arguments can be made that this is historical Jerusalem (see Zech 14:8). Context, however, would seem to point to spiritual Babylon, the subject of chapters 17–18. Some would identify the city with Rome, and also with good reason in light of the first-century historical context and chapter 18. I believe it would certainly include Rome, but it is more. Babylon in Revelation is the city of man that stands in opposition to the city of God, the new Jerusalem (Rev 21–22). Babylon falls completely, and all the cities of her world fall with her. God remembers her; she is not forgotten. She will drink in full measure "the cup filled with the wine of His fierce anger." What Jesus drank for His own (Mark 10:38-39), she will be forced to drink herself.

Verse 20 is a simple statement of cosmic upheaval and eschatological trauma. It recalls the cosmic disturbance of the sixth seal in 6:12-14. Here is a snapshot meant to leave a lasting impression of a world now experiencing in totality the fury and wrath of its Creator.

The cosmic storm of God's wrath reaches its climax and culmination with great hailstones of one hundred pounds falling to earth and on people (16:21). We have seen this before (Josh 10:11; Ezek 38:18-22). The heaviest hailstone on record in modern times was a mere 1.93 pounds! The earth, what little remains, will be pummeled and pulverized. Tragically, but now expected, men curse God for His righteous judgment (16:9,11). Beaten, they again blaspheme. Conquered, they curse. One last time they shake their fist in God's face and curse His name. Judgment day has come. The results are certain. The response of humanity is stunning. So great is their hatred for God, they curse His name with their final, dying breath.

Conclusion

At the cross God demonstrated His wrath and poured it out on His beloved Son. His great love for sinners was on full display. In the great tribulation He will pour out His wrath on rebellious and unrepentant sinners who curse His name. There will be no middle ground in that day. There is really no middle ground today. What will you do?

Will you believe in Him or blaspheme Him?

Will you confess Him or curse Him?

Will you repent or continue to rebel?

The choice is yours, and the choice is mine. The time to make the choice is now. Time will soon be gone for all of us. Judgment day is on its way to planet Earth.

Reflect and Discuss

1. Why will no one be able to accuse God of being unfair when they receive His judgment?
2. Have you ever felt like you were being treated unfairly by God? How does this feeling line up with the testimony of Scripture?
3. How do these chapters give hope and encouragement to God's people?
4. Read through Exodus 15:1-8. What parallels do you see between that text and Revelation 15:2-4?
5. What does it mean to have a high view of God? How can you cultivate a high view of God? How can we communicate that view to others?
6. Why are the glory and the judgment of God so often seen together? How do these two aspects of His character relate?
7. Why do people fail to repent even upon seeing God's judgment? How might this inform our evangelism and disciple making?
8. The passage tells us that the time of God's gracious patience with mankind will come to an end. How should this influence our missionary drive and strategy?
9. What does it mean to stay alert and remain clothed in preparation for Christ's return? What are some marks of being prepared? Unprepared?
10. Why do people continue to curse God, even to their dying breath? How were you changed from cursing to praising God?

Are You a Babylonian, Seduced by This World?

REVELATION 17:1-18

Main Idea: God allows wickedness to wreak havoc on the world, but He eventually defeats those who oppose Him in worldliness and rebellion.

I.   **This World Is Seductive: It Will Attract You (17:1-5).**
II.   **This World Is Murderous: It Takes Innocent Life (17:6).**
III.   **This World Is Resilient: It Keeps Coming Back (17:6-8).**
IV.   **This World Is Organized: It Has a Plan (17:9-10).**
V.   **This World Is Powerful, but Its Time Is Short (17:11-13).**
VI.   **This World Is Foolish: It Opposes the Lord of Lords and King of Kings (17:14).**
VII. **This World Is Self-Destructive: It Will Not Last (17:15-18).**

Revelation has been called "a tale of two cities." One is Babylon, which represents this evil world and opposes the things of the one true God. Its character and destiny are described in detail in chapters 17–18. The other city is the new Jerusalem. Its glory and goodness are described in Revelation 21–22. At this point in the book, we are again confronted with inescapable questions: Which God will you worship? Which city will you love and live for? We all must answer these questions. In a real sense this is where Revelation has been taking us all along. As John Piper well says,

> That's the goal of everything the [angels have] been revealing. That's what the whole book of Revelation is about. That's the point of all God's judgments, all God's dealings with the world. All God's plans for history from beginning to end have this one goal—WORSHIP GOD! Don't worship the wealth of Babylon, don't worship the power of Babylon, don't worship the pleasures of Babylon, and don't even worship the holy messenger who brings you the news that Babylon has fallen forever. WORSHIP GOD! ("Worship God")

Unfortunately humans are too easily allured and trapped by this world. We do not see it for what it really is and where it ultimately leads.

261

What we need is to have it exposed. We need to have it uncovered and shown to be what it truly is. Babylon and all it represents will be destroyed. The new Jerusalem and all it represents will last forever. Why would any sane person choose Babylon over the new Jerusalem? This text answers that question.

This World Is Seductive: It Will Attract You
REVELATION 17:1-5

Revelation 17–18 is an extension of the bowl judgments of chapter 16. John is told by one of the angels "who had the seven bowls" to come so that he might see "the judgment of the notorious prostitute," the great whore "who sits on many waters" (17:1). We are told in verse 15 the waters are the peoples of the world.

This harlot is said to lead the kings, the rulers of the world, into sexual immorality. The image is one of spiritual adultery and idolatry. Not only does she seduce the leaders of the world, but common people, "those who live on the earth," are drunk with the wine of her sexual immorality (17:2). The lust for power, material possessions, sex, and pleasure has intoxicated the world. No one under the sun (see Ecclesiastes) has escaped her enticing allurements. The prostitute has captivated their hearts and taken over their lives. As 1 John 2:16 explains, "the lust of the flesh, the lust of the eyes, and the pride in one's lifestyle" have become our gods. This is a description of a world where the American dream is ultimate. And we must be careful because it is not hard to imagine that you and I will wake up on that day and realize that we have all become Babylonians!

Once again John is carried away in the Spirit (1:10; 4:2; 17:3; 21:10) into a desert to see a vision (17:3). He sees the notorious prostitute "sitting on a scarlet beast that was covered with blasphemous names and had seven heads and 10 horns." This is the beast, the antichrist, of chapter 13. The woman is beautifully and seductively dressed "in purple and scarlet, adorned with gold, precious stones, and pearls" (17:4). She is quite attractive, like any beautiful adulteress (Prov 5:2; 6:20-25; 7:16-27). Yes, she is beautiful and attractive, but she bites and brings death. She holds "a gold cup in her hand filled with everything vile and with the impurities of her prostitution" (17:4). Johnson says, "The golden cup filled with wine alludes to Jeremiah's description of Babylon's worldwide influence in idolatry (Jer. 51:7). Her cup is filled with 'abominable things'" (*Revelation*, 1983, 155). The idols of heart and life are filled to the brim as she shares them with a senseless humanity that falls into a drunken stupor, no longer able to see real truth, beauty, and goodness found only in God and His salvation through the Lamb.

In verse 5 the identity of the harlot is revealed. Like the Roman prostitutes of the day, she has a headband, and here that headband is a mystery about to be revealed: "Babylon the Great, the mother of prostitutes and of the vile things of the earth." This is not literal Babylon on the Euphrates, a city that had been of no real significance for centuries. Regarding a specific city, it is better to see it as referring to Rome in that day, but its significance is greater than just Rome. This prostitute is "that great system of godlessness that leads people away from the worship of God and to their own destruction" (Mounce, *Revelation*, 311). It is an ever-present reality, a seductress that exists and entices in every age and every generation. It is a this-world perspective. Seduced by the sirens and idols of the day, we run madly down a path of spiritual and eternal suicide. Proverbs 6:32-33 rings true for this mad, mad world:

> *The one who commits adultery lacks sense; whoever does so destroys himself. He will get a beating and dishonor, and his disgrace will never be removed.*

The World Is Murderous: It Takes Innocent Life
REVELATION 17:6

Because Babylonianism is driven by self-interest, it is willing to sacrifice others to promote its own benefits and prosperity. We see this all across the globe with abortion, euthanasia, genocide, and infanticide. Life is increasingly discounted at both its beginning and its end, as well as for the economically, ethnically, and socially marginalized.

However, in verse 6 it is revealed that the notorious prostitute has set her sights throughout history on the people of God and the followers of Jesus. Indeed, this whore is "drunk on the blood of the saints and on the blood of the witnesses to Jesus" (18:24; see Isa 49:26). In the New Testament alone the seeds of martyrdom were planted by John the Baptist, Stephen, James, and Antipas. From those seeds has flowed the blood of saints for 20 centuries. And the more blood this world drinks, the more it wants. Its intoxicating effects consume it and drive it to want more and more and more. The twentieth century was the bloodiest in Christian history. We should expect the twenty-first to be worse. Mounce again is helpful: "Although the Neronian massacre after the great fire of AD 64 may have been in the back of John's mind, the drunken prostitute pictures the final days of persecution at the end of the age" (*Revelation*, 312). As we move toward the end of history, we can expect the blood of martyrs to flow like a river, even a flood, among the nations. It may be your calling and my calling. Are we willing to embrace it? Philippians 1:21 is a wonderful reminder that it is worth it to die for Christ!

This World Is Resilient: It Keeps Coming Back
REVELATION 17:6-8

The vision of the notorious prostitute amazed John (17:6). The angel, however, said he would explain things to him concerning both the woman and the beast who carries her (17:7). Verse 8 is the beast's parody on the life, death, and resurrection of Jesus and the description of the Lamb (1:18; 2:8; see also 1:4,8; 4:8). We see this in 13:3,14 as well. And yet there is embedded here an important truth that Christians of every age must understand. Throughout history multiple antichrists (1 John 2:18) have risen from the abyss in the form of the beast for their reign of terror. They have a time, they die, and then amazingly they appear again only to be destroyed. The pattern repeats itself again and again and will continue until the antichrist, the beast, brings the cycle to an end. The priorities and values of this world system make themselves felt and known in empires and men consumed with the idols of this world. The beast has been Egypt, Babylon, Medo-Persia, Greece, Rome, the Ottomans, the Soviet Union, communist China, and now the Western world. It has been Anticochus Epiphanes, Nero, Domitain, Genghis Khan, Shaka Zulu, Mussolini, Hitler, Stalin, Mao, Pol Pot, Idi Amin, Kim Il Sung, Saddam Hussein.

Granted, all kingdoms and personalities were not equally evil and wicked. All, however, loved the prostitute more than they love God. And lest we think we are off the hook, remember verse 2: "Those who live on the earth"—regular, ordinary people like you and me—have become drunk with the wine of her seduction. Generation after generation, we give life and power to the beast as we love the practices, values, and ways of this world. Indeed, John informs us that "those who live on the earth whose names have not been written in the book of life from the foundation of the world will be astonished when they see the beast that was, and is not, and will be present again." The beast and the things of this world sparkle in our eyes and grip our hearts. First John 2:17 sounds an important warning: "And the world with its lust is passing away, but the one who does God's will remains forever." Babylonianism will not last. The American dream is headed for destruction.

This World Is Organized: It Has a Plan
REVELATION 17:9-10

There is a divine rhyme and reason to the ebb and flow of history, because history is His story, the story of Messiah. The drama of redemption and restoration is unfolding according to God's sovereign plan. John tells us we need wisdom to unravel the mystery of "Babylon the Great, the mother of prostitutes [i.e., a whore who gives birth to more whores] and of the vile things of the earth" (17:5).

There is no unanimity among Bible interpreters on verses 9-12. Godly men and women understand the details differently. The fact that we need wisdom is an understatement! Now, most agree that the phrase "the seven heads are seven mountains" is a reference to Rome in the first-century context. The city was known as "the city on seven hills." Seven would also communicate great power and authority, something that is true of every coming of the beast. Verse 10 adds another interpretive challenge: The seven heads "are also seven kings: Five have fallen, one is, the other has not yet come, and when he comes, he must remain for a little while." Efforts to identify these seven kings with seven Roman emperors have not worked. Viewing them as seven secular empires similar to Daniel 2 and 7 is more promising in my judgment, though I hold my view with great tentativeness. In Israel's history five kings or kingdoms had fallen and passed off the scene: Egypt, Assyria, Babylon, Medo-Persia, and Greece. The one who "is" would obviously be Rome. And the one that "has not yet come" is the future kingdom of the antichrist. His kingdom will draw from the characteristics of the previous six. Once again the number seven would communicate completeness or perfection in power. The manifestation of this kingdom "will remain only a little while." Yes, the beast as a man and kingdom will embody the brutality, greatness, splendor, strength, and wickedness of these great empires. But like all other worldly empires, it will have its day and come to an end. Brilliantly organized and with a plan for world domination, it will be impressive for a time, a very brief time, as it stands in pale comparison to the eternal and everlasting kingdom of God. The world has a plan, but God's plan will endure forever.

This World Is Powerful, but Its Time Is Short
REVELATION 17:11-13

Verses 11 and 12 extend the explanation of verses 9-10. The beast is said to belong to the seven kings, particularly the seventh in my view, but he is also an eighth king himself. But as we were also told in verse 8, the beast goes to destruction. Again, his kingdom will not last. It cannot deliver on its false promises. Perhaps it is at the midpoint of the tribulation, following its apparent death and resurrection, that the beast achieves its lust for worldwide conquest and domination. MacArthur says, "The Antichrist's kingdom is said to be both the seventh and eighth kingdoms because of his supposed demise and resurrection. He is the seventh before and the eighth king after his 'resurrection'" (*Study Bible*, 2016). However, what all interpreters of Revelation can agree on is this: This king and his kingdom are going down. They will be destroyed. The beast will be beaten.

Verse 12 adds an additional detail and explanation: the 10 horns (17:3,7) are 10 future kings yet to receive their royal authority. However, when they do, we are again informed it will be for a short duration, described as "with the beast for one hour." These 10 kings, whoever they are, will serve alongside the beast. Verse 13 informs us they will actually "have one purpose, and they give their power and authority to the beast." Later they will have one purpose in carrying out the will of God in the destruction of the prostitute.

Isaiah 40:8 reminds us, "The grass withers, the flowers fade, but the word of our God remains forever." This world system, Babylonianism, will come again and again to seduce, attack, and destroy the people of God. It is influential and powerful. It is intimidating and prosperous. It is enticing and persuasive. It gives every appearance of the promise of victory, of the winning team: Get on board or get crushed. Join the team or be called a fool. Worship the beast and whore with the prostitute, or live a wasted life.

However, the Bible makes clear that "eat, drink, and be merry for tomorrow you die" is a satanic lie! Tomorrow, we will stand before the King of kings and Lord of lords and give an account for the life He gave each one of us—the life many will waste. The world lasts only a little while

(17:10), for one hour (17:12), and it is headed for destruction (17:8,11). This is not the winning team. It is headed for devastating defeat.

This World Is Foolish: It Opposes the Lord of Lords and King of Kings
REVELATION 17:14

This world chooses the wrong opponent. It takes on the wrong adversary. Verse 14 is an interjection that anticipates the second coming of Jesus described in 19:11-21 (see esp. 19:16). It is also a simple summary of Armageddon (16:16) and the final battle. The beast and his kingdom, in a spiritual suicide mission, attack the warrior Lamb, the Lamb who is also a Lion (Revelation 5). It is no contest! The Lamb will conquer them, for "He is Lord of lords and King of kings." The title is well known, pointing back to Deuteronomy 10:17; Psalm 136:2-3; Daniel 2:47. It is a title reserved only for God. In *1 Enoch* 9:4 our God is called "Lord of lords, God of gods, King of kings, and God of the ages." There is no God like our god, and this world has played the fool in opposing Him and His kingdom.

We are told He brings with Him those who "are called, chosen, and faithful." This is the army of 19:14. This description highlights the biblical balance of divine sovereignty and human responsibility. Called and chosen is God's part; faithful is our part. Thankfully, even our faith and faithfulness are kept by the power of God (Jude 24-25). Interestingly, we are not designated a role or assignment. I suspect it is because we are only spectators in the final conflict. Our Lord and King won the battle without our help in His first coming; I believe it will be the same at His second!

The World Is Self-Destructive: It Will Not Last
REVELATION 17:15-18

The transitory nature of this world system, Babylon, has been alluded to several times in chapter 17. Now the truth is driven home in graphic finality. When a man is finished with a prostitute, he does not marry her or take her home to his mother. What we see in the movie *Pretty Woman* (1990) is a dishonest myth. Men do not go to prostitutes to love them but to use them. In Revelation the prostitute has had a massive influence that covers the earth, as verse 15 makes clear. But suddenly it is over. She is finished. An abrupt turnabout will be made by the "10

horns" (17:16) who are the 10 kings. The language recalls the words of
Ezekiel 23:11-35.

They will awaken from their drunken stupor with the woman, whose
charm and seduction will have lost its lure. They have a new love in the
antichrist. Love for the woman will turn to "hate" from the 10 kings and
the beast (17:16). They will strip her of all the wealth she has confiscated
throughout the world. They will make her "desolate and naked" (17:16).
The beast and his kings will turn on her. Evil will attack evil once more
but with the greatest ferocity the world will ever see. They tear away her
personal support, position, power, and prestige, and expose her moral
corruption. They will "devour her flesh" (17:16) like dogs devoured the
corpse of Jezebel (see 1 Kgs 21:23; 2 Kgs 9:30-37). They will "burn her
up with fire." In a moment she is old news never to be seen again. Her
demise will be greatly lamented by those who have loved and whored
with her, as chapter 18 plainly teaches.

This hostile action, her destruction, will be initiated by God: "For
God has put it into their hearts to carry out His plan" (17:17)—that is, to
rid the world of "the world." The kings believe they are carrying out their
own program for conquest, but actually they will accomplish God's providential program. Having destroyed the woman, the antichrist will unite
the world's religious, economic, and political systems under his control.
The 10 kings will agree to "give their kingdom to the beast until God's
words are accomplished" (17:17). God's prophetic program will reach
its intended goal as He sovereignly allows the kingdoms of this world to
come under the beast's control until the end of the tribulation. The angel
concludes his revelation by identifying the woman simply as "the great
city that has an empire over the kings of the earth" (17:18). For obvious
reasons, the early church believed the verse was speaking of Rome.

A great anti-God system will continue, both as power (economic
and political) and cult (religion), united in one figure, the antichrist.
The woman is the "great city," Babylon in its religious, political, economic, and social significance. It refers to a diabolical worldly system.
Babylon cannot be confined to a city in the past or future, such as Rome
or Babylon, Washington or London, Moscow or Beijing. It is a trans-
historical system of satanic evil, an extension of ancient Babylon, forming an evil world system throughout history and during the tribulation.
After the destruction of the woman, all its power will reside in the antichrist, who will manifest all of its satanic evils in its fullness. Evil devours
evil because God puts it in their heart. It is inevitable.

Conclusion

My friend C. J. Mahaney has well said, "Today, the greatest challenge facing [evangelical, Bible-believing] American [Christians] is not *persecution from* the world, but *seduction by* the world" ("Is This Verse," 22). The Christian apologist C. S. Lewis would add,

> We are half-hearted creatures, fooling about with drink and sex and ambition when infinite joy is offered to us, like an ignorant child who goes on making mud pies in the slum because he cannot imagine what is meant by the offer of a holiday at the sea. We are too easily pleased. (*Weight of Glory,* 25–26)

Babylon offers mud pies in the slum. The new Jerusalem ruled by the King of kings and the Lord of lords offers a glorious holiday at a crystal sea that will last forever. Do not be too easily pleased. Do not be seduced by a world that can never deliver what is truly lasting and ultimately satisfying.

Appendix: Cast of Characters in Revelation 17 (Swindoll, *Insights,* 229)		
Phrase/Image	**Scripture**	**Explanation**
The notorious prostitute	17:1-8	The evil, satanically led, organized system that stands in constant opposition to God and His kingdom; the source of all false economies, governments, and religions, drawing its inspiration from idolatry, pride, self-sufficiency, and a denial of God's grace
Many waters	17:1,15	Nations and people groups around the world under the influence of this false system
The beast	17:3,8,11-14	The antichrist, ruler of the end-time worldwide empire and object of worship
"Was, and is not, and is about to come up from the abyss"	17:8,11	The antichrist will imitate Christ's death and resurrection in order to amaze the world and win its political and religion allegiance (13:3-4). This description contrasts with the divine Christ, "who is, who was, and who is coming" from heaven to rule forever (1:8).

Seven heads	17:3,7,9-10	Seven world empires that stood in opposition to God and His people—five that were in John's past (Egypt, Assyria, Babylon, Medo-Persia, and Greece), one that existed in John's present (Rome), and one that will arise in the future (empire of the antichrist). Certainty here is not absolute—much debated.
Seven mountains	17:9-10	Ancient Rome built on seven hills. It came to represent the city of man in contrast to the city of God.
The eighth king	17:11	The antichrist, who is one of the preceding kings, is also an "eighth." This may refer to two phases of his rule—before his pseudo "death and resurrection" (the "seventh" king) and after this deceptive feat when Satan turns his local political career into a global empire (as the "eighth" king)
Ten horns	17:3,7,12	Ten political powers that will unite to empower the antichrist, turning all worldly authority over to him
"Called, chosen, and faithful"	17:14	When Christ returns as King of kings and Lord of lords to overcome the beast and the kings of the earth, He will be accompanied by the "called, chosen, and faithful." This same group is called the "armies that were in heaven . . . wearing pure white linen" (19:14). The New Testament commonly uses the terms "called," "chosen," and "faithful" to describe the Lord's saints.

Reflect and Discuss

1. Compare and contrast the image of Babylon as described in this chapter with the new Jerusalem as described in Revelation 21.

2. How does this description of Babylon resemble the American dream?

3. When examining your own heart, what are some of the things of this world that tend to distract you from God and His good plan for you?

4. How do the many antichrists relate to the antichrist of Revelation? What antichrists can you observe in the world today?

5. The kingdom of the beast cannot last. It fails to deliver on its promises of domination and victory. How have you seen the empty promises of sin and rebellion lead to ruin?

6. Compare Revelation 17:14 with Psalm 2. What parallels do you see?

7. How does Revelation 17:14 show the balance between God's sovereignty and our responsibility? What other passages would you point to that illustrate this balance?

8. What does the beast's turn against the prostitute tell you about Satan's character? About his end goal?

9. What does it mean that we are too easily pleased by the things of this world? What kind of pleasure should we strive for?

10. How can Christians pursue faithfulness to Christ when so much of our society seems caught up in "Babylonianism"? How can we protect against the prostitute's seduction?

A Funeral Song for a Prostitute

REVELATION 18:1-24

Main Idea: As God destroys the sin and wickedness that marks this world, those who have loved this world will experience bitter disappointment and divine judgment.

I. **Stanza 1: God Severely Judges the Notorious Prostitute (18:1-8).**
    A. This worldly system is judged for its demonic nature (18:1-2).
    B. This worldly system is judged for its idolatries (18:3).
    C. This worldly system is judged for its sinfulness (18:4-5).
    D. This worldly system is judged for its pride (18:6-8).

II. **Stanza 2: The Earth Greatly Laments over the Notorious Prostitute (18:9-19).**
    A. Rulers weep over her sudden judgment (18:9-10).
    B. Businessmen and businesswomen mourn for their loss (18:11-17).
    C. Shipping will grieve over her destruction (18:17-19).

III. **Stanza 3: Angels Rightly Sing of the Utter Destruction That Is the Destiny of the Notorious Prostitute (18:20-24).**
    A. There will be no record of her (18:21).
    B. There will be no rejoicing over her (18:22).
    C. There will be no rebuilding of her (18:22).
    D. There will be no reflection of her (18:23).
    E. There will be no recovery for her (18:23).
    F. There will be no respect for her (18:23).
    G. There will be no redemption for her (18:24).

What makes you cry? What causes you to weep uncontrollably? What breaks your heart? I often say we will talk about what we love. I also believe we will cry over the loss of what we love. In this chapter we observe the world weeping over the death of a prostitute. However, this prostitute was using others just as others were also using her. The people of this world were glad to let her use them because they became drunk with the passion of her sexual immorality (18:3,4,9). In fact, she made them rich, provided them a life of luxurious living (18:3,9). But with her death all was lost. All she gave them was suddenly, in a moment, taken away. When it was too late, they saw that the prostitute, this worldly system of desires and idols, was a deceptive mirage. Sensual pleasures, material possessions, a life of luxury, and the promises of power and satisfaction were completely, suddenly, utterly, and eternally destroyed. Sin is deceptive. It will destroy and it will be destroyed. Security is not found in this world. Security is found only in Christ.

Revelation 18 is a requiem, a funeral dirge, a song of lamentation and sorrow over the demise and destruction of Babylon. Ladd notes that the Old Testament "background for this section is found in the prophetic dirges over the fall of Tyre (Ezek 26–28) and of Babylon (Isa 13–14; 21; Jer 50–51)" (*Commentary*, 235). It is a song that has been sung through the ages by those who gave their all to this world, only to be sadly disappointed with the results. We find echoes of its sentiments in modern songs such as Peggy Lee's "Is That All There Is?" in which she laments the failure of life's pleasures to satisfy her high expectations. Though the Scriptures make clear that God and God alone is able to satisfy our longings, they are equally clear that Babylon can only deliver disappointment.

Stanza 1: God Severely Judges the Notorious Prostitute
REVELATION 18:1-8

Payday has arrived for Babylon the great (17:16-20). She is no longer great, for God put it in the hearts of the antichrist and his followers to destroy and devour her. Now songs will be sung about her. Three dirges or laments are recorded in verses 9-20. These three sad songs are bracketed by two angel songs (2-3,21-24) that demonstrate God's justice in taking down this arrogant and proud and wicked system.

This System Is Judged for Its Demonic Nature (18:1-2)

John sees another angel sent by God ("coming down from heaven") who has "great authority," so great that "the earth was illuminated by his splendor" (18:1). Having come from God's presence, he radiates the glory of God. He has an announcement to make with a mighty voice: "It has fallen, Babylon the Great has fallen!" (14:8; see 17:5). This proud and evil system of worldly desires, lust, pleasures, and priorities is finished. Though this is a future event, it can be stated in the past tense because its fall is certain. The repetition adds emphasis and finality. It is a signed, sealed, and settled reality (see Isa 21:9; Jer 51:8).

The great city is now nothing more than a haunt, a home for three things: demons or unclean spirits, unclean birds, and every unclean and detestable beast. Duvall says, "Rather than the honorable garden city that God envisions, Babylon has become just the opposite; a desolate, demonic wasteland, completely devoid of image-of-God life" (*Revelation*, 233). Keener adds, "Becoming a dwelling place of demons is a suitable judgment for a power once mobilized by demons (Rev 16:14; see 9:20)" (*Revelation*, 423).

This Worldly System Is Judged for Its Idolatries (18:3)

Sexual immorality is often a picture of spiritual adultery. It communicates a love affair with the idols of this world. The nations are drunk in their passion for these idols. The kings or rulers of the earth have crawled into bed with these god-substitutes. The merchants of the earth were seduced by the alluring power of her luxurious lifestyle. The peoples of the earth consort with the whore of wealth unaware of her infections and fatal diseases. The idols of this life have cast a spell over the human race, and we bow and worship. Unless we are called, chosen, and faithful in the Lamb (17:14), we have no hope of breaking the hold she has on us.

This Worldly System Is Judged for Its Sinfulness (18:4-5)

John hears "another voice from heaven." It is a call for God's people to "come out" and separate themselves from the world. Failure to flee (see 1 Cor 6:18) will result in taking part in her sins and sharing in her plagues. Isaiah 52:11 says, "Leave, leave, go out from there! Do not touch anything unclean; go out from her, purify yourselves, you who carry the vessels of the LORD." Jeremiah 51:45 adds, "Come out from among her, My people! Save your lives, each of you, from the LORD's burning anger." Revelation 18:5 explains verse 4: "Her sins are piled up to heaven." Peterson says, "Her sins stink to high Heaven" (*The Message*). And she is not forgotten or unnoticed by the Lord: "God has remembered her iniquities." He sees and knows all that the woman has done.

Share in her sins and you share in her punishment. Stay with her and you will suffer with her. Her sins are piled up to heaven. They have reached heaven's doorstep. God is fully aware of what the sins and iniquities are and who has committed them. Jeremiah 51:9 clearly is in the background of this oracle:

> *We tried to heal Babylon, but she could not be healed. Abandon her!*
> *Let each of us go to his own land, for her judgment extends to the sky*
> *and reaches as far as the clouds.*

The time for healing is past. The time for fleeing is now.

This Worldly System Is Judged for Its Pride (18:6-8)

The judgment of Babylon is repeatedly addressed in the Old Testament (Ps 137:8; Jer 50:14-15,29; 51:24,26). God will now pay back the wicked city of man for all it has done. In fact, she is to receive double for what she did to others. That could possibly convey the idea of paying her back both for what was in her heart and for what she actually did. Still, as Ladd notes, "The idea of rendering double for one's deeds is an Old Testament idiom indicating punishment in full measure (Jer 16:18; 17:18)" (*Commentary*, 238).

Verses 7-8 extend the argument of her judgment. She glorified herself and lived in luxury. Therefore "give her that much torment and grief." After all, she boasted in her heart claiming, "I sit as a queen; I am not a widow, and I will never see grief." Her sin demands righteous retribution because of her "self-glorification, sensuous luxury, and prideful arrogance, the very opposite of humble dependence on the Lord and sacrificial love within a community (e.g. Prov. 29:23; Isa. 5:15; 1 Pet. 5:6)" (Duvall, *Revelation*, 234). Her boast recalls ancient Babylon's boast in Isaiah 47:7-8:

> *You said, "I will be the mistress forever." You did not take these things*
> *to heart or think about their outcome. So now hear this, lover of*
> *luxury, who sits securely, who says to herself, "I exist, and there is no*
> *one else. I will never be a widow or know the loss of children."*

Because of her boast, she will receive "in one day" the plagues of "death and grief and famine. She will be burned up with fire." All of this is a certainty because "the Lord God who judges her is mighty" (see Isa 47:9). No one and nothing can prevent her certain destruction. Her pride truly is her downfall. Osborne well notes,

> One does not have to read many magazines or watch many
> movies to realize the extent to which sinners today guzzle "the

wine of passion for immorality." One must realize that divine judgment is not too far away. Those who willingly participate in such immorality will also participate in the judgment to come. Those who live for greed and luxury will also face an angry God for seeking only "the treasures of earth" and ignoring "the treasures of heaven" (Matt. 6:19-20). Jesus warned them well (and this includes materialistic Christians): "What sorrows await you who are rich, for you have your only happiness now" (Luke 6:4 NLT). (*Revelation*, 659–60)

Stanza 2: The Earth Greatly Laments over the Notorious Prostitute
REVELATION 18:9-20

Whatever we hate will also reveal what we truly love. The earth dwellers, those who lived for the priorities and values of this world, hated God and loved the prostitute. Consumed by greed and self-interest, their narcissism controlled their desires, their passions, their worldview. Suddenly, all that they have lived for is gone, taken in a moment. It is more than they can bear. Yes, they mourn the death of Babylon, but mostly they sorrow over their own loss. In the end, all of life is about themselves, not others.

Verses 9-20 comprise three dirges or laments over the sudden fall and destruction of Babylon. The kings or rulers (18:9-10), the merchants or businessmen (18:11-17), and all connected to the industry of shipping (18:17-19) weep and mourn over the fall of their idol, their god. The words of these verses recall the words of Ezekiel 27 and the sorrow expressed over the destruction of the city of Tyre. Mounce notes,

> Fifteen of the twenty-nine commodities listed in Rev. 18:12-13 are also found in Ezek. 27:12-22. The same three groups of mourners are all referred to in the Ezekiel passage, although their reactions to the fall of the cities differ somewhat—the mariners cry bitterly (vv. 29-30), the kings shudder with horror (v. 35), and the merchants hiss (v. 36). (*Revelation*, 331)

Rulers Weep over Her Sudden Judgment (18:9-10)

The rulers of the earth went to the bed of the prostitute and were intimate with her. What she offered they wanted and gave their lives to. She satisfied their earthly desires with her idols ("sexual immorality"), and they "lived luxuriously with her." Her destruction ("the smoke of her burning") causes them to "weep and mourn." The one they once called lover, they now remove themselves from. "They will stand far off in fear of her torment" (18:10,15,17). They do not run to her rescue because they were only using her as she used them. She might have been their lover, but she was never truly loved.

Fearful now of getting too close, lest they also are consumed by her destruction, they sing their song of lament, "Woe, woe, the great city, Babylon, the mighty city! For in a single hour your judgment has come." The famous city, great and strong, is reduced to ashes by our God in a moment, in a "single hour." Like the magnificent twin towers of the World Trade Center, this ungodly, Christless worldly system of idols and wickedness comes crashing down in no time at all. Shock and horror are the only words that capture man's reaction. What they lived for is suddenly taken from them. What they trusted in is suddenly gone and gone forever. These rulers played the fool, but they are not the only ones.

Businessmen and Businesswomen Mourn for Their Loss (18:11-17)

With the fall and destruction of this worldwide economic system, chaos ensues. New York, London, Hong Kong, Tokyo, Beijing—all the markets of the world—tank and bottom out. Stuff is available, but no one has the resources to purchase it. All "the merchants of the earth"—the Wall Street wizards—can do is "weep and mourn over her, since no one buys their merchandise any longer" (18:11). Malls are empty. Shops are shut up. They never saw it coming.

Verses 12-13 list 29 items of value and wealth falling into seven different categories:

- Precious metals and stones (gold, silver, precious stones, pearls)
- Fabrics for expensive clothing (fine linen, purple, silk, scarlet cloth)
- All kinds of ornaments and decorations (scented woods, ivory, costly wood, brass, iron, marble)
- Fragrances (cinnamon, spice, incense, myrrh, frankincense)
- Foodstuffs (wine, oils, flour, grain)
- Animals (cattle and sheep, horses and carriages)
- Humans (slaves)

Regarding this last category, Mounce notes that "it is estimated that there were as many as 60,000,000 slaves in the Roman Empire" (*Revelation*, 334). There could be no clearer evidence of the depth of the utter depravity of man. Souls of men were viewed as nothing more than human livestock for service and even entertainment.

The fruit they longed and lived for, the return on their investment, is all gone! "All your splendid and glamorous things are gone." Indeed, all they have lived for is gone and lost; "they will never find them again" (18:14). This is the first of seven double negatives in the remainder of this chapter. This one is actually a triple negative. It literally says, "No more, not, they will not be found."

Like the kings of the earth (18:10), the merchants "will stand far off in fear of her torment" (18:15). They will continue "weeping and mourning" (see 18:11). Like the kings they will cry, "Woe, woe" over the great city that looked so fine (18:16)! Recalling verse 10, they are amazed that something so great, luxurious, and rich could be "destroyed" in "single hour" (18:17). No one ever anticipated anything like this. We thought she would live forever, failing to realize only the one who does the will of God lives forever.

Shipping Will Grieve over Her Destruction (18:17-19)

A third and final group—"every shipmaster, seafarer, the sailors, and all who do business by sea"—join the kings and merchants. Like their earthly companions they "stood far off" and cried at the sight of her destruction (18:17-18). They then ask a new question: "Who is like the great city?" (see Ezek 27:32). This is reminiscent of the praise given to the beast in 13:4. Who could have imagined this? She was glorious but now she is gone. She was rich but now she lies in ruins. She was everything but now she is nothing. Wealth is great while it lasts, but therein lies the problem: it does not last.

Like the others they weep and mourn (18:9,11,15). Further, "they threw dust on their heads" as an outward sign of their mourning (18:19). They too cry, "Woe, woe, the great city." We "became rich from her wealth," but "in a single hour she was destroyed." David Platt is right: "If you love this world, it will pass away, and it will take you with it. You will not only lose true pleasure; you will lose your life. . . . You will perish with this world" ("Danger").

Stanza 3: Angels Rightly Sing of the Utter Destruction That Is the Destiny of the Notorious Prostitute
REVELATION 18:20-24

Adrian Rogers used to say, "We become like what we worship. True worship will make us more like God." We will love what He loves and hate what He hates. God hates the evil and murderous city of man known as Babylon, and so should we. Thus, we have a completely different perspective on her judgment and destruction, as verse 20 shows. We "rejoice" with all of heaven and the saints, apostles, and prophets because "God has executed your judgment on her!" The prayer of 6:10 is answered. Rejoicing is not over the eternal and spiritual death of lost souls but over the justice and righteousness of God's judgment. Further, God avenges, not man (see Rom 12:19).

The stage is set for the final stanza of chapter 18, a song sung by a single angel. The refrain will become a familiar one voiced six times: "No more" (ESV) or "never." In Greek, the refrain is the emphatic double negative: "Never, never again!"

There Will Be No Record of Her (18:21)

A "mighty angel" appears for the third time (5:2; 10:11) and throws a large millstone into the sea. It plunges to the bottom never to be seen again, a sign of Babylon's judgment and destiny. The great city will be violently thrown down "never to be found again." She is gone forever. There will be no record of her.

There Will Be No Rejoicing over Her (18:22)

Music ceases. Harpists, musicians, flute players, and trumpeters "will never be heard in you again." Song and dance stop because there is nothing for the earth dwellers to celebrate. An eerie silence envelopes the fallen world.

There Will Be No Rebuilding of Her (18:22)

Craftsmen never practice their trades. The sound of the mill and everyday labor stops. No one works. Industry is at a standstill. The economy has collapsed with an economic depression unlike anything the world has ever seen.

There Will Be No Reflection of Her (18:23)

No one will have to turn out the lights on Babylon because "the light of a lamp will never shine in you again." Darkness will drape the destroyed city as she is abandoned and forsaken. No one visits her anymore. No one parties here anymore. It is dark here, all dark.

There Will Be No Recovery for Her (18:23)

The hope of new life, a rebirth, is not in her future. No one falls in love or marries anymore. "Weddings are a thing of the past. The merry sounds of bridal festivities have forever been silenced" (Mounce, *Revelation*, 339).

There Will Be No Respect for Her (18:23)

The prostitute's judgment is just. Her merchants were filled with arrogance and pride as "the nobility of the earth." Not anymore! And all nations were deceived and led astray by her sorcery, her magic spells. She bewitched the nations and led them into destructive foolishness. Now that she is exposed, no one has any regard or respect for her. Her merchants were great but not anymore. Her sorceries worked for a time but never again.

There Will Be No Redemption for Her (18:24)

This whore is familiar with blood, but not the saving blood of Christ. No, in her the blood of prophets and saints is found. The blood of Christian martyrs that ran through the streets of Rome has continued to run through her streets around the world for 20 centuries (see 17:6). However, that day will soon be over. Their blood cries for justice like righteous Abel, and God has heard them. And her guilt cries for judgment, and God hears that too!

Conclusion

The Babylon of the Bible might well be called "Vanity Fair" today. Indeed, in poetic rhyme, Ella Wheeler Wilcox describes a world that promised much but in the end, delivered very little. She unwittingly notes that it is the brow with thorns that is the victor! Her words could be a commentary on Revelation 17–18.

VANITY FAIR
In Vanity Fair, as we bow and smile,
As we talk of the opera after the weather,
As we chat of fashion and fad and style,
We know we are playing a part together.
You know that the mirth she wears, she borrows;
She knows you laugh but to hide your sorrows;
We know that under the silks and laces,
And back of beautiful, beaming faces,
Lie secret trouble and dark despair
In Vanity Fair.

In Vanity Fair, on dress parade,
Our colors look bright and our swords are gleaming,
But many a uniform's worn and frayed,
And most of the weapons, despite their seeming,
Are dull and blunted and badly battered,
And close inspection will show how tattered
And stained are the banners that flaunt above us.
Our comrades hate, while they swear to love us;
And robed like Pleasure walks gaunt-eyed Care
In Vanity Fair.

In Vanity Fair, as we strive for place,
As we rush and jostle and crowd and hurry,
We know the goal is not worth the race—
We know the prize is not worth the worry;
That all our gain means loss for another;
That in fighting for self we wound each other;
That the crown of success weighs hard and presses
The brow of the victor with thorns—not caresses;
That honors are empty and worthless to wear,
In Vanity Fair. (*Kingdom of Love,* 137–38)

Reflect and Discuss

1. What examples can you give of people looking to Babylon to provide satisfaction, joy, and meaning?

2. This chapter shows the inability of sin to provide lasting pleasure. How have you seen the deceptiveness of sin in its failure to provide lasting joy and security?

3. Consider the grounds for Babylon's judgment in 18:1-8. Which of these is most likely something that marks your life?

4. How do Christians heed the warning of 18:4 without separating entirely from non-Christians?

5. Judgment in this passage is all the more severe because of the prostitute's pride. Why is God so opposed to arrogance and pride?

6. How is our heart revealed by what we weep over? What causes you to weep?

7. Why does love for this world lead to destruction with the world?

8. How does the worship of God make us more like God, and the worship of idols and Satan make us more like them? Have you found yourself molding to a person or thing you care most about? What is it?

9. Discuss how the dark description of Babylon's judgment makes you feel. Is there rejoicing? Sadness?

10. This passage provides a strong warning against falling in love with this world. What role does warning play in our evangelism and missions?

Heaven's Hallelujah Chorus

REVELATION 19:1-10

Main Idea: The just judgment, righteous character, and perfect plan of God should lead us to passionate worship of and witness to Jesus Christ.

I.   **Praise God for His Salvation (19:1-5).**
II. **Glorify God for His Bride (19:6-8).**
III. **Worship God for the Witness of Jesus (19:9-10).**

In this "tale of two cities" that is the book of Revelation, Babylon represents the evil world system that focuses on earthly and temporal values (Rev 17–18), while the new Jerusalem focuses on heavenly and eternal values (Rev 21–22). Of course, Revelation may also be called "a tale of two women": the prostitute of Babylon and the bride of the Lamb. The two come together in Revelation 19:1-10. Their future destinies could not be more radically different. Choosing which one you love and belong to is crucial.

A single word captures the heart of this text: "Hallelujah." It appears in verses 1, 3, 4, and 6. Surprisingly, the word appears nowhere else in the New Testament. In 1741 George Friederich Handel (1685–1759) wrote *Messiah*, the most famous oration of which is the "Hallelujah Chorus." It is a tradition around the world that when it begins the congregation stands and remains standing until its completion. In heaven, however, they respond differently. There they fall down and worship (19:4). They worship "God, who is seated on the throne" because He has judged "the notorious prostitute" (19:1-5), prepared the bride (the church) for the marriage supper of the Lamb (19:6-8), and directed all of heaven and earth to keep their attention on Jesus (19:9-10). Heaven's "Hallelujah Chorus" is a response to the command of 18:20, and it anticipates the second coming of Jesus (19:11-21), His millennial reign (20:1-6), Satan's final judgment (20:7-10), the great white throne judgment (20:11-15), and the establishment of the new heaven, new earth, and new Jerusalem (Rev 21–22).

There has been a lot of bad news in the Apocalypse, but praise be to God, good news, great news, has arrived! The response of those who love and follow the Lamb is nothing less than unabated, unhindered, enthusiastic praise and worship. This is a day we have all longed for, and it is finally here!

Praise God for His Salvation
REVELATION 19:1-5

Verse 1 begins with the connecting phrase, "After this." In light of God's judgment of Babylon in chapters 17–18, the following celebration and worship take place "in heaven." John heard "something like the loud voice of a vast multitude." This multitude may be angels or the church triumphant or both. Their worship is anything but quiet and reserved. It is loud and enthusiastic. They sing "Hallelujah," which means "praise Yahweh" or "praise the Lord." Mounce notes, "The Hebrew form introduces a number of Psalms (106, 111–13, 117, 135, 146–50)" (*Revelation*, 337).

Six items are cited in verses 1-2 for this praise of Yahweh, this praise of the Lord: His salvation, His glory, His power, His true and just judgments, His judgment of the notorious prostitute (i.e., Babylon), and His avenging the blood of His servants. Verse 3 records the second hallelujah as "a sort of heavenly encore that heightens measurably the dramatic quality of the scene" (ibid., 337–38). God is praised because the notorious prostitute's "smoke ascends forever and ever!" God is not vindictive or capricious in His judgment of Babylon. He is totally true and just. John Piper is right when he says,

> If God turned a deaf ear to sin and evil and injustice and suffering in this world, He would not be true, and He would certainly not be just. God here is rightfully and wholeheartedly praised for His justice." ("Worship God!")

Verses 4-5 record the third hallelujah and add to our heavenly choir "the 24 elders and the four living creatures." Clearly angels and humans are of one mind and heart in their adoration and worship of God. Here they fall down and worship together "God, who is seated on the throne" (see Rev 4–5). They cry, "Amen!" So be it! We agree! They cry, "Hallelujah!" Praise the Lord! This exclamation of praise is the last we see of the 24 elders and the four living creatures. They exit the scene worshiping the One who is worthy.

From the throne a voice speaks. It could be an angel, one of the four living creatures, or even one of the elders. The text does not specify *who*, but it records *what*: "Praise our God, all His slaves, who fear Him, both small and great!" There is no discrimination or segregation in this worship. John Piper captures powerfully the praise and worship resounding throughout heaven for the awesome and all-encompassing salvation that belong to our God and all His servants, all His sons and daughters. It is the same praise and worship that should resound in our churches anytime we gather in the name of our great God. He says,

> Corporate worship . . . is the declaration in the midst of Babylon that we will not be drawn into her harlotries, because we have found in God the satisfaction of our souls. In his presence is fullness of joy and at his right hand are pleasures forevermore. Corporate worship is the public savoring of the worth of God and the beauty of God and power of God and the wisdom of God. And therefore worship is an open declaration to all the powers of heaven and to all of Babylon that we will not prostitute our minds or our hearts or our bodies to the allurements of the world. Though we may live in Babylon, we will not be captive to Babylonian ways. And we will celebrate with all our might the awesome truth that we are free from that which will be destroyed. ("Worship God!")

Glorify God for His Bride
REVELATION 19:6-8

In verses 1-5 we have glorified a God of salvation, glory, and power (19:1), a God whose judgments are always true and just, a God who judges evil, corruption, and immorality, a God who avenges the blood of His servants (19:2), and a God who welcomes all who fear Him, small and great (19:5). Now our text moves to glorify God for two additional reasons: He is an almighty God who reigns as sovereign Lord over all things (19:6), and He is "a God who arranged from all eternity for the marriage of his Son Jesus to a countless host of saved sinners, purified and beautified by his own blood" (19:7-8) (Piper, "Worship God!")

John again (see 19:1) "heard something like the voice of a vast multitude." He further describes it as something "like the sound of cascading waters, and like the rumbling of loud thunder." The sound is deafening. It was like a mighty waterfall, an awesome cascade of thunders. They shout or sing the fourth and final hallelujah. And why do they shout their praise as loud as they possibly can? Because "our Lord God, the Almighty, has begun to reign." Once again this great title, which appears nine times in Revelation, is used to identify God by His power and might (1:8; 4:8; 11:17; 15:3; 16:7,14; 19:6,15; 21:22). Mounce notes, "The previous 'Hallelujahs' (vv. 1, 3, 4) pointed back to the destruction of Babylon in chapter 18. The 'Hallelujah' of v. 6 points forward in anticipation of the coming wedding of the Lamb." He further notes that the title "Almighty" literally means "one who holds all things in his control" (Mounce, *Revelation*, 339). This is an omnipotent, all-powerful God who is inaugurating His universal, visible, and permanent reign over all things. What is a reality in heaven is now about to become a reality on earth. The prayer of Matthew 6:10—"Your kingdom come. Your will be done on earth as it is in heaven"—has been granted!

With the arrival of the reign of God comes also the long-awaited day of the marriage of the Lamb, the Lord Jesus, and His bride, the church. This is the occasion for rejoicing, exultation, and the giving of glory to "our Lord God, the Almighty." The image of marriage symbolizing the relationship of God and His people appears several times in the Scriptures (Isa 54:5-7; Hos 2:19; 2 Cor 11:2; Eph 5:21-33). Providing helpful historical context, Mounce again notes:

> In biblical times a marriage involved two major events [or three if you count the processional], the betrothal and the wedding. These were normally separated by a period of time during which the two individuals were considered husband and wife and as such were under the obligations of faithfulness. The wedding began with a procession to the bride's house, which was followed by a return to the house of the groom for the marriage feast. By analogy, the church, espoused to Christ by faith, now awaits the parousia when the heavenly groom will come for his bride and return to heaven for the marriage feast that lasts throughout eternity. (*Revelation*, 340)

Verses 7-8 speak of the preparation of the bride for her wedding day. Through sanctification by the Word and Spirit, she has made herself ready (see Eph 2:10). This is the only time in Revelation where the saints are described as making themselves ready, preparing themselves as the bride of Christ for His coming. How do we prepare ourselves and get ready for that day? I believe the book of Revelation itself provides the answer.

- The bride prepares herself by remaining faithful to Christ in a fallen and evil world.
- The bride prepares herself by enduring hardship in the midst of suffering.
- The bride prepares herself by trusting God in the face of martyrdom.
- The bride prepares herself by obeying God to take the gospel to all tribes, languages, peoples, and nations.

As Philippians 2:12 says, we are to "work out [our] own salvation with fear and trembling." But don't miss what Philippians 2:13 says, for it matches up perfectly with Revelation 19:8. Philippians tells us, "For it is God who is working in you, enabling you both to desire and to work out His good purpose." And in Revelation 19:8 we read, "She was given fine linen to wear, bright and pure. For the fine linen represents the righteous acts of the saints." Who, we might ask, granted her the permission to clothe herself in this way? God did! This is what is called a "divine passive," where God is the implied agent behind the action. Ladd says it perfectly:

> While the bride must make herself ready for the marriage, her glorious raiment is not something she can acquire for herself; it must be granted her, i.e., given to her as a divine gift. . . . The fine linen, bright and pure, stands in sharp contrast to the brilliant robes of the harlot. The wedding garment is a simple white garment which has been washed and "made . . . white in blood of the Lamb" (Rev 7:14). (*Commentary*, 249)

Worship God for the Witness of Jesus
REVELATION 19:9-10

John Piper is again spot-on when he says,

> [Worship] is what the whole book of Revelation is about. That's the point of all God's judgments, all God's dealings with the world. All God's plans for history from beginning to end have this one goal—WORSHIP GOD! Don't worship the wealth of Babylon, don't worship the power of Babylon, don't worship the pleasures of Babylon, and don't even worship the holy messenger who brings you the news that Babylon has fallen forever. WORSHIP GOD!

[The church] is an alien outpost in Babylon. And we
exist to reassert God's rightful place wherever it has been
prostituted to secular commerce or secular education or
secular entertainment or secular media or secular arts or
secular sports. All the people of God, exiled in Babylon, are
called to be filled with the Spirit of prophecy (Acts 2:17f),
and the Spirit of prophecy is the testimony of Jesus (Revelation
19:10)—the testimony that Jesus is the Lord of the universe
and that means Lord over every area of secular life in Babylon.

But as an alien outpost in Babylon we know what's
coming. And we know what the worship of heaven is going
to be like when Babylon comes down, and God stands forth
to vindicate his Son. And we know from verse 10 that the
reason this has all been revealed to us ahead of time is that we
might WORSHIP GOD. God lets John hear the celebration
of heaven so that in his exile and his suffering he might join
in and worship God. And John wrote it down in a book so
that we might listen to the worship of heaven and join in.
("Worship God!")

John is given a command by an angel to "write." He is to record
the fourth of the seven "blessings" in Revelation (1:3; 14:13; 16:15;
19:9; 20:6; 22:7,14). Those who participate in the marriage supper of
the Lamb are "fortunate" or blessed. This stands in striking contrast to
those who are judged at the "the great supper of God" in verses 17-18
at the second coming of Jesus. The angel adds his own words of affirmation and confirmation: "These words of God are true." There is no
deceit, deception, falsehood, or lying in these words. As is always true of
God's words, these words are true.

John is overwhelmed by all of this. He falls at the feet of the angel
to worship him (19:10). This is sin. This is idolatry, even if the being is
an angel. John receives a quick and stiff rebuke: "Don't do that." Three
reasons are given. First, because "I am a fellow slave with you and your
brothers who have the testimony of Jesus," who hold also to the faithful witness given by Christ. Second, because you must instead "worship
God." The clear implication is we are to worship God and only God. As
1 John 5:21 says, "Little children, guard yourselves from idols."

Third, because "the testimony about Jesus is the spirit of prophecy." The idea, I believe, is that the true spirit of prophecy always bears

witness to Jesus. The true spirit of prophecy always points to Jesus. MacArthur says,

> The central theme of Old Testament prophecy and New Testament preaching is the Lord Jesus Christ. Until the coming of His Kingdom, all who proclaim the gospel must be faithful to the testimony of Jesus, the saving gospel message, which was His message. (*Revelation 12–22,* 207)

David Levy adds,

> In this book, prophecy is designed to unfold Christ's character, glory, purpose, and program. Therefore, 'Worship God' alone (v. 10)! With these words, the scene is set for the manifestation of Jesus Christ as the glorified King of king and the Lord of lords. *Hallelujah!* ("Marriage Supper," 26)

Conclusion

Scott Duvall provides nine excellent theological observations that capture the key themes of Revelation 19. I believe they serve us well as concluding truths on which we should meditate and reflect. I hope they will inspire even greater worship for "our Lord God, the Almighty."

- God's people are called to rejoice at the demonstration of God's righteous judgments.
- Evil power centers are guilty of arrogance, deception, and murder.
- God will avenge the suffering of His people.
- God is to be praised for His just and true judgments as reflections of His righteous and faithful character.
- God deserves praise and glory for beginning His universal reign.
- Jesus relates to His people like a husband to his bride.
- God's people, in contrast to the notorious prostitute, are clothed in righteous acts.
- Angels, like believing humans, are fellow servants who hold to the testimony of Jesus.
- God alone deserves worship, for He (by His Spirit) is the source of the prophecy [the prophetic message] about Jesus. (*Revelation,* 251)

Once more we see, it really is all about Jesus. That has always been God's plan. Nothing will keep it from coming to pass.

Reflect and Discuss

1. What attributes of God lead you to worship?
2. Why is it right to praise God for His judgment?
3. In what ways does corporate worship in local churches reflect the worship of God in heaven?
4. What role do corporate worship gatherings have in God's cosmic plan? How should this shape your attitude toward gathering with the church? Your preparation?
5. How does Revelation 19 show us that Jesus' prayer in Matthew 6:10 is being granted?
6. How does marriage in the Bible reflect the gospel? If you are married, what aspects of your marriage need to conform to this pattern?
7. Consider the suggestions in this chapter for how the bride of Christ readies herself for marriage. In which of these aspects do you see the most victory in your life? In which aspects do you see the most need for growth?
8. What does Revelation 19:8 reveal about our role in remaining faithful to Christ? about God's role?
9. In what sense is the entire book of Revelation about worship?
10. Based on Revelation 19:10, how can we tell if worship is true and right?

The Return of the King
(Jesus Is Coming Again)

REVELATION 19:11-21

Main Idea: When Jesus returns, He will do so in power and glory as He executes justice on all who reject and oppose Him.

I. **King Jesus Will Return in Glory and Power (19:11-16).**
    A. His appearance is glorious (19:11-13).
    B. His army is holy (19:14).
    C. His authority is unparalleled (19:15-16).
II. **King Jesus Will Judge All Who Rejected Him (19:17-18).**
    A. There will be no escape (19:17).
    B. There will be no discrimination (19:18).
III. **King Jesus Will Defeat the Enemies Who Oppose Him (19:19-21).**
    A. Jesus will capture His enemies (19:19-20).
    B. Jesus will slay His enemies (19:21).

The greatest and most influential person ever to live was Jesus of Nazareth. A survey of the Bible reveals that His life can be outlined around seven major events:

1. The **incarnation**, when the Word became flesh (John 1:14).
2. His **baptism**, where He was immersed by John, anointed by the Spirit, and declared by His Father to be the Messiah (Matt 3:13-17).
3. His **temptation** in the wilderness for 40 days, where He accepted His destiny as a suffering servant Messiah (Matt 4:1-11; see Isa 52:13–53:12).
4. His **crucifixion** on the cross, where He bore the wrath of God and paid the full penalty of sin providing salvation for all who would trust in Him (Matt 27; Mark 15; Luke 23; John 19).
5. His bodily **resurrection**, whereby God declared His acceptance of Christ's sacrifice and victory over death, hell, Satan, and sin (Matt 28; Mark 16; Luke 24; John 20–21; Acts 1; 1 Cor 15).

6. His **ascension** back to heaven (Luke 24; Acts 1), where He intercedes for us at God's right hand (Heb 7:25) and reigns as Lord and King (Phil 2:9-11).
7. His **second coming**, where He will establish His universal and cosmic reign as King of kings and Lord of lords (Rev 19:11-21).

This last event has captivated the expectations and hearts of Christians for almost two thousand years. All who know King Jesus as Lord and Savior join with the apostle John in praying the prayer of Revelation 22:20: "Come, Lord Jesus!"

The second coming of Jesus Christ refers to the historical, visible, and bodily return of the Son of God to the earth. This return will be a great and glorious return in power. It will take place at the end of the tribulation period (Rev 6–18), and the millennial kingdom will immediately follow (Rev 20:1-6). The enemies of Christ will be totally defeated at His return.

Key texts of this event include Daniel 7:13-14; Zechariah 14:1-11; Matthew 24:29-31,36-44; 25:1-26; Mark 13:24-27; Luke 21:25-28; Acts 1:9-11; Revelation 11:15-19; 14:14-20; 16:12-21; and 19:11-21. Key terms include *parousia*, which means "presence, coming, or arrival"; *apocalypse*, which means "unveiling or revelation"; and *epiphany*, which means "manifestation or appearing."

These passages and concepts help us understand some of the specifics of the nature of Christ's coming:

- It will be **personal** (Zech 14:3-5; Matt 24:30; Acts 1:9-11).
- It will be **historical** (Zech 14:3-5; Matt 24:30; Acts 1:9-11).
- It will be **visible** (Matt 24:30; Acts 1:9-11).
- It will be **physical** (Matt 24:30; Acts 1:9-11).
- It will be **victorious** (Zech 14:3-5; Rev 19:11-21).
- It will be **cosmic** in its benefits (Rom 8:18-25).

These passages also help identify, with some specificity, the precise purpose of His coming: It will be to judge Satan, sin, and the system of the world (Rev 17–18; 19:11-21). It will be to establish the universal, visible manifestation of His kingdom (Phil 2:9-11; Rev 20:1-6). It is to provide motivation for faithful service for the Christian community in each and every generation (Matt 24:42–25:46; 2 Thess 2:13-17; 1 John 3:1-3).

Additionally, these texts reveal the climactic events of His coming, including the battle of Armageddon (Rev 14:14-20; 16:12-21; 19:17-21), the sheep and goats judgment (Matt 25:31-46), the resurrection of the saints (Rev 20:4),and the establishment of His thousand-year reign or millennial kingdom (Rev 20:1-6).

Given these characteristics, it is instructive to highlight the contrast between the first and second comings of King Jesus:

The First and Second Comings of Jesus Christ	
His First Coming	**His Second Coming**
He rode a donkey.	He will ride a white horse.
He came as the Suffering Servant.	He will come as King and Lord.
He came in humility and meekness.	He will come in majesty and power.
He came to suffer the wrath of God for sinners.	He will come to establish the kingdom of God for His saints.
He was rejected by many as the Messiah.	He will be recognized by all as Lord.
He came to seek and save the lost.	He will come to judge and rule as King.
He came as God incognito.	He will come as God in all His splendor.

From the above, there is a clear and obvious contrast in His first and second coming, but there is also a certain continuity that Graeme Goldsworthy captures beautifully:

> Christ does not return to do some new or different work. His return in glory will be to consummate the finished work of his life, death and resurrection. At his coming he will be revealed in all his glory to all principalities and powers. That which the believer now grasps by faith will be open to every eye. . . . Although the Lamb will ever be the Lamb, for the glorified Christ is exalted on account of his sufferings, nevertheless the majesty of the Lion will shine forth from the Lamb at His second coming. (*Lamb and the Lion,* 28)

Jesus Will Return in Glory and Power
REVELATION 19:11-16

Revelation 19–22 is the way the Bible is supposed to end, the way our hearts long for it to end. John Piper puts it so well:

> There are two appearings of Christ—one is called an appearing of grace, the other called an appearing of glory (Titus 2:11-13). . . . The Christ who will come in glory is

the Christ who came in grace. . . . What God's grace has
begun in our lives through the first coming of Christ his
glory will complete in our lives through the second coming.
("Our Hope")

The apostle John's vision of the second coming of Christ focuses
primarily on one major aspect of His return: His complete and total
victory over all the powers of evil. He sees our King coming as the conquering warrior Messiah "in bloodstained garments, destroying all hostile and opposing powers with his mighty sword. . . . In his cross and
resurrection, Christ won a great victory over the powers of evil; by his
second coming, he will execute that victory" (Ladd, *Commentary*, 252–
53). There is not a more glorious description of our coming King in
the whole Bible than verses 11-16. Three facets of His return are highlighted in these verses.

His Appearance Will Be Glorious (19:11-13)

Heaven opens and we see a rider on a white horse. This is not the rider
of 6:2 who represented the spirit of conquest embodied ultimately in
the beast of 13:1-10. This rider is the Lord Jesus Christ. This is the return
of the King! The white horse symbolizes victory and possibly purity. This
rider also has five names, four that are revealed and one that is concealed. Here He is called "Faithful and True" (1:5; 3:14). "Faithful" conveys dependability, reliability, trustworthiness. "True" affirms that He is
authentic, genuine, the real thing. What He says you can believe. When
He acts you can trust Him. In fact, as the faithful and true One, He can
do what no other King, ruler, or warrior can do: "He judges and makes
war in righteousness." Ladd notes, "The present tense of the verbs indicates the permanent character of Messiah in all his acts" (*Commentary*,
253). He is always faithful, true, and righteous in whatever He does,
including making war.

Verse 12 adds three further characteristics of the returning King.
First, His eyes are "like a fiery flame," which communicates His penetrating judgment and insight (see 1:14; 2:18; see also Dan 10:6). Jesus peers
into the depths of our souls. He sees every act, every thought, every
emotion. He knows you as no one else knows you. He knows you better
than you know yourself. Such a reality should thrill you and terrify you.
It should humble you. He knows you in all of your sin, depravity, and
wickedness. And yet He loves you and cares for you. To know you and

me as He does and yet still love us is simply another evidence of His amazing grace.

A second characteristic is noted: "[M]any crowns [or diadems] were on His head." These are the crowns of royalty, the crowns of absolute, complete, and total sovereignty. Swindoll notes,

> This image of the multi-crowned King Jesus inspired Matthew Bridges in 1852 to pen a majestic hymn that God's people still love to sing:

> Crown Him with many crowns,
> The Lamb upon His throne:
> Hark! How the heav'nly anthem drowns
> All music but its own!
> Awake, my soul, and sing
> Of Him who died for thee,
> And hail Him as thy matchless King
> Through all eternity. (*Insights,* 249)

The third characteristic of Jesus mentioned in verse 12 (echoed in verse 16) is that "He had a name written that no one knows except Himself." This is His third name and also His concealed name. "That he also has a secret name means that the human mind cannot grasp the depths of his being" (Ladd, *Commentary,* 254), which means for all of eternity we will grow in our knowledge and wonder of this great Redeemer King!

Verse 13 adds two more descriptions to this awesome vision. First, "He wore a robe stained with blood." Given the context and the parallels in Isaiah 63:1-6 and Revelation 14:20, the blood of His enemies would be the most natural reading. However, we also see in Revelation the importance of the blood of the martyred saints (6:10; 17:6; 18:24) and the blood of the redeeming Lamb (5:9). Perhaps it is God's intention to remind us that His enemies will be judged, the saints will be vindicated, and the redemption of the Lamb will be remembered for all of eternity. Of this much I am certain: We should never forget that without the shedding of His blood, the precious blood of the Son of God, there is no forgiveness for our sins.

Second, the fourth name of the returning King is revealed: "His name is the Word of God" (see John 1:1; 1 John 1:1). As the Word of God, He is God's perfect communication and revelation. When you look at Jesus, you are looking at God. When you listen to Jesus, you are hearing the voice of God. As the author of Hebrews reveals, in these last days, God "has spoken to us by His Son" (Heb 1:2).

His Army Is Holy (19:14)

When the King returns, He will be accompanied by His armies. The plural tips us off that both angels and believers are present, though the saints are the main army in view here. Angels are said to come with Christ in Zechariah 14:5; Matthew 13:40-42; 16:27; 24:30-31; 25:31-32; Mark 8:38; Luke 9:26; 1 Thessalonians 3:13; 2 Thessalonians 1:7; and Jude 14-15. Believers are said to return with the King in 1 Thessalonians 4:14 and Revelation 17:14. But here verse 14 reflects verse 8, which is clearly a reference to the redeemed. Believers clothed in the imputed righteousness of Christ and their righteous deeds come "on white horses, wearing pure white linen."

We should not miss the observation that they "followed Him." When we return with Christ, He will be out front. He will lead the way. We will not be participators in the battle, only spectators. King Jesus did not need our assistance or help when He came the first time to redeem sinners, and He will not need our assistance or help when He comes the second time to reign as Sovereign. Holy armies come with Him and are following Him. He fights the battle for us. He again wins the day on behalf of those who love and trust Him.

His Authority Is Unparalleled (19:15-16)

Three images—a sword, a staff, and a winepress—depict the unparalleled authority of the returning King. Old Testament references once again drive the argument of these verses. "A sharp sword came from His mouth" draws from Isaiah 11:4 (see Rev 1:16; 2:12,16; also 2 Thess 2:8). His powerful word is the means by which He will "strike the nations with it. He will shepherd them with an iron scepter." This draws from Psalm 2:8-9 (see Rev 2:26-27; 12:5; also Isa 11:4). Further, "He will also trample the winepress of the fierce anger of God, the Almighty." This harks back to Isaiah 63:1-6 (see Joel 3:13-14; Rev 14:19-20; 16:19). He can judge the world in such vivid wrath because He is "God, the Almighty," the Sovereign God (1:8; 4:8; 11:17; 15:3; 16:7,14; 19:6; 21:22). He can do all of this because on His robe along the thigh He has a name, a fifth name: "King of kings and Lord of lords" (17:14; see also Deut 10:17; Dan 2:47). He and He alone is the sovereign King and Lord. He has no equal and no competition. He possesses full divine authority and absolute power over all things (Matt 28:16-20). This is who He is. This is He who is coming. It is a day His followers look, pray, and sing for!

David Jeremiah is right: "When we sing, 'All hail the power of Jesus' name! Let angels prostrate fall; Bring forth the royal diadem, and Crown Him Lord of all,' we are proclaiming His coming again" (Jeremiah and Carlson, *Escape*, 224).

King Jesus Will Judge All Who Reject Him
REVELATION 19:17-18

As the apostle Paul anticipated his approaching execution, he wrote, "There is reserved for me in the future the crown of righteousness, which the Lord, the righteous Judge, will give me on that day, and not only to me, but to all those who have loved His appearing" (2 Tim 4:8). And the apostle John wrote as the end of his life drew near, "[W]hat we will be has not yet been revealed. We know that when He appears, we will be like Him because we will see Him as He is" (1 John 3:2).

It is sad, tragic, and heartbreaking beyond words that unbelievers do not get to share or enjoy the believer's reward. For them there is no hope, only horrible and terrifying destruction and judgment.

There Will Be No Escape (19:17)

John Piper says, "The second coming is like lightning and vultures" ("Second Coming"). He notes Christ's coming "will be globally unmistakable. It will be as publicly unmistakable as lightning" (Matt 24:27). And the second coming of Christ will be "like vultures [who] come on a corpse" (Matt 24:28).

> When the world is ready for judgment as road kill is for the vultures, then he will come in great wrath. . . . This will not be private, secret, or pleasant for unbelievers. He will come on the clouds of heaven with power and great glory (Matt 24:30). And the judgment will be like vultures sweeping in on the corpse of human rebellion. (Piper, "Second Coming")

The apostle John sees an angel. The sun is to his back giving him an ominous appearance. He cries in a "loud voice" to "all the birds," the vultures "flying high overhead." They are called to "come, gather together for the great supper of God." This supper is much different from the marriage supper of the Lamb in 19:9. There the saints are called to come and celebrate with the Lord. Here sinners are called and condemned by the Lord for a "bird feast," a vulture's banquet where they are the entrée. It is a great supper because all rebellious sinners on earth will be present. Try as they might, there is no escape.

There Will Be No Discrimination (19:18)

Verses 17-18 draw from Ezekiel's prophecy against Gog (Ezek 39:17-20). Scott Duvall solemnly notes,

> Everyone will participate in one of two eschatological feasts: the righteous joining in the wedding supper of the Lamb or the wicked becoming the feast at the great supper of God. God will judge the wicked from every social category (6:15; 13:16); social status or rank will not be enough to exempt the ungodly from judgment. (*Revelation*, 258).

Kings, captains, and mighty men will be judged. Free and slave will be judged. Just as our God is indiscriminate in His offer of salvation (Acts 10:34), He is also without discrimination in His judgment. A day of universal, righteous reckoning is coming. Everyone will be held accountable for their rejection of the Lamb.

King Jesus Will Defeat the Enemies Who Oppose Him
REVELATION 19:19-20

The long-awaited Battle of Armageddon (14:14-20; 16:12-16) will be a disappointment to those expecting a good fight because it will be over in a flash. It will last but a moment. Swindoll says, "Let's cut to the chase: Before anybody on earth can utter the word 'Armageddon,' the battle will be over. When God determines the end has come, it's curtains" (*Insights*, 254). Martin Luther in his classic hymn "A Mighty Fortress Is Our God" wrote of how our God deals with Satan and his devices: "One little word shall fell him." When the King returns, this is exactly what will happen!

Jesus Will Capture His Enemies (19:19-20)

The beast of 13:1-10 (antichrist) gathers with his armies to war against the returning King. So swift and complete is the defeat of this evil army that our text does not even describe it! It simply reports the results. Both the beast and the false prophet are captured (19:20). The deceptive ministry and lying propaganda of the false prophet is specifically addressed. Through false miracles or "signs" he had deceived the followers of the beast. This is a reminder that not everything that appears to be a miracle is a miracle, and not everything that is a miracle is a miracle from God. These two are the first inhabitants of eternal hell, "the lake of fire" (20:14-15; 21:8). These verses do not have a hint of annihilation. Their eternal destiny is one of conscious torment and eternal separation from God. Revelation simply confirms the witness of Jesus (Matt 13:40-42; 25:41-46; Mark 9:42-48), who said more about the reality of hell than anyone else in the Bible. *Captured* and *condemned* are two words that describe the future of all who say no to God's grace revealed in Jesus Christ.

Jesus Will Slay His Enemies (19:21)

Here is a further and final unforgettable picture of the destiny of those who have said no to God. It details in tragic words what these people who are alive on earth can expect when Jesus comes again. They are killed by the divine sword coming from the mouth of Christ. The birds will gorge on their flesh. This apocalyptic imagery can only approximate the horrors that lost humanity will experience then and later at the final judgment at the great white throne (Rev 20:11-15). The Bible teacher John Philips says it well:

> Then suddenly it will all be over. In fact, there will be no war at all, in the sense that we think of war. There will be just a word spoken from Him who sits astride the great white horse. Once He spoke a word to a fig tree, and it withered away. Once He spoke a word to howling winds and heaving waves, and the storm clouds vanished and the waves fell still. Once He spoke to a legion of demons bursting at the seams of a poor man's soul, and instantly they fled. Now He speaks a word, and the war is over. The blasphemous, loud-mouthed Beast is stricken where he stands. The false prophet, the miracle-working windbag from the pit is punctured and still. . . . Another word, and the panic-stricken armies reel and stagger and fall down dead. Field marshals and generals, admirals and air commanders, soldiers and sailors, rank and file, one and all—they fall. And the vultures descend and cover the scene. (Quoted in Swindoll, *Insights*, 253)

David Platt sums up well all we have seen in this passage of Scripture:

What a powerful picture of Christ—on a white horse, faithful and true, the righteous Judge and Messianic warrior who sees all, knows all, and judges all, crowned with diadems and shrouded in mystery. He comes to conquer God's enemies once and for all, to end the history of the world with the revelation of God's Word, to rule the nations as He brings the wrath of God upon this world dominated by sin and Satan. He is King of kings and Lord of lords. ("The Hallelujah Chorus")

Conclusion

"The Incomparable Christ"

Author Unknown

More than nineteen hundred years ago there was a Man born contrary to the laws of life. This Man lived in poverty and was reared in obscurity. He did not travel extensively. Only once did He cross the boundary of the country in which He lived; that was during His exile in childhood. He possessed neither wealth nor influence. His relatives were inconspicuous, and had neither training nor formal education. In infancy He startled a king; in childhood He puzzled doctors; in manhood He ruled the course of nature, walked upon the billows as if pavements, and hushed the sea to sleep. He healed the multitudes without medicine and made no charge for His service. He never wrote a book, and yet all the libraries of the country could not hold the books that have been written about Him. He never wrote a song and yet He has furnished the theme for more than all the songwriters combined. He never founded a college, but all the schools put together cannot boast of having as many students. He never marshalled an army, nor drafted a soldier, nor fired a gun; and yet no leader ever had more volunteers who have, under His orders, made more rebels stack arms and surrender without a shot fired. He never practiced medicine, and yet He has healed more broken hearts than all the doctors far and near. . . . The names of the past proud statesmen of Greece and Rome have come and gone. The names of the past scientists, philosophers, and theologians have come and gone; but the name of this Man abounds more and more. Though time has spread [almost two thousand] years between the people of this generation and the scene of His crucifixion, yet He still lives. Herod could not destroy Him, and the grave could not hold Him. He stands forth upon the highest pinnacle of heavenly glory, proclaimed of God, acknowledged by angels, adored by saints, and feared by devils, as the living, personal Christ, our Lord and Savior. And He is coming again! Are you ready?!

Reflect and Discuss

1. Discuss the differences between Jesus' first and second comings. Why did he not come in majesty and power the first time?
2. Despite the differences, how could you explain how Jesus' first and second comings are part of the same work?
3. How have you seen the faithfulness of Christ in your life (Rev 19:11)? His trueness?
4. Jesus' "name written that no one knows except Himself" shows that we can never exhaustively know and understand him. How has your knowledge of Christ grown the longer you have walked with Him?
5. How do Jesus as the "Word of God" and Scripture as God's Word relate? Are they the same? different?
6. Why do the armies accompany Jesus in Revelation 19:14 if they are not going to fight with Him?
7. How do unbelievers try to escape the judgment of God? What tactics do people employ to absolve themselves of their sin?
8. What does Revelation say to those who try to use their social or economic status to avoid judgment and condemnation?
9. Can Revelation be used to support the claim of annihilation for those who are condemned? How does this passage speak to the issue?
10. How does the picture of the man Jesus Christ, as presented in this passage, set Him apart from every other man or woman who ever lived?

The Millennial Kingdom of Jesus Christ

REVELATION 20:1-10

Main Idea: After the tribulation Christ will establish His millennial kingdom with His saints; then He will finally and forever judge Satan and his followers for their rebellion.

I.   Before the Kingdom Satan Is Bound (20:1-3).
II. During the Kingdom the Saints Will Reign (20:4-6).
III. After the Kingdom Sinners Will Be Defeated (20:7-10).

Introduction

In Acts 1:6, just before He ascended, Jesus' disciples asked Him, "Lord, are You restoring the kingdom to Israel at this time?" The kingdom about which they were asking, the kingdom in which Jesus Christ will be universally acknowledged as King of kings and Lord of lords, is that kingdom discussed in Revelation 20. It is the millennial kingdom, the thousand-year reign of Christ on the earth.

The tribulation, with its seal, trumpet, and bowl judgments, has ended (Rev 6–18). Israel has experienced a great end-time revival (Rev 7:1-8; see Rom 11:25-26). The nations, the people groups of the world, have come to Christ (Rev 7:9-17). Antichrist (the beast) and the false prophet have been revealed, defeated, and cast into the lake of fire (Rev 19:19-21). Babylon, that evil, organized religious, political, social, and economic world system that stands in opposition to God, has been destroyed (Revelation 17–18). Armageddon has taken place (Rev 14:14-20; 16:16-21; 19:17-21), and Jesus has come again to the earth to rule and reign for a thousand years as its rightful Master, Lord, and King (Rev 19:11-16).

The doctrine of the millennium, mentioned only here in Revelation 20, has generated significant controversy throughout the history of the church. Sadly, Christians have too often divided unnecessarily over the issue. Basically three major views have been held by various students of Scripture.

Premillennialism. The word *millennium* comes from the Latin words *mille* (thousand) and *annus* (year). The prefix *pre-* before the word *millennialism* refers to the time of Christ's second coming as it relates to the millennium, and thus *premillennialism* is the position that teaches the millennium will be preceded by Christ's return to the earth. Sometimes premillennialists are referred to as "chiliasts." The word *chiliasm* comes from the Greek word *chilioi*, meaning "a thousand." Premillennialism holds to the following points:

- Christ will return to the earth at the end of this age, at the end of the great tribulation, with His saints to reign for a thousand years as King.
- In the millennium Israel will experience the blessings God promised to Abraham and David pertaining to Israel's land, nationality (seed), and king (throne). New Testament believers will likewise share in these covenant blessings having been grafted into the one people of God (Rom 11).
- The church today is not completely experiencing the fulfillment of the promises made to Israel. Certain aspects of these covenants have been inaugurated, but others await future eschatological fulfillment.
- The millennial kingdom is the thousand-year period in which Jesus Christ will rule over the earth as the promised Messiah, the seed of David (2 Sam 7:14-16). This kingdom will be inaugurated at His second coming and therefore at the end of the tribulation (Rev 19:11-21). The millennium is an intermediate kingdom of a thousand years before the establishment of the eternal state (Rev 20:1-6; 21–22).

Amillennialism. The prefix *a* means "no," and thus *amillennialism* holds that there will be no *literal* reign of Christ on earth for a thousand years. It is sometimes called "realized" millennialism. The basic tenets of amillennialism are these:

- The millennium or kingdom reign of Christ and His saints is in existence for the period of time between Christ's first and second coming. We are in the millennium right now.
- The kingdom is either realized in the church on earth (Augustine's view now perpetuated by the Roman Catholic Church) and/or the saints in heaven (B. B. Warfield's view). There will be no future reign of Christ on the earth prior to the new heaven and new earth, and the word *thousand* is a symbolic number indicating a long period of time.

ESCHATOLOGY: MAJOR VIEWS OF THE MILLENNIUM IN REVELATION 20:1-10			
	PREMILLENNIALISM "SECOND COMING *BEFORE* THE MILLENNIUM"	POSTMILLENNIALISM "SECOND COMING *AFTER* THE MILLENNIUM"	AMILLENNIALISM "*NO LITERAL MILLENNIUM*"
Definition	Christ's second coming will occur *before* the millennium.	Christ's second coming will occur *after* the millennium.	There will be *no* literal historical reign of Christ on earth for 1,000 years. His second coming ushers in the eternal state.
Characteristics	Christ will return at the end of this age to reign for 1,000 years. In the millennium the nation Israel will experience the blessing God promised to Abraham and David. New Testament believers are grafted in to share in the covenant blessings. The church today is not completely experiencing the fulfillment of the promises made to Israel. The millennium is an intermediate kingdom of 1,000 years in which Christ reigns before the establishment of the eternal state.	The church is not the kingdom, but it will bring in the kingdom by the preaching of the gospel. Christ will not be on the earth during the kingdom. He will rule in the hearts of His people but will return after the millennium. There will be no literal 1,000-year millennium. The church, not Israel, will receive the fulfillment of the promises to Abraham and David in a spiritual sense.	The kingdom reign of Christ and His saints is in existence for the period of time between Christ's two advents. The kingdom is realized in the church on earth and/or the saints in heaven. The promises to Israel about a land, seed, and throne are completely fulfilled now in a spiritual sense in the church. The promises to Israel were conditional, and Israel did not meet those conditions. Christ is ruling now; Satan is bound between Christ's two advents.
Advocates	Clement, Polycarp, Ignatius, Tertullian, Cyprian, Tyndale, some Anabaptists, Moravians, Mennonites, John Wesley, Ryrie, Walvoord, Graham, Criswell, Moore, Grudem, Erickson, Mohler, Swindoll, and MacArthur.	Daniel Whitby, Jonathan Edwards, Charles Wesley, Charles Hodge, A. A. Hodge, Augustus Strong, B. H. Carroll, G. W. Truett.	Origen, Augustine, Roman Catholic Church, John Wycliffe, Martin Luther, John Calvin, Zwingli, B. B. Warfield, L. Berkhof, G. Beale, W. Hendriksen.

- The promises to Israel about a land, seed, and throne are being fulfilled now in a spiritual sense in the church.
- God's promises to Israel were conditional and have been transferred to the church because Israel did not meet the condition of obedience.
- Christ is ruling now in heaven where He is seated on the throne of David, and Satan is presently bound between Christ's two advents. This binding relates primarily to Satan's inability to stop the preaching and spread of the gospel to the nations.

Texts cited to support this view include:

How can someone enter a strong man's house and steal his possessions unless he first ties up the strong man? Then he can rob his house. (Matt 12:29)

The Seventy returned with joy, saying, "Lord, even the demons submit to us in Your name." He said to them, "I watched Satan fall from heaven like a lightning flash. Look, I have given you the authority to trample on snakes and scorpions and over all the power of the enemy; nothing will ever harm you." (Luke 10:17-19)

He disarmed the rulers and authorities and disgraced them publicly; He triumphed over them by Him. (Col 2:15)

Postmillennialism. The prefix *post* means "after," and thus *postmillennialism* means that Christ's second coming will occur after the millennium. The tenets of this view are these:

- The church is not the kingdom, but it will bring in the kingdom (a utopian, Christianized condition) to the earth by preaching the gospel. Many liberals argue from this principle that the millennium will come through human effort and natural process (e.g., evolutionary progress). They do not expect a literal and historical second coming, while evangelical postmillennialists certainly do expect one (see below).
- Christ will not be on the earth during the kingdom. He will rule in the hearts of His people, and He will return to the earth after the millennium.
- The millennium will not necessarily last for a literal thousand years. The word *thousand* is symbolic of a long period of time. This is similar to amillennialism.

- The church, not Israel, will receive the fulfillment of the promises to Abraham and David in a spiritual sense.

Though this view is not popular today, it has been hugely influential in the history of the church, including playing a significant role in launching the modern missions movement. Persons in the contemporary scene associated with what is called "theonomy," "dominion theology," and "reconstructionism" do hold a postmillennial position.

Before I defend my view, let me again clarify that this is not a doctrine we should divide over. We should discuss it. We should debate it. But we should not divide over it. Good, godly men and women who believe the Bible differ on this issue. Some of my closet friends hold a different view. I greatly love and respect them. I learn from them, even if I do not agree with them.

Having clarified that, I do think premillennialism is the best position to explain what the Scriptures are saying. It is the view that best honors a normal, historical, grammatical hermeneutic while still recognizing the prophetic and apocalyptic nature of Revelation. Chapter 20, obviously, follows chapter 19, and so the millennium follows the Second Coming. The word *millennium* occurs six times in verses 1-7. Never in Scripture when the word *year* is used with a number is its meaning not literal. The two resurrections mentioned in verses 4-7 clearly speak of physical, bodily resurrections. All of this supports premillennialism. This approach to Scripture means the promises about Christ returning to establish on earth His millennial reign of a thousand years are to be taken in the normal sense.

Yes, His kingdom is in existence now (John 3:3,5: Acts 28:31) in heaven and in the hearts of men, but it will be present and fully manifested on the earth during the millennium. Thus, His kingdom is both "now" and "not yet"—realized and yet future.

Additionally, the promises to Israel have not been transferred to the church. The church has been grafted into these promises, as Romans 11 clearly affirms. The complete fulfillment of the Abrahamic covenant, Davidic covenant, and new covenant have not taken place yet. The church and Israel, though distinct, are related to one another in God's plan of redemption personally, nationally, and cosmically. Since the church began on the day of Pentecost, the church is in some sense separate from the nation Israel. Normal grammatical interpretation thus makes a warranted distinction between Israel and the church. However, as Ephesians 1–3 teaches, there is now one people of God, which constitutes the church, the eschatological people of God gathered and realized for all eternity.

Premillennialism makes the most sense because of its consistency in interpretation. Since the prophecies about Christ's first advent were fulfilled literally, the prophecies about His second advent can be expected to be fulfilled in the same way.

In the Psalms and Prophets, a future, eschatological kingdom patterned after but surpassing the model of the Davidic kingship is predicted. This kingdom is a universal kingdom of peace and prosperity with the anointed Messiah ruling over the whole earth (Pss 2; 21; 45; 72; 96; 98; 110; Isa 2:2-4; 9:6-7; 11:1-10; 24–25; 40:3-11; 43:15; 44:6,22-23; 65:17-25; Jer 23:1-6; 33:14-26; Ezek 34:23-31; 37:24-28; Dan 2; 7; Amos 9:11-15; Mic 4:1-8; 5:1-5; Zech 9:9-10; 14:9,16-17; Mal 1:11,14).

The new covenant (Isa 59:20-21; Jer 31:31-34; 32:37-42; Ezek 11:17-21; 16:60-63; 36:24-34; 37:21-28) in particular makes promises of this coming kingdom that are yet to be fully realized. It states that God will cause Israel to repent and be obedient (Isa 59:20; Ezek 36:27,31; 37:24). God will cleanse and forgive Israel (Ezek 16:63; 36:25,29; 37:23). The Holy Spirit will permanently indwell all His people (Isa 59:21; Ezek 36:27; 37:14). Israel will be permanently established forever in their land as a nation (Jer 31:35-37; 32:41-44; Ezek 36:28; 37:25). God will be worshiped by Israel and will place His presence among them forever (Jer 32:38; Ezek 37:26-28).

Additionally, the words of Jesus support premillennialism best. Note His promise to the 12 apostles in Matthew 19:27-28:

> Then Peter responded to Him, "Look, we have left everything and followed You. So what will there be for us?"
>
> Jesus said to them, "I assure you: In the Messianic Age, when the Son of Man sits on His glorious throne, you who have followed Me will also sit on 12 thrones, judging the 12 tribes of Israel."

Consider also His words to the apostles in Acts 1:6-7:

> So when they had come together, they asked Him, "Lord, are You restoring the kingdom to Israel at this time?"
>
> He said to them, "It is not for you to know times or periods that the Father has set by His own authority."

He does not deny or correct their hope for a future kingdom. Rather, He simply says they will not be told *when* that kingdom is coming.

Lastly, Paul's teaching concerning future Israel in Romans 11:25-29 fits best within a premillennial framework. There he teaches that there is still a distinction between Israel and the church, even if Jew and Gentile who trust in Jesus are part of the one people of God.

Given this premillennial framework, let us now examine the text and note particular features of Christ's kingdom on the earth. There is really good news for God's people in these verses.

Before the Kingdom, Satan Is Bound
REVELATION 20:1-3

Christ has returned and defeated the forces of evil on the earth (19:11-21). John now sees "an angel coming down from heaven," coming down to earth. The phrase "I saw" occurs repeatedly at the end of Revelation (19:11,17,19; 20:1,4,11; 21:1). The most natural reading is to see this indicating chronological sequence and progression. These things happen one after the other (Mounce, *Revelation*, 361).

Second Coming → Millennium → Final Rebellion → Great White Throne → Eternal State

The millennium is the beginning of God's restorative work "on the way" to the new heaven, new earth, and new Jerusalem of chapters 21–22.

The angel from heaven "has the key to the abyss." The key indicates authority. The abyss is mentioned seven times in Revelation (9:1,2,11; 11:7; 17:8; 20:1,3). MacArthur notes that in Revelation, the abyss, or pit, is always a "reference to the temporary place of incarceration for certain demons. The abyss is not their final place of punishment; the lake of fire is (Matt. 25:41). Nevertheless it is a place of torment to which the demons fear to be sent (Luke 8:31)" (*Revelation 12–22*, 234). The angel also has in his hand "a great chain" (20:1). The huge chain is for a huge prisoner and carries the ideas of binding and confinement.

This angel now seizes the one who was his former master before he rebelled against God (see Ezek 28:14; see above on Rev 9:1-5, pp. 180–85). Four names or titles are given that describe his character and devices (see 12:9). He is "the dragon," mentioned 12 times in Revelation. He is terrifying, powerful, cruel, dangerous, and vicious. He is "that ancient serpent," which recalls Genesis 3 (see 2 Cor 11:3) and the garden of Eden. He is our ancient enemy who deceived Adam and

Eve ushering in the fall. He is "the Devil," meaning the slanderer, the accuser. He is "Satan," meaning the adversary, the enemy, our opponent. This is our archenemy who hates us and lives for our misery, our death, our destruction. Osborne says, "In this context the list of names might almost be official, as if the legal sentence is read to the condemned prisoner as he is being thrown into prison" (*Revelation*, 700).

Because this angel has the delegated authority of God, he can take authority over the one who "is prowling around like a roaring lion, looking for someone he can devour" (1 Pet 5:8). Note the four steps taken to bind and confine our ancient foe: he "bound him for 1,000 years," he "threw him into the abyss," he "closed it," and he "put a seal on it." Satan's activity, even his presence on earth, is completely curtailed and brought to a halt for the entire millennium. His deceptive work among the nations is stopped for a thousand years!

Only after the millennium is finished is he released, and then for only "a short time" (20:3). This short-lived release from captivity is discussed in verses 7-10. Mounce makes a perceptive and telling observation at this point when he says,

> Apparently a thousand years of confinement does not alter Satan's plans, nor does a thousand years of freedom from the influence of wickedness change people's basic tendency to rebel against their creator. (*Revelation*, 363)

What an indictment once again on the wicked hearts of evil demons and evil humanity!

During the Kingdom, the Saints Will Reign
REVELATION 20:4-6

John provides only a brief description of activity of the millennial kingdom in these verses. Additional insights, as previously noted, are found in texts like Isaiah 11:1-11; 65:17-25; Jeremiah 31:31-34; Joel 3:17-21; Amos 9:11-15; and Micah 4:1-5. John sees thrones and "people seated on them who were given authority to judge." Matthew 19:28 teaches that the 12 apostles will sit as judges over the 12 tribes of Israel. First Corinthians 6:3 speaks of believers judging angels. Revelation 2:26 says the saints will have authority over the nations. And Revelation 5:10 teaches that the followers of the Lamb "will reign on the earth." These could refer to glorified saints ruling over natural-born persons in the millennium. In any event, these pictures are all good news for the believer, even if the precise details remain a mystery.

John then sees a second group: martyred saints. These are described as those who "had been beheaded [i.e., executed] because of their testimony [or witness] about Jesus and because of God's word." Further, they had not "worshiped the beast or his image, and [they] had not accepted the mark on their foreheads or their hands." These tribulation saints had remained faithful and true to the Lamb. "They did not love their lives in the face of death" (12:11). These faithful believers were previously seen in chapters 6 and 13. They are now rewarded for their faithfulness as they are gloriously resurrected! They come to life in bodily resurrection and are also granted the privilege to reign with Christ as coheirs for a thousand years (see Rom 8:17).

John calls this "the first resurrection." It is a bodily resurrection in *kind* and the first resurrection in *time*. "The rest of the dead," unbelieving humanity, are not resurrected until after the millennium when they will stand before God at the great white throne judgment (20:11-15). Believers in Jesus enjoy the first resurrection unto glorified eternal life. Unbelievers experience the second death (i.e., eternal separation from God) at the final judgment. The term *second resurrection* never occurs in Scripture.

Verse 6 provides a beautiful summary as to the destiny of the followers of the Lamb. They are called both "blessed" (i.e., happy, fortunate) and "holy" (i.e., set apart for God) since they participate in the first resurrection, the glorification of the body unto eternal life. But it does not end there! Three additional blessings are bestowed on the redeemed: (1) Over these "the second death [i.e., eternal and spiritual death] has no power"; (2) they "will be priests of God and of the Messiah," serving their great God during the millennium and for all eternity; and (3) they "will reign with Him for 1,000 years."

John MacArthur, drawing on various biblical texts, provides a wonderful summary of what life will be like in the millennium:

> A final blessing for the participants in the first resurrection is that they will reign with the Lord Jesus Christ for a thousand years, along with believers who survived the Tribulation. Politically and socially, the rule of Christ and His saints will be universal (Ps. 2:6-8; Dan. 2:35), absolute (Ps. 2:9; Isa. 11:4), and righteous (Isa. 11:3-5). Spiritually, their rule will be a time when the believing remnant of Israel is converted (Jer. 30:5-8; Rom. 11:26) and the nation is restored to the land God

promised to Abraham (Gen. 13:14-15; 15:18). It will be a time
when the Gentile nations also will worship the King (Isa. 11:9;
Mic. 4:2; Zech. 14:16). The millennial rule of Christ and the
saints will also be marked by the presence of righteousness
and peace (Isa. 32:17) and joy (Isa. 12:3-4; 61:3,7). Physically,
it will be a time when the curse is lifted (Isa. 11:7-9; 30:23-24;
35:1-2,7), when food will be plentiful (Joel 2:21-27), and when
there will be physical health and well-being (Isa. 33:24; 35:5-6),
leading to long life (Isa. 65:20). (*Revelation 12–22,* 239)

The millennium will be a wonderful time under the cosmic and universal
reign of King Jesus.

After the Kingdom, Sinners Will Be Defeated
REVELATION 20:7-10

These verses record what can be called "the final battle" between God
and Satan, good and evil. Osborne points out,

> There are five aspects of this scene: the release of Satan, his
> deception and gathering of the nations for the final battle,
> their surrounding God's people, fire descending from heaven
> to devour the nations, and the casting of Satan into the lake of
> fire. (*Revelation,* 710)

Why does our God allow the evil one a final desperate grasp at power? I
believe the answer is twofold. First, to demonstrate the evil intentions of
Satan that consume him now and forever. Second, to reveal that even in
a near perfect environment with no Satanic temptation, man is capable
of and willing to rebel against his gracious and loving God.

At the beginning of the millennium, two types of persons are on
the earth: believers with glorified bodies and believers with nonglorified bodies who survived the tribulation. Nonglorified believers can and
will have children. These persons, like all persons, will have the opportunity to say yes or no to Jesus. Outwardly it appears virtually all will
say yes. Inwardly, however, in their heart, many will say no. When the
opportunity comes to rebel against the most wonderful leader the world
has ever known, they will jump at the chance. Their doom, however, is
sealed even before the rebellion begins.

Satan is released from his prison (v. 7). Immediately he goes out
with a twofold agenda: to deceive the nations and to gather a great

army to war against the Lord (v. 8). "Gog and Magog" is a reference to
Ezekiel 38–39. Here the phrase stands for the enemies of God among
the nations of the world. They march on "the beloved city" (v. 9), the
city of Jerusalem, where King Jesus reigns over His worldwide kingdom.
Before they can achieve their goal, however, "fire came down from
heaven and consumed them." In a flash, in a moment, the final battle
is over. An army "like the sand of the sea" is vaporized instantaneously!
"Like Armageddon a thousand years earlier (19:11-21), the 'battle' will
in reality be an execution" (MacArthur, *Revelation 12–22*, 242).

Our text ends with Satan finally receiving his just reward: he is
"thrown into the lake of fire and sulfur where the beast [i.e., antichrist]
and the false prophet are." There this unholy trinity's eternal destiny is
to be "tormented day and night forever and ever." Their just judgment
is literal. It is eternal. No reprieve. No relief. No second chance. No end.

Conclusion

There is a lot to take in from Revelation 20, exegetically, theologically,
and even personally. Osborne provides a helpful overview that addresses
all three of these, reminding us that God is holy and sin is serious. God
will not tolerate sin and evil forever. Their end is in sight. Osborne
writes:

> In 20:4-6 . . . the saints sit on thrones and judge the nations
> for the thousand-year period. In 20:5-6 the contrast between
> saint and sinner comes to the fore, and this has strong
> evangelistic potential. Every non-Christian must be aware that
> only believers will experience the "first resurrection." For the
> unbelievers the only "resurrection" they will experience will be
> the one that leads to the "second death," but that will have no
> "power" over the Christian. The believer will know only "life,"
> but the unbeliever will have only eternal "death."
>
> God allows Satan and his followers to have one last gasp,
> yet the purpose there is to prove beyond any doubt that the
> hold of depravity over the sinner is total. Though the nations
> have had a thousand years to experience the [benevolent]
> authority of Christ, as soon as Satan is released they flock
> after him. This tells the reader that God's only response
> must be eternal punishment. The power of sin is eternal
> over those who have rejected Christ again and again, as seen

in the repeated repudiations of God's offer of repentance throughout this book (9:20-21; 16:9,11), culminating in the final refusal after experiencing the reign of Christ for a thousand years. So God can respond to eternal sin only with eternal torment. Thus, as the enemies of God and the saints surround his people, he sends fire from heaven to devour them as a prelude to the eternal fire that will be their destiny.

At that time Satan joins the other two members of the false trinity (19:20) in the lake of fire, where their followers will soon join them. God's justice demands this response. Those who are offended by such teaching have too low a realization of the terrible nature of sin and the natural response that divine holiness must have toward it. We must remember the many times in this book that God sought their repentance, and those who did repent (11:13) no longer faced such judgment. But God cannot abide sin, and his reaction must be swift and final. (*Revelation*, 717)

Final judgment will be swift. It is truly final. Are you prepared? Are you ready? Only those who follow Christ will be.

Reflect and Discuss

1. What do you see are some of the strengths and weaknesses of the premillennial view of the end times?
2. What do you see are some of the strengths and weaknesses of the amillennial view of the end times?
3. What do you see are some of the strengths and weaknesses of the postmillennial view of the end times?
4. Do you agree that the premillennial position makes the most sense of the biblical data?
5. How is God's sovereign power and authority shown in this passage?
6. Why do people continue to sin even when Satan is bound?
7. What does it mean that believers will reign with Christ? How will our reign relate to His?
8. In what ways is the millennial reign like the garden of Eden before the fall?
9. Why does God release Satan for a final rebellion?
10. Is it just for God to punish someone (even Satan!) for eternity? Why?

Why the Doctrine of Hell Is No Laughing Matter

REVELATION 20:11-15

Main Idea: Jesus will defeat all the enemies of God forever by sending them to eternal punishment in hell.

I.   Unbelievers Will Stand Before the Sovereign God of the Universe (20:11).
II. Unbelievers Will Be Judged for Their Righteousness, Not the Imputed Righteousness of Christ (20:12-13).
III. Unbelievers Will Spend Eternity Separated from God in the Lake of Fire (20:14-15).

It was once a Bible doctrine people believed and feared. It was never far from their minds or absent from serious conversations. But times have changed. American church historian Martin Marty says, "Hell disappeared. No one noticed" ("Hell Disappeared," 381–98). Alan Bernstein, professor of medieval history at the University of Arizona, says, "Hell today is enveloped in silence" ("Thinking About Hell," 78). Even among evangelicals there is a noticeable absence. The respected theologian Donald Bloesch notes, "The doctrine of hell has passed out of conversation and preaching, even in conservative evangelical churches" (Swindoll, *Insight*, 48). Still, hell has not really disappeared so much as it has been ignored or redefined or lampooned. I think Jeffery Sheler is on to something when he writes, "The netherworld has taken on a new image: more of a deep funk than a pit of fire" ("Hell," 45).

So today it is "earthly infernos" that get all the attention. As Ross Douthat writes,

> Hell means the Holocaust, the suffering in Haiti. . . . And
> if it's hard for the modern mind to understand why a good
> God would allow such misery on a temporal scale, imagining
> one who allows eternal suffering seems not only offensive but
> absurd. ("A Case for Hell")

Perhaps no one says it more clearly than theologian Clark Pinnock when he writes,

Let me say at the outset that I consider the concept of hell as endless torment in body and mind an outrageous doctrine, a theological and moral enormity, a bad doctrine of the tradition which needs to be changed. How can Christians possibly project a deity of such cruelty and vindictiveness whose ways include inflicting everlasting torture upon his creatures, however sinful they may have been? Surely a God who would do such a thing is more nearly like Satan than like God, at least by any moral standards, and by the gospel itself. ("Destruction," 246–47)

A quick Internet search for quotes about hell yields millions of hits, including the following:

- "What is hell? I maintain that it is the suffering of being unable to love." —Fyodor Dostoyevsky, *The Brothers Karamazov*
- "Maybe this world is another planet's hell." —Aldous Huxley
- "We are each our own devil, and we make this world our hell." —Oscar Wilde
- "Hell is—other people!" —Jean-Paul Sartre, *No Exit*
- "What is hell: Hell is oneself.
  Hell is alone, the other figures in it
  Merely projections. There is nothing to escape from
  And nothing to escape to. One is always alone." —T. S. Eliot
- "There are moments when even to the sober eye of reason, the world of our sad humanity may assume the semblance of Hell." —Edgar Allan Poe
- "An intelligent hell would be better than a stupid paradise." — Victor Hugo, *Ninety-Three*
- "I believe I am in Hell, therefore I am." —Arthur Rimbaud
- "Hell isn't other people. Hell is yourself." —Ludwig Wittgenstein
- "'No sight so sad as that of a naughty child,' he began, 'especially a naughty little girl. Do you know where the wicked go after death?'
  'They go to hell,' was my ready and orthodox answer.
  'And what is hell? Can you tell me that?'
  'A pit full of fire.'
  'And should you like to fall into that pit, and to be burning there forever?'
  'No, sir.'

'What must you do to avoid it?'
I deliberated a moment: my answer, when it did come was
objectionable: 'I must keep in good health and not die.'"
— Charlotte Brontë, *Jane Eyre*

It is often said that Jesus spoke more often about hell than any other
person in the Bible. That is true. The Greek word *gehenna* is found 12
times in the New Testament and is always translated as "hell." Christ
used the word 11 times (Matt 5:22,29,30; 10:28; 18:9; 23:15,33; Mark
9:43,45,47; Luke 12:5). The only other mention is in James 3:6 in reference to the tongue. Christ warned his listeners to be afraid of *gehenna*
(Matt 5:22) and claimed that only God has the power to cast humans
into it (Luke 12:5). He testified that both the soul and the body could
enter *gehenna* (Matt 10:28). The unsaved could go there with two eyes
(Matt 18:9; Mark 9:47), two hands (Mark 9:43), and two feet (Mark
9:45). It is a place marked by fire (Matt 5:22). In His contrast between
the sheep (the saved) and the goats (the unsaved), Jesus said that the
unsaved eventually would go into "the eternal fire prepared for the
Devil and his angels" (Matt 25:41). Summarizing the teachings of Jesus
on hell, using Matthew 25:31-46 as a primary text, Don Whitney says that
Jesus taught the following:

- Hell is real.
- Hell is separation from God.
- Hell is for all the "accursed ones."
- Hell is eternal.
- Hell is fire.
- Hell is a prepared place.
- Hell is eternity with the Devil and his angels.
- Hell is inevitable if you have never come to Christ.
- Hell is inescapable once you are there.
- Hell is avoidable if you will repent and believe in Jesus Christ.
  ("Hell Is Real")

Add to this Luke 16:19-31, the story of the rich man and Lazarus,
and it becomes clear that our Lord believed hell was real. He leaves
no room for either *universalism*—the teaching that all will eventually be
saved—or *annihilationism*—the teaching that all who are lost will simply
cease to exist.

We know Jesus believed in hell because *He taught it*. We also know Jesus believed in hell because of *the cross*. Robert Murray M'Cheyne got it exactly right:

> The dying of the Lord Jesus is the most awakening sight in the world. Why did that lovely One that was from the beginning the brightness of His Father's glory, and the express image of His Person, degrade Himself so much as to become as a small "corn of wheat," which is hidden under the earth and dies? Why did He lie down in the cold, rocky sepulcher? Would Christ have wept over Jerusalem if there had been no hell beneath it? Would He have died under the wrath of God if there were no wrath to come? Oh! Triflers with the gospel— and polite hearers, who say often, "Sir, we would see Jesus," but who never find Him—go to Gethsemane, see His unspeakable agonies; go to Golgotha, see the vial of wrath poured upon His breaking heart; go to the sepulcher, see the "corn of wheat" laid dead in the ground. Why all this suffering in the spotless One if there is no wrath coming on the unsheltered, unbelieving head? (*Works*, 320)

The coming of the Son of God into this fallen world and the bloody cross testifies there is a hell.

There is one major objection to address before we investigate our text. **Why would a good God punish forever a finite offense at a particular moment in time?** This seems unjust or at the least all out of proportion. I believe the answer is twofold. *First*, sin against God is far more serious than most imagine. Sin is an act of insurrection against an infinitely worthy and holy Sovereign. Sin is not a slap to the face of a mouse. It is a repeated slap in the face of the King of the universe. *Second*, as Russell Moore says,

> Hell is the final handing over of the rebel to who he wants to be, and it is awful. The sinner in hell does not become morally neutral. . . . We must not imagine the damned displaying gospel repentance and longing for the presence of Christ. They do not in hell love the Lord their God with heart, mind, soul, and strength. Instead, in hell, one is now handed over to the full display of his nature apart from grace. And this nature is seen to be satanic (Jn. 8:44). The condemnation continues

forever and ever, because the sin does too. ("Why Is Hell Forever?")

Now, what do we learn of this terrible, perhaps better "terrifying," doctrine in Revelation 20:11-15? Why is hell truly no laughing matter?

Unbelievers Will Stand Before the Sovereign God of the Universe
REVELATION 20:11

Following the millennial kingdom (20:1-6) and the final defeat of the Devil (20:7-10), John sees another vision. John MacArthur calls it "the most serious, sobering, and tragic passage in the entire Bible" (*Revelation 12–22*, 245). It is a vision of "a great white throne," the place of final eternal judgment. That it is white symbolizes the holiness and purity of the One on the throne, His glory and majesty. This is our great God in all His power and sovereignty.

Though God the Father and God the Son share the heavenly throne, Scripture would seem to indicate it is the Lord Jesus who will preside at this ominous event.

> *The Father, in fact, judges no one but has given all judgment to the Son. . . . For just as the Father has life in Himself, so also He has granted to the Son to have life in Himself. And He has granted Him the right to pass judgment, because He is the Son of Man.* (John 5:22,26-27)

> *He commanded us to preach to the people and to solemnly testify that He is the One appointed by God to be the Judge of the living and the dead.* (Acts 10:42)

> *Therefore, having overlooked the times of ignorance, God now commands all people everywhere to repent, because He has set a day when He is going to judge the world in righteousness by the Man He has appointed. He has provided proof of this to everyone by raising Him from the dead.* (Acts 17:30-31)

> *They show that the work of the law is written on their hearts. Their consciences confirm this. Their competing thoughts will either accuse or excuse them on the day when God judges what people have kept secret, according to my gospel through Christ Jesus.* (Rom 2:15-16)

I solemnly charge you before God and Christ Jesus, who is going to judge the living and the dead, and because of His appearing and His kingdom. (2 Tim 4:1)

King Jesus sits on the eternal throne of judgment. The risen and glorified Christ is the One to whom and before whom all will give an account. As the scene unfolds, the universe's "uncreation" is described in striking imagery. From the presence of the Son both "earth and heaven fled." Before the eternal state of chapters 21–22 begins, Isaiah 51:6 says, "The heavens will vanish like smoke, the earth will wear out like a garment, and its inhabitants will die like gnats. But My salvation will last forever, and My righteousness will never be shattered."

Matt Chandler provides an insightful observation in the context of what is beginning to unfold before our eyes:

> If God is most concerned about his name's sake, then hell
> ultimately exists because of the belittlement of God's name,
> and, therefore, our response to the biblical reality of hell
> cannot, for our own safety, be the further belittlement of God's
> name. . . . Someone who says hell cannot be real, or we can't
> all deserve it even if it is real, because God is love is saying that
> the name and the renown and the glory of Christ aren't that
> big of a deal. (Chandler and Wilson, *Explicit*, 44–45)

When sinners stand before God at the great white throne, they will realize the name and the renown and the glory of Christ is a big deal. They will be standing before the sovereign God of the universe.

Unbelievers Will Be Judged for Their Personal Righteousness, Not the Imputed Righteousness of Christ
REVELATION 20:12-13

Acts 10:34 teaches that "God doesn't show favoritism." There will be no ethnic, social, or economic discrimination at the great white throne. Now, I do believe there will be a spiritual discrimination. And though good Bible students disagree, I also think there is a distinction between the great white throne judgment and what is called the judgment seat of Christ. Jesus Christ is the Judge at both. However, those who are judged and for what they are judged is radically different, as shown in the following chart:

Contrasting the "Judgment Seat of Christ" and the "Great White Throne Judgment"		
Issue	Judgment Seat of Christ (The Bema Seat of Judgment)	Great White Throne Judgment
Persons Judged	Believers only who have the imputed righteousness of Christ	Unbelievers only who have only their own righteousness
Key Scriptures	Romans 14:10 1 Corinthians 3:10-15 2 Corinthians 5:10	Revelation 20:11-15
Basis of the Judgment	Faithfulness in Christ and resultant good works (even to the motivations)	Rejection of Christ and thus one's own righteousness
Results	Rewards or loss of rewards, but not loss of salvation, which is secure	Eternity in hell, the "lake of fire"

John here only sees "the dead" (i.e., the spiritually dead; see Eph 2:1-3), those who died apart from Christ. They are called "the dead" four times in these verses. The words "dead" or "death" appears a total of seven times. Further, it is "the great and the small, standing before the throne." One's status in this life will have no bearing at this judgment. John then sees books (plural) opened. These are the books of works, which contain every action, thought, and emotion of all unsaved persons. To say it is something akin to a heavenly video recorder is not enough. It is more than that. In fact, the theology of a comprehensive judgment for all persons finds repeated biblical support:

Wouldn't God have found this out, since He knows the secrets of the heart? (Ps 44:21)

For God will bring every act to judgment, including every hidden thing, whether good or evil. (Eccl 12:14)

For the Son of Man is going to come with His angels in the glory of His Father, and then He will reward each according to what he has done. (Matt 16:27)

For nothing is concealed that won't be revealed, and nothing hidden that won't be made known and come to light. (Luke 8:17)

On the day when God judges what people have kept secret, according to my gospel through Christ Jesus. (Rom 2:16)

Because their name was "not found written in the book of life" (20:15) and because in unbelief they rejected the perfect imputed righteousness of Christ, they now stand spiritually naked, fully exposed before the all-seeing, omniscient Judge of the universe. And no one escapes, as verse 13 makes clear. The sea, often an image of the evil turmoil of this world system, forfeits its dead. Death, that which claims the body, gives up its dead. Hades, that which claims the soul, gives up its dead. With resurrected bodies fit for hell, peoples from every corner of the earth will stand before righteous King Jesus.

Verse 12 tells us an important theological truth: the spiritually dead are "judged according to their works by what was written in the books [of works]." Verse 13 reinforces this truth: "[A]ll were judged according to their works." Here is a theological principle we must not miss: At the great white throne, every single person will be judged fairly and equally. But the people there will not all receive the same penalty and punishment. Everyone will be "thrown into the lake of fire" (20:15; 21:8), but there will be varying degrees of punishment and suffering. You see, revelation brings responsibility. The more you know and reject, the greater and more severe is your judgment. You may ask where such an idea comes from, and the answer is simple and important: from Jesus. Hear the words of Christ:

If anyone will not welcome you or listen to your words, shake the dust off your feet when you leave that house or town. I assure you: It will be more tolerable on the day of judgment for the land of Sodom and Gomorrah than for that town. (Matt 10:14-15)

Woe to you, Chorazin! Woe to you, Bethsaida! For if the miracles that were done in you had been done in Tyre and Sidon, they would have repented in sackcloth and ashes long ago! But I tell you, it will be more tolerable for Tyre and Sidon on the day of judgment than for you. And you, Capernaum, will you be exalted to heaven? You will go down to Hades. For if the miracles that were done in you had been done in Sodom, it would have remained until today. But I tell you, it will be more tolerable for the land of Sodom on the day of judgment than for you. (Matt 11:21-24)

He also said in His teaching, "Beware of the scribes, who want to go around in long robes, and who want greetings in the marketplaces, the front seats in the synagogues, and the places of honor at banquets. They devour widows' houses and say long prayers just for show. These will receive harsher punishment." (Mark 12:38-40)

Yes, there will be degrees of torment in the lake of fire, but do not be deceived. Everyone in hell will suffer terribly in a place where no good thing is present. And why is no good thing present? Because God is not there in His grace, love, and mercy. Randy Alcorn is right: "The unbeliever's 'wish' to be away from God turns out to be his worst nightmare" ("Banished"). C. S. Lewis would add, "To enter heaven is to become more human than you ever succeeded in being on earth; to enter hell is to be banished from humanity" (*Problem of Pain*, 127–28).

Unbelievers Will Spend Eternity Separated from God in the Lake of Fire
REVELATION 20:14-15

Human language is incapable of describing both the glories of heaven and the horrors of hell. Take all the images that appear in the Bible, including "the lake of fire" (20:14-15) and "the lake that burns with fire and sulfur" (21:8), multiply it ten billion times, and you will still not give an adequate description of those who experience the second death. Jonathan Edwards tried to illustrate the horror:

> The pit is prepared. The fire is made ready. The furnace is now hot, ready to receive them. The flames do now rage and glow. The glittering sword is whet, and held over them, and the pit has opened her mouth under them. . . . O sinner! Consider the fearful danger you are in. ("Sinners")

Christians, too, should consider the peril of hell and be spurred towards faithfulness in missions and evangelism:

> It is an unworthy motive to preach on hell to frighten people into the family of God. . . . We preach it because it tenders the hearts of the Christians and creates within them a concern for the lost people. . . . No redeemed child of God can look through the eyes of the scriptures at the awful glaring destiny of the lost and not have a grave concern about the sinners on their way to eternal damnation. . . . The mantle of the prophet

falls upon the shoulders of a preacher who can look through the eyes of this great doctrine at a lost world. (Autrey)

"Death and Hades" (i.e., body and soul joined together) are cast into hell, the lake of fire. "This is the second death." Spiritual death. Eternal death. Permanent separation from God forever. Alone. Trapped. Imprisoned. No way out. No second chance. What an awful and great punishment! Yes, in one sense God is there (see Ps 139). However, the lost will have no sense of His gracious presence, only His terrible wrath.

Finding their names absent from the book of life, they are all, each and every one, "thrown into the lake of fire." Language like this leaves no room for any form of universal salvation, a second chance, or annihilation of the wicked. This is the eternal infliction of punishment resulting in the physical and spiritual and mental misery mentioned by Jesus (Matt 25:41,46). The wicked will be tormented without rest, day and night, forever (Rev 14:11), for "it is appointed for people to die once—and after this, judgment" (Heb 9:27). This day is coming, and it will be impossible to avoid it.

Conclusion

Dorothy Sayers was a close friend of C. S. Lewis. She died in 1957. When it comes to the doctrine of hell, she was filled with insight and wisdom. We do well to consider her words:

> There seems to be a kind of conspiracy, especially among middle-aged writers of vaguely liberal tendency, to forget or to conceal, where the doctrine of hell comes from. One finds frequent references to the "cruel and abominable doctrine of hell," or "the childish and grotesque mediaeval imagery of physical fire and worms . . ."
>
> But the case is quite otherwise; let us face the facts. The doctrine of hell is not "mediaeval": it is Christ's. It is not a device of "medieval priestcraft" for frightening people into giving money to the church: it is Christ's deliberate judgment on sin. The imagery of the undying worm and the unquenchable fire derives, not from "medieval superstition," but originally from the Prophet Isaiah, and it was Christ who emphatically used it. . . . One cannot get rid of it without tearing the New Testament to tatters. We cannot repudiate

Hell without altogether repudiating Christ. (*Matter of Eternity*, 86)

Accordingly, the great patristic preacher John Chrysostom wisely advised, "If we think always of hell, we shall not soon fall into it" (*Homilies*, 476). And Charles Spurgeon would add, "Think lightly of hell, and you will soon think lightly of the cross. . . . He who does not believe that God will cast unbelievers into hell will not be sure that He takes believers into heaven" ("Future Punishment").

In an interview the great heavyweight boxing champion Muhammad Ali said, "The most important thing about life is what's gonna happen when you die. Are you gonna go to heaven or hell, that's eternity." He then added, "[It] just scares me to think I'm gonna die one day and go to hell" ("World Heavyweight Champion"). Muhammed Ali is wise to have such a fear, because the doctrine of hell is no laughing matter.

Reflect and Discuss

1. Why do you think talking about hell has fallen out of practice in contemporary culture? among many Christians?
2. How does the cross show us that Jesus believed in the reality of hell?
3. Why is eternal punishment for sins just on God's part?
4. What is the connection between hell and the glory of God?
5. How would your life look different if you lived in light of eventually giving an account to God for every thought, word, and deed?
6. What does it mean that "revelation brings responsibility" in regards to eternal punishment?
7. In what sense is God absent from hell if He is omnipresent?
8. How should Christians preach the doctrine of hell to unbelievers?
9. What are some of the various ways some have been tempted to soften the doctrine of hell? How does Revelation 20 dismiss those possibilities?
10. Contrast heaven and hell, according to the Bible. In what ways are they polar opposites of each other?

What Will Eternity Be Like?

REVELATION 21:1-8

Main Idea: God will establish a new heaven and a new earth, where Christ will spend eternity among His redeemed people in perfect and constant communion.

I. We Will Enjoy a New Heaven and a New Earth (21:1-2).
II. We Will Live in Intimate and Personal Communion with Our God (21:3).
III. We Will No Longer Experience the Horrible Effects of Sin (21:4).
IV. We Will Rest in the Sure Promises of God (21:5-6).
V. We Will Live as God's Adopted Children with No Fear of the Second Death (21:7-8).

One of the most wonderful promises in the whole Bible is that persons who have put their faith in Jesus Christ will spend all of eternity with God in a place called heaven. Paul reminds us in Philippians 3:20, "Our citizenship is in heaven." Hebrews 12:22 affirms, "Instead, you have come to Mount Zion, to the city of the living God (the heavenly Jerusalem)." This is our future home and our future hope, and that ought to make a difference in our lives today.

Throughout my life I have often heard statements to this effect: "He is so heavenly minded that he is no earthly good." There is only one thing wrong with that statement: It is not true! The fact is those who are the most heavenly minded are the most earthly good. That is why Colossians 3:1-2 teaches us, "So if you have been raised with the Messiah, seek what is above, where the Messiah is, seated at the right hand of God. Set your minds on what is above, not on what is on the earth." C. S. Lewis beautifully echoes the truth of Scripture when he writes,

> A continual looking forward to the eternal world is not (as some modern people think) a form of escapism or wishful thinking, but one of the things a Christian is meant to do. It does not mean that we are to leave the present world as it is. If you read history, you will find that the Christians who did most for the present world were just those who thought most

of the next. The Apostles themselves, who set on foot the conversion of the Roman Empire, the great men who built up the Middle Ages, the English Evangelicals who abolished the Slave Trade, all left their mark on Earth, precisely because their minds were occupied with Heaven. It is since Christians have largely ceased to think of the other world that they have become so ineffective in this. Aim at Heaven and you will get earth "thrown in:" aim at earth and you will get neither. (*Mere Christianity*, 134)

Revelation 21–22 brings us to the end of the Apocalypse and to the end of the Bible. It is a fitting conclusion to the historical drama of redemption that began in Genesis 1–3. In fact, it is interesting to compare the beginning of Genesis with the end of Revelation. Parallels and differences are too important to ignore.

Genesis	Revelation
Heaven and earth created (1:1)	New heavens and earth recreated (21:1)
Sun created (1:16)	No need of the sun (21:23)
The night established (1:5)	No night there (22:5)
The seas created (1:10)	No more seas (21:1)
The curse announced (3:14-17)	No more curse (22:3)
Death enters history (3:19)	Death exits history (21:4)
Man driven from paradise (3:24)	Man restored to paradise (22:14)
Sorrow and pain begin (3:17)	Sorrow, tears, and pain end (21:4)
The Devil appears (3:1)	The Devil disappears (20:10)

Indeed, one of the most wonderful things about the Bible is that in its first two chapters the Devil is not there, and in its last two chapters the Devil is not there. Examine Genesis 1–2, and you will find no mention of the ancient serpent. Examine Revelation 21–22, and you will likewise find no mention of Satan. He is not there. He is in the lake of fire (20:10), where he will be imprisoned for all eternity.

These final two chapters unfold clearly in a threefold division: 21:1-8; 21:9–22:5; and 22:6-21. They logically and theologically follow the second coming (19:11-21), the millennium (20:1-6), the final rebellion (20:7-10), and the great white throne judgment (20:11-15). The eternal destiny of the redeemed is so radically different from the eternal destiny of the lost. Only new and wonderful things are in the future for those who love God and trust in His Son. A new day is coming! As the old hymn says, "When we all get to heaven, what a day of rejoicing that will be!" What, then, is in store for those who live under the reign of this King? What will eternity be like?

We Will Enjoy a New Heaven and a New Earth
REVELATION 21:1-2

John sees "a new heaven and a new earth," since "the first heaven and the first earth had passed away." Duvall notes, "This final 'and I saw' passage (cf. 19:11,17,19; 20:1,4,11,12; 21:1) serves as the high point of the whole letter" (*Revelation*, 280). John draws on the language of Isaiah 65:17 and 66:22. Heaven is mentioned more than five hundred times in the Bible and right at 50 times in Revelation (MacArthur, *Revelation 12–22*, 262). Three heavens are mentioned in the Bible (see 2 Cor 12:2-4):

- the earth's atmosphere, where the clouds are and the birds fly;
- the starry heavens, where the planets, sun, and stars reside; and
- the unique dwelling place of God, where good angels and saints will live forever and ever.

That heaven has not yet been created, and no one is there right now. Believers who die do immediately go to be with the Lord (2 Cor 5:8), but that is an intermediate place of blessing, not our final heavenly home. Revelation 21–22 describes our eternal abode, the third heaven.

John also says there is no sea. Greg Beale notes there are five uses of the "sea" in the Apocalypse. They are:

1) The origin of cosmic evil (especially in light of the OT background; so 4:6; 12:18; 13:1; 15:2), 2) the unbelieving, rebellious nations who cause tribulation for God's people (12:18; 13:1; Isa. 57:20; cf. Rev. 17:2,6), 3) the place of the dead (20:13), 4) the primary location of the world's idolatrous trade activity (18:10-19), 5) a literal body of water, sometimes mentioned together with "the earth," . . . in which the sea as a part of the old creation represents the totality of it (5:13; 7:1-3; 8:8-9; 10:2,5-6,8; 14:7; 16:3 . . .). (*Revelation*, 1,042)

He believes all five are probably in view here as being excluded from the new earth, though I am not sure about his fifth option. As beautiful bodies of water were a part of God's original creation, I believe they will also be a part of the new creation.

Verse 2 sees the descent of "the Holy City, new Jerusalem." She is pure, spotless, and without blemish in character. She comes down as a wonderful gift of grace. And she is "prepared like a bride adorned for her husband," the Lamb, the Lord Jesus. She will be described in greater detail in 21:9–22:5. Significantly, she is both a place and a people. God's people, as Scripture reveals, have long awaited this day and moment (Gal 4:26; Heb 11:8-10; 12:22; 13:14).

Now we should address an important question: Will God renovate the old creation, as Romans 8:19-22 seems to teach, or will He completely recreate a new creation, as 2 Peter 3:10-13 appears to affirm? This is not an easy question to answer. Might it be that there is something of a transformation of the old order through the destruction of the old order? I think we are on good ground to affirm some type of continuity between the old order and the new order, though the new will be radically superior. Perhaps the judgment of 2 Peter 3 is one of cleansing rather than total destruction (Osborne, *Revelation*, 730n4). What we can say for certain is, "There will be a whole new reality, a new kind of existence in which all the negatives of the 'first' (Gen 1) world will be removed, all the discoloration by sin will be gone" (ibid., 730).

We Will Live in Intimate and Personal Communion with Our God
REVELATION 21:3

This is one of the most wonderful promises in the Bible. In a real sense this is what the Bible has been pointing toward throughout its 66 books. Again John hears "a loud voice," something we hear more than 20 times in Revelation. This voice comes with divine authority and power, for it comes from God's throne. The voice announces that God's dwelling place (or tabernacle) is with man! God will permanently and forever pitch His tent (see John 1:14) among His redeemed people. His "shekinah glory" will make its home in and among His peoples. The plural "peoples" is preferred here, as heaven will be a kingdom diversity home for all the *ethnē's* (granted, the Greek uses the related word *laoi* here). It will be wonderfully multicultural and multiethnic. There will be no segregated subdivisions in the new Jerusalem!

God's tabernacle is His people. He tabernacles among His peoples (see Lev 26:11-13). And the great promise of this verse only gets better: "God Himself will be with them and be their God." "God Himself" is emphatic. Our great God will be with us, in our midst, as our God. As Mounce beautifully puts it, "It is with the redeemed peoples of all races and nationalities that God will dwell in glory" (*Revelation*, 383). Matthew 5:8 says, "The pure in heart are blessed, for they will see God." That great promise is now fulfilled. It becomes reality in the fullest measure.

Often I am asked, "In heaven, will we see God?" Revelation 21:3 says, "Absolutely!" And 22:4 seals the deal!

We Will No Longer Experience the Horrible Effects of Sin
REVELATION 21:4

I have often referred to this verse as one of the most precious in all of Scripture and with good reason. I almost always read it at funeral services because it is filled with so much hope and assurance. This sinful, fallen world has left so many people beaten and broken. The pain it inflicts often overwhelms us, almost crushing us. This verse promises us that in eternity all that causes pain and sorrow will forever be taken away!

Verse 4 identifies five things that will be absent in eternity: tears, death, grief, crying, and pain. Wiped out forever are the horrible consequences and effects of sin. Revelation 7:17 previously promised, "For the Lamb who is at the center of the throne will shepherd them; He will guide them to springs of living waters, and God will wipe away every tear from their eyes." And hear also the words of Isaiah 25:8-9:

> He will destroy death forever. The Lord GOD will wipe away the tears from every face and remove His people's disgrace from the whole earth, for the LORD has spoken.
>
> On that day it will be said, "Look, this is our God; we have waited for Him, and He has saved us. This is the LORD; we have waited for Him. Let us rejoice and be glad in His salvation."

Adrian Rogers used to say, "Death is only a comma to a Christian—not a period!" Scott Duvall says, "Like a compassionate parent caring for a suffering child, God will wipe away our tears" (*Revelation*, 282). Yes, in eternity all the former things associated with the fallen world will pass away and they are never coming back.

We Will Rest in the Sure Promises of God
REVELATION 21:5-6

The One "seated on the throne" speaks again (see v. 3), and once more His words bless, comfort, excite, and bring joy to His peoples. "Look" signals that a special announcement is about to follow. The declaration comes: "I am making everything new." The promises of verse 4 are just an inkling of all that God is going to do for His people, His bride. A quick survey of chapters 21–22 identifies at least 12 sure promises we can rest in:

1.	God makes a new heaven, earth, and Jerusalem.	21:1-2
2.	Chaos and disorder are no more.	21:1
3.	God will live with His people personally.	21:3; 22:4
4.	The effects of sin are eradicated and done away with.	21:4,8,27; 22:3
5.	All the legitimate desires of our heart will be satisfied.	21:6
6.	Our inheritance of heavenly blessings will be plentiful and permanent.	21:7
7.	The splendor of the new Jerusalem will be magnificent.	21:9-21
8.	The glory of God will permeate our dwelling place.	21:22-23
9.	Nations will be guided by God.	21:24,26
10.	Protections and peace are perfectly present.	21:25; 22:4-5
11.	Productivity will be bountiful and breathtaking.	22:1-2
12.	Perpetual, perfect service will be our calling.	22:3

These promises are not conditional, potentially true, or tentative. John is told, "Write, because these words are faithful and true" (see 19:9; 22:6). Just as the Living Word is "Faithful and True" (19:11), so also the written Word is "faithful and true."

The new creation has come. The Word of God is faithful and true. Verse 6 affirms, "It is done!" It is finished. It is complete. And who can say this? The sovereign God and ruler of the universe who declares

Himself to be "the Alpha and the Omega, the Beginning and the End" (see 1:8,17; 22:13; also Isa 44:6; 48:12). He is the A and Z. He is the Lord over both ends of history and all that is in between. David Platt says, "He had the first word in history, and He will have the last word in history" ("Consummation").

Because He is Himself eternal life, He can give eternal life to others. That is what He has done for all who have trusted in His Son (John 3:16), and that is what is intended by the beautiful image of the "water as a gift to the thirsty from the spring of life." John 7:37-38 says,

> *On the last and most important day of the festival, Jesus stood up and cried out, "If anyone is thirsty, he should come to Me and drink! The one who believes in Me, as the Scripture has said, will have streams of living water flow from deep within him."*

If you are thirsty, come to Christ and be satisfied. It will cost you nothing. Jesus has already paid it all. Satisfied forever and it cost you not a thing—what a magnificent picture of God's amazing grace! Charles Spurgeon said it this way:

> What does a thirsty man do to get rid of his thirst? He drinks. Perhaps there is no better representation of faith in all the Word of God than that. . . . So, dear Soul, whatever your state may be, you can surely receive Christ, for He comes to you like a cup of cold water! ("Good News")

We Will Live as God's Adopted Children with No Fear of the Second Death
REVELATION 21:7-8

This introduction to the new creation of eternity concludes with a word of blessing in verse 7 and a word of warning in verse 8. The blessing is for the overcomers who trust in Christ. The warning is for sinners who are headed to the lake of fire without Christ. The one who conquers or overcomes is a popular theme in the writings of John. In 1 John 5:4-5 he writes,

> *Whatever has been born of God conquers the world. This is the victory that has conquered the world: our faith. And who is the one who conquers the world but the one who believes that Jesus is the Son of God?*

And in the letters to the seven churches in Revelation 2–3 our Lord makes a promise to "the victors" in each church:

Church	Text	Promise
Ephesus	2:7	You will have access to the tree of life.
Smyrna	2:11	You will not be hurt by the second death.
Pergamum	2:17	You will be given hidden manna, a white stone, and a new name.
Thyatira	2:26-27	I will give you authority over the nations and the morning star.
Sardis	3:5	Clothed in white garments, your name will never be blotted out of the book of life, and I (Christ) will confess you before My Father and before His angels.
Philadelphia	3:12	I will make you a pillar in the temple of My God, and I will write on you the name of My God, the name of the new Jerusalem, and My own new name.
Laodicea	3:21	You will sit with Me on My throne.

To those wonderful promises our Lord has added the promise of eternal life via the springs of water in verse 6. Now he adds the promise of a gracious heritage: "I will be his God, and he will be My son." Throughout all of eternity we will be the adopted heirs of a perfect heavenly Father (see Rom 8:14-17; Gal 4:4-7). Patterson notes,

> While God has but one ontological Son . . . he has many children by adoption (Rom 8:15,23; Gal 4:5). And the children who by faith have been adopted into the family of God are just as much the heirs and joint heirs as the supernatural Son of God. (*Revelation*, 366)

Tragically, this is not the destiny of those who never trust in Christ for salvation. An irreversible judgment and justice is all they can expect. God provides a selective, not exhaustive, list of persons who will not be in heaven in verse 8. Eight specific sins are noted that characterize the lives of those who will spend eternity separated from God in the lake of fire, who experience the second death. The "cowards" are individuals who, because of fear, will not confess Christ openly when confronted with persecution (see Heb 10:38-39). The "unbelievers" or faithless are those who deny Christ by their conduct and speech. The "vile" or detestable are those polluted by gross acts of idolatry. "Murderers" are malicious, savage killers (especially those who kill the tribulation saints). "Sexually immoral" are those who lived sexual lifestyles contrary to God's plan and purpose. "Sorcerers" are those who mix drugs with the practices of spirit worship, witchcraft, and magic. "Idolaters" are worshipers of idols and images (this practice especially will be prevalent when the world bows to the antichrist's image). "All liars" are those who habitually deceive others. None of these people will have access to the new Jerusalem. They will spend eternity "in the lake that burns with fire and sulfur, which is the second death" (see Keener, *Revelation*, 489–90).

Conclusion

So many wonderful things can be said about eternity one hardly knows where to start and end. Chuck Swindoll is helpful and uses negation to highlight 12 things that will not be present in eternity, things we will not miss:

1. No more sea—because chaos and calamity will be eradicated (21:1).
2. No more tears—because hurtful memories will be replaced (21:4).
3. No more death—because mortality will be swallowed up by life (21:4).
4. No more mourning—because sorrow will be completely comforted (21:4).
5. No more crying—because the sounds of weeping will be soothed (21:4).
6. No more pain—because all human suffering will be cured (21:4).
7. No more thirst—because God will graciously quench all desires (21:6).
8. No more wickedness—because all evil will be banished (21:8,27).
9. No more temple—because the Father and Son are personally present (21:22).
10. No more night—because God's glory will give eternal light (21:23-25; 22:5).
11. No more closed gates—because God's doors will always be open (21:25).
12. No more curse—because Christ's blood has forever lifted that curse (22:3). (*Insights*, 273)

Ecclesiastes 3:11 says God "has put eternity in their hearts." It is great to know that what God has planted in our hearts—this longing in our souls—will be fully and completely satisfied in the new heaven and new earth. We each have a longing for eternity in our soul that only God can fill. Come and taste the Lord. You will find He is better and more wonderful than you ever hoped or imagined. He is that good.

Reflect and Discuss

1. Do you think it is possible to be "so heavenly minded" that we become "no earthly good"? What is the real problem with people who are accused of this?
2. Compare the first few chapters of Genesis and the last few chapters of Revelation. What strikes you about the parallels and differences?
3. What is significant about there being "no sea" in the new heavens and the new earth? How does this give you hope in this life?
4. Why is it significant that Christ's bride is both a place and a people?
5. How should the continuity between this world and the new creation affect the way we relate to this creation?
6. How do you practice communion with God now? How will communion with God in eternity be similar and different?
7. Reflect on the various ways you have seen the brokenness of this fallen world. Now read Revelation 21:4 and consider how God will set all things right.
8. Which of the promises of God in Revelation 21–22 do you most long for? Why?
9. Which of the characteristics in Revelation 21:8 is the most applicable warning for you, and how can you heed this warning today?
10. What is one thing about your life or ministry that can be changed to be more "heavenly minded" to be more effective for "earthly good"?

The Glory and Majesty of the New Jerusalem

REVELATION 21:9–22:5

Main Idea: In eternity God's people will enjoy perfect fellowship and communion with God in His perfect city.

I. **The New Jerusalem Will Be like a Perfect City (21:9-21).**
   A. It is the beautiful bride of the Lamb (21:9-14).
   B. It is the most holy place where God is glorified (21:15-21).
II. **The New Jerusalem Will Be like a Perfect Temple (21:22-27).**
   A. It is characterized by God's presence (21:22).
   B. It is characterized by God's protection (21:23-26).
   C. It is characterized by God's purity (21:27).
III. **The New Jerusalem Will Be like a Perfect Garden (22:1-5).**
   A. We will be nourished by our God (22:1-2).
   B. We will worship our God (22:3).
   C. We will see our God (22:4).
   D. We will reign with our God (22:5).

Our world has changed a lot over the past five hundred years. Most of us cannot really imagine just how different things were, though some interesting reminders give us a clue. Here are some things I read concerning the 1500s.

Most people got married in June because they took their yearly bath in May and still smelled pretty good by June, hence the popularity of *June weddings*. However, they were starting to smell, so brides carried a bouquet of flowers to hide the body odor.

Baths consisted of a big tub filled with hot water. The man of the house had the privilege of going first and enjoying the nice clean water; then came all the sons and other men, then the women, and finally the children—last of all the babies. By then the water was so dirty you could actually lose someone in it—hence the saying, *"Don't throw the baby out with the bathwater."*

Most houses had thatched roofs—thick straw, piled high, with no wood underneath. It was the only place for animals to get warm, so all the dogs, cats, and other small animals (mice, rats, and bugs included!)

lived in the roof. When it rained, it became slippery, and sometimes the animals would slip and fall off or out the roof—hence the saying, "*It's raining cats and dogs.*"

However, there was nothing to stop things from falling into the house. This posed a real problem in the bedroom where bugs and other droppings could really mess up your nice clean bed. Hence, a bed with big posts and a sheet hung over the top afforded some protection. That's how *canopy beds* came into existence.

The floor was dirt. Only the wealthy had something other than dirt, hence the saying, "*dirt poor.*"

Most people had little meat, but sometimes they could obtain pork, which made them feel special. When visitors came over, they would hang up their bacon to show off. It was a sign of wealth that a man could "*bring home the bacon.*" They would cut off a little to share with guests and would all sit around and "*chew the fat.*"

Lead cups were used to drink ale or whiskey. The combination would sometimes knock people out for a short time. Someone walking along the road would take them for dead and prepare them for burial. They were laid out on the kitchen table for a couple of days, and the family would gather around and eat and drink and wait to see if they would wake up—hence, the custom of holding a *wake.*

England is an old country and not very large. They started running out of places to bury people. So they would dig up coffins and take the bones to a "bone house" and reuse the grave. When reopening these coffins, one out of 25 coffins was found to have scratch marks on the inside, and they realized they had been burying people alive. So they thought they would tie a string on the wrist of the corpse, lead it through the coffin and up through the ground and tie it to a bell. Someone would have to sit out in the graveyard all night (the "*graveyard shift*") to listen for the bell; thus, someone could be "*saved by the bell*" or was considered a "*dead ringer.*"[4]

Yes, things have changed quite a bit in five hundred years. But these changes pale in comparison to the differences between the way things are now and how they will be in the new heaven, the new earth, and the new Jerusalem. In 21:1-8 John gave us a glimpse of the glory of eternal life. Now in 21:9–22:5 the apostle is given a magnificent vision of heaven's capital, the new Jerusalem. As we examine these verses, we will see

---

[4] Source unknown. I am aware some of these observations are disputed.

that the new Jerusalem is described as a perfect city (21:9-21), a perfect temple (21:22-27), and a perfect garden (22:1-5). Revelation 21–22 is a picture of Eden regained and more.

The New Jerusalem Will Be like a Perfect City
REVELATION 21:9-21

Heaven will be heaven because of Jesus. We will enjoy Him intimately and forever! We will also experience the many ways He showers us with blessings of grace and goodness. In eternity our Lord relates to us in various ways as an evidence of His love. In verses 9-21 He provides a perfect city, a unique city. This city is also a bride (21:2), and she is the most holy place as well. As a bride the city is a sacred spouse. As the most holy place the city is sacred space.

It Is the Beautiful Bride of the Lamb (21:9-14)

"Then one of the seven angels, who had held the seven bowls filled with the seven last plagues" (Rev 15–17:1) comes and speaks to John telling him to "come" that he might show him "the bride, the wife of the Lamb" (21:9). For the fourth time John is carried away in the Spirit (see 1:10; 4:2; 17:3), this time "to a great and high mountain." This stands in vivid contrast to his vision of Babylon in 17:3 where he was taken into the wilderness to see the prostitute. Here he will see the glory of the Lamb's bride, "the holy city, Jerusalem, coming down out of heaven from God, arrayed with God's glory" (21:10-11). The new Jerusalem is a great city, a holy city, a heavenly city, the Lamb's city. John details her glory, "God's glory," in verses 11-14.

His description is accurate but also inadequate given the limitations of human language. "Arrayed with God's glory," John tells us its radiance is "like a very precious stone, like a jasper stone, bright as crystal." Duvall says, "It is a translucent stone, perhaps opal or even a diamond, specifically associated with the light and glory of God (21:11)" (*Revelation*, 298). The city "had a massive high wall," a symbol of security and stability. It has "12 gates," a sign of great access since there are three in each direction of the compass (21:13). At the 12 gates are "12 angels," divine honor guards who protect the gates even though "its gates will never be shut by day" (21:25 ESV). Each of the gates contains all "the names of the 12 tribes of Israel's sons" (21:12). God is faithful in His covenantal promises to Abraham and his descendants (see Gen 12:1-3). Verse 14 further describes the wall by noting it has 12 foundations on which are written "the 12 names of the Lamb's 12 apostles." This recalls Ephesians 2:20 where Paul writes that the church is "built on the foundation of the apostles and prophets, with Christ Jesus Himself as the cornerstone." Swindoll rightly notes concerning the 12 tribes and 12 apostles, "Thus, the city will be the dwelling place of the united people of God—Old and New Testament believers—whose salvation rests on the completed work of Jesus Christ" (*Insights*, 283).

It Is the Most holy place Where God Is Glorified (21:15-21)

The angel of verse 9 now measures the city with "a gold measuring rod" (21:15). Verses 15-17 reveal it is laid out like a cube. This recalls and reflects the most holy place, or holy of holies (1 Kgs 6:20; 2 Chr 3:8-9). This is "the place of divine presence. A city foursquare would be the place where God has taken up residence with his people" (Mounce, *Revelation*, 392). Osborne wisely states, "The number is obviously symbolic. . . . It signifies not only perfection but a city large enough to hold all the saints down through the ages, the saints from 'every tribe, language, people and nation' (5:9; 7:9; cf. 21:4, 26)" (*Revelation*, 753).

Verses 18-21 describe both the incredible magnificence and the inestimable value of this city. The wall is built of jasper, and the city is described as being of "pure gold like clear glass" (21:18). "The foundations of the city wall were adorned with every kind of precious stone" detailed in verses 19-20. There are 12 total, which "correspond roughly to the gems on the breastplate of the high priest" (Duvall, *Revelation*, 289). Additionally, "the 12 gates are 12 pearls; each individual gate was made of a single pearl" (21:21). Their value simply cannot be calculated. And the great street of the city, which no doubt leads to the throne of God, is "pure gold, like transparent glass" (v. 21). Mounce points out, "Like the priests of the Old Testament (1 Kings 6:30) who ministered in the temple, the servants of God walk upon gold" (*Revelation*, 395).

The New Jerusalem Will Be like a Perfect Temple
REVELATION 21:22-27

The city imagery now flows into temple imagery as the internal characteristics and blessings of the holy city Jerusalem are described. This is a temple city, one that is marked by the undiluted perfections of deity!

It Is Characterized by God's Presence (21:22)

John looks, and to his amazement he sees no temple in the city. Now this is not a contradiction with other verses in Revelation, where there was a temple (7:15; 11:19; 14:15,17; 15:5-8; 16:1,17). This is the eternal state, the new Jerusalem, and there is a temple—it is the "Lord God the Almighty and the Lamb." The Lord and the Lamb are its temple. Symbol gives way to blessed reality. The temple *represented* God's presence, but believers now *have* God's presence. And we will have it forever. We will have Him forever.

It Is Characterized by God's Protection (21:23-26)

This temple city is permeated by the Lord's presence and glory. Therefore, "the city does not need the sun or the moon to shine on it, because God's glory illuminates it, and its lamp is the Lamb." The "light of the world" will be the light who illuminates this temple city (John 8:12).

Verse 24 informs us that "the nations will walk in its light, and the kings of the earth will bring their glory into it." The multiethnic, multicultural nature of eternity is on beautiful display in the glorious light of our God. And these nations and governments present in eternity will be at perfect peace with one another because they all have the same Father, worship the same Lord, and are indwelt by the same Spirit. In this temple city the "gates will never close because it will never be night there." No darkness, evil, or terror. Indeed, the redeemed from all the people groups of the world "will bring the glory and honor of the nations into it" (21:26). Keener notes for us,

> This is the most positive vision of the future possible: Whereas Gentiles once trampled the temple city (11:2), now they honor it, coming to worship God (15:4; cf. Ps. 102:15; Zech. 14:16-19). . . . They offer their glory to God in light of God's greater glory (21:23), forsaking idolatry. (*Revelation*, 498)

It Is Characterized by God's Purity (21:27)

Verse 27 begins with a double negative in Greek. We could say, "But no nothing profane will ever enter it." Nothing unclean, no one who is detestable, no one who is false or deceitful will enter this temple city. No, "only those written in the Lamb's book of life," made pure and holy by the cleansing power of the blood of the Lamb, will be allowed in. Our God is a holy God, and only the holy live with Him forever.

The New Jerusalem Will Be like a Perfect Garden
REVELATION 22:1-5

The temple city is also a garden city, which reminds us of Eden. In imagery drawn from both Genesis 1–2 and Ezekiel 47:1-12 we see the image of a garden bracketing the entire Bible (Duvall, *Revelation*, 298). Four wonderful blessings belong to all who will live forever in this Eden regained.

We Will Be Nourished by God (22:1-2)

"The river of the living water" (see Gen 2:10; Ezek 47:1-2), a river "sparkling like crystal," a glorious and life-giving water, flows "from the throne of God and of the Lamb" (22:1). There is no death in this garden city, only eternal life. The Lord and the Lamb on the throne guarantee it. This crystal clear river flows "down the middle of the broad street of the city" (i.e., the street of gold from 21:21). And on both sides of the river is "the tree of life," the heavenly counterpart to the earthly tree of life in the garden of Eden (see Gen 2:4; 3:22-24). It too is a picture of eternal life but also abundant life with its "12 kinds of fruit, producing its fruit every month." In fact, "The leaves of the tree are for the healing of the nations" (22:2). This is another symbolic reminder that there is no pain, sorrow, or death in this heavenly city (see 21:4). We are perfectly cared for and nourished, as Adam and Eve were in the garden before the fall.

We Will Worship Our God (22:3)

The curse is vanquished forever (see Gen 2:16-17; 3:14-24). Remarkably, the curse is replaced by "the throne of God and of the Lamb" in this beautiful garden city. Genesis 3 is reversed, undone forever. All that we lost in the fall we get back and more. What is the only rightful response to all of God's goodness and grace? "His slaves will serve Him." The Greek word *latreuo* translated as "serve" here carries the idea of service through worship or worship through service. Nothing about heaven will be boring or dull. We will honor our God in delightful and joyful service that is our spiritual worship (see Rom 12:1). "Service of worship will be eternal and complete, for it is worship of God and the Lamb" (Osborne, *Revelation*, 774).

We Will See Our God (22:4)

Verse 4 contains an amazing twofold promise for the child of God. It seems too good to be true! First, we will see our God and experience perfect fellowship with Him. Second, His name will be on our foreheads, and we will enjoy a perfect relationship with Him. I love the comments of Scott Duvall on this verse:

> Now, in the new holy of holies, the entire priestly community will experience the greatest blessing of all: they will see the face of God. Moses was not allowed to see God's face, but saw only his back (Exod. 33:20, 23; cf. John 1:18; 1 John 4:12), but God's people have always longed to see the Lord (e.g., Pss. 11:7; 17:15; 27:4; Matt. 5:8; 1 John 3:2; Heb. 12:14). The old priestly blessing/prayer for the Lord to "make his face shine on you" and "turn his face toward you" (Num. 6:25-26) finds its ultimate fulfillment here. God's people will also bear his "name," meaning they will belong to him, imitate his character, and live safely in his presence (see 2:17; 3:12; 7:3; 14:1). (*Revelation*, 301)

We Will Reign with Our God (22:5)

Verse 5 tells us that "in the New Jerusalem God is ever present, and his glory makes unnecessary all other sources of light" (Mounce, *Revelation*, 400). "Night will no longer exist" (see 21:25), and "people will not need lamplight or sunlight" (see 21:23). We will see His face, and He will "make His face shine on" us (Num 6:25). We will reign with Him forever and ever (see 2:26-27; 3:21; also 2 Tim 2:12). MacArthur summarizes well what those who follow the Lamb have to look forward to:

> The eternal capital city of heaven, the New Jerusalem, will be a place of indescribable, unimaginable beauty. From the center of it the brilliant glory of God will shine forth through the gold and precious stones to illuminate the new heaven and the new earth. But the most glorious reality of all will be that sinful rebels will be made righteous, enjoy intimate fellowship with God and the Lamb, serve Them, and reign with Them forever in sheer joy and incessant praise. (*Revelation 12–22*, 288)

Conclusion

Few doctrines generate more questions than the doctrine of heaven. For some of those questions the Bible provides a clear answer. Others we can only speculate about or plead ignorance. Below are some of the more common questions with brief answers. Though the Bible does not tell us everything we would like to know, it tells us more than enough to let us know eternity with our God is going to be wonderful!

Questions About Heaven

Will babies go to heaven? Yes. Anyone who has not reached an age of moral responsibility or accountability will be the gracious recipient of God's mercy and salvation. This truth would also apply to those who because of some mental handicap are also incapable of moral discernment of right and wrong. God's grace, I believe the Bible affirms, will extend to all such persons (Akin and Mohler, "Children").

Will we know one another in heaven? Yes. We will maintain our personal identity in heaven. Men will be transformed, glorified men; women will be transformed, glorified women. It is even possible that we will possess our individual names in heaven. In other words, all of you will be you and all of me will be me. Personality and individuality do exist beyond the grave (1 Cor 13:12).

Do those in heaven have any knowledge of what is happening on earth right now? The Bible is not clear. Some believe 1 Samuel 28:16-18; Luke 15:7,10; and Hebrews 12:1 teach that persons in heaven have a knowledge of what is taking place on earth. Certainly God and the angels have knowledge of what is taking place on earth. As for believers who are now in heaven, there is no conclusive answer. We simply do not know.

Will we be aware of loved ones who are not in heaven? I do not know. The Bible teaches in Revelation 21:4 that there will be no tears, nor sorrow, nor pain in heaven. It is possible we will see them as God sees them. It is also possible He wipes away our memories of them.

Will there be marriage in heaven? No. Jesus said in Matthew 22:30, "For in the resurrection they neither marry nor are given in marriage but are like angels in heaven."

Will there be sex in heaven? That is a most interesting question and has received various answers by theologians. The Roman Catholic philosopher and theologian Peter Kreeft argues that there will be sex in heaven because humans are sexual beings and they will maintain their sexual identity throughout eternity. With respect to the issues of sexual intercourse, he says,

> I think there will probably be millions of more adequate ways to express love than the clumsy ecstasy of fitting two bodies together like pieces of a jigsaw puzzle. Even the most satisfying earthly intercourse between spouses cannot perfectly express all their love. If the possibility of intercourse in heaven is not actualized, it is only for the same reason earthly lovers do not eat candy during intercourse: there is something much better to do. ("Sex in Heaven")

He concludes by arguing, "This spiritual intercourse with God is the ecstasy hinted at in all earthly intercourse, physical or spiritual" (ibid.).

Will Jesus be the only person of the Trinity we shall see in heaven? No. The Bible makes clear in Revelation 21–22 that we shall see God in all of His fullness. In other words, we will see that there is only one God, yet this one God exists as three persons: Father, Son, and Holy Spirit (see Matt 5:8; 1 John 3:2).

Will Jesus still have the scars in His hands, feet, and side in heaven? Yes. We will see that these are the only man-made things in heaven!

Can you eat all that you want in heaven and not get fat? Yes. In heaven, with a glorified body, everything will be processed perfectly and everything will be enjoyed supremely.

Will angels escort us to heaven? Based on Luke 16:22, there is reason to believe that when a believer dies, an angel will escort him or her into the presence of God.

Will we go to heaven as it eternally exists or to an intermediate state of blessedness when we die? The Bible teaches that we go immediately into the presence of God into an intermediate state, sometimes called "paradise" in the Bible. Therefore, we are with God though we are not in our final resting place.

Do people who commit suicide go to heaven? If a person has trusted Jesus Christ as their Lord and Savior, they will go to heaven. Suicide is a sin, but it is not the unpardonable sin.

Will animals go to heaven? The Bible is not clear as to whether animals go to heaven, though we have every reason to believe there will be animals in the new heaven, the new earth, and the new Jerusalem. Romans 8:19-23 speaks of the whole creation groaning and waiting for its redemption. Certainly animals would fall into this category, and they also are a part of God's good creation.

Why do even Christians sometimes fear death and going to heaven? Because death is unnatural and was never intended by God for us. If Adam and Eve had never sinned, they would have never died. Therefore, there is a sense in which the fear of death is understandable, even for those who know they are going to be with God. Yet the Bible is also clear that through Christ we can overcome that fear. To be absent from this body is to be immediately present with Him (2 Cor 5:8).

Will we know everything in heaven? Of course not. Often people confuse heaven and deity. We will still be human in heaven and therefore finite (but immortal by God's sustaining power). As a result, our knowledge will be finite. One of the joys of heaven will be that we will go on forever and ever learning more and more and more about the greatness and the glory of our God.

Will we all be equal in heaven? No. The Bible teaches that there are both degrees of punishment in hell and degrees of reward in heaven. However, there will be no jealousy in heaven. Every vessel will be completely filled concerning its capacity. No one will have more than they are capable of holding and no one will have less than they are capable of holding. Everyone will be satisfied perfectly with who they are and what they have. Thomas Watson said, "Though every vessel of mercy shall be full, yet one vessel may hold more than another" (*Body of Practical Divinity*, 475).

Will we have emotions in heaven? Yes. Just as we now exist as whole persons with mind, will, and emotion, so in heaven mind, will, and emotion will function perfectly as we enjoy fully all that these various components of the human personality provide.

Will we be free to sin in heaven? No. We will be free *not* to sin in heaven. Just as God is completely free in His will and sinless, so we in our glorified state will be completely free and sinless. We will be free to be our true selves as God created us to be, and that involves both full freedom and the absence of sin.

What will we possess in heaven? Nothing and everything! There appears to be no private property in heaven, no ownership. Yet we will all possess its fullness, goodness, truth, beauty, love, life, and most of all, God. These things make heaven heaven.

Will we wear clothes in heaven? Probably. However, the Bible seems to indicate the possibility that our clothing will be a natural outgrowth of our glorified humanity. In heaven light is the supreme entity, and it reigns in all of its fullness. Remember, Adam and Eve were naked in the garden before the fall, and they were not ashamed.

How big is heaven? Heaven is big enough so that billions and billions of saved people are never crowded yet small enough so that no one ever gets lost or feels alone.

Is heaven serious or funny? Yes. In heaven there will be joy and happiness, seriousness and solemnity. All of these things will indeed constitute our experiences in heaven.

Will we be bored in heaven? Absolutely not. In heaven we are with God, who is infinite. We will never come to the end of knowing Him, loving Him, exploring Him, and growing in our knowledge of Him. In heaven, even though it is eternity, each day will be a new day as we learn more and more about the magnificence and glory of our great God.

Will we age in heaven? No. But we will be fully complete, mature, perfect, and whole.

Will there be ethnic segregation in heaven? No. In heaven our oneness in Christ and the realization of our family relationship will come to perfect fruition.

Will injuries, deformities, and other physical disabilities disappear in heaven? Yes. Amputees will have their limbs restored; the paralyzed will be healed, the blind will see, and the mentally disabled will be given full intelligence and cognitive ability.

Will we be able to do the supernatural and miraculous in heaven? Probably. We will have a glorified body like Jesus. We will be like Adam and Eve before the fall but better.

Will there be government in heaven? Yes. It will be a theocracy (i.e., God ruled)! Revelation 21:24 says, "The nations will walk in its light, and the kings of the earth will bring their glory into it." Thus, God's sovereign rule will be perfectly realized and manifested in heaven among angels and humans.

Will there be music and singing in heaven? Yes, and with great variety I am sure.

What language will we speak in heaven? We will speak every language with perfect clarity and complete understanding.

What will heaven look like? Beautiful and glorious! It transcends human description.

Will we work in heaven? Yes, and it will be the most satisfying and fulfilling labor we have ever known. We will never get tired or tire of the work.

Will we play sports in heaven? Why not? Zechariah 8:5 says, "The streets of the city will be filled with boys and girls playing in them."

Will we be—or be like—angels in heaven? No and yes. *No*, because we are humans and the object of God's redeeming love. Further, we will judge angels, according to 1 Corinthians 6:3, having authority over them. But *yes*, we are like the angels in that in heaven we will not marry and procreate.

What will we look like in heaven? Perfect! We will have a transformed, glorified body in heaven that is incorruptible, glorious, powerful, and spiritual (1 Cor 15:42-44)! In fact, it will be a body like the body of the resurrected and glorified Jesus (Phil 3:20-21; 1 John 3:2-3).

Of course, the most important question one could ever ask about heaven is this: *How does one go to heaven?* And the answer is simple and yet incredibly difficult. It is simple for us, but it was incredibly difficult and costly to God. By repenting of sin and placing one's faith and trust completely and only in Jesus Christ as Lord and Savior, one can be saved and go to heaven. Jesus said in John 14:6, "I am the way, the truth, and the life. No one comes to the Father except through Me." Trust in Christ and only Christ, and your eternal home will be heaven.

Reflect and Discuss

1. How drastically has the world changed in your lifetime? What are some examples of such changes? How do these help you imagine the difference between our time and the new creation?
2. What are the parallels between the most holy place in the Old Testament and the new Jerusalem? What do these parallels tell us about this city?
3. What does it mean that God and the Lamb are the temple in the new Jerusalem?
4. Why do you think John emphasizes "the nations" in Revelation 21–22?
5. In what ways does this city look like the garden of Eden? How is it different?
6. What does the garden imagery in this passage tell us about the mission of God in the whole Bible?
7. What is the connection between service and worship in the Christian life? How do you practice both of these?

8. Why is seeing the face of God the greatest blessing of all in the new creation?

9. What questions do you wrestle with about the doctrine of heaven? Does the Bible give clear answers to your questions? Hints? Is it silent?

10. How does the doctrine of the new heavens and the new earth contradict popular conceptions about heaven among Christians or the wider culture?

God's Final Invitation

REVELATION 22:6-21

Main Idea: Christ invites all who will hear to turn from their sin, trust Him as Lord and Savior, eagerly await His coming, and walk faithfully before Him until He comes.

I.   Invitation 1: Obey the Word of God (22:6-7).
II. Invitation 2: Be True to the Worship of God (22:8-9).
III. Invitation 3: Proclaim the Truth of God (22:10-11).
IV. Invitation 4: Pursue the Will of God (22:12-15).
V.   Invitation 5: Respond to the Invitation of God (22:16-17).
VI. Invitation 6: Heed the Warning of God (22:18-19).
VII. Invitation 7: Pray for the Coming of God (22:20-21).

Our God takes delight in inviting the peoples of the world, who are made in His image, to come and be satisfied in Him. Time and again throughout the Bible we see God extending an invitation to come and enjoy who He is and all that He provides. Sometimes these invitations are extended through God's servants; other times they come directly from God Himself:

> *Proclaim Yahweh's greatness with me; let us exalt His name together.* (Ps 34:3)

> *Come and see the wonders of God; His acts for humanity are awe-inspiring. He turned the sea into dry land, and they crossed the river on foot. There we rejoiced in Him.* (Ps 66:5-6)

> *Come, let us shout joyfully to the Lord, shout triumphantly to the rock of our salvation! Let us enter His presence with thanksgiving; let us shout triumphantly to Him in song.* (Ps 95:1-2)

> *"Come, let us discuss this," says the Lord. "Though your sins are like scarlet, they will be as white as snow; though they are as red as crimson, they will be like wool."* (Isa 1:18)

> *Come, everyone who is thirsty, come to the waters; and you without money, come, buy, and eat! Come, buy wine and milk without money*

*and without cost! Why do you spend money on what is not food, and
your wages on what does not satisfy? Listen carefully to Me, and eat
what is good, and you will enjoy the choicest of foods. Pay attention
and come to Me; listen, so that you will live. I will make an everlasting
covenant with you, the promises assured to David.* (Isa 55:1-3)

Follow Me . . . and I will make you fish for people. (Matt 4:19)

*Come to Me, all of you who are weary and burdened, and I will give
you rest. All of you, take up My yoke and learn from Me, because I am
gentle and humble in heart, and you will find rest for yourselves. For
My yoke is easy and My burden is light.* (Matt 11:28-30)

*Then the King will say to those on His right, "Come, you who are
blessed by My Father, inherit the kingdom prepared for you from the
foundation of the world."* (Matt 25:34)

*Then, looking at him, Jesus loved him and said to him, "You lack one
thing: Go, sell all you have and give to the poor, and you will have
treasure in heaven. Then come, follow Me."* (Mark 10:21)

*Listen! I stand at the door and knock. If anyone hears My voice and
opens the door, I will come in to him and have dinner with him, and
he with Me.* (Rev 3:20)

And finally, in the last book of the Bible, the last chapter in the book,
we are told in verse 17,

*Both the Spirit and bride say, "Come!" Anyone who hears should say,
"Come!" And the one who is thirsty should come. Whoever desires
should take the living water as a gift.*

At the very end our God one last time invites people to come to Him
and be saved.

Last words are important words. Indeed, last words are intended
to be lasting words, words that make an impression, words that will stay
with the listener or the reader. In Revelation 22:6-21 we come to the
last words in the book of Revelation, the last words of the Bible. God's
written Word comes to an end, and so what we find here is of utmost
importance to God. It also should be of utmost importance to us. Two
themes are dominant: the *reliability and authenticity* of the book and the
imminence of the end.

As the Apocalypse comes to an end, God sends forth His final invitation. Actually, I believe seven invitations are embedded in these final words of the Bible. Here we will discover words of affirmation, encouragement, command, and warning. As our Lord repeatedly challenged the seven churches in chapter 2–3, anyone who has an ear should listen!

Invitation 1: Obey the Word of God
REVELATION 22:6-7

Revelation 22:6-21 is the epilogue to the book that contains various speakers and subjects. Duvall notes that it has

> important parallels with the prologue in 1:1-8, and three central themes that reinforce the overall message of the book: (1) the book is an authentic prophecy from God (22:6-8,10,16,18-19), (2) Jesus Christ's return is imminent (22:6-7,10,12,20), and (3) those who obey the prophecy will be blessed (22:7,9,11,14,17,18-19). (*Revelation*, 304)

The angel who began talking to John in 21:9 (also 22:1) tells him, "These words," the words of the Revelation, are "faithful and true." They are reliable, dependable. You can trust these words. After all, their source is "the Lord, the God of the spirits of the prophets," who inspired and moved them to write (see 2 Pet 1:20-21). Further, in this book, the Lord sent "His angel to show His slaves what must quickly take place." This recalls the first verse of the book. What you have received is clearly divine revelation. It is from God.

In verse 7 the Lord Jesus speaks directly once again (see 16:15) addressing the imminence and certainty of His second coming: "Look, I am coming quickly." Some form of the word "come" appears seven times in this final chapter. In light of His "anytime return," what should our response be? We should "[keep] the prophetic words of this book." We should diligently and consistently obey God's Word. Those who do are promised to be blessed (see 1:3).

Here then is how we should live in anticipation of the return of the King. Let the Word of God live in your daily life. Let Scripture guide you and shape you. Let it do its powerful work as it, by the Spirit, transforms you into the image of the Lord Jesus. Dennis Johnson says it well in his commentary on Revelation:

Scripture is not a passive cadaver, waiting for curious medical students to dissect it in their quest for information. It is a living, double-edge sword that proceeds from the mouth of the triumphant Son of Man and pierces the thoughts and intents of our hearts. It is a hammer that shatters, a seed that grows, rainfall that never returns to its Giver without accomplishing the mission on which he sent it. Scripture has a job to do in us. (*Triumph of the Lamb*, 334)

Invitation 2: Be True to the Worship of God
REVELATION 22:8-9

John affirms he is the one who both "heard and saw these things," the messages and visions of Revelation. Understandably, they were over-whelming. John honestly confesses, "When I heard and saw them, I fell down to worship at the feet of the angel who had shown them to me." Immediately, the angel commands him, "Don't do that!" The angel knows that to worship anything other than God is idolatry. He explains to John, "I am a fellow slave with you, your brothers the prophets, and those who keep [i.e., obey] the words of this book." He, too, is a servant of our great God. Therefore, John, watch out! Think clearly! Always remember: "Worship God!"

John had already received this same warning in 19:10. But like us he had not learned his lesson. Once more he has to be reminded of the basic truth of Exodus 20:3 and the first commandment: "Do not have other gods besides Me." From this we are once again shown that to take a good thing (like an angel) and turn it into a god thing is to make it into a bad thing (an idol). MacArthur clearly and simply reminds us, "God alone is the only acceptable person to worship. The Bible forbids the worship of anyone else, including angels, saints, the Virgin Mary, or any created being (see Col. 2:18)" (*Revelation 12–22*, 296).

Invitation 3: Proclaim the Truth of God
REVELATION 22:10-11

Unlike the prophet Daniel who was told, "[K]eep these words secret and seal the book until the time of the end" (Dan 12:4), John is told, "Don't seal the prophetic words of this book." Why is his command different?

Because "the time is near." Christ could return at any moment. Eternity is drawing closer. For all of us, it is only a heartbeat away. We dare not silence the Word of God by disobedience, indifference, laziness, or neglect. We must preach it and teach it continually and faithfully. A time is coming when the opportunity to respond to the gospel and the Word of God will be no more.

Verse 11 echoes Daniel 12:9-10, which says, "Go on your way, Daniel, for the words are secret and sealed until the time of the end. Many will be purified, cleansed, and refined, but the wicked will act wickedly; none of the wicked will understand, but the wise will understand." Revelation 22:11 contains four commands that serve as warnings and encouragement. It affirms that a day is coming when change will no longer be possible. That is true eschatologically, but it is also true personally. How we respond to the truth of God's Word in this life will confirm our character and determine our destiny for all eternity. Negatively, the unrighteous will still do evil, and the filthy will forever be filthy. On a positive note, the righteous will still do right, and the holy will still be holy. One's character will be set, forever fixed in a final condition and disposition. Those in hell will have no heart and passion for God. Those in heaven will delight in their emulation of their Lord. These truths must be told. We dare not be silent. Souls are at stake. Eternal destinies hang in the balance.

Invitation 4: Pursue the Will of God
REVELATION 22:12-15

Verse 12 contains a third affirmation of the imminent return of Christ: "Look! I am coming quickly." And when He comes, He is bringing his "reward" with Him (see Isa 40:10). He will "repay each person according to what he has done." Jeremiah 17:10 reminds us, "I, Yahweh, examine the mind, I test the heart to give to each according to his way, according to what his actions deserve." Mounce notes, "The reward will be spiritual blessedness to the righteous but judgment for those who are evil. It is the quality of a person's life that provides the ultimate indication of what that person really believes" (*Revelation*, 407). Verse 13 makes clear the One who will render the judgment is fully qualified. He is the "Alpha and Omega," the A to Z (see 1:8; 21:6), "the First and the Last, the Beginning and the End." He sees all and He knows all. Nothing you ever think, feel, or do escapes Him.

There is in verse 14 a seventh and final blessing for the one who loves and obeys God, for "those who wash their robes." Those who have been washed by Christ in justification continue to wash their robes in sanctification (see John 13:10). Duvall notes that in the first century context this washing "refers to persevering in faithfulness to Christ and refusing to compromise with the world, even in the face of tribulation" (*Revelation*, 306). These who are faithful in following the Lamb are promised access or "the right to the tree of life" as well as access to the holy city Jerusalem "by the gates." Eternal life in the eternal city is in their future forever.

Verse 15 stands in striking contrast to verse 14. Those whose destiny is the lake of fire are described as those "outside" the holy city. The list here recalls 21:8. Mounce's comments are instructive:

> John describes six (or perhaps seven, depending upon how one views the two kinds of liars) types of evildoers who are excluded from the city. The term "dog" is used in Scripture for various kinds of impure and malicious persons. In Deut. 23:17-18 the term designates a male cult prostitute. In the Jewish culture of first-century Palestine it was used in reference to the heathen (Matt. 15:22ff), and in Phil. 3:2 Paul turns the tables and applies it to the Judaizers. Those who practice magic arts, the sexually immoral, murderers, idolaters, and all liars are to be excluded along with the dogs. To love and practice falsehood is to be totally devoid of truthfulness. These have become like their leader, Satan, "who leads the whole world astray" (Rev. 12:9; also 13:13-15; 16:14). (*Revelation*, 408)

Invitation 5: Respond to the Invitation of God
REVELATION 22:16-17

Jesus authenticates the message of Revelation in verse 16. He, Himself, sent His angel "to attest these things to [John] for the churches." And this Jesus is the Root (i.e., source) and the Offspring (i.e., descendant) of David (see Isa 11:1,10). He is before David as God and comes from David as man. He is the root and fruit of David! He is the God-man who is also "the Bright Morning Star" (see Num 24:17). The Christology of the end of Revelation is staggeringly high and exalted.

Verse 17 contains the great invitation of Revelation. It could be said to be the great invitation of the Bible. It is a fourfold invitation to all persons of the world to come and be saved.

1. The Holy Spirit says come!
2. The bride, the church of Jesus, says come!
3. The one who hears is told to extend the invitation to come!
4. The one who is thirsty is invited to come.

All who desire the eternal living water of life are invited to come and be saved without price because Jesus has already paid it all. Isaiah 55:1 says,

> *Come, everyone who is thirsty, come to the waters; and you without money, come, buy, and eat! Come, buy wine and milk without money and without cost!*

Jesus said in John 7:37, "If anyone is thirsty, he should come to me and drink!" Charles Spurgeon, in reflecting on both the content and location of verse 17, wisely says,

> To my mind, the solemnity of this invitation lies partly in the fact that it is placed at the very end of the Bible and placed there because it is the sum and substance—the aim and objective of the whole Bible. It is like the point of the arrow and all the rest of the Bible is like the shaft and the feathers on either side of it. We may say of the Scriptures what John said of his Gospel, "These are written"—all these books that are gathered together into one library called the Bible— "These are written that you might believe that Jesus is the Christ, the Son of God. And that believing you might have life through His name." So far as you are concerned, this blessed Book has missed its purpose unless you have been led by it to come to Christ!
>
> It is all in vain that you have a Bible, or read your Bible, unless you really "take the water of life" of which it speaks. It is worse than vain, for if it is not a savor of life unto life to you, it shall be a savor of death unto death! Therefore, it seems to me that this is a very solemn invitation because all the books of the Bible do, in effect, cry to sinners, "Come to Jesus." ("Oft-Repeated Invitation")

Invitation 6: Heed the Warning of God
REVELATION 22:18-19

As the book of Revelation draws to a close, God issues "a severe warning against adding to or taking away from its prophetic message" (Mounce, *Revelation*, 409). The warning is all-inclusive: "everyone." It is also comprehensive: do not add to the book (22:18), and do not subtract from the book (22:19). To tamper with and distort God's Word—in this context meaning the Apocalypse but by implication all 66 books of the Bible—is to invite God's judgment into your life.

On the one hand, add to the book, and the Lord Jesus will add the plagues of Revelation, a hyperbole indicating the severity and harshness of the judgment. On the other hand, take away from the words of the book, and Jesus "will take away [your] share of the tree of life and the holy city" (see Deut 4:2; 12:32; Gal 1:6-7). MacArthur once more provides a pastoral and theological perspective on these two verses:

> No true believer would ever deliberately tamper with Scripture. Those who know and love God will treat His Word with the utmost respect. They will say with the psalmist, "O how I love Your law!" (Ps. 119:97; cf. Pss. 119:113, 163, 167; John 14:23); and, "I delight in Your law" (Ps. 119:70; cf. Pss. 1:2; 119:77, 92, 174). That does not, of course, mean that believers will never make errors in judgment or mistakenly interpret Scripture incorrectly or inadequately. The Lord's warning here is addressed to those who engage in deliberate falsification or misinterpretation of Scripture, those whom Paul denounces as peddlers of the Word of God (2 Cor. 2:17). (*Revelation 12–22*, 310)

The bottom line is clear: Believers love the Word but unbelievers hate the Word. Believers obey the Word but unbelievers disobey the Word. Believers receive the Word but unbelievers reject the Word.

Invitation 7: Pray for the Coming of God
REVELATION 22:20-21

Revelation and the Bible are at their end. One last time the risen Lamb, the Lord Jesus Christ speaks. His last words are brief but sure. Coming in the form of testimony, our God and King promises, "Yes, I am coming quickly." Certainly, without a doubt, His coming is imminent, so be ready. As James 5:9 says, "Look, the judge stands at the door."

Now, given that this promise was made almost two thousand years ago, some sneer and scoff. They mock and ridicule. But doubters would be wise to read 2 Peter 3:1-10 to get heaven's perspective on the kindness, love, and patience that has delayed His coming. Hearing this promise from the lips of Christ Himself, John is quick to respond and to respond with enthusiasm. "Amen!" So be it. Yes! I agree. So, "come, Lord Jesus!"

Titus 2:13 calls us to wait and look for "our blessed hope, the appearing of the glory of our great God and Savior Jesus Christ" (ESV). Taken as a whole, the end of Revelation calls us to a clear and simple threefold posture: watch, wait, and witness. Persecution, trials, and suffering may be a threefold companion, but do not grow weary in well doing. God sees and He knows. And He is with you and working through you to advance His kingdom among the nations. How do we know? Just look at the last verse in the Bible, Revelation 22:21. There is our prayer and promise, "The grace of the Lord Jesus be with all the saints." To this we say with the apostle John, "Amen." We agree. We believe.

Conclusion

From the moment sin entered history, God has been on a rescue mission to save sinners. Our God is a saving God pursuing lost souls for His glory and the good of the nations. It is therefore not surprising at all that His Word concludes with a final invitation to sinners to come to Jesus and be saved.

Some years ago *The New York Times* ran a story about the popularity of the Mayberry Day festivals in Mount Airy, North Carolina, where thousands flock to celebrate "a place that never was, a place they choose to believe once existed." Why the make-believe, why the continued nostalgia over a mythical town in a television series? The article concludes with this thought:

> People come . . . less to escape than to search. . . . "All of this tells me that people are really looking for something," says a 73-year-old barber by the name of Hiatt. "They want to know if there really was a place where people trusted each other, where there's peace and serenity." (Sack, "Mt. Airy Journal")

Well, the Bible teaches that such a place does exist. It is not in a place called Mayberry. It is in a place called heaven and in a person named Jesus. To that place and to that person God extends a final invitation for all to come (22:17).

Reflect and Discuss

1. When was the first time you heard the invitation and call of God? How did you respond?
2. If you were asked by someone why the Bible can be trusted, how would you answer them? How does Revelation 22 answer that question?
3. How can you bring your life into greater alignment with God's Word as you anticipate His second coming?
4. What good things in your life are you tempted to turn into objects of worship, much like John worships the angel in this passage?
5. John is told to proclaim God's truth because the end is near. With whom do you need to share the gospel, since their acceptance or rejection of Christ in this life will determine their eternal destiny?
6. Contrast Revelation 22:14 with those who believe all that is necessary to enter heaven is to go to church, pray a simple prayer, or perform a religious ritual.
7. In what sense is the entire Bible, like Revelation 22:17, an invitation? What is it an invitation to do?
8. What are some ways we can take away from the Scriptures, whether intentionally or unintentionally? What are some ways we can add to them?
9. How is one's reception of the Word of God really a clear dividing line between believers and unbelievers? Is your life marked by reception, obedience, and love for the Word or by apathy, disobedience, and rejection?
10. Conclude your study by praying for the Lord to come quickly and establish His kingdom that will last forever.

WORKS CITED

Akin, Daniel L. *10 Who Changed the World*. Nashville, TN: B&H, 2012.

———, Bill Curtis, and Stephen Nelson Rummage. *Engaging Exposition*. Nashville, TN: B&H Academic, 2011.

———, and R. Albert Mohler Jr. "Why I Believe Children Who Die Go to Heaven." Accessed March 29, 2016. http://www.danielakin.com/wp-content/uploads/2004/08/Why-I-Believe-Children-Who-Die-Go-to-Heaven.pdf.

Alcorn, Randy. "Banished from Humanity." Accessed March 29, 2016. http://www.desiringgod.org/articles/banished-from-humanity.

Allen, John L. *The Global War on Christians: Dispatches from the Front Lines of Anti-Christian Persecution*. New York: Image, 2013.

Alter, Charlotte. "Deaths of Christian 'Martyrs' Doubled in 2013." *Time Magazine*, January 8, 2014. Accessed June 6, 2016. http://world.time.com/2014/01/08/deaths-of-christian-martyrs-doubled-in-2013.

American Humanist Association. "Humanist Manifesto I." Accessed March 29, 2016. http://americanhumanist.org/humanism/humanist_manifesto_i.

———."Humanist Manifesto II." Accessed March 29, 2016. http://americanhumanist.org/humanism/humanist_manifesto_ii.

Autrey, C. E. 1957 Texas Baptist Evangelism Conference.

Barclay, William. *The Revelation of St. John*. Rev. ed. Daily Bible Study Series. Philadelphia, PA: Westminster, 1976.

Barton, Bruce B. *Revelation*. Edited by Grant R. Osborne. Life Application Bible Commentary. Wheaton, IL: Tyndale, 2000.

Beale, G. K. *The Book of Revelation: A Commentary on the Greek Text*. The New International Greek Testament Commentary. Grand Rapids, MI: Eerdmans, 1999.

———. "Why Is the Number of the Beast 666?" Accessed March 29, 2016. http://www.thegospelcoalition.org/article/why-is-the-number-of-the-beast-666.

Beasley-Murray, G. R. *The Book of Revelation.* Grand Rapids, MI: Eerdmans, 1981.

Belz, Mindy. "Taking on the Thugs." *WORLD,* November 6, 1999.

Bernstein, Alan. "Thinking About Hell." *The Wilson Quarterly* 10, no. 3 (1986): 78–89.

Bloesch, Donald. *Insight,* December 29, 1986–January 5, 1987.

Bradley, Omar. *Collected Writings.* Vol. 1. Washington, DC: GPO, 1945.

Bruce, F. F. *New Testament History.* Garden City, NY: Doubleday, 1972.

Bultmann, Rudolf. *The Presence of Eternity: History and Eschatology.* New York: Harper, 1957.

Carson, D. A. "Rev. 5." Accessed March 29, 2016. http://resources.the gospelcoalition.org/library/revelation-5-en.

Chambers, Oswald. *My Utmost for His Highest.* Updated edition. Grand Rapids, MI: Discovery House, 1992. October 17.

Chandler, Matt, and Jared C. Wilson. *The Explicit Gospel.* Wheaton: Crossway, 2012.

Chrysostom, John. *The Homilies of S. John Chrysostom . . . on the Epistles of S. Paul the Apostle to the Philippians, Colossians, and Thessalonians.* Oxford: J. Parker, 1879.

Cobb, James G. *Reformation's Rib: Celebrating Katherine von Bora.* Lima, OH: CSS, 2001.

Criswell, W. A. *Expository Sermons on Revelation.* 5 vols. Grand Rapids, MI: Zondervan, 1962.

Dever, Mark. "We Shall Overcome." Sermon preached at Capitol Hill Baptist Church, Washington, D.C., March 22, 2009. Accessed March 29, 2016. http://www.capitolhillbaptist.org/sermon/we -shall-overcome.

Douthat, Ross. "A Case for Hell." *The New York Times,* April 24, 2011. Accessed March 29, 2016. http://www.nytimes.com/2011/04/25 /opinion/25douthat.html.

Duvall, J. Scott. *Revelation.* Teach the Text Commentary Series. Grand Rapids, MI: Baker, 2014.

Edwards, Jonathan. "Sinners in the Hands of an Angry God." Accessed March 29, 2016. http://edwards.yale.edu/archive?path=aHR0c DovL2Vkd2FyZHMueWFsZS5lZHUvY2dpLWJpbi9uZXdwaGlsby9 nZXRvYmplY3QucGw/Yy4yMTo0Ny53amVv.

Estep, William Roscoe. *The Anabaptist Story.* Grand Rapids, MI: Eerdmans, 1975.

Fee, Gordon D. *Revelation: A New Testament Commentary.* New Covenant Commentary Series. Eugene, OR: Cascade, 2011.

Fischer, Michael. "The Fiery Rise of Hindu Fundamentalism." *Christianity Today,* March 1, 1999.

George, Timothy. "The Nature of God: Being, Attributes, and Acts." In *A Theology for the Church.* Rev. ed. Edited by Daniel L. Akin, Bruce Riley Ashford, and Kenneth Keathley. Nashville, TN: B&H Academic, 2014.

Glaze, R. E., Jr. "Nicolaus and the Nicolaitans." In *Biblical Illustrator,* January 1980.

Goldsworthy, Graeme. *The Lamb and the Lion: The Gospel in Revelation.* Nashville, TN: Thomas Nelson, 1985.

Graham, Billy. *Approaching Hoofbeats: The Four Horsemen of the Apocalypse.* Waco, TX: Word, 1983.

Graves, David. "Local References in the Letter to Smyrna (Rv. 2:8-11), Part 2: Historical Background." *Bible and Spade* 19, no.1 (2006), 23–31.

Hamilton, James M. *Revelation: The Spirit Speaks to the Churches.* Preaching the Word. Wheaton, IL: Crossway, 2012.

Harder, James. "U.N. Faithful Eye Global Religion." *Insight,* October 2–9, 2000.

Harris, Joshua. *New Attitude.* Accessed March 29, 2016. http://the rebelution.com/blog/2013/01/the-room-by-joshua-harris-2#. Vkoj4K72D_Q.

Havner, Vance. *Repent or Else!* Westwood, NJ: Revell, 1958.

Helyer, Larry R., and Richard Wagner. *The Book of Revelation for Dummies.* Hoboken, NJ: Wiley, 2008.

Hendriksen, William. *More than Conquerors: An Interpretation of the Book of Revelation.* Grand Rapids, MI: Baker, 1940.

IMB Global Research. Accessed March 29, 2016. http://public.imb .org/globalresearch/Pages/default.aspx.

Jeremiah, David, and Carole C. Carlson. *Escape the Coming Night.* Dallas, TX: Word, 1997.

Johnson, Alan F. "Revelation." In *Hebrews–Revelation.* Expositor's Bible Commentary. Edited by Frank E. Gabelein and J. D. Douglas. Grand Rapids, MI: Zondervan, 1981.

———. "Revelation." In *Hebrews–Revelation.* Rev. ed. Expositor's Bible Commentary. Edited by Tremper Longman and David E. Garland. Grand Rapids, MI: Zondervan, 2006.

———. *Revelation.* Bible Study Commentary. Grand Rapids, MI: Zondervan, 1983.

Johnson, Dennis E. *Triumph of the Lamb: A Commentary on Revelation.* Phillipsburg, NJ: P&R, 2001.

Keener, Craig S. *Revelation.* NIV Application Commentary. Grand Rapids, MI: Zondervan, 2000.

Kistemaker, Simon. *Exposition of the Book of Revelation.* New Testament Commentary. Grand Rapids, MI: Baker Academic, 2001.

Kreeft, Peter. "Is There Sex in Heaven?" Accessed March 29, 2016. http://www.peterkreeft.com/topics/sex-in-heaven.htm.

Ladd, George Eldon. *A Commentary on the Revelation of John.* Grand Rapids, MI: Eerdmans, 1972.

Lawless, Charles E. *Disciplined Warriors: Growing Healthy Churches that Are Equipped for Spiritual Warfare.* Grand Rapids, MI: Kregel, 2002.

Levy, David. "The Church Compromised." *Israel My Glory,* December 1994/January 1995.

————. "The Marriage Supper of the Lamb." *Israel My Glory,* June/July 1998.

————. "The Scroll with Seven Seals." *Israel My Glory,* October/November 1995.

Lewis, C. S. *Mere Christianity.* 1952. Repr., San Francisco, CA: HarperSanFrancisco, 2001.

————. *The Problem of Pain.* 1940. Repr., San Francisco, CA: HarperSanFrancisco, 2000.

————. *The Weight of Glory: And Other Addresses.* 1949. Repr., San Francisco, CA: HarperSanFrancisco, 2000.

MacArthur, John. *Revelation 1–11.* Chicago, IL: Moody, 1999.

————. *Revelation 12–22.* Chicago, IL: Moody, 2000.

Mahaney, C. J. "Is This Verse in Your Bible?" In *Worldliness: Resisting the Seduction of a Fallen World.* Edited by C. J. Mahaney. Wheaton, IL: Crossway, 2008.

Manley, Stevan. *Church Herald and Banner,* November 3, 2000.

Marty, Martin E. "Hell Disappeared. No One Noticed. A Civic Argument." *Harvard Theological Review* 78 (1985): 391–98.

"The Martyrdom of Polycarp." Edited and translated by Massey Hamilton Shepherd Jr. Pages 141–60 in *Early Christian Fathers,* edited by Cyril C. Richardson. First Touchstone edition. New York, NY: Simon & Schuster, 1995.

McGinn, Bernard. *Antichrist: Two Thousand Years of the Human Fascination with Evil.* San Francisco, CA: HarperSanFrancisco, 1994.

M'Cheyne, Robert Murray. *The Works of Rev. Robert Murray M'Cheyne: Complete in One Volume.* n.p.: Robert Carter, 1874.

Moore, Russell D. "Why Is Hell Forever?" Accessed March 29, 2016. http://www.russellmoore.com/2011/03/21/why-is-hell-forever.

Morris, Leon. *The Revelation of St. John: An Introduction and Commentary.* Tyndale New Testament Commentary. Grand Rapids, MI: Eerdmans, 1969.

Mounce, Robert H. *The Book of Revelation.* Rev. ed. New International Commentary on the New Testament. Grand Rapids, MI: Eerdmans, 1997.

Newell, Marvin J., ed. *Expect Great Things: Mission Quotes that Inform and Inspire.* Pasadena, CA: William Carey Library, 2013.

Nicholson, J. Boyd. "Hold Fast to the Gospel." *Uplook* 64, no. 11 (November 1997): 11–13.

Osborne, Grant R. *Revelation.* Baker Exegetical Commentary on the New Testament. Grand Rapids, MI: Baker Academic, 2002.

Patterson, Paige. *Revelation.* New American Commentary. Nashville, TN: B&H Academic, 2012.

Pinnock, Clark H. "The Destruction of the Finally Impenitent." *Concordia Theological Review* 4 (1990): 243–59.

Piper, John. "Angels and Prayer." Sermon preached at Bethlehem Baptist Church, Minneapolis, MN, January 12, 1992. Accessed March 29, 2016. http://www.desiringgod.org/messages/angels-and-prayer.

———. "Christ: The Lion and the Lamb." Sermon preached at Bethlehem Baptist Church, Minneapolis, MN, March 23, 1986. Accessed March 29, 2016. http://www.desiringgod.org/messages/christ-the-lion-and-the-lamb.

———. "Is the United States Talked About in the Book of Revelation?" Accessed March 29, 2016. http://www.desiringgod.org/interviews/is-the-united-states-talked-about-in-the-book-of-revelation.

———. "Our Hope: The Appearing of Jesus Christ." Sermon preached at Bethlehem Baptist Church, Minneapolis, MN, May 18, 1986. Accessed March 29, 2016. http://www.desiringgod.org/messages/our-hope-the-appearing-of-jesus-christ.

———. "The Second Coming Is like Lightning and Vultures." Sermon preached at Bethlehem Baptist Church, Minneapolis, MN, March 18, 2009. Accessed April 7, 2016. http://www.desiringgod.org/articles/the-second-coming-is-like-lightning-and-vultures.

———. "Things Are Worse and Better Than They Seem." Sermon preached at Bethlehem Baptist Church, Minnapolis, MN, June 6, 1993. Accessed March 29, 2016. http://desiringgod.org/messages/things-are-worse-and-better-than-they-seem.

———. "Worship God!" Sermon preached at Bethlehem Baptist Church, Minneapolis, MN, September 15, 1991. Accessed March 29, 2016. http://www.desiringgod.org/sermons/worship-god.

———. "A Year End Look at Jesus." Sermon preached at Bethlehem Baptist Church, Minneapolis, MN, December 27, 1992. Accessed March 29, 2016. http://www.desiringgod.org/messages/a-year-end-look-at-jesus-christ.

Platt, David. "Consummation of the Kingdom." Sermon preached at the Church at Brook Hills, Birmingham, AL, October 28, 2012. Accessed March 29, 2016. http://www.radical.net/resources/sermons/consummation-of-the-kingdom.

———. "The Danger of Worldly Desires." Sermon preached at the Church at Brook Hills, Birmingham, AL, October 7, 2012. Accessed March 29, 2016. http://www.radical.net/resources/sermons/the-danger-of-worldly-desires.

———. "Fighting from (Not for) Victory." Sermon preached at the Church at Brook Hills, Birmingham, AL, September 23, 2012. Accessed March 29, 2016. http://www.radical.net/resources/sermons/fighting-from-not-for-victory.

———. "The Hallelujah Chorus." Sermon preached at the Church at Brook Hills, Birmingham, AL, October 14, 2012. Accessed March 29, 2016. http://www.radical.net/resources/sermons/the-hallelujah-chorus.

———. "How Do We Worship God in His Wrath?" Sermon preached at the Church at Brook Hills, Birmingham, AL, September 30, 2012. Accessed March 29, 2016. http://radical.net/resources/sermons/how-do-we-worship-god-in-his-wrath.

———. "The Life of the Christian and the Coming of the Kingdom." Sermon preached at Church at Brook Hills, Birmingham, AL, September 16, 2012. Accessed March 29, 2016. http://www.radical.net/resources/sermons/the-life-of-the-christian-and-the-coming-of-the-kingdom.

Riddlebarger, Kim *The Man of Sin: Uncovering the Truth About the Antichrist.* Grand Rapids, MI: Baker, 2006.

Robertson, A. T. *Word Pictures in the New Testament.* 6 vols. Nashville, TN: Broadman, 1930.

Rogers, Adrian. *The Wit and Wisdom of Adrian Rogers*. Memphis, TN: Love Worth Finding Ministries, 2006.

———. *Adrianisms: The Wit and Wisdom of Adrian Rogers*. Vol. 2. Memphis, TN: Love Worth Finding Ministries, 2007.

Rogers, Cleon L., and Fritz Rienecker. *The New Linguistic and Exegetical Key to the Greek New Testament*. Grand Rapids, MI: Zondervan, 1998.

Sack, Kevin. "Mount Airy Journal: Reality Plays a Bit Part on Mayberry Days." *The New York Times*, September 29, 1997. Accessed March 29, 2016. http://www.nytimes.com/1997/09/29/us/mount-airy-journal-reality-plays-a-bit-part-on-mayberry-days.html.

Sayers, Dorothy. *A Matter of Eternity*. Edited by Rosamond Kent Sprague. Grand Rapids, MI: Eerdmans, 1973.

Schaeffer, Francis A. *Death in the City*. Chicago, IL: InterVarsity, 1969.

Sheler, Jeffrey L. "Hell Hath No Fury." *U.S. News & World Report* 128, no. 4 (2000).

Simcox, Thomas C. "The Greatest Sacrifice." *Israel My Glory*, March–April 2014.

Smalley, Stephen S. *The Revelation to John: A Commentary on the Greek Text of the Apocalypse*. Downers Grove, IL: InterVarsity, 2005.

Spurgeon, Charles. "Future Punishment a Fearful Thing." Sermon preached at the Metropolitan Tabernacle on March 25, 1866. Accessed March 29, 2016. http://www.spurgeongems.org/vols10-12/chs682.pdf.

———. "Good News for Thirsty Souls." Sermon preached at the Metropolitan Tabernacle, London, July 4, 1880. Accessed March 29, 2016. http://www.spurgeongems.org/vols25-27/chs1549.pdf.

———. "The Harvest and the Vintage." Sermon preached at the Metropolitan Tabernacle, London, September 17, 1876. Accessed March 29, 2016. http://www.spurgeongems.org/vols49-51/chs2910.pdf.

———. "The Oft-Repeated Invitation." Sermon preached at the Metropolitan Tabernacle, London, July 10, 1881. Accessed March 29, 2016. http://www.spurgeongems.org/vols46-48/chs2685.pdf.

———. "Saints Guarded from Stumbling." Sermon preached at the Metropolitan Tabernacle, London, February 19, 1893. Accessed March 29, 2016. http://www.spurgeongems.org/vols37/chs2296.pdf.

———. "Song for the Free—Hope for the Bound." Sermon preached at the Metropolitan Tabernacle, London, November 20, 1887.

Accessed March 29, 2016. http://www.spurgeongems.org/vols31-33/chs1992.pdf.

Swindoll, Charles R. *Insights on Revelation*. Grand Rapids, MI: Zondervan, 2011.

———. *Making New Discoveries*. Anaheim, CA: Insight for Living, 1996.

Tenney, Merrill C. *Interpreting Revelation*. Grand Rapids, MI: Eerdmans, 1957.

Tertullian. *Apology, De Spectaculis*. Cambridge, MA: Harvard, 1960.

Thielicke, Helmut. *Man in God's World*. New York: Harper & Row, 1963.

"Vicar of Baghdad: Four Iraqi Christian Kids Beheaded After Refusing to Convert to Islam, Telling ISIS Militants 'No, We Love Jesus.'" *Christian Post*, December 2, 2014.

Walvoord, John F. *The Revelation of Jesus Christ: A Commentary*. Chicago, IL: Moody, 1966.

Watson, Thomas. *A Body of Practical Divinity*. n.p.: T. Wardle, 1833.

White, John Wesley. "Hope: Can the World be Saved?" Accessed March 29, 2016. http://www.preaching.com/sermons/11565472.

Whitney, Donald. "Hell Is Real." Accessed March 29, 2016. http://biblical spirituality.org/wp-content/uploads/2011/02/matthew25.mp3.

Wiersbe, Warren W. *Be Victorious*. Wheaton, IL: Victor, 1985.

Wilcox, Ella Wheeler. *Kingdom of Love: And, How Salvator Won*. Chicago, IL: Conkey, 1901.

Wilson, Mark W. *Charts on the Book of Revelation: Literary, Historical, and Theological Perspectives*. Grand Rapids, MI: Kregel, 2007.

Woods, Deane. "The Lamb in the Apocalypse." *Israel My Glory*, May/June 2005.

"World Heavyweight Champion." *The Islamic Bulletin*. Accessed July 8, 2016. http://www.islamicbulletin.org/newsletters/issue_28/muhammad_ali.aspx.

SCRIPTURE INDEX